CAPT. CHRISTOPHER LEVETT STEERING HIS SHALLOP INTO HOG-ISLAND-ROADS, 1623.

his noble attendance rowing by us in their canoes."

Portland
in the Past

WITH

HISTORICAL NOTES OF OLD FALMOUTH

William Goold

HERITAGE BOOKS
2015

HERITAGE BOOKS

AN IMPRINT OF HERITAGE BOOKS, INC.

Books, CDs, and more—Worldwide

For our listing of thousands of titles see our website
at
www.HeritageBooks.com

A Facsimile Reprint
Published 2015 by
HERITAGE BOOKS, INC.
Publishing Division
5810 Ruatan Street
Berwyn Heights, Md. 20740

Copyright © 1886 William Goold

Printed for the author
by B. Thurston & Company
Portland, Maine
1886

International Standard Book Numbers
Paperbound: 978-0-7884-0688-1
Clothbound: 978-0-7884-6234-4

PREFATORY NOTE.

THIS volume has been long in preparation, and ought to be correct, and yet I do not claim that it is entirely free from errors. Such total exemption can hardly be expected of a work of the kind. It should be recollected that the published prospectus did not promise a history of the town — that has been written by an abler hand. A writer in the Historical and Genealogical Register says, " He who gleans history after William Willis will find a barren field." My object has been to prepare a volume of reliable local history, new as nearly as practicable, which should be entertaining as well as instructive. I have not especially sought to trace the pedigree of those of whom I have written. I believe with Shakespeare that

> " Honors best thrive
> When rather from our acts we them derive,
> Than our foregoers."

I have abundant material and memoranda for further labor in this field of local history, which I shall continue to prosecute.

THE AUTHOR.

ILLUSTRATIONS.

CONTENTS.

8 CONTENTS.

PORTLAND IN THE PAST,

WITH HISTORICAL NOTES OF OLD FALMOUTH.

CHAPTER I.

CAPTAIN CHRISTOPHER LEVETT'S COASTING TRIP. HE ESTABLISHED A
PLANTATION ON AN ISLAND AT CASCO, AND BUILT A HOUSE, THE
FIRST WITHIN THE PRESENT BOUNDS OF PORTLAND, IN 1623. ITS
PROBABLE LOCATION. GOVERNOR ROBERT GORGES, KNIGHT, WITH
HIS SHIP THE SWAN, SPENT THE FOLLOWING WINTER IN THE HAR-
BOR. HIS CHAPLAIN, REV. WILLIAM MORRELL, WROTE A POEM
DESCRIPTIVE OF NEW ENGLAND.

THE first European who discovered, appreciated, and
described the beauties and capabilities of what is now the
city and harbor of Portland and Falmouth was Christopher
Levett. He came here from the Isles of Shoals, where he
landed from England in 1623. His first visit to the main
land was to Piscataqua. From thence he coasted with two
boats and ten or more men to Cape Elizabeth, Casco Bay,
and on to Boothbay. Here he turned back to the western
part of Casco Bay, as the most suitable place he had found
for a permanent plantation, and for the beginning of a city.
He had a grant of six thousand acres of land, to be located
where he might choose east of Piscataqua. Levett's project received the approbation of King James.*

* It seems that Levett had decided, before leaving England, to call his
city York. In Sainbury's State Papers, Vol. I., p. 45, is this minute of
the Council. "May 5, 1623. Christopher Levett to be a principal
patentee, and to have a grant of 6000 acres of land." "June 26, 1623.

Levett built a house, fortified it, and spent the winter and the next summer in it. He left ten men in his house while he went to England for his wife, and the people to form his colony. There is no account of his return. Four years after (1628) he published in London an account of his travels, a description of the coast, and of his settlement at what is now Portland. His description of its marked natural features is so minute that there is no mistaking the rivers and islands of Casco Bay and Portland harbor. The title to Levett's narrative is " A voyage into New England, begun in 1623 and ended in 1624, performed by Christopher Levett, his majesty's Woodward of Somersetshire, and one of the council of New England. London, 1628." It is addressed to " the Duke of Buckingham, the Earl of Arundel, Earl of Warwick, the Earl of Holderness, and the rest of the Council of New England." Of this book there is but one copy of the original edition known to exist in this country, and that is owned by the New York Historical Society.*

As Levett's book relates wholly to the coast of Maine, and much of it to Casco Bay at a very early period, I shall make some extracts from it. In his preface Levett says, " Being but a young schollar though an ancient traveler by sea." He begins his narrative as follows: " May it please your Lordships, that whereas you granted your commission unto Capt. Robert Gorges, Governor of New England, Capt. Francis West, myself, and the Governor of New Plymouth,

The king judges well of the undertaking in New England, and more particularly of a design of Christopher Levett, one of the council for settling that plantation, to build a city and call it York."

* A copy from the book was obtained and printed by the Maine Historical Society in their second volume of collections in 1837.

as councillors with him, for the ordering and governing said
territories."

This was an attempt to establish a general government
over the New England colonies and scattered plantations,
to restrain the lawless adventurers who were swarming here
for fishing and for traffic with the Indians, which was very
profitable, in which many frauds were practiced, to the damage of those who had a legal right to the trade.

In Sir Ferdinando Gorges "Brief Narration," he says:
"Hereupon my son, Robert Gorges, being newly come out
of the Venetian war was the man they pleased to pitch upon,
being one of the company, who between my Lord Gorges
and myself was speedily sent away into the Bay of Massachusetts, where he arrived about the beginning of August
following, Anno 1623."

The Council of New England on the 30th of December,
1622, "granted to Robert Gorges, youngest son of Sir Ferdinando Gorges, Knight, and his heirs," ten miles on the
coast adjoining Massachusetts Bay on the east, and extending thirty miles into the country.*

Governor Bradford of New Plymouth in his history says:
"He [Governor Gorges] gave us notice of his arrival [at
Cape Cod] by letter, and before we could visit him, sails
for the eastward with the ship he came in, but a storm
arising, they bore into our harbor, are kindly entertained,
and stay fourteen days."

Soon after Governor Gorges went to Piscataqua. Here
Levett met him, having gone there from the Isles of Shoals,
where he says he first landed. Levett says he stayed at
Piscataqua "with Mr. Thompson about one month, in which

* Willis, p. 93. Robert Gorges married a daughter of the Earl of
Lincoln.

time I sent for my men from the east, who came over in
divers ships.* At this place I met the Governor (Robert
Gorges), who came thither in a bark he had of Mr. Weston
about twenty days before I arrived in the land. The Governor then told me that I was joined with him in commission
as a councilor, which being read, I found it was so, and he,
in the presence of three more of the council, administered
unto me an oath."

In pursuing Levett's narrative we shall find it mentioned
incidentally that Governor Gorges either accompanied him
or met him with his ship at Cape Newagen, and at Casco Bay.
Levett says: "After the meeting of my men, I went a coasting in two boats with all my company. In the time I staid
with Mr. Thompson I surveyed as much as possible I could,
the weather being unseasonable and very much snow."

He next describes the Piscataqua, the Agamenticus (at
York), and Cape Porpoise. He says: "About four leagues
further east there is another harbor called Sawco, where I
found my other boat. There I stayed five nights, the wind
being contrary, having much rain and snow and continual
fogs. We built a wigwam of poles, and covered it with our
boat sails. The greatest comfort next unto that which was
spiritual was this: we had fowl enough for killing, wood
enough for felling, and good fresh water enough for drinking. We had crane, goose, ducks, and mallard, with other
fowl, both broiled and roasted."

Levett describes the Pool, and says: " In this place there
is a world of fowl." He continues: "This river I am told
by the savages comes from the chrystal hill, as they say, one
hundred miles in the country, yet it is to be seen at the sea-

* Probably some of those of his fathers, the elder Gorges who had
a fishing station at Monhegan.

side, and there is no ship arrives in New England either west so far as Cape Cod, or to the east so far as Monhegan, but they see this mountain the first land if the weather is clear." *

Levett describes the two next rivers east of the Saco about six miles apart, and says: "There is no coming in for ship or boat by reason of a sandy breach which lieth along the shore and makes all one breach." This was evidently Old Orchard and Spurwink. He next describes Portland harbor and Casco Bay. "And now in its place I come to Quack, which I have named York; at this place there fished divers ships of [from] Weymouth this year. It lieth about two leagues to the east of Cape Elizabeth. It is a bay or sound between the main and certain islands which lieth in the sea about one English mile and a half. There are four islands which make one good harbor.† There is very good fishing and much fowl, and the main as good ground as any can desire. There I found one river, wherein the savages say there is much salmon, and other good fish. In this bay there hath been taken this year four sturgeons‡ by fisher-

---

* This seems to favor the point in dispute, that the mountains seen by Rosier from his anchorage near Monhegan, toward which he and Weymouth steered their course, were the White Mountains.

† These four islands yet "make one good harbor." They are named "Bang's, Peak's, House and Hog."

‡ In Maverick's manuscript Description of New England in 1660, recently discovered in the British Museum, he mentions the "town of Newbury on the river 'Meromac.' . . . . The river is broader than the Thames at Deptford, and in summer abounds with sturgeon, salmon, and other fresh water fish. Had we the art of taking and saving the sturgeon it would prove of very great advantage, the country affording vinegar, and all other materials to do it withall." In no case before have I seen any mention of the manner of saving the sturgeon, but supposed it was with salt, smoke, or both; but this mention of "vinegar" shows what

men who drive only for herrings (for bait), so that it is likely there may be good stores taken, if there were men fit for that purpose.* This river I made bold to call by my own name, Levett's river, being the first to discover it. How far this river is navigable I can not tell; I have been but six miles up it, but on both sides is good ground."

The place described by our explorer, called "Quack," and named by him "York," was evidently Portland harbor. The distance which he estimates it to be from the extreme point of Cape Elizabeth (a name as old as the discovery) alone would fix its identity. The protection from the sea described as "four islands," renders it unmistakable. The name "Quack" was probably the fishermen's contraction of some longer Indian name. Governor Winthrop invariably wrote "Pascataquack" as the name of the river Piscataqua, and Martha's Vineyard was called by the Indians "Capawack."

In Rev. Elijah Kellogg's vocabulary of words in the language of the Quoddy Indians, written while he was a missionary in the employ of the society for propagating the gospel among them, March, 1828, he says the Indian word for red

---

saved it. It was packed in kegs, and shipped to Spanish markets. Edmond Mountfort, who leased the sturgeon fishery at ancient Augusta (Small Point harbor) of the proprietors in 1718, failed in his enterprise, and had his rent returned. Perhaps this was for the want " of the art," or the vinegar mentioned by Maverick. In Captain John Smith's narrative of his voyage to New England, he says he got "some sturgeon, but it was too tart of the vinegar, which was of my own store."

* The privilege of the sturgeon fishery in some localities afterward became very valuable. The fish were cut up, cured and shipped to Spanish markets. There was an extensive business carried on at Topsham by Thomas Purchase, on the Androscoggin a century later, and the sturgeon fishery at ancient "Augusta," at Cape Small Point, was leased to Edmond Mountfort, afterward of Falmouth.

is *macquack*. The steep ledges on the shore of the neck may have been more stained red by iron than now, which caused the Indians to call the shores and harbor " Macquack."

Levett evidently ascended Fore river to its source at Capisic and Stroudwater, and to cover his six miles he must have reckoned from Spring Point (Fort Preble), which is really its mouth ; but it has not been known by his name since.

" In the same bay I found an other river, up which I went three miles, and found a great fall of water, much bigger than the fall at London bridge at low water, further a boat cannot go, but above the fall the water runs smooth again.* Just at this fall of water the Sagamore, or King, hath a house where I was one day, when there was two Sagamores more, their wives and children, in all about fifty, and we were but seven. They bid me welcome, and gave me such victuals as they had, and I gave them tobacco and aqua-vitæ (rum). After I had spent a little time with them, I departed, and gave them a small shot, and they gave me an other. And the great Sagamore of the east country, whom the rest do acknowledge to be chief amongst them, he gave unto me a beaver skin, which I thankfully received, and so in great love we parted. On both sides of this river there is goodly ground. . . . . . . In the way between York (Quack) and Sagadahock lieth " Cascoe" a good harbor, good fishing, good ground, and much fowl."

Where Quack or York leaves off and " Cascoe " begins is not easy to determine, evidently some of the near small harbors of the bay he calls " Cascoe," which, like the star of

---

* The great fall of water at low tide at London (old) bridge was not natural. It was caused by the massive piers between the nineteen narrow arches which obstructed the current. It had stood six centuries, and in 1831 a new structure of five arches, and costing ten millions of dollars, was completed, having occupied seven years in building. In the description of the river with its fall, its distance from the bay, any one familiar with the locality would readily recognize the Presumpscot.

empire, has moved westward and included Quack.   Levett
continues :

" For Sagadahock I need say nothing of it, there hath been heretofore enough said by others, and I fear too much.   But the place is
good.   The next place I came to was Cape Manwagan (southwest
part of Boothbay), a place where nine ships fished this year.   But I
like it not for a plantation, for I could see little good timber and less
good ground.   There I staid four nights in which time there came
many savages with their wives and children and some of good
account amongst them, as Menawarmet, a Sagamore; Cogawesco the
Sagamore of Cascoe and Quack, now called York; and Somerset, a
Sagamore who has been found very faithful to the English, and hath
saved the lives of many of our nation; some from starving, others
from killing (being killed).*   Then I sent for the Sagamores, who
came, and after some compliments they told me that I must be their
cousin and that *Captain Gorges* was so, which you may imagine I
was not a little proud of to be adopted cousin to so many great kings
at one instant, but willingly accepted it. †   And so passed away a
little time very pleasantly. . . . . When they were ready to depart
they asked me where I meant to settle my plantation.   I told them I
had seen many places at the west and intended to go farther to the
east before I could resolve.   They said that there was no good place;
and the best time for fishing was then at hand, which made me the
more willing to retire, and rather because Cogawesco, the Sagamore

* This chief is probably the same one who deeded land to John Brown
at Pemaquid two years after under the name of " Capt. John Somerset."
I think it probable that Levett gave him the name.   In his title page
to his voyage he represents himself as " His Majesty's Woodward of
Somersetshire," — of course Levett was a resident of that county.   He
is subsequently several times favorably mentioned by Levett, and afterwards at Somerset's request named a son of his.

† This is the first mention of Captain Gorges, the Governor-General, in
the journal, since Levett left Piscataqua, but it shows conclusively that
he was, or had recently been there, as he had never been in the country
before, and of course could not have made their acquaintance.   Perhaps
he had been in his ship to visit Monhegan, twelve miles off the coast,
where his father had a fishing station.

of Cascoe and Quack, told me if I would sit down at either of these places, I should be very welcome, and that he and his wife would go along with me in my boat to see them, which courtesy I had no reason to refuse, because I had set up my resolution before to settle my plantation at Quack, which I named York, and was glad of this opportunity that I had gained the consent of them who, as I conceive, hath a natural right of inheritance as they are the sons of Noah.

"The next day the wind came fair, and I sailed to Quack or York, with the king, queen, and prince, bow and arrows, dog and kettle in my boat, his noble attendance rowing by us in their canoes.* When we came to York the masters of the ships came to bid me welcome. † The woman, or reputed queen, asked me if those men were my friends. I told her they were. Then she drank to them and told them they were welcome to her country, and so should all my friends be at any time. She drank also to her husband and bid him welcome to her country too, for you must understand that her father was the Sagamore of this place, and left it to her at his death, having no more children.

"And thus after many dangers, much labor and great charge, I have obtained a place of habitation in New England, where I have built a house, and fortified it in a reasonable good fashion, strong against such enemies as are those savage people.

"Whilst I stayed in this place I had some little truck, but not much, by reason of an evil member in the harbor, who being covetous of truck, used the matter so that he got the savages away from me. And it is no wonder he should abuse me in this sort, for he

* This was the first royal procession borne on the waters of Portland harbor, which was participated in by Englishmen. The next was at the embarkation of the Prince of Wales in 1860, who also had "his noble attendance rowing by," but this was the only similarity to that of the native royal family.

† Probably one of these was the ship of Governor Gorges, as Levett mentions his presence here at the time in the interview with the belligerent captain of the trading ship. Another may have been the ship in which Levett or his men came over. They used the savages kindly, and gave them meat, drink and tobacco.

hath not spared your Lordships and all the council for New England.
He said unto the Governor that the Lords had sent men over into
that country to make prey of others.* . . . . He said he cared not
for any authority in that place, and though he was forbidden to
truck, yet would he have all he could get, in spite of who should say
to the contrary, having a great ship with seventeen pieces of
ordnance and fifty men. And indeed his practice was according to
his words, for every Sunday, or once in the week, he went himself or
sent a boat up the river and got all the truck before they could come
down to the harbor."

It was the presence of such unprincipled traders as this
on the coast that caused Governor Gorges to abandon the
project of establishing a general government in New England. It is evident from the language of Governor Bradford
that the Governor-General spent the winter with councilor
Levett at his house, or in the Governor's own ship here.
Bradford says, p. 153, " and toward the spring they (Governor Gorges and Mr. Weston) came to agreement after they
had been to the eastward." Levett also uses this expression
in his narrative. " On a time the Governor was at my house
and brought a savage."

Local historians seem to have overlooked these allusions
by Levett to the presence of " My Lord Gorges," the Governor-General at Cape Manwagan and at Casco.

The Mr. Thomas Weston named was a London merchant
largely concerned in the New England fishery. He it was
who went over to Leyden in the spring of 1620 and induced
the Pilgrims " not to meddle with the Dutch, or too much to
depend on the Virginia company; for if that failed they
came to resolution that he and such merchants as were his

---

* The rehearsal by Levett of what the " evil member in the harbor "
said to the Governor shows conclusively that Governor Gorges was also
present in the harbor.

friends (together with their own means), would set them forth; and they should make ready and neither fear want of shipping nor money, for what they wanted should be provided." Bradford continues, mentioning 'the formation of the Council of Plymouth, and says : " Unto which Mr. Weston and ye chief of them began to incline it was best for them to go; as for other reasons, so chiefly for ye hope of present profit to be made by ye fishing that was found in the country." So it seems those people did not come over solely for " conscience sake " as has been by some writers represented. The preamble to the articles of confederation of the colonies in 1643 (Bradford History, p. 416), commences thus: " Whereas we all came into these parts of America with one and ye same end and aim; namely, to advance the kingdom of our Lord Jesus Christ and to enjoy ye liberties of ye gospel in purity with peace."

The Massachusetts colonies were founded with still more special reference to the fisheries. We are told in Winslow's " Briefe Narrative of the True Grounds and Causes of the First Planting of New England," that when the Puritans sent agents from Leyden to King James to gain his consent to their going to America, the King at once asked " what profit might arise." They answered in a single word : "Fishing." " So God have my soul," remarked the King, " 'tis an honest trade; 'twas the apostles' own calling." The Pilgrims sought out a place for the settlement which " seemed to offer some advantages both for whale and cod fishery," and for two years were sustained in their struggles for food chiefly by the fish which they caught in their slight nets, and the mollusks which they dug upon the shore.

Their forced landing-place was a good enough place to nurse their consciences, but not so good a place as Maine for

obtaining a living, although we have seen that some who
came to the eastern country of Maine came because they had
no conscience.   Robert Cushman wrote to the brethren at
Leyden under date London, June 11, 1620, giving an account
of the charter of the ship.   " And so advising together
(with Mr. Weston) we resolved to hire a ship, and have
tooke a liking to one till Monday, about 60 last (180 tons),
for a greater we cannot get except it be too great, but a fine
ship it is."   This was the Mayflower of blessed memory.   I
write this of Mr. Weston because I shall prove that he was
one of Levett's distinguished party that wintered at his plantation or on shipboard in what is now the harbor of Portland.

On his arrival in New England Governor Gorges had orders
to call Weston (who was here before him) to account for procuring a permit from the crown with the assistance of Sir
Ferdinando Gorges, to " transport many pieces of great ordnance for New England, pretending great fortification here
in ye country.   The which when he had obtained he went
and sold them beyond seas for his private profit."   After
some provocation, the Governor seized Weston's ship and
ordered him on shore.   Bradford says, " Mr. Weston had notice to shift for himself, but it was conceived he knew not
whither to go, or how to mend himself, and so stirred not,
. . . . and toward the spring they came to agreement after
they *had been to the eastward* and ye Governor restored him
his vessel again, and made him satisfaction in buiscuit and
meal and such like provisions, for what he had made use of
that was his."   Weston must have wintered in the ship or
with Levett at his house.

Another member of this winter party was an Episcopal
clergyman, chaplain to Governor Gorges.   Dr. Belknap in
his American Biography thus notices him: " He (the Gov-

ernor), brought over with him as chaplain William Morrell, an Episcopal clergyman. This was the first essay for the establishment of a general government in New England, and Morrell was to have a superintendence in ecclesiastical as Gorges had in civil affairs; but he made no use of his commission, and only mentioned it in his conversation about the time of his departure. This Mr. Morrell appears to have been a diligent inquirer into the state and circumstances of the country, its natural productions, the manners and customs and government of the natives. The result of his observations he wrought into a poem which he printed in both Latin and English. The Latin is by no means destitute of classical merit. The description itself is just and animated, and the English translation (considering the date of it), is very tolerable."

Dr. Belknap was a learned and polished writer, whose opinion of a poetical production is worth something.

Next to Rev. Richard Seymore, chaplain to the Popham colony, who arrived at Sagadahock in 1607, Mr. Morrell was the first minister of the Church of England who came to New England to remain and to officiate in his sacred office.*

---

* The Rev. William Morrell's poem on "New England" was reprinted in the first volume of the Collections of the Massachusetts Historical Society, 1806, p. 125. It is a poem of nearly four hundred lines. He opens thus:

"NEW ENGLAND."
"Fear not, poor muse, 'cause first to sing her fame,
    That yet scarce known, unless by map or name;
    A grandchild to earth's paradise is born,
    Well limbed, well nerved, sweet, yet forlorn."

These are the closing lines :
    "If heaven grant these, to see here built I trust,
    An English kingdom from this Indian dust."

Of course the Governor kept his chaplain in his ship (the Swan) with him, and also of course services according to the book of common prayer of the English Church (of which all the Gorges family were members), were held regularly on the Sabbath on board the ship or at councilor Levett's house during that winter where probably the whole company assembled, including Levett, the Governor, the men numbering nearly forty ; and notably including an ordained minister of the Church of England, the Governor-General of New England, and one of his councilors, with probably other officers, and the merchant who more than any other, assisted the Pilgrims to come over, and who chartered the Mayflower for the voyage only three years before.

If the foregoing suppositions are correct, these divine services were the first held by Europeans within the limits of ancient Falmouth. Bradford, in his history of Plymouth says : " The Governor (Gorges) and some that depended upon him, returned, for England having scarcely saluted ye country in his government, not finding the state of things here to answer his quality and condition." Rev. Mr. Morrell returned home one year after the Governor. The real cause of the return of Gorges was probably the complaints made to the government of oppression by those owning ships in the fishery here, by which there was danger of the council losing their charter. Sir Ferdinando Gorges was three times summoned to the bar of Parliament to defend the charter, in which he was finally successful. Bradford's History of Plymouth, p. 141, 1623, says : " About ye latter end of June came in a ship with Captain Francis West, who had a commission to be Admiral of New England, to restrain interlopers and such fishing ships as came to fish and trade without a license from the Council of New England, for which they should pay a round sum of money. But he could do no good of them, for they were too strong for him, and he found the fishermen to be stubborn fellows. And their owners, upon complaint made to the Parliament, procured an order that fish should be free." The bill did not receive the royal assent. The question of the fisheries occasioned an earnest debate in Parliament, and the great patent of New England was denounced as a monopoly. Lord Coke said to Sir Ferdinando Gorges "Shall none visit that coast for fishing? This is to make a monopoly upon the seas which were wont to be free. If you alone are to pack and dry fish, you attempt a monopoly of the wind and sun."

In his "Brief Narration," the elder Gorges, in relation to the Governor's return, says: "Believing that the supplies he expected would follow according to the undertakings of divers his familiar friends, who had promised as much. But they hearing how I sped in the House of Parliament withdrew themselves, and myself and friends were wholly disabled to do anything to purpose. This coming to my son's ears, he was advised to return home till better occasion should offer itself unto him."

But to return to Levett's narrative: He says in his title-page that his voyage ended in 1624, but nowhere does he say at what time of the year he left his plantation for England, but from his recital of conversation at an interview with the sagamores at his house, we learn what were his intentions. He says:

" A little before my departure there came these Sagamores to see me: Sadamoyt, the great Sagamore of the east country; Manawormet, Oppasunwit, Skedraguscett, Cogawesco, Somerset, Conway, and others. They asked me why I would be gone out of their country? I was glad to tell them my wife would not come thither except I did fetch her. Then they run out upon her in evil terms and wished me to let her alone, and take an other. I said she was a good wife, and I had children by her, and I loved her well; so I satisfied them. Then they told me that I and my wife and children, with all my friends, should be heartily welcome into that country at any time. Then they must know how long I would be wanting. I told them so many months. They asked me what I would do with my house; I told them I would leave ten of my men there until I came again."

Levett probably remained until the fishing ships left in the fall, to be with his men to overlook their work of preparing for his permanent residence.

The last and largest part of Levett's book is taken up with an account of the Indians, the country, and the benefits of emigration, both to England and the emigrants, and thus concludes: "And if we will endure poverty in England wilfully, and suffer so good a country as this is to lie waste, I am persuaded we are guilty of a grievous sin against God, and shall never be able to answer for it." Undoubtedly the same reasons that induced Governor Gorges to abandon the country, prevented the return of Levett, — the uncertainty about the fate of the charter and the liberty conceded by the government to traders to the coast. Levett was evidently well educated. His book is written in better style than most of the productions of the travelers of his time.

Interest is naturally felt to ascertain where Levett located his habitation, but this must be left to conjecture, assisted by some evidence lately made public. He had a large unoccupied area to choose from. His first thought would be safety, and next the natural advantage of good fresh water, sheltered landing, and good soil. All of these he could secure by a settlement on Hog Island.

After a careful examination of the upper islands of the harbor I am convinced that Hog Island was the one pitched upon by Levett for his plantation, and where he built his house and passed the winter of 1623-4. That Levett pitched upon an island for his home is confirmed by Robert Trelawney's letter to Sir Ferdinando Gorges (Trelawney Papers, p. 103), complaining of Cleeves for setting down where he did. In 1636 he wrote that Cleeves "said that it was formerly granted to one Levett, and by him to one Wright. . . . . whereas, Levett never took that as a part of his patent, but an island in the bay of Casco." This was written only twelve years after Levett's occupation, and would of course be correctly stated by a gentleman of Trelawney's character.

In a manuscript description of New England lately discovered in the British Museum, evidently written by Samuel Maverick in 1660, although without name or date is this relating to Casco Bay. After describing Pemaquid and Sagadahock which was evidently done by some official authority, the author proceeds:

"Casco Bay. Between Sagadahocke and Cape Elizabeth, lying about seven miles asunder is Casco Bay. About the year 1632 * there was a Patent granted to one Capt. Christopher Levett for 6000 acres of land which he took up in this bay near Cape Elizabeth, and built a good house and fortified well on an island lying before Casco River. This he sold and his interest in the Patent to Mr. Ceeley, Mr. Jope and Company of Plymouth (England), in this Casco Bay and many scattering Families settled. There was a Patent granted for this Bay some years since by the title of the Province of Ligonia to Colonel Alexander Rigby afterwards a judge and under his Government the people lived some years, till of late the Government of the Massachusits hath made bold to stretch its jurisdiction to the middle of

* Maverick's date should be 1622.

3

this Bay, and as lying in their way have taken in a dozen Governments more." *

To me it appears probable that the sandy cove west, and near the old farmhouse on the south side of Great Hog Island was the place where Levett harbored his boats and built his house; and the near safe anchorage was where Governor Gorges' ship — the Swan — spent the winter. No spot visited by the Rev. Chaplain Morrell would be more likely to inspire a poet to write of

" The beautiful shores of New England."

Shell fish must have been plenty in this cove, as there is on the shore a continuous shell-bank composed mostly of clam shells. This undoubtedly was a favorite resort for the Indians, and the Sagamore Cogawesco piloted Levett to this cove in his own boat. A special inducement to Levett to choose this place was the abundance of spring water on both Hog Islands. Tradition points to this as the earliest settlement on the islands, and the apple trees and unknown graves indicate it to be that.

The farm on the south side of Hog Island is probably the oldest clearing for settlement within the bounds of ancient Falmouth. Tradition has always pointed to this spot as one of the first occupied here. On DeBarres' chart of the coast, the survey for which was made by the British government in 1760, this farm and the buildings are distinctly and prominently marked in connection with the

---

* When Winthrop and his company arrived in 1630 Maverick was settled at Noddles Island, now East Boston. This manuscript fixes the date of his arrival to be in 1622. He was then about twenty-two years old. Maverick was a Church of England man. The long residence of Maverick on these shores gives his Description of New England great value with historians.

ancient anchorage of "Hog Island Roads." On the arrival of Mowatt and his squadron, Parson Smith noted, "1775, November 16th, a fleet of six vessels of war anchored at *the Island*." It is well known from those who witnessed it, that these vessels anchored first in Hog Island Roads. Parson Smith indicates that this was *the Island* best known.

> " Here the dark forest's midnight shade began
> To own the power of cultivated man;
> Here is the shore, whose wide-extended breast
> First gave its borders for the wanderers rest."

In writing to Trelawney from Richmond's Island in 1640, Winter makes this memorandum (Trelawney Papers p. 251), "Edmond Baker of Newton Ferrers which dwelt at the house in Casco ten years since." There must have been a house at Casco at the time named, 1630. The editor of the Trelawney Papers supposes that this was the house built by Levett and that it was on House Island, and that the house gave the island its name. This supposition is rendered improbable by a deed of the western half of the island to the United States by John Green Walden in 1808 (Cumberland Records, Book 53, p. 581), in which the island is called "*Howes alias House Island*," indicating that its name was derived from a former owner or occupant named "Howe." From *Howes* to *House* is an easy and probable transition. These men, Thomas Alger, Edmond Baker, and Nicholas Rouse, who "dwelt in the house at Casco," were probably of the party of ten which Levett left there in 1624 to keep the house until his return. Others would be likely to join the Trelawney Colony, whose descendants yet remain in the vicinity of Spurwink. If this could be established it would prove the continued occupation of the soil of old Falmouth by Levett's company, the first who built here.

Levett's account of his voyage was published in 1628. The year previous he had not abandoned his project of building a city at Casco, as it is recorded that in 1627 he induced the King to issue a proclamation for a contribution to be taken in the churches to aid him in his intention "to build a city and call it by the name of York." Nothing definite is known of him after this. Winthrop mentions that a Captain Levett died in 1628 on his way to England. If this had been Christopher, the councilor of the New England Company and the associate of the Gorges family, it would have been so noted by the Governor.

CHAPTER II.

SPURWINK AND RICHMOND'S ISLAND. WALTER BAGNALL. HIS TREAS-
URE. RICHARD BRADSHAW, RICHARD TUCKER AND GEORGE
CLEEVES AT SPURWINK. TRELAWNEY AND GOODYEAR'S PATENT;
IT DID NOT CONVEY ABSOLUTE TITLE TO RICHMOND'S ISLAND.
JOHN WINTER. RAISING OF CORN; MILLS FOR GRINDING. THE
FIRST VESSELS BUILT IN FALMOUTH. GOATS, HOGS, AND THE FIRST
NEAT CATTLE.

AFTER the brief settlement by Levett and his men in
1623–4, the next occupation of any part of old Falmouth
by a European was Richmond's Island, by Walter Bagnall,
in 1628. He had only one associate, servant or assistant,
which, is not known, Winthrop calls him John P——. He
was a trader with the Indians, and probably with the fishing
ships, from whom he must have obtained his supplies. Boston was not settled until three years later. The Indians
were then numerous at Spurwink and Casco in summer.
In 1636, Trelawney wrote to Sir Ferdinando Gorges that
" this was one of their [the Indians] greatest rendezvous."

Bagnall was killed on the third of October, 1631, by
Squidraset and his company, an Indian sagamore whom
Levett mentions. There is a creek in the present town of
Falmouth, bearing the name of this chief; it is variously
spelled.

Charles Francis Adams, in a note to the New English
Canaan, supposes Bagnall to have been formerly a servant
to Morton at Merry Mount. Morton says, "a servant of
mine in five years was thought to have a thousand pounds
in ready gold, gathered by beaver; when he died, what ever

29

became of it?" Winthrop says "this Bagnall was some
time servant to one in the Bay, and these three years had
dwelt alone in said Isle, and had gathered about four hundred pounds, most in goods; he was a wicked fellow, and
had much wronged the Indians." Adams says Morton
alone in the bay at that time, had any number of servants.
Perhaps the fact of Bagnall having served Morton at Merry
Mount, was Winthrop's authority for calling him "a wicked
fellow." Governor Wiggin of Piscataqua notified Winthrop of the murder at Richmond's Island, and urged him
to send twenty men to revenge it. Winthrop wrote, "The
Governor thought best to sit still awhile." This expression
of the Massachusetts Governor strengthens the conjecture
that the murdered man was from Merry Mount, and an
Episcopalian.

Bagnall first set down on the island without a title, but
according to the council records a grant of the island was
made to him in 1631, three months after his death. This
grant indicates that Bagnall was not the despicable fellow
described by Winthrop, or else he had powerful friends in
England. Bagnall was killed October 3d, 1631, and not
until August, 1632, was any movement made to punish the
murderers. At that date the General Court took action in
the matter, and passed this order: "In consideration that
further justice ought to be done in this murder, the court
order that a boat sufficiently manned be sent with a commission to deal with the plantation at the eastward, and to
join with such of them as are willing thereto for examination of the murder, and for apprehending such as shall be
guilty thereof, and to bring the prisoners into the Bay."

About this time a noted pirate captain named Dixy Bull
was committing depredations along the coast, and Massa-

chusetts colony fitted out of an expedition against him.* Captain Clapp is quoted by Prince as saying:

" There arose up against us one Bull, who went to the eastward trading, turned pirate, took a vessel or two, plundered some planters there abouts, and intended to return into the Bay, and do mischief unto our magistrates here in Dorchester, and other places. But as they were weighing anchor [at Pemaquid] one Mr. Shurt, his men, shot from the shore and struck the principal actor dead, and the rest were filled with fear and horror. These men fled eastward, and Bull got into England; but God destroyed this wretched man. Thus the Lord saved us from their wicked device against us."

In July 1633, in a letter to Trelawney, Winter mentions the depredations of Dixy Bull at Pemaquid, and says he intended to visit Richmond's Island, and take away their men and provisions, and asks to have some pieces of ordnance sent from England to defend the plantation. Two pieces of ordnance arrived in the ship Hunter in June of the next year. In an inventory of goods at Richmond's Island in 1639, the following arms are named: " Three pieces of ordnance — two sakers, one demi culverin, with carriages, besides a variety of small arms." At the island, above the landing, in a semi-circle facing the anchorage, are several indentations in the earth with projecting knolls toward the landing, which probably mark the places where these pieces of ordnance were mounted.

---

* From the account of William Pincheon, treasurer of the Massachusetts Colony:

1632 " Paid Mr. Alcock for a fat hog to victual the pinnace for the taking of Dixy Bull	3 10 0	
Paid Goodman Lyman for a fat hog for the same use	3 10 0	
Paid Mr. Shurt of Pemaquid by order of Court for provisions for the pinnace, 26¼ lbs. Beaver	13 2 6	
Paid Lieutenant Mason for his service in the pinnace by order of Court	10 0 0	

On the return of this expedition, which was jointly fitted out by the Massachusetts and Piscataqua colonies, they stopped at Richmond's Island to bring the guilty parties "into the Bay." The murderer, Squidraset, did not wait around the island for punishment, but when the expedition arrived, as ordered by Governor Winthrop, he was probably at his home at the lower falls of the Presumpscot; but Black Will of Nahant was at the island enjoying his clam-bakes, and not expecting injury. Him the Massachusetts folks seized and hung for a murder of which he was innocent. The Bay people probably acted upon the principle of hang-ing a proxy if it was more convenient, as on a former occa-sion, as related by Morton in his New English Canaan. He represents that the Pilgrims hanged an old and bedridden pauper who could not labor, in place of a culprit who was a useful cobbler and could not be spared so well.

Wood in his New England Prospects calls this Indian sagamore "Duke William." Lewis, the historian of Lynn, calls him "Poquanum, or Dark-skin," and says he was Sagamore of Nahant. There are depositions in Salem court records, which prove that he was known by the familiar name of "Black Will," and that in 1630 he sold the prom-ontory of Nahant to Thomas Dexter for a suit of clothes.

On the eleventh of May, 1855, Richmond's Island being then owned by Dr. John Cummings, his farmer with his two boys were plowing on the harbor side of the island, and about four rods from the high bank a stone pot was discov-ered in the bottom of the furrow. It was laid aside, and afterward examined, when it was found to be filled with earth at the top, and gold and silver coins at the bottom in separate parcels, and a gold ring in the middle space. There were twenty-seven silver coins, all shillings and six-penny pieces, of the reign of Elizabeth. There were four shillings and sixteen six-penny pieces, the oldest of these was 1564, of the reign of James I. There were four shillings and one sixpence; the oldest date 1606, of the reign of Charles I; one shilling and one sixpence bearing the date of 1625. The gold coins numbered twenty-one: ten sovereigns and three half sovereigns, of the time of James I.; seven sovereigns of Charles I.; one Scottish coin dated 1602, which is the only gold coin bearing a date. The total standard value of the coins was one hundred dollars. The pot in which the treasure was found would hold about a quart, and was globe-shaped, with a small bottom and top.

The ring found in the pot with the coin is a wedding signet-ring of fine gold, weighing eight pennyweights and four grains. The signet is oval, three-fourths by five-eighths of an inch in size. On the outer side of the surface is an ornamental border, in the center the letters G. V. Inside is engraved the word " United," then the figure of two united hearts, and the words, " Death only partes." The workmanship is remarkably good, the letters well formed and sharply cut. The metal is bright and the preservation perfect. This ring is an object of remarkable interest, and is now in the possession of the son of Mr. Cummings. A number of the coins are in the cabinet of the Maine Historical Society, and in the sixth volume of the society's collections is a full description of the several coins, the ring, and the circumstances of their discovery, by Hon. William Willis. A careful spading of the locality where the treasure was found failed to reveal anything of more value than broken pottery, glass bottles, spikes, nails, and an iron spoon, showing that it was the site of a house without a cellar. Mr. Willis attributed the ownership of the treasure

to Walter Bagnall. If that is correct the deposit had lain
in its place about two and a quarter centuries, and yet
neither the coins nor the ring were corroded.

While Bagnall was occupying the island, Richard Bradshaw was settled on the mainland at Spurwink, of whom
little is known, except what we learn from George Cleeves.
In his declaration in his action against Winter for trespass
in 1640, he made oath to the following statement: "Joining himself with Richard Tucker, then of Spurwink, who
had also a right of inheritance there, the which he bought
and purchased for a valuable consideration, of Richard
Bradshaw, who was formerly *settled there* by Capt. Walter
Neale, by virtue of a commission by some of the Lord's
patentees." *

The word "settled" was one much used at that time, and
in this connection implied a house and home. I think it is
a fair inference that Bradshaw had a house at Spurwink,
which he conveyed to Tucker with the "right of inheritance." When George Cleeves came, he probably built
another house. In a letter to Trelawney, Winter mentions,
["Trelawney Papers" page thirty-two], the occupation of
"the house old Cleeves built."

Two years after the taking possession of Richmond's
Island by Walter Bagnall, and one year before his death,
Richard Tucker settled on the east side of Spurwink river,
in the place of Bradshaw. Here were extensive marshes,
both salt and fresh, furnishing immediate pasturage and hay
for cattle, without the laborious process of felling and burning the trees, which must be done before any hay-crop
could be raised on upland. From whence Tucker came is

---

* Walter Neale arrived in this country in 1630, and returned to England
in 1633. He came out to take charge of the company at Piscataqua.

unknown. He was joined the same year by George Cleeves, who came from Plymouth, England. There was a large house on their plantation, and here they pursued the usual occupations of planters on the coast, such as farming, fishing, fowling, and trading with the natives, whom their successor, Trelawney, says came here in great numbers. Unfortunately for Tucker and Cleeves, who supposed that they had a title under a proclamation of King James, in December, 1631, a grant was made by the Council of Plymouth in England, which included, with an enlargement of two thousand acres in 1636, all the land from Spurwink to the river of Casco. This grant was in the names of Robert Trelawney and Moses Goodyear, merchants of Plymouth in England, and covered all the present town of Cape Elizabeth, on which they established an extensive plantation and fishery. As this was one of the principal business places on the coast at the time, I will give a description of the island and the antecedents of its chief proprietor.

During the reign of the Second Charles, the merchants trading to New England pursued their business under great difficulties and discouragements. The Dutch commander, Van Tromp, swept the English Channel with a broom at his mast-head, indicating his purpose. Another pest was the Turkish pirates who came from Sallee, in Morocco. In spite of the weak naval police maintained in the Channel by England, these pirates carried on a regular trade. First, they would capture a ship, confiscate the cargo, sell the crew as slaves, and then allow all who could, to obtain a ransom through friends at home, amounting to from thirty to three hundred pounds. So regular had this system become in 1625, that the master and wardens of Trinity House reported to the Privy Council that there were from twelve hundred to fourteen hundred Englishmen, captives in Sallee; the greater part taken within thirty miles of Dartmouth, Plymouth, and Falmouth. Within our own century the Barbary pirates have been one of the dreaded dangers to traders to Europe and the Mediterranean, and the expedition for their chastisement, served to develop the naval skill and gallantry of our own Edward Preble, who earned the reputation of being the "father of the American navy." Nor were Dutch cruisers and the pirates of Morocco the only dangers lying in wait for the English mariners in those days. The dangerous headlands and shoals were not marked by the present aids to navigation. It was not until 1664 that Sir John Coryton, at the suggestion of Winstanly, petitioned the Trinity House for liberty to erect lighthouses on Ramhead and the Eddystone. When erected, the best means to light those towers was judged to be by fires of bituminous coal.

During the early part of the seventeenth century the English Port of Plymouth sent to the New England coast most of the trading and fishing ships which returned in the fall, often by the way of Spain, where cargoes of fish and staves found a ready market. Those sailing for England direct, carried besides fish of all kinds, pipe staves, oar rafters of ash, and furs. Naturally enough Sir Ferdinando Gorges who lived at Butshead and the Trelawneys of Ham brought their trade to their own port of Plymouth.

The family of Trelawney had furnished mayors for the city of Plymouth for many years, when the office was one of great dignity and authority in the west of England. Robert Trelawney, the Third, who had succeeded to the mayoralty, was born at Plymouth in 1598; was married in 1623, and had a large family of children. On the first of

December, 1631, Robert Trelawney and Moses Goodyear, another Plymouth merchant, obtained of the "President and Council of Plymouth," a grant of land which is thus described in the "Indenture," leaving out some superfluous words:

"All those lands lying along the sea coast eastward, between the land before granted, to the land of the said Captain Thomas Cammock [Black Point], and the bay and river of Casco; together free liberty to and for the said Robert Trelawney and Moses Goodyear to fowl and fish, and stages, kayes, and places for taking, saving, and preserving of fish, to erect, make and maintain, and use in, upon, and near the island commonly called Richmond's Island . . . . paying therefor yearly for ever unto the President and council for every one hundred acres of the said land in use twelve pence lawful money of England." The consideration named was "That the said Robert Trelawney, Moses Goodyear, and their associates have adventured and expended great sums of money in the discovery of the coasts and harbors of those parts, and are minded to undergo a further charge in settling a plantation in the *main land*." * From the phraseology of the grant, it was the intention to convey the right to occupy the island for the taking and curing of fish only; and that absolute title to the soil was conveyed only to the "main land," where it was the intention of "settling a plantation." Trelawney

* The English records say that in 1629 letters of marque " were granted to Nicholas Opie and Robert Trelawney as owners of the Confidence of Plymouth, of fifty tons, Master Lawrence Johnson, and her pinnace of thirty tons." These and others of Trelawney's ships probably had been on our coast and their masters were familiar with the island, which afterwards under the ownership of Trelawney, became the seat of a large fishing and European trade.

and Goodyear, the grantees, appointed John Winter of
Plymouth, England, their agent to manage their plantation,
he to have one-tenth of the profits, and a salary. Winter
had "fished at Casco," was then in the country, and was
undoubtedly the explorer and prime mover in obtaining the
patent, which was sent over to him, and he immediately
entered upon his agency, but Goodyear's name does not
appear in the business.

Captain Thomas Cammock whose grant is mentioned as
joining that of Trelawney and Goodyear on the west
obtained it the same year. Jocelyn who came passenger
from England with him in 1638, says Cammock was "a near
kinsman of the Earl of Warwick."

The "Trelawney Papers," being a voluminous correspondence between the agent and owner of Richmond's Island
and Spurwink plantation, has been (August, 1884) published, edited by Mr. James P. Baxter. In his introduction
he gives the following explanation of the way by which they
came into the possession of the Maine Historical Society.
"Some time in the year 1872, the late John Wingate Thornton of Boston, while looking over an English catalogue,
noticed a document advertised therein, which was said to
bear the autograph of Robert Trelawney, a name in which
he was interested on account of its associations with the
locality where he was born, which he knew had once been
held by Robert Trelawney, a Plymouth, England, merchant.
. . . ." By correspondence Mr. Thornton learned that
these papers were in the possession of the Rev. C. T. Col-
lins Trelawney, who finally presented them to the Maine
Historical Society. Mr. Thornton died while editing the
papers for publication, when the task was undertaken by
Mr. Baxter, who has arranged a work with explanatory

notes, which shows his industry and talent as a historian, and which has given a new interest to this locality of a plantation of a bygone age.

Trelawney and Goodyear intended their grant to include a shipping port, as well as a plantation, and therefore commenced to build on the island. Soon after taking possession Winter turned his attention to the ejection from their grant of Tucker and Cleeves. Cleeves said in his declaration after their occupation, "for two years or thereabouts this dependent, John Winter, came and pretended an interest there by virtue of a succeeding patent surreptitiously obtained, and so by force of arms expelled and thrust away the plaintiff from his house, lands and goods." This action against Winter for trespass was brought in 1640, as soon as regular courts were established by Sir Ferdinando Gorges. The verdict was as follows: "The jury find for the plaintiff the house and land enclosed, containing four acres or thereabout, and give him eighty pounds for damage, and twelve shillings and sixpence for costs of court." Cleeves and Tucker had removed to Casco Neck, and although they recovered for their improvements, Winter held the land. We will now leave Tucker and Cleeves in their new home, and follow for a while the fortunes of the Trelawney plantation under John Winter's administration. Winter set vigorously about his fishing and shipping port on the island, and in improving the Tucker and Cleeves plantation at Spurwink opposite. We get from his letters to his employer the extent and description of his buildings. In June, 1634, he wrote: "I have built a house here at Richmond's Island that is forty feet in length, and eighteen feet broad within the sides, beside the chimney, which is large, with an oven in each end of him, and he is so large that we can place our kettle within the clavell piece. We can brew,* bake, and boil our kettle all at once in him, with the help of another house that I have built, under the side of our house, where we set our sieves and mill, and mortar, to break our corn and malt and to dress our meal in. I have two chambers in him, and all our men lies in one of them, and every man hath his close-boarded cabin [berth], and I have room enough to make a dozen close-boarded cabins more if I have need of them; and in the other chamber I have room enough to put the ship's sails into, and all our dry goods which are in casks; and I have a store-house in him that will hold eighteen or twenty tons of cask, which we put our bread and beer into, and every one of these rooms is closed with locks and keys unto them. At the main [Spurwink] we have built no house, but our men live in the house that the old Cleeves built."

In a letter from Rev. Robert Jordan to Robert Trelawney of Plymouth, England, July 2d, 1642, is this: "The act will declare itself to you or any man of judgment, that you should have Spurwink houses and land was consented to by all." The word "houses" shows that there was more than one house then on the plantation.

The mention by Winter of the mill and mortar, calls to

---

* This "brewing" was then an important part of kitchen work; neither tea nor coffee were in use, and beer of home brewing was the common drink. In George Cleeves' complaint to the court against Robert Jordan for ejecting him from his house at Casco in 1661, he enumerates among others the following as a grievance: "And the more to vex and grieve me he brought with him one of his own men who was stark drunk, taking my kettle and pot being full of wort for beer, ready to turn up, and threw it about the house, and carried away said kettle and pot, and detaineth them to this day." In Winter's inventory in 1640, the "brewing vessels" are mentioned.

mind the importance attached by the early settlers to Indian corn, and the means available to make it into meal for cooking. Corn mills operated by hand power, after the corn had been broken in a mortar, were the usual means of reducing the hard kernel to meal and hominy for bread, samp, and other various dishes. This corn mill mentioned by Winter is included in an invoice of goods sent from England in 1634 by Trelawney. There were then no water mills, nor wind mills for grinding corn east of Boston. Governor Winthrop's journal mentions in October 1632, that Captain Thomas Cammock of Black Point, Scarborough, and Edward Godfrey of Piscataqua [Kittery], arrived in Boston in a pinnace with sixteen hogsheads of corn to be ground there at the wind mill. The Pemaquid, Monhegan, and Sheepscot settlements were dependent upon the same mill mentioned by Winthrop, to grind their corn. In writing to Trelawney in June 1634, Winter mentions "sieves, mill, and mortar, to break our corn." In July 1639, Winter wrote to his principal, "I want a mill to grind English grain. When we have got some English grain it is a great trouble and hindrance of time to go 30 leagues to mill to grind it. Here is never a mill in all the country but in the Bay" [Massachusetts]. In 1642, in Winter's inventory of property at Richmond's Island he mentions "one steel mill, one other hand mill, two grinding stones, one pair of stampers for Indian corn." In 1643, he mentions "one mill that goeth with a horse." This is, I think, the only mention of a horse by Winter at the plantation.

Indian corn was an important article of diet and commerce in the first settlement of this country. The English found the Indians subsisting upon it for a large part of the year. Father Rasle, in a letter from Norridgewock in 1723,

4

to his brother, says of the Indians, " They catch the river fish as they ascend in the spring, and dry them, and live on them all the time they are planting their fields. They do not give their corn the last tillage until Corpus Christi day ; after this they deliberate as to what spot on the seashore they shall go to find something to live on until the harvest, ordinarily at the fifteenth of August." While taking the alewives for food, the Indians also caught enough to dress their corn land, putting one or two in each hill.

Bradford in his history of Plymouth says, in 1621, " As many as were able began to plant their corn, in which ser-vice Squanto (the friendly Indian) stood them in great stead, showing them both the manner of setting it, and after how to dress and tend it. Also he told them except they got fish and set with it (in these old grounds) it would come to nothing ; and showed them that in the middle of April they should have store enough come up the brook." Edward Winslow's " Account of the Indians in Purchase," says, " The corn will not be procured without good labor and diligence, especially in seed time, when it must also be watched by night to keep the wolves from the fish, till it be rotten, which will be in fourteen days ; yet men agreeing together, and taking their turns, it is not much." To such an extent was the fertilizing of the land with fish carried, that in 1639 the Plymouth colony restrained, by a penalty, the using of any cod or bass fish for manuring the ground.*

There was an Indian corn field on the north side of the Presumpscot river below the falls of Ammoncongan ; it is

---

* Hutchinson, Vol. I., p. 90, and Historical Collections, Vol. II., p. 91. " Large quantities of herring had been taken from the streams of Cape Cod to fertilize the soil, up to 1718, when it was ordered that no herrings shall be taken in future to fish corn."

mentioned in the deed of the "mile square" from Cunna-teconnett and Warrabitu, native chiefs, to George Munjoy in 1666. "Beginning at the great falls [Saccarappa], and extending down the river to the lowest part of the *town planting ground.*" Christopher Levett who was here in 1623, and visited an Indian settlement at the lower falls of the Presumpscot, says: "On both sides of the river there is goodly ground." It was probably cleared or he would not have mentioned its quality. Tradition fixes this land as an Indian planting ground, which seems probable as the land in both these localities in old Falmouth was suitable for corn, and at the foot of the falls was plenty of fish in the spring for food for the planters and to "fish the corn."

It was not known until 1762 that a good crop of corn could be obtained from burnt land. Colonel Isaac Parsons of New Gloucester observed the condition of the ground where a growth of hard wood had been burnt off — that it was light and there was nitre with the ashes. He concluded that it contained the ingredients necessary for a crop of corn and was loose enough without plowing, as had always been supposed to be indispensable, and that it must be hilled up to make it stand. Colonel Parsons tried the experiment in the year named of opening the sod among the stumps, with the corner of a hoe and dropping in the corn and then let the turf fall back in its place. The corn came up thrifty, and grew as well as in plowed land. At the proper time the rank "fire weeds" were hacked down with the hoe, and the result was an abundant harvest of sound corn. This manner of raising corn came to be practiced in all the eastern country, and more than doubled the corn crop in the then District of Maine, with a great saving of labor. This simple mode of planting required a strong faith in the old settlers, and was slow in coming into general practice, but it made it possible for the new settler to raise a sustaining crop the first year after the felling of the growth. This discovery, with the fall of Quebec three years before, ending the Indian wars, was the means of hastening the settlement of the whole eastern country.

The following from the Eastern Herald, printed in Portland September 10, 1792, will give an idea of the importance of the new method of raising corn without plowing. The paper says, " General Wadsworth ·thinks he has raised more than one thousand bushels of corn this season on burnt land that is now out of the way of the frost, at a place called Great Ossipee [Hiram], about thirty-six miles from this town." The fear of the frost was not the only anxiety of the early settler for his corn crop. As soon as it was "full in the milk," the bears, raccoons, squirrels, crows, jays, and several other birds, seemed to think it grew especially for their food, and each feared that he should not get his proper share. The most troublesome were the bears and coons, as they came in the night. A few years ago I was staying at a farmhouse in Albany, N. H., in October. I noticed several fires in the evening above on the mountain side, and was told they were built there nightly to keep the bears from the corn.

Trelawney had sent out some goats for the plantation, July, 1634. Winter wrote, " We had an ill hap of your goats sent ; the dogs killed one ewe goat, and the ram goat was chased into the woods by our great boar." In June, 1636, Winter says, " There is no Indians comes near us that we know since they killed our pigs." Jocelyn says, " goats were the first small cattle they had in the country. He was counted no boddy that had not a ' trip ' or flock of goats.

A he goat gelt at Michaelmas and turned out to feed will be fat in a months time, and is as good meat as a wether." In 1639, Winter writes, " One must be always to follow the pigs at the main [Spurwink] or else we shall lose them all. There be divers would have goats but they lack money about these parts. I could willingly sell a score of goats for we overlay this island too much, and if I put them on the main the wolves will have them all." In July, 1639, there were sixty-two goats on the island, young and old. In December Winter says; " I think I shall kill four or five and twenty fat hogs this season. I make account to send some pork into the Bay [Massachusetts] to sell. Our swine at first coming here would feed themselves in the woods and would weigh two hundred weight. Now we are faine to feed most of them and they do not weigh above one hundred and sixty pounds, the best." In June, 1640, there were on the island and main land seventy-six goats and kids, seventy swine and forty-five young pigs. In 1638, Winter complained that " wolves and bears do kill many and maketh the pigs fearful to stay any way in the woods for all, I have a man to follow after them." Jocelyn who was at Black Point in 1637, says, " hogs are here innumerable every planter hath a herd. When they feed on shell fish and the like as they do that are kept near the sea and by fishers stages, they taste fishy and rank, but when they are fed on white oak acorns or Indian corn there is no better pork in the world."

The raising of hogs was a prominent source of profit at the Spurwink plantation. In 1634, Winter wrote to Trelawney : " I would that you had sent us no more beef nor pork by the James, for I hope we shall have pork enough here-

after to serve our turn for victualing. We have good store
of pigs young and old, if it please God to prosper no worse
hereafter. We have near about two hundred marked, but
we loose some in the woods for the want of one to look
after them. We must have a man to keep them hereafter.
I could wish you would get one that hath used to keep pigs,
that he may be careful of them, for I hope we shall find
some profit of them. We have about fifty sows young and
old, that will be breeders and hereafter they will increase
apace. . . . . We gave them no meat [food] at all this
winter, but they did get their meat themselves and kept
themselves in very good case for this was a very fair winter,
and we have at the main [Spurwink plantation], store of
acorns and clams in the river, that the pigs feed upon."
The next year 1635, Winter wrote, " I think we lost last
winter between fifty and sixty pigs young and old, and we
had ninety that did live all the winter, though somewhat
changeable; but yet, of them you shall find good profit
hereafter. I hope we shall kill fifty at least this winter, and
good swine I hope they will be; they are now running in
the woods fat and worth killing."

On his return to Richmond's Island after a visit to England, Winter wrote to Trelawney under date of June, 1636 :
" We have had great loss on our pigs since I went away,
which our men says Indians killed many, and they say the
wolves have killed others, and some died of the winter. As
yet I can hear no other way how they came to an end, but
howsoever the loss is great. They do acknowledge they had
at Michaelmas three hundred, and they say they killed but
forty, and they think they have now alive betwixt fifty and
sixty, but I could not see above forty since I came hither;

therefore you may not expect to trust on victualing here upon flesh the next year." *

The venture of the goats and hogs at the plantation proved so encouraging that on Winter's return passage from a visit to England he brought some neat cattle. In a letter to Trelawney dated at the island on the twenty-third of June, 1636, he says, " I praise God we brought our cattle here safe with us, and I have got a bull to go with them and they prove very well here upon the island.† Since my coming here I have received eight young yearlings more which your brother [Edward Trelawney] bought in the Bay [Massachusetts] and as he writes they are of the Dutch breed."

I think there is no mention of horses at the plantation,

---

* From York records we take the following : " The humble petition of William Cutt and —— Cutting, showeth that John Reynolds, contrary to an act in Court that no wimin shall live on the Isle of Shoals, hath brought his wife thither, with an intention there to live and abide. And hath also brought upon Hog Island a great stock of goats and hogs which doth not only spoil much fish, to the great dammage of several others and likewise many of your petitioners, but also doth spoil the spring of water that is on that island, making it unfit or unserviceable for any manner of use, which is the only relief and sustenance of all the rest of the island.

" Your petitioners therefore pray that the said Reynolds may be ordered to remove his said goats from the island forthwith. Also that the act of the Court before mentioned may be put in execution for the removal of all wimen inhabiting there — and your petitioners shall ever pray." The order of the Court was that Reynolds should remove his swine from the island within twenty days. " And as for the removal of his wife (if no further complaint against her) she may yet enjoy the company of her husband. These dated the 20th of October, 1647."

† These were the first neat cattle ever brought to the territory afterward forming the town of Falmouth. The first cattle brought to Plymouth was only twelve years before — 1624.

but in September, 1638, Trelawney instructed Winter that
he had put on board the ship Hercules at Plymouth, England, bound to Richmond's Island, ten bushels of oats and
four trusses of hay, and ordered the captain to call at the
Isle of Mayo, one of the Cape Verds, and take on board six
asses to make a plow team, and sent harnesses for them
and the irons for a plow and harrow. These animals arrived
and are mentioned in the inventory of stock on the plantation.

There were a large number of ships trading to Richmond's
Island. The Hercules and Margery were owned by the
proprietors. The Richmond was built at the island and
another larger ship was built at the mouth of the Spurwink.
There were many ships chartered and sent here from Eng-
land. Among these were the Hope of Dartmouth, Bonny
Bess, Samuel, White Angel, Star, Exchange of Bristol,
Fellowship of Barnstable, Speedwell, True Love, Welcome,
Agnes, Fortune of London, Friendship, Heart's-Desire of
Abson, Holy Ghost, Lion, Mary-Rose, and Peter — the three
last from Barnstable, and Agnes of Antony. The Peter,
Capt. George Luxton of Barnstable, was at Casco Bay sell-
ing liquor in 1640. The Richmond which was launched at
the island in June, 1637, took pipe staves at Casco Bay for
her first cargo.

Among the scores of ships employed in the trade from
Richmond's Island by Trelawney and Winter was one called
the Speedwell. Not only from her name, but from the language of Winter to his principal concerning the vessel, I
think she was unquestionably the historical old Dutch ship
of the Pilgrims. "The smale ship" (of sixty tons) which
Governor Bradford says in his History of Plymouth, "was
bought and fitted in Holland, which was intended to help to

transport them, and to stay in the country and attend upon fishing, and such other affairs as might be for the good of the colony when they came there." In the Speedwell those from Holland left Delft Haven and arrived at Southampton in July, 1620, "where they found the bigger ship [the Mayflower] come from London, lying ready with all the rest of their company."

On the fifth of August the Pilgrims sailed from Southampton in the two ships, the Mayflower and Speedwell, for the New World. Bradford says: "Being thus put to sea, they had not gone far, but Mr. Reynolds the master of the lesser ship complained that he found his ship so leaky as he durst not put further to sea till she was mended. So the master of the bigger ship (called Mr. Joans) being consulted with, they both resolved to put into Dartmouth, and have her searched and mended, which was accordingly done to their great charge and loss of time and fair wind. She was here thoroughly searched from stem to stern; some leaks were found and mended, and now it was conceived by the workmen and all, that she was sufficient, and that they might proceed without either fear or danger. So with good hopes, from hence they put to sea again, conceiving they should go comfortably on, not looking for any more lets of this kind; but it fell out otherwise; for after they had gone to sea again above one hundred leagues without the Land's End, holding company together all this while, the master of the small ship complained his ship was so leaky as he must bear up or sink at sea, for they could scarce free her with much pumping. So they came to consultation again, and resolved both ships to bear up back again, and put into Plymouth, which accordingly was done. But no special leak could be found, but it was judged to be the general weakness of the ship, and that she would not prove sufficient for the voyage. Upon this it was resolved to dismiss her and a part of the company, and proceed with the other ship." From the volume of "Trelawney Papers," lately published by the Maine Historical Society, we learn that the weak old ship did "prove sufficient" afterward for a voyage to New England and to return.

John Winter, the agent at Richmond's Island, wrote to Trelawney in England on the eleventh of June, 1635, as follows: "Sir: It may please you to understand that the Speedwell arrived here on the twenty-sixth of April. By her I received your order for despatching her away for Bilboa. . . . . I have no other intent as yet but to come away in the Speedwell, for I think the company (men whose term of service had expired) will not come home in her otherwise; they tell me so plainly. The ship is an old leaky vessel still, — and our men are very unwilling to come home in her. You made choice of a very bad ship to come this way, but I assure myself that God of his mercy can bring us as safe home in this weak ship, as he can in a stronger if it please him."

This voyage of the Speedwell was made fifteen years after her failure to accompany the Mayflower. Would there probably be two Speedwells in the west of England within this time, both "old leaky vessels"? If this was not the Speedwell of the Pilgrims, why this expression of Winter, "The ship is an old leaky vessel *still*"? It implies that the ship had a bad reputation, which was known by Trelawney, Winter and their men. Her failure with the Mayflower was an event that all remembered. The "merchant adventurers" of Plymouth furnished the Pilgrims with the means to purchase the Speedwell in Holland, and when she proved insufficient they of course took her off their hands and had her repaired. True to her tradition the Speedwell sprung a leak in the harbor at Richmond's Island. Winter wrote on the twenty-sixth of June: " This letter not being sealed before an ill hap befel us of a great leak, which broke open upon us the night before we were ready to come to sea, that our men did pump between eight and nine hundred strokes a glass [an hour] — that we were compelled to take out most of our fish again and haul the ship ashore to stop the leak, the next strake from the garboard, in a seam and knot of the plank; but at present the ship is from the ground, and tight, and all the fish in that we took out."

The "smale ship" of ill omen did carry her passengers and cargo safe home. John Jocelyn says Winter was " a brave and discreet man." — his men must have believed him more than that when they thought his presence would save a leaky ship.

The historic Speedwell may have swung at her anchor in Portland harbor, as it often occurred before the improvement of the island harbor, when the wind was strong from certain points, that vessels were compelled to leave their anchorage and take shelter in Portland or Winter harbor, according to the direction of the wind.

Shipbuilding was one of the industries intended to be followed at Richmond's Island. A shipyard was established and carpenters brought out from England. It must have been slow work when all the wales and plank were sawed by hand for the lack of a saw mill. The long invoices of goods, materials and tools, which came from the proprietor in England, contains "whip saws, thwart saws, addzes, etc." Whipsaws are yet seen in use in the small shipyards of eastern Maine and the Provinces, to divide crooked timber or that which is too long for the mill. The log is rolled from a side-hill on to a high frame, or lifted by a purchase on to high horses. The " top sawyer " stands on the log and the "pitman" underneath, to draw the saw down. It is only made to cut in its descent. There is no *frame* to the saw as noted in the Trelawney Papers.

In May, 1636, Winter returned from a visit to England. He had left the plantation in charge of Narius Hawkins and Edward Trelawney, brother of the proprietor. While Winter was with his principal, evidently they had decided to build a small vessel for a coaster to the Isles of Shoals, where they had a fish house, or Boston, or to take a cargo to England if occasion required. In June, Winter wrote to Trelawney, " I do propose to build our bark about twenty-five or thirty tons; therefore you may please to send cables, canvass for sails, and ropes for rigging of her. Carpenters at home can direct you what will be needful for a bark of that burthen. You shall do well to have the carpenter that cometh in the ship a shoreman and to order it so with him that he may worke with our carpenter the time they are in the country." In another letter of the same month he asked to have " two or three murderers [cannon] and several small arms for the bark."

But in no letter which has been preserved is there any further mention of the building of the bark until eighth of July, 1637, when Winter wrote, " our new bark was launched on the tenth of June, but as yet no masts or yards made for her, nor deck calked." We learn that although the bark was so small she was to be square rigged, that is, with " yards," and had been one year in building, and bore the name of the island. She first made a trip to Massachusetts with Narius Hawkins as captain, and made one trip after mackerel in 1638.

June, 1639, Mr. Winter records a disaster to the Richmond which proved her strength. "Narius Hawkins last voyage in her for corn [to Virginia] she received a great storm at sea and with the stripe [stroke] of a sea laid the bark upon the side, her ballast shifting in the hold, and before they could right her they were fain to cut their mainmast by the board, and they lost all their sails and rigging of their mainmast, yet I praise God the bark took no hurt but proceeded in her voyage, and returned me home about fifty-one or fifty-two hogsheads of Indian corn." Winter mentions a great storm about Christmas, 1638, which swept away or stove all their boats, but "the Richmond here rode that storm and rode it very well without damage to anything." He never failed to say a good word for the Richmond.

On the tenth of July, 1639, Winter wrote to Trelawney, "The Richmond, God willing, is to come home to Plymouth, Stephen Nichols master, and as I had no fish, I thought good to load her with pipe staves. She departed this day to go up to Casco to take her lading." I have gleaned these notes of the Richmond from the "Papers" as she was the first vessel built within the bounds of ancient Falmouth, and next to Popham and Gilbert's bark Virginia ("a pretty pinnace of about some thirty ton," built at Sagadahoc in 1607), she was the first vessel built in what is now our State. For the history of Falmouth's first ship so far, we are indebted to the Trelawney volume. In the Public Record office in London we get another glimpse of her career in these brief entries. "These are to certify that there is landed at Falmouth [England] to his majesties use out of the Richmond of Plymouth, belonging to Mr. Robert Trelawney." Here follows an invoice of powder, muskets, swords and stores, and continues "on the fourteenth of

January, 1642." Another entry reads, "saved for his majesties use on board the Richmond of Plymouth six hundred and eighty-one ounces of plate, one gold hatband ninety-nine links, three ounces weight, being goods of R. Trelawney." And again, "received at St. Michael's Mount [Cornwall], out of the Richmond one hundred and fifty bushels of wheat, the goods of R. Trelawney." The confiscated bark was pressed into the service by the Parliament, and in the king's name was employed to convey away the property of the staunch old Cavalier her owner; and this is the last written history of the Richmond.

The success of the new bark (she is also spoken of as a "ship"), seems to have encouraged her builders to lay down the keel of a larger vessel. The next season, July 30th, 1638, Winter wrote, "our carpenter hath drawn out a draught for a new vessel, and says he cannot work by the draught you sent." Again he says, "the proportion of our new vessel is forty-eight foot by the keel, eighteen foot at the beam and eleven foot in the hold." July 8th, 1639, the master carpenter, Stephen Sargent wrote, "As for your new ship there was nothing provided for her when I came over here. Now we have gotten to your Island most of her timber and bends, some plank, and her beams are over here. For burden she will be one hundred tons. Except you send two good workmen to him who is here already, she cannot be built against our time be expired."

> "Covering many a rood of ground,
> Lay the timber piled around."

By the same ship, Winter wrote: "Our plank must have most of next summers drouth to season it. Our trees for most part of the plank were cut two years since. If I can get good plank, I hope we shall have a strong ship. I propose to bring her to two decks with a forecastle and quarter deck — nine foot in the hold and four and one-half foot betwixt the decks. The timber was all moulded before I had your last letter by the Hercules, otherwise I should have brought her to twenty tons greater."

Winter wrote to his partner from the Isles of Shoals on the twenty-first of June, 1641: "My being here at present is to get some pitch and some liquor casks and some other necessaries for our new ship. She was launched the fifteenth of this month. She swimbed as upright as might be when she was launched and very stiff of her side. We had much work to do on her when she was launched; both decks to calk, the hatches to make, her head to set up, her masts to make and her boat to build. We have had two ship carpenters, and two house carpenters since March, besides our own carpenters, and would have got more if I could have got them for money. After our higher deck is calked, and our mainmast in, I do propose to get in our fish as fast as I can, while the carpenters are doing the other work." The captain's name was Sargent and the mate's, Douglas.

On the twenty-ninth of June, 1641, Trelawney wrote to Winter from London during the long Parliament, of which he was a member, and which he mentions as "like to continue many years," although he sided with the king. He further says, "I hope my new ship by this time will be fully laden for Bilboa. I have caused an insurance to be made on her. God send her well." Mr. Trelawney's attention was absorbed in the contest between Charles the First and the Parliament. He thus closes the letter to Winter, "I resolve within a few days to go and see my wife and children which I have not done almost these nine months. I have not else but my love to you and Mrs. Winter, and to your daughter and all your company. Pray God ever to bless you, preserve and keep you. So to God I commend you and rest. Your assured loving friend, ROBERT TRELAWNEY." This is, I think, the last letter in the collection from Mr. Trelawney. A few months after it was written, he was arrested and imprisoned for an alleged treasonable speech, and died in confinement.

On the twenty-ninth of July, 1641, Winter wrote that the ship was ready for sea, and gave the items of her cargo but did not mention her name, therefore we cannot trace her career or fate. In a letter from Winter, July,. 1641, to Trelawney, he says, "our ship was but then launched but was not brought into the harbor." She was probably built at the mouth of the Spurwink.

At the commencement of the plantation the owners prepared for the purchase of the furs collected by the Indians. Few came to the island, and boats were sent east with suitable goods to barter for furs but they were not successful, and this branch of the intended trade was abandoned. In writing to Sir Ferdinando Gorges in 1637, complaining of Cleeves, he says, " He [Cleeves] has so enraged them [the Indians] against us that never any of them since his removal, have ever come near my people, though before it was one of their greatest rendevous."

John Josselyn, gentleman, who was at Richmond's Island in 1638, wrote out his travels in which he thus describes the importation of wine to the Maine coast fisheries. " At the end of his voyage the merchant comes in with a walking tavern, a bark laden with the blood of the rich grape, which they bring from Fayal, Madrid, Canaries, with brandy, rum, the Barbadoes strong-water, and tobacco."

In 1639, Winter wrote, " The ship that Trustum Bowes is

on, came from the Canaries laden with wine, strong waters, and sugar, and comes to a bad market. Great store of sack and strong waters comes in all the ships that come hither." There must have been a wine cellar at the island for the preservation of these wines at an even temperature. Winter mentions in 1643, the charge by Cogan, his commission merchant in Boston, for "bringing twelve buts of wine up to the cellar, and helping of it into the cellar, and for cellarage." In 1638, the Richmond took from Robert Trelawney to "the Bay [Massachusetts] thirty-four pipes of wine, fifty jars of oil, and earthern ware" with Winter's pious prayer, "God send it to a good market."

The fish cured and shipped at Richmond's Island, and indeed on the whole coast were of several kinds and cured in different manners. The favorite article for export was dry cod. "Core fish" were thoroughly salted in pickle, and packed without drying. Fish oil under the trade name of "Traine" was also an important staple in the fishery. "Dum fish" were those stained by imperfect drying. In the cargo of nearly every ship were hogsheads of "fish peas." These were the spawn or eggs of fish salted. Some kinds resemble peas and are as large. They are now known to commerce by the same name. Fish peas are erroneously noted in the volume of "Trelawney Papers" as a vegetable. Striped bass were a favorite fish with the fishermen in their season and were dried. The largest part of the fish cured at the island were shipped direct to Bilboa, Spain, some to the Canary Islands, and to Portugal. Wines were usually the return cargo to England, and much of it came to Richmond's Island and was sold to Boston and Piscataqua merchants.

In Winter's report to his principal of his proceedings in

5

June, 1634, he says, "I have made trial of fishing all this
year. I have a boat at sea always when there is weather for
them to go to sea. They did never miss a week but they
were at sea two or three days, and had always fish; sometimes thirty fishes, sometimes forty fishes, and sometimes
half a hundred; only two weeks of Christmas time we did
forbear,* but the 7th of January all three boats were to sea
again."

* These two weeks kept as a Christmas festival at Richmond's Island
is in strong and favorable contrast with the manner of passing that holi-
day season by the Pilgrims at Plymouth. In November, 1622, the ship
Fortune arrived at Plymouth with thirty-five passengers " to live in the
plantation. Most of them were lusty young men and wild enough."
Governor Bradford in his journal describes the suppression of all
attempt at Christmas sports at Plymouth. "On ye day called Christmas-
day ye Governor called them out to work (as was used) but ye most of
this new company excused themselves and said it went against their con-
sciencies to work on that day. So ye Governor told them that if they
made it a matter of conscience he would spare them till they were better
informed. So he led away ye rest and left them; but when they came
home at noon from their work he found them in ye street at play, openly;
some pitching ye bar, and some at stool ball and such like sports. So
he went to them and took away their implements, and told them that
was against *his* conscience, that they should play and others work. If
they made it a matter of devotion, let them keep their houses, but there
should be no gameing or reveling in ye streets, since which time nothing
hath been attempted that way at least openly."

CHAPTER III.

CHURCH OF ENGLAND MINISTERS AT RICHMOND'S ISLAND. RICHARD GIBSON. ROBERT JORDAN. DESCRIPTION OF RICHMOND'S ISLAND. FATAL SHIPWRECK.

In June, 1636, Winter went to England in the ship Speedwell as we have seen, leaving the plantation and fishery in charge of Narius Hawkins, a man of various attainments. He sometimes went skipper of a fishing boat; he was also a navigator, and went master of the new bark Richmond to Spain, and had just returned from that voyage. Edward Trelawney, brother of the principal proprietor, was at the plantation and had a joint care with Hawkins. In January while Winter was away, Edward Trelawney wrote to his brother of the state of the establishment and the employes and thus concluded: "But above all I earnestly request you for a religious, able minister, for its most pitiful to behold what a most heathen life we live." When Winter returned in May following he probably brought with him the desired minister. In October Winter wrote, "our minister is a very fair conditioned man, and doth keep himself in good order, and instructs our people well, if please God to give us grace to follow his instruction." As this was the first minister stationed in the old Falmouth limits, he claims more than a passing notice. The young clergyman's name was Richard Gibson. He had just taken the degree of A.B. at Magdalen College, Cambridge. Winter had at the island a daughter Sarah. Willis says an only one, but the "Papers" show that he had another one married in England. If we may judge from the clothing ordered by the father from England

59

the island belle was well dressed at the Sunday service held by the young minister. In reading the annals of the island we must conclude that as the minister would be the only suitable match in her exile, the Reverend Richard Gibson was chosen by the father, with the idea of a possible union between him and the fair Sarah.

Former historians have traced a tradition that there was a chapel of the English Church at the island, but there is no mention of one in the "Papers." The tradition probably had its origin in the fact that in the court records of York county is an inventory of the property at the island when Winter died, in which "communion vessels" are named. In 1639, among the effects at the plantation are named "the communion vessels and the tablecloth for the communion table as it was, and the ministers bed clothes." Probably some room or loft was fitted up for a chapel. The annual salary of Mr. Gibson was twenty-five pounds, and there is mention of contributions by visiting ship's companies, and by the employes of the establishment. The first hint of any dissatisfaction with the minister was in a letter of Gibson's to Trelawney in June, 1638, in which he says, "Your people here were willing to have allowed me twenty-five pounds yearly out of their wages so I could continue amongst them *wholly*, but Mr. Winter opposed it, because I was not so sought unto as he expected." * In another letter in July, 1639, Gibson says to Trelawney, relating to his intercourse with Winter, "Since the arrival of the Hercules he hath entertained me very coarsely, and with much discourtesy so that I am obliged to remove to Piscataqua for maintenance."

* Gibson had been preaching half the year at Saco which accounts for his expression to Trelawney, "so that I could continue amongst them *wholly*."

And further on he says, "but it is a case which you know not, nor can remedy." This expression seems to support the theory that Winter had been hopeful that Gibson would marry his daughter and was disappointed. In the spring of 1638, Winter wrote to Trelawney to know if he had promised Gibson that he might be absent from the plantation one half the year, and adds, "He [Gibson] is now to have a wife, and will be married very shortly unto one of Mr. Lewis' daughters of Saco." Winter's knowledge of Gibson's intended marriage seems to have soured him against the minister. "The Hercules" was probably the ship which brought Mary Lewis from England, whom Gibson afterward married.

The History of Saco and Biddeford, page eighty, says, "As we find 'the church Point' mentioned in the boundaries of an estate at Winter Harbor, in 1642, it is quite probable that a small church was erected there." There is evidence in a letter written by Thomas Jenner, a dissenting minister of Saco, to Governor Winthrop, dated April 2, 1641, and preserved in Governor Hutchinson's papers, that there was Church of England worship there. Jenner had evidently been cautioned by Winthrop against imprudent interference with the church people, and this letter is a reply. Jenner says: "Nor have I inveighed in the least measure against the Church of England (to my remembrance), but have been (and still am) very fearfull to give one word of distaste about those things but altogether seek to gain them to Christ. True I do acknowledge that after I had been here for the space of a month or six weeks and perceiving them very superstitious (performing mans invention rather than instituted worship of God), now that I might gain their good esteem of God's pure ordinances, and

make them see the evil and folly of their superstition and
will worship, I made choice of Psalm 19 and 7 to handle it
at large. . . . . Now I thank God it took a general good
impression except Mr. Vines and one more who told me I
struck at the church of England though I mentioned her
not."

Folsom says, "Mr. Jenner was the first puritan minister
that preached in Maine." Hence Winthrop's tender-footed
caution to him. If the people of Maine had been all
heathen, he could not have expressed more pity for their
"superstition." He remained at Saco only two years. This
letter by Jenner was written a month after Winter mentioned that Jordan was at his island, and had been for three
months, and had been two years with Purchase "his kinsman." Jordan undoubtedly succeeded Gibson in the ministry at Saco, and when Jordan left for the island the people
were left without a minister. This destitution was thought
by Winthrop and the Bay people, to be a providential opening for a missionary of their own to instruct the Maine
people in their spiritual and political duties, hence Winthrop's instructions. During his two years' residence at
Winter Harbor, (for that and Saco were the same), Jordan
must have visited the flourishing settlement at Richmond's
Island, only five or six miles off, where was stationed a
brother minister of the established church, and where ships
were frequently arriving from his own home. On these
visits of course he was entertained by Winter and his family; this acquaintance with Jordan, and his knowledge that
Gibson was about to marry Miss Lewis, probably caused
Winter's "discourtesy" which Gibson complained of.

Another little church with refined attendants which would
require the care of Mr. Jordan, was at Black Point. The

only evidence that there was an Episcopal church there in Jordan's time, as chaplain at the island, is found in John Josselyn's book. He came from England in 1638, to visit his brother, Judge Henry Josselyn, at Black Point and remained one year and six months. They were sons of Sir Thomas Josselyn. Josselyn came again to Black Point in 1663, and remained eight and a half years. In his book he says, in writing of a strange flame pointed out to him by some Indians, "I saw it plainly, mounting into the air over *our church* which was built upon a plain a little more than a half a quarter of a mile from our dwelling house." The Josselyn house was near the "Ferry rocks." If this church had belonged to any other sect than the established Church of England, Josselyn would have called it meeting-house, but he says "*our church*," and the Josselyns were strict Episcopalians. It is by gathering up these threads of casual mention that enables us to weave the web of local history. Mr. Jordan's spiritual charge extended over all the settlements from the Saco river to Sagadahoc, so far as to baptize the children and probably to read the burial service for the dead. Mr. Gibson undoubtedly performed the same service in the same places in his time.

There is documentary evidence that Mr. Jordan officiated at the New Casco settlement east of Presumpscot river. He was enjoined from exercising the ordinance of baptism by the General Court of Massachusetts, in 1660; not on account of his unworthiness, but on account of the form used, which was according to the book of Common Prayer. There was then no minister who represented the ruling theology of Massachusetts nearer than at Wells, and the interests of religion were considered paramount to all others. The General Court thought it better for the children to go unbaptized than that the rite should be performed according to the Prayer book. The record is as follows: " Whereas it appears to this court by several testimonies of good repute that Mr. Robert Jordan did in July last, after exercises were ended on the Lord's day, in the house of Mrs. Macworth in the town of Falmouth, then and there baptize three children of Nathaniel Wallis, of the same town, to the offence of the government of this Commonwealth; this court, judging it necessary to bear witness against such irregular practices, do therefore order that the secretary, by letter in the name of this court, require him to desist from any such practices for the future, and also that he appear before the next General Court to answer what shall be laid against him for what he hath done for the time past."

Mr. Gibson wrote to Governor Winthrop under date of Jan. 14, 1639, as follows: " By the providence of God and the council of friends I have lately married Mary, daughter of Mr. Thomas Lewis of Saco. Howbeit so it is at present, that some troublous spirits out of misapprehension, others, as is supposed for hire, have cast an aspersion upon her." * Gibson asks the Governor to call before him certain persons in Boston who came over in the same ship with her, as to the truth of the accusations and to give him the result. The two closing lines of this letter establish his spirit of Christian resignation. They are in these words: " If these imputations be justly charged upon her, I shall reverence God's afflicting hand, and possess myself in patience under God's chastening." Mr. Gibson officiated at Richmond's Island three years and six weeks. Several of

---

* This scandal concerning Gibson's wife may have had its origin at the plantation, prompted by disappointment at his choice.

Winter's men, without his consent, left the island in 1636, and took up a residence at Piscataqua (Portsmouth), and in 1640, they, with others, built an Episcopal church and parsonage. It was these men, undoubtedly, who induced Mr. Gibson to become their minister. Mr. Trelawney seems to have continued his friendship to him in his new charge; he sent him a jar of olive oil as a present, and in his will, executed in 1640, he remembered him by a gift of forty shillings.

In 1640, Gibson brought an action against John Bonighton of Saco for slander of himself and wife, and recovered a verdict of six pounds, six shillings and eight pence and costs. In 1642, Gibson was preaching at the Isles of Shoals. He was prosecuted by the Massachusetts government for his ministerial acts under the Church of England but punishment was remitted, "he being about to leave the country." He seems to have been a worthy man and maintained his religious faith and forms amid all his persecutions until he returned to England. Even John Winthrop spoke well of him. He was a staunch churchman, and next after Chaplain Robinson, who came to Casco with Governor Robert Gorges in 1623, he was the first clergyman who held divine service regularly in old Falmouth.

While Mr. Gibson was at Piscataqua, he was summoned to Boston to answer to the charge of marrying and baptizing at the Isles of Shoals. The laws of the Massachusetts colony forbade the practice of the clerical duties to any of the Church of England. Winthrop says of Gibson, "He being wholly addicted to the hierarchy and discipline of England did marry and baptize at the Isles of Shoals which was found within our jurisdiction." Mr. Gibson had written a letter to Mr. Larkham, a minister at Dover, denying the title of Winthrop's colony to those shores. On presenting himself at Boston in answer to the summons, Gibson was imprisoned. After several days confinement, he made a full acknowledgement of all he was accused of and submitted to the court. Whereupon, continues Winthrop, "in regard he was a stranger, and was to depart the country within a few days he was discharged without fine or other punishment." As this was considered great lenity by the Puritan Governor, he felt compelled to excuse himself. Mr. Gibson would not stay long where he had no rights of his religion, and undoubtedly soon returned to England.

About the same time that Mr. Gibson left Richmond's Island, another young clergyman of the English Church came to Saco. This was the Reverend Robert Jordan; one who, as a minister and as a man, came to be very prominent in the old township of Falmouth. The "Trelawney Papers," page 269, in an editorial note has a copy from the register of Oxford University saying that Robert Jordan entered Baliol College, June 15, 1632, and was then nineteen years old; was the son of Edward Jordan of the city of Worcester, of "plebian rank." The age given to young Jordan would fix the year of his birth to be 1613. In his testimony before Judge Josselyn of Scarborough in 1660, he said he was then forty-nine which would fix his birth-year in 1611. In his deeds of land Jordan calls himself "Presbyter."

Winter, on the second of August, 1641, wrote to Trelawney this: "Here is one Mr. Robert Jordan a minister which hath been with us this three months, which is a very honest, religious man by anything I can yet find in him. I have not yet agreed with him for staying here, but did refer it till I did hear some word from you. We were long without a minister, and were but in a bad way, and so we shall be still, if we have not the word of God taught unto us some times. The plantation at Pemaquid would willingly have him, on the desire he might be there one-half the year, and the other half to be here with us. I know not how we shall accord upon it as yet. He hath been here in the country this two years, and hath always lived with Mr. Purchase which is a kinsman unto him."

During the long contest between Charles I. and his Parliament, Robert Trelawney was a zealous and outspoken Royalist, and as such he was a second time elected to the House of Commons for Plymouth, and yet his parliamentary career was brief. His first election was in 1640. He was expelled from the House and committed to prison as was alleged, for having said in private discourse in the city to a friend that " the House could not appoint a guard for themselves without the consent of the king under pain of high treason," which was proved by a fellow who pretended to overhear him, when the person himself with whom the conference was held declared that he said " it might be imputed to them for high treason." Trelawney was confined at Winchester House, then used as a state prison by the House of Commons. It was situated at Southwark, at the west end of London Bridge. He was once released and was offered an opportunity to retract, but refused; by so doing he would have virtually pleaded guilty to the false charge. He was again committed and his petition to be allowed bail to visit his sick wife was refused, and she died while he was in confinement. His estates were confiscated and his favorite bark Richmond, built at Richmond's Island, for which she was named, was seized and loaded with his confiscated property including " six hundred and eighty-one ounces of plate, and one gold hatband of ninety-nine links,

three ounces in weight, being the goods of R. Trelawney."
At a subsequent trip she loaded with wheat belonging to his
estate. His bereavement, and the loss of his estates broke
the spirit of the brave Devonshire squire, and he died in
prison in 1645, at the early age of forty-five years. He
made his will in prison on the twenty-fourth of August,
1643, in which a very large estate is disposed of, much of it
for charitable purposes. The place of Trelawney's burial is
unknown, nor is there any authenticated portrait of him. I
shall be pardoned for occupying so much space by a notice
of one who, although he was never there, yet, but for his
unjust imprisonment and consequent death, would have
probably made Richmond's Island and the mouth of the
Spurwink the permanent center of a large trade. His business enterprise there was flourishing, while all other parts of
ancient Falmouth were but a comparative wilderness. Mr.
Trelawney's estates were undoubtedly restored to his children by Charles II., on his return to the throne, as his public
legacies were paid and his descendants still occupy his house
at Ham.

When the proprietor was imprisoned in London, returns
for cargoes shipped at Richmond's Island ceased to come
from Plymouth, and the busy fishing port languished. The
plantation was in debt to Winter for his tenth of the profits
and his stipend. Unlike his predecessor in the chaplaincy
at the island, Robert Jordan became interested in Sarah
Winter and perhaps in prospective inheritance. Robert Jordan and Sarah Winter were married as a natural result.

John Winter made his will naming Robert Jordan his
executor. Winter died at Richmond's Island the same year
with his patron Robert Trelawney. Jordan pursued the
business on his own account. Three years after (1648), he,

as Winter's executor, petitioned the General Assembly of Ligonia, representing that he had "emptied himself of his proper estate" in paying Winter's legacies, and that "the mostness" of Winter's estate was in the hands of the executors of Robert Trelawney, and "that your petitioner may have secured and sequestered unto himself and for his singular use what he hath of the said Trelawney in his hands." At a session of the Assembly held at Casco Bay, December 18, 1648, "it was ordered that it shall be lawful for the said petitioner Robert Jordan to retain, occupy to his proper use and profit, to convert all the goods, lands, cattle and chattels belonging to Robert Trelawney deceased, whatsoever, by what party or parties soever, unless the executors of the said Robert Trelawney shall redeem and release them by the consent and allowance of the said Robert Jordan, his heirs, executors, administrators, and assigns." This order was in accordance with the report of a committee, of which George Cleeves, Winter's and Jordan's old enemy, was chairman. He was magnanimous and agreed with his associates in their report. Jordan prepared his accounts and submitted them to the commissioners appointed by the Assembly. This pyramid of indebtedness showed much tact by Jordan in the piling up. The last item and capstone, was a legacy given to Mr. Winter by Mr. Trelawney in his will, of twelve pounds. This claim for the legacy may have been lawful, but we at this day would be better pleased if our townsman had omitted it in his account. Jordan's claim, as executor of Winter, against the Trelawney estate amounted to more than twenty-three hundred pounds; while the whole plantation, consisting of many thousand acres, with the cattle and property on the island, was appraised at only six hundred pounds, leaving a balance apparently due Jordan of seventeen hundred pounds. The order of the Assembly reads, "The remainder of this debt being left by us recoverable by any just cause of law according to conveniency." This act of the Assembly, and the value fixed by the appraisers on the Trelawney property, made Jordan as Josselyn says (about same time) of the Boston merchants, " *damnable rich.*"* We must conclude that "lobbying" near the sessions of legislative bodies is not of modern invention.

The son and heir of Trelawney, Jordan says in his petition, was then "seven or eight years old." The civil war and general derangement in England, "The fatal year of '48" as John Trelawney wrote fifty years after, prevented Trelawney's executors or heirs from attempting to redeem the Spurwink property. In 1692 John Cóok of Boston wrote to Sir Jonathan Trelawney, Lord Bishop of Exeter, offering to assist in the recovery of the property or to purchase the claim. Several such offers from New England were made to the descendants of Trelawney, who had become a prominent family in the kingdom.

From time to time Massachusetts passed acts extending the time for the recovery " of houses or lands " in the eastern country after the ending of the war with the Indians. In 1715 the time was extended: "To all persons beyond sea shall be allowed the term of ten years from the publication of the act to pursue their claim, and challenge to any houses or lands." This act fixed the limit of the time when it would be legal to commence proceedings to 1725. Colonel Samuel Waldo enclosed this act to one of Trelawney's heirs in 1738, yet the heirs seem to have become sensible of their

---

* In his remarks on the Massachusetts colony in 1673, Henry Josselyn says " The grose Goddons, or great masters, as also, some of their merchants, are damnable rich."

great loss by neglect, and continued to write to this country for information until 1809, when the correspondence ceased.* It was four years after Winter's death when the General Assembly of Ligonia gave Jordan all of the Trelawney property, real and personal, in the Province. He had continued to keep up the establishment on the island but after obtaining legal possession Jordan removed to the Cleeves house at Spurwink. The location of this house has not been determined. The editor of the "Trelawney Papers" has located it on his map opposite the island.

In 1723, soldiers were stationed at several points in Falmouth. The record says, "At Spurwink, at Mr. Jordan's where a ferry is kept, three men under the care of a corporal." This was a fortified house of a son of the elder Jordan. The original house was burnt by the Indians when the Reverend Robert Jordan left it in 1675. The son would be likely to build over the same cellar and near the same well used by his father. I think probabilities point to the shore of the Spurwink, near the ferry landing, as the site of the original farm buildings. Ambrose Boaden kept the ferry, and lived at the opposite ferry landing.

Notwithstanding the great labors and cares required by his large landed property and the island establishment, he seems to have still continued his duties to his mother

* The Captain Tate of a mastship, mentioned in the Trelawney correspondence, was not the first George as noted in the Trelawney volume, page 431, but his son Samuel, who died in Portland at the house of his son-in-law, Joseph H. Ingraham, in 1814. Mr. Willis says he died in London, which is an error. The note in the Trelawney volume makes Admiral Tate grandson of the first George — he was his son. The Trelawney lands are now held under the award of the Assembly with no other valid title.

church, and the people, even at a distance, according to his
ordination vows. The baptizing the children of Nathaniel
Wallis at the house of Mrs. Macworth "after the exercises
were ended on the Lord's day," for which he was imprisoned
in Boston two years after his Trelawney claim was settled,
and this service was held fifteen miles from his home.

A valuable and interesting relic of Mr. Jordan's ministry,
is the baptismal font, undoubtedly used in the baptism of
the Wallis children, which he probably brought with him
from England. It is not mentioned with the other chapel
furniture in the frequent inventories of the island property
when Gibson was there, nor in Mr. Jordan's time, which
renders it conclusive that it was his private property. It is
first mentioned in the inventory of the estate of Robert,
oldest son of John, who was the oldest son of Reverend Robert Jordan. He received the gift deed of Richmond's Island
from his father dated at Portsmouth, 25th of January, 1677.
The inventory of the estate of Robert, grandson of Reverend Robert Jordan, was taken at Falmouth (probably at
Richmond's Island), on the 9th of July, 1750. Among the
items is, "one brass basin, two shillings eight pence." This
estate was administered upon by John, eldest son of the
deceased owner, who married Abigail Coombs at New
Meadows, Brunswick, and lived there, and all of his nine
children settled in Brunswick and Harpswell. Peter, the
oldest son, died at Brunswick, in 1830, and in virtue of his
right as the oldest son, undoubtedly held the basin; and
from his children it was purchased by Seth Storer, Esq., of
Scarborough, a descendant of Reverend Robert Jordan.
The Reverend H. G. Storer at my request favored me with
the following letter of explanation.

REV. ROBERT JORDAN'S BAPTISMAL BASIN.

SCARBOROUGH, Sept. 10, 1883.

My Dear Sir:

The only evidence we have of the genuineness of the Jordan "Baptismal Font" is family tradition, and such probable confirmation thereof as is furnished by the font itself. As to its *certain* history I can only report as follows:

About thirty years ago Mr. John McKeen of Brunswick, informed my father that the Reverend Robert Jordan's baptismal font was in the possession of a Jordan family then resident of Harpswell, to whom it had been handed down as an heirloom left by the oldest son of the Reverend Robert Jordan to his own eldest son; and then successively held by the eldest son of *that branch* of the Jordan family, until it reached in due course the head of the Jordan family then living in Harpswell. Mr. McKeen had satisfied himself that this history was reliable, and that the basin was the identical font of the Reverend Robert Jordan for which reason he was very desirous to secure it for the Maine Historical Society, and was only waiting for some funds from the society to aid him in the attempt.

As my father was a grandson of Colonel Tristam Jordan of Saco, and as much attached to his kinsfolk as a Scotch Highlander to his clan, he was greatly interested in the "find" reported by Mr. McKeen; and a year or two thereafter, finding himself in Harpswell, he hunted up the Jordan family there and found the font; venerable from the accumulated verdigris, but carefully preserved in the hands of a widow Jordan. How long her husband had been dead I do not know, nor did my father report his christian name; but he had left behind him two sons who were fishermen, and then absent from home in pursuit of their vocation.

After some considerable negotiation and hesitation Mrs. Jordan, in consideration of the fact that neither of her sons had ever manifested any interest in the font as a family relic, and would not care to retain it, and being herself in straitened financial circumstances, consented to convey it to my father for the sum he offered, as a representative of the Jordan family. The express and vital condition of the sale was that the font should never go out of the possession of Robert Jordan's descendants. My father, a year or two before his decease committed the font to the care and keeping of the

6

Maine Historical Society, expressly *in trust*, and upon these terms the society now hold it.

Respectfully yours,

H. G. Storer.

This font is now undoubtedly two and a half centuries old. There are no marks of hammering nor soldering on it, but it was probably cast from bell metal. It is nineteen inches across the top, and three and one-half inches deep. It is ornamented with figures of foliage made with a graver, by hand; and shows that it was not made for any common use.

At the breaking out of Philip's war in 1675, the Reverend Mr. Jordan with his neighbors was compelled to flee from Spurwink, by the Indians who burnt his house. He took refuge at Piscataqua. His will was executed at Great Island, now Newcastle, on the twenty-eighth of January, 1678. He never returned to his plantation, but died at Great Island in 1679, aged sixty-eight years. His descendants are widely scattered and must now be numbered by thousands.

Richmond's Island is off the south shore of Cape Elizabeth half a mile distant at the nearest point. It is about one mile long and three-fourths of a mile wide at the broadest part, and contains some over two hundred acres. At the suggestion of Captain Green Walden of the U. S. Revenue service, a petition was forwarded to Congress, which since has from time to time made appropriations for the building of a breakwater on the bar connecting the island with the main shore, which was bare at low water. This work is nearly completed, and has perfected a harbor of refuge for vessels when they could not make Portland harbor. If this breakwater was leveled on top it would make a useful driveway to the island. Before it was built the anchorage was unsafe in a storm from some points.* The island probably received its name from the Duke of Richmond who was a member of the Council of Plymouth. Winter wrote in 1639: "We had a great storm before Christmas which sunk all our boats but one; two drove away, we never saw them again. One split in pieces, all the rest much torn. Five mainsails and six foresails were lost."

In the summer of 1639 a maid-servant of Winter was drowned in crossing the bar. Her employer, Winter, in a letter to Trelawney relates the circumstances of the accident in these words: "The maid Thompson had a hard fortune. It was her chance to be drowned coming over the bar after our cows, and very little water on the bar — not above a foot. We cannot judge how it should be except that her hat did blow from her head and she to save her hat, stepped on the side of the bar. A great many of our company saw when she was drowned and ran with all speed to save her, but she was dead before they could come to her." Peter Gullett, another servant, died at the island in October, 1736. In a field at the west of the present house are evident marks of graves. This was probably the ancient burying ground where these people were buried.

The most fatal shipwreck that ever occurred on the shores or waters of old Falmouth was at Richmond's Island. On the evening of the twelfth of July, 1807, the schooner Charles, Captain Adams, a regular packet sailing between Portland and Boston, was on the passage from Boston, and in a fog

---

* The breakwater was commenced in 1872 and finished 1881 at a cost to the United States of one hundred and ten thousand dollars. In its construction sixty-eight thousand one hundred and seventy-six tons of granite grout were used.

she struck on Watts' Ledge at the eastern end of the island, in a very heavy surf which broke over the vessel. Of the twenty-two persons on board, mostly passengers, sixteen perished. Among them were the Captain, Caleb Adams, his wife, and a son of Nathan Sargent, with several others of Portland. Captain Adams reached the rocks once and returned to save his wife, when both were drowned. Two ladies from Boston, Mrs. Mary Stonehouse, Mrs. Hayden and her child were among the lost. Their grave-stones with pathetic inscriptions, and the stones in memory of the Captain and his wife are near the east corner of the eastern burial ground. Seven of the first recovered bodies were brought to town and carried into the meeting-house of the Second Parish. On the fourteenth, impressive services were held over them and an able discourse was delivered by the pastor Reverend Elijah Kellogg. No fatal calamity was ever so sensibly felt by the people of the town.*

The once busy shipping-port and plantation of Richmond's Island, the seat of a large trade, where church service was held regularly on the Sabbath, and the festivals of Easter, Whitsuntide, Michaelmas, and Christmas, were celebrated

---

* In Southgate's history of Scarborough is an account of the flight from justice of a murderer who took refuge on Richmond's Island. " On the fifteenth of February, 1749, William Dearing of Blue Point in a fit of sudden passion, cruelly murdered his wife by striking her with an ax. No provocation had been offered on the part of Mrs. Dearing who was an amiable woman, and a worthy member of the Black Point church. Of all those who loved her none appeared to have regretted her death so much as her murderer. He was apprehended the next day and lodged in jail, whence he escaped to Richmond's Island where he stayed three weeks, being secretly fed and otherwise provided for by his friends in this town, until he took passage for Halifax. The remembrance of his crime drove him mad, and having been placed in confinement he soon ended his life by dashing his head against a spike in the wall of his cell."

as in Old England, has become a single island farm. The harbor of refuge for ships where the historic "Speedwell" of the Pilgrims has swung at anchor, remains, much improved. The river Spurwink with its marshes, once the Nile of Falmouth and Scarborough with George Cleeves as the sphinx to guard its mouth, yet flows in a lazy current to the sea. The origin of its name is an open. question — it is not known in England. On its shores undoubtedly are the descendants of Christopher Levett's men, whom he left on his plantation at Casco in 1624. Casco, where Winter sent his ships to load staves for Spain, has become the principal haven for ships, and Richmond's Island is now the out-port.

We will now resume the following of the fortunes of Cleeves and Tucker after their ejection from Spurwink by Winter.

Where all was open to them they would naturally choose a spot to continue their farming where returns could be obtained with as little delay as possible, and which would require the least labor to fit it for a crop. Undoubtedly Levett's men bestowed much labor on his plantation, as it was intended for a permanent residence. Not only did they all work on it the first summer, but he left ten of them to keep it and prepare for his return. It must have occupied the second season for farming, before he decided not to return. In these two seasons a farm could be well started with such a number of men. Levett's "fortified" house was undoubtedly standing when Cleeves and Tucker were ejected from their Spurwink farm. The Indians were then friendly as we have seen by Levett's narrative. At his last interview he told the natives how many months he would be absent, "at which they rejoiced exceedingly and then agreed among themselves that when the time should be expired which I spoke of for my return, every one at the place where he lived would look to the sea, and when they did see a ship they would send to all the sagamores in the country and tell them that poor Levett was come again." Therefore they would have no motive to destroy his house. It was only seven years after Levett's men left, when Cleeves and Tucker came from Spurwink. A plantation so recently under cultivation by such a strong force must offer advantages to new comers over the wild wilderness. Trelawney says in his letter to Sir Ferdinando Gorges that Cleeves claimed under "one Wright who occupied under one Levett." Whether Wright ever occupied the Levett farm or not, we have no means of knowing. That Cleeves and Tucker planted on Hog Island is proved by the deed from Gorges to Cleeves and Tucker in 1637. After describing the land on the neck he says, "as also one island adjacent to said premises, and now in the tenor and *occupation* of said George Cleeves and said Richard Tucker, commonly called and known by the name of Hogg Island."

Trelawney who was in England when he wrote to Gorges complaining of Cleeves, seems not to have known that Cleeves and Tucker claimed and occupied the island. The harbor and islands must have been familiar to Cleeves and Tucker when they lived at Spurwink, which was only ten miles off, and fishing and shooting were necessary employments. It is a fair inference that Cleeves and Tucker occupied Levett's house and farm while preparing their own on the Neck, and perhaps for more than one year. This would prompt Cleeves as Trelawney wrote, to claim under Levett. The name of the island may have been applied from Cleeves' and Tucker's herd of swine kept there. We have seen that it was the practice to keep herds of these animals at large, and what place so well adapted to the purpose as an island? Some have supposed that the name of the island was derived from the name of a shell-fish, the quahaug, but the shell-heaps remaining do not contain shells of these bivalves. There was undoubtedly good reason for the adoption of the name. The island is known and called by its original name in the Coast Pilot and all government charts and publications, and there should be as good a reason assigned for any alteration. The very useful domestic animal, the hog, has furnished a name for numerous islands on the coast of New England, and furnished a principal article of food for the early settlers. New England could not have been settled without him or a similar animal. Winter accused Cleeves of killing his hogs; of course he would not go to Spurwink to do it. Winter may have had a herd on some one of the near islands as he claimed all in the harbor. In his complaint against Winter, in 1640, eight years after he left Spurwink, Cleeves says, "Being moved by envy or some other sinister cause, hath now for these three years past, and still doth interrupt me to my great hindrance, thereby seeking my ruin and utter overthrow."

That Cleeves and Tucker were the first settlers on Falmouth neck there can be no doubt. Henry Josselyn a magistrate of Black Point, where he had lived since 1635, testified in August, 1659, as follows: "Henry Josselyn examined sweareth that upwards of twenty years Mr. George Cleeves has been possessed of that tract of land he now liveth on in Casco Bay, and was the first that planted there, and for the said lands, had a grant from Sir Ferdinando Gorges, as Sir Ferdinando acknowledged by his letters which was in controversy between Mr. Winter agent for Mr. Robert Trelaw-

ney of Plymouth merchant, and the said Cleeves, and they
came to trial by law at a court held at Saco, wherein the
said Winter was cast, since which time the said Cleeves hath
held the said lands without molestation."

By comparing several documents on York records we find
that the Cleeves and Tucker house was a little west of, and
near the north corner of Fore and Hancock streets.   It must
have been very near to the lot occupied now by a three story
house in which Henry W. Longfellow the poet was born.
In a deed in 1681, Mary Munjoy mentions the house in these
words.   " Bounded by a strait line from the mouth of a runnet water on the easterly side where Mr. Cleeves' house
formerly stood."   This runnet of water sixty years ago
would by some be called a brook.   It was the natural discharge from the several springs on the side of the hill, a
part of whose waters had been conveyed in aqueducts of
bored logs to various localities, and yet it discharged much
clear water on to the hard sandy beach, which was utilized to
fill ships' water casks.   We know that the foliage of trees
gathers the watery vapor and brings it to the ground in the
form of rain, when the space not overshadowed by trees shows
no sign of having been wet.   In Cleeves' and Tucker's time
when the top of the hill was covered by a forest, these "run-
nets of water," which occupy so conspicuous places in old
deeds and plans of land, were full and would now be called
brooks.

The deposition of John Alliset, given in Boston in 1736,
confirms the location of the Cleeves house, and also that of
George Munjoy.   " John Alliset, aged about eighty years,
testifieth and saith, that he formerly lived in Falmouth in
Casco Bay, and that he well knew Mr. George Cleeves and
Mr. George Munjoy, and Mary his wife, with whom he lived

eight years, and that there is a certain run of water about twenty rods distant from Fort Point, laying about north from said Fort Point. [The western end of the Grand Trunk passenger station now covers the point.] That he well remembers that Mr. George Cleeves had a house and lived therein ; which house was between the said Fort Point and the said run of water; and that Mr. George Munjoy had a house and lived therein, which was upon the northeasterly side of said run of water ; that he also well remembers that there was a meeting-house built on a point of Mr. Munjoy's land, bearing about northeast or easterly from said Munjoy's house." This point is now included in the property of the Portland Company.

This reduced run of water which marked the western boundary of Mary Munjoy's share of the Cleeves farm, was in about 1847 arrested in its natural course to the harbor and conveyed in pipes — a part to supply the station of the Grand Trunk railroad, another part to supply the Boston steamboats, and a third outlet was on Fore street at its natural crossing where casks were filled at a small price by Bethuel Sweetsir, and were carted away for all purposes, and yet the fountain was not, nor is it yet exhausted.

Cleeves conveyed his homestead to John Philips in 1659 and described it as "all that tract, parcel, or neck in Casco Bay, and now in possession of me the said George Cleeves, on which my dwelling-house standeth by the meets and bounds herein expressed, that is to say to begin at the point of land commonly called Machagony, and being north-easterly from my said house and so along by the water side from the house south-westerly to the south west side of my cornfield." In 1681 the house had disappeared, perhaps it was burned in the sacking of the town three years before.

At the date above, Mary Munjoy, daughter of Philips, who had purchased the Cleeves farm four years previous, when the house is mentioned as standing, claimed the land, and the government of Massachusetts confirmed it to her by the following description: "The easterly end of said neck of land whereupon her husband's house formerly stood, bounded by a straight line from the mouth of a runnet of water on the easterly side where Mr. Cleeves's house formerly stood, and so on to the old barn on top of the hill." This old barn stood near the easterly corner of the burying ground.

"My dwelling-house" mentioned by Cleeves could not have been the original house built by Cleeves and Tucker in 1632-3. That, of course, was of necessity hurriedly constructed of logs, and also, of course, of small capacity. In 1643 Cleeves had returned from England with a commission as Deputy President of the newly established province of Ligonia. He held the first court at Saco. In December, 1648, President Cleeves held a court at Casco. There was no other building to hold it in but the houses of the settlers, and of course the house of the Deputy President of the province (which extended from Sagadahock to Cape Porpoise), would be the most suitable, and President Cleeves had had five years of official life to make it so. The log hut which had served to shelter him and his partner for fifteen years was out of the question, and a new one becoming the new dignity of the owner must be erected, and as sawmills had been built in the province, the house would be a frame house. The old house would naturally be occupied until the new one was ready, which must stand on a new site. If the original building spot was well chosen the new house would stand near. If there was a better location the new house would occupy it. So we see that the exact site of the

first house on the neck is very uncertain. In support of the
supposition that the house mentioned in the deed to Philips
in 1659, was not the original house, I quote from Cleeves'
" complaint " against Jordan to the General Court of Massachusetts in May, 1661. " He sues me again for delivery of
my house, goods, and cow, and recovered against me, and
hath taken them from me and holds them, the house being
prized at eight pounds which but a little before cost me sixty
pounds." This was twenty-seven years after the building of
the first house, which would hardly with propriety be called
a "little time," nor could the cost of the log house have
been sixty pounds. To me this is conclusive evidence that
the original log house had disappeared or had been left to
Tucker and that a frame house of larger dimensions and
better suited for the residence of the chief magistrate of a
Province whose coast line was sixty miles in extent, had
been erected.

After Cleeves and Tucker had occupied Hog Island and
Falmouth Neck four years, without specific title, Winter
began to claim the land, arguing that the Presumpscot was
the original " Casco River." In 1636, Cleeves went to England and obtained from Sir Ferdinando Gorges a deed of
the Neck and Island. It was a limited title expiring at the
end of two thousand years. The consideration was one
hundred pounds sterling. As this was the first deed of the
Neck I will insert the description and tenure as received by
Cleeves and Tucker from Gorges. " All that part purport
and portion of lands begining at the further most point of
a neck of land called by the Indians, Machegonne, and now
and forever, hence forth, to be called or known by the name
of Stogummor, and so along the same westerly as it tendeth
to the first fall of a little river issueing out of a very small

pond [Capissic,] and from thence over land to the falls of
Pesumsca, being the first falls in that river upon a strait
line, containing by estimation from fall to fall, nearabout an
english mile, which to gether with the said neck of land that
the said George Cleeves and the said Richard Tucker have
planted for divers years already expired, is estimated in the
whole to be fifteen hundred acres or there abouts. As also
one island adjacent to said premises and now in the tenor
and ocupation of the said George Cleeves and Richard
Tucker commonly called or known by the name of Hogg
Island, which said premises with their appurtenances are not
already possessed or passed to any other person or persons
whatsoever, but now granted by me and this my special order
for confirmation thereof under my hand and seal, all now
are and hereafter shall be deemed reputed and taken to be
parts, parcels, and members of the province of New Somer-
settshire in new England aforesaid, ... to the end and
full term of two thousand years fully to be complete and
ended; to be holden of the said Ferdinando Gorges and his
heirs Lord or Lords of the said province of New Somersett-
shire, as of his or their mannor of Willitton and free mannors
in free and common soicage by fealty only for all manner of
services, and the yearly rent of two shillings the hundred for
every hundred acres thereof, be it wood, meadow, pasturage,
or tillage." Formal possession was given to Cleeves and
Tucker by Arthur Macworth by appointment June 8, 1637.

The furthermost point of a neck of land called by the
Indians "Machegonne," I should take to be the most easterly
point of the neck now called Fish Point. The name given
by Gorges, "Stogummer," never was attached in practice to
any locality here, but the name "Mannor of Willitton" is
worth preserving. The "first falls of a little river" must

have been those on the Capissic near Stroudwater, but the length of the back line of the tract instead of being "near about an English mile" is nearer four miles. The number of acres is also very much underestimated, either through ignorance or intentionally.

On the eighth of June, 1637, Gorges gave Cleeves a commission "for the letting and settling all or any part of his lands or islands lying between the Cape Elizabeth and the entrance of Sagadahock river, and so up into the main land sixty miles." By virtue of this commission Cleeves leased for sixty years to Michael Mitton, in December of the same year, Pond Island, now Peaks Island. This name evidently came from a pond of fresh water which is never dry, on the eastern end of the island. Cleeves in the conveyance declared that it was subsequently to be known as Michael's Island. It since has successively borne the names of Munjoy's, Palmer's, and Peaks Island. Mitton probably came from England with Cleeves on his return; he afterward married Cleeves' only child, Elizabeth. Cleeves arrived in May, 1637, bringing a commission from Gorges to several persons, including himself, to govern his province of New Somersetshire. There is no evidence that any served but Cleeves. He also brought a warrant from the King and Council for searching out the great lake Iracoyce, and the sole trade of beaver, and by agreement with the owners for the settling of Long Island. These important commissions, although of little profit, show Cleeves to have been possessed of good address and that he had the confidence of the large landed proprietors in England. The "great lake Iracoyce" of which fabulous accounts were circulated in England of the wealth of furs to be obtained there, is still in doubt. Cleeves brought home a commission under the privy signet for searching out the lake and for its sole trade in furs, by articles of agreement between himself, the Earl of Sterling, and Viscount Canada. Of his efforts in that direction nothing has come down to us, but his commissions show that he was not considered in England to possess the despicable character attributed to him by some writers.

CHAPTER IV.

AFTER the Spurwink and Richmond's Island settlements, the next within the limits of Falmouth was commenced at the mouth of Presumpscot river. The principal man of this hamlet was Arthur Macworth. In a deed to him by Richard Vines of Saco, agent of Gorges, dated 1635, Macworth is described as "having been in possession there many years." The property conveyed is described in the deed as "all the tract of land lying in Casco Bay on the north east of the river Presumsca which now and for many years is and hath been in the possession of said Macworth, being at the entrance of said river where his house now standeth on a point of land commonly called and known by the name of Menickoe, and now and forever to be called and known by the name of Newton, and thence up the said river to the next creek below the first falls, and so over the land to the great bay of Casco, until five hundred acres be completed; together with one small Island over against, and next to his house." The deed was witnessed by George Cleeves, Richard Tucker, and Robert Sankey of Saco.

Mr. Willis supposed that Macworth arrived at Saco with Vines in 1630, and remained a short time there. He was appointed by the deed from Gorges in 1637, to deliver possession to Cleeves and Tucker of Casco neck, and was long a magistrate. His second wife was the widow of Samuel Andrews, formerly of London, who was probably one of Vines' company and died at Saco about 1687, leaving a son James, for many years a reputable inhabitant of Falmouth. Arthur Macworth died in 1657 at his home at the point, leaving two sons, Arthur and John, and several daughters. The sons probably died without issue, as the name became extinct here after the removal of Mrs. Macworth, who died in Boston after 1676. Her daughters married William Rogers, Abraham Adams, Francis Neale and George Felt. They left many descendants. Mrs. Macworth's will was dated at Boston, May 20, 1676, and is recorded in Suffolk county. Arthur Macworth and his wife were much attached to the Church of England. Reverend Robert Jordan frequently held services at their house. Here he committed the offence of "baptizing the children of Nathaniel Wallis after the service was ended," for which he was imprisoned at Boston by the Massachusetts authorities in 1660. It is very probable that Reverend Richard Gibson held divine service at the Macworth house before Jordan came to Richmond's Island. The name "Newton" given by Gorges to Macworth's plantation never prevailed. The point on the east side of the river where his house was, and the island opposite, were called by his name which has been corrupted to Mackey's Point and Island. The creek which was the northern limit of the plantation still retains the ancient name of "Sciterygusset" which was the name (variously spelt), of an Indian sagamore living there, and mentioned by Christopher Levett who was here in 1623, and the same who was at the head of the party who killed Bagnall at Richmond's Island in 1631, for which crime another sagamore, Black Will, suffered two years after.

In 1639, Gorges organized a civil government, appointed a deputy and councilors who held a court at Saco in June, 1640, which was the first general assembly ever held in the province. The proceedings of this court are a part of the ancient records of York county. Thomas Gorges, a cousin to Sir Ferdinando, was appointed Steward General and arrived during the summer, and held a court at Saco on the eighth of September, at which there were nine jury trials. George Cleeves, although a prominent man in the new province, did not receive any appointment under the new organization, although Mitton, his son-in-law, was appointed constable of Casco. The reason why Cleeves was neglected was that he was opposed in politics to Gorges, who was a royalist and his officers in the province were nearly all of the same faith. The religious government was according to the Church of England. An order was passed at Saco that all the inhabitants "who have any children unbaptized should have them baptized as soon as any minister is settled in any of their plantations."

The government of the province of New Somersetshire seemed now to promise permanency, but in 1642 the civil war broke out in England and extended to the colonies, destroying all that Gorges had labored so long to establish. He was a firm Episcopalian, and joined the king's party with all the energy for which he was noted. Although he was more than seventy years old, he joined the royal forces, and was taken prisoner in 1645; was imprisoned and died in 1647.

During the civil war in England, Cleeves thought he saw an opportunity to further his interests and punish his enemies. In 1643, he went to England, and in April of that year (probably by Cleeves' suggestion) Colonel Alexander

Rigby, a republican member of Parliament, purchased of
the surviving proprietors the charter of the province of
Ligonia.   It was a dormant title, and with the royal party
in the ascendant would have been of little value, but with
an ardent republican member of Parliament as proprietor, it
could be turned to account by Cleeves, who was appointed
first deputy by Rigby.   In this transaction it was proved in
court that Cleeves, when in England, affixed the names of
the principal inhabitants of his vicinity to a petition to
Parliament without their knowledge or consent, and when
called to an account on his return, he admitted the fact and
said he did it at the suggestion of Parliament.   The origin
of this province of Ligonia, was a grant from the Council of
Plymouth in 1630 to John Dy and others of forty miles
square, lying between Cape Elizabeth and Cape Porpoise,
including both.   It was first called the Plough patent from
the ship Plough which brought the first settlers to Winter
Harbor in 1631.   Cleeves arrived in Boston from England
in 1643, with his commission from Rigby to act as Deputy
Governor of the new province.   Knowing that he should
encounter the Gorges' government, Cleeves petitioned the
General Court of Massachusetts to afford him assistance.
This they declined to do, but consented that the Governor
should write an unofficial letter in his behalf as he was of
their party, but they feared a failure of his government.
The letter from Governor Winthrop did not have the
desired effect on the Gorges officials, who opposed the
organization of the Rigby government, making two parties.
Those of Casco principally joined Cleeves although some
dissented; notably, Arthur Macworth, who lived at the
mouth of the Presumpscot.   His was one of the names
which Cleeves used unwarrantably in England.   Macworth

supported Vines who was elected Deputy Governor for the next year. Cleeves wrote to Vines that he would submit their case to the government of Massachusetts, until a final determination could be obtained from England. Vines not only refused the reference, but imprisoned the bearer of the letter, Richard Tucker, and required a bond that he would appear at court, and also for his good behavior, as the conditions of release.

After this violence Cleeves and his party, about thirty in number, wrote to the Governor of Massachusetts for assistance, and offered to join the confederacy of the United Colonies. The Governor returned an unfavorable answer, objecting that "they had an order not to receive any but such as were in a church way." Cleeves continued to maintain a feeble sway and must have finally submitted to the Gorges' government had not Rigby's party been triumphant in England. Vines continued to hold his court at Saco, with Arthur Macworth as one of the assistants. In assessing the expenses of the court, Saco paid eleven shillings, Casco ten shillings, while Kittery, which included Berwick, paid two pounds and ten shillings. This assessment shows the relative number of inhabitants and taxable property of these settlements. In 1646, after mutual threatenings the parties of Vines and of Cleeves agreed to refer the subjects of contention to the court of assistants of Massachusetts. At the appointed time Cleeves and Tucker appeared in Boston for the Rigby government and Henry Josselyn of Black Point for Gorges, but the hearing was without result. Soon after, the decision of Commissioners for Plantations in England arrived declaring Rigby to be the rightful owner of the province of Ligonia. The Commissioners further ordered that all the inhabitants of said province should yield obedience to Rigby, and Massachusetts was required, if need be, to support his authority. Gorges was now dead and Republicanism was in the ascendant in England.

Cleeves was now triumphant over his adversaries, and assumed undisputed sway in the whole province of Ligonia, including the settlements of Casco, Richmond's Island, Spurwink, Black and Blue Points, Saco, and Winter Harbor. As Deputy President Cleeves immediately commenced to make grants in all parts of the province. The old opponents of Cleeves seemed now to have submitted gracefully, and courts were holden, but only scraps of the records have been preserved. A court was held at Casco in September and December of 1647. At the September term of the court, Robert Jordan petitioned for the allowance of his claim against Trelawney, as executor of the will of John Winter, his father-in-law, of Richmond's Island. The court was styled the "General Assembly of the province of Lygonia." The proceedings of the Assembly in September, 1648, are subscribed by George Cleeves, Deputy President, William Royall, Henry Watts, John Cossons, Peter Hill, and Robert Booth. Royall and Cossons were from Westcustogo, now Yarmouth. Hill and Booth were from Saco, and Watts was from Scarborough.

Rigby, who was one of the Barons of the Exchequer at home, and chief proprietor of Ligonia, died in August, 1650. After the news of this event the old opposition to Rigby's government was revived. His son, Edward Rigby, who had become the proprietor, wrote to those disaffected, saying that he should soon send back Cleeves to his government and also a kinsman of his own. Cleeves had probably been called to England by the death of the elder Rigby, and did not return until the winter of 1653.

The government of Massachusetts, seeing the disordered state of affairs in Maine in 1652, seriously undertook to establish a claim to the province as far east as Casco Bay. The excuse was a new discovery of the meaning of their eastern boundary as described in the charter. After a new running, the eastern limit was, by the commissioners, decided to be "a grayish rock at highwater water mark cleft in the middle." This rock is the ancient monument between Falmouth and North Yarmouth. The principal inhabitants west of Saco river had already reluctantly submitted to the jurisdiction of Massachusetts, but those east of Saco opposed the claim of Massachusetts on political and religious grounds. They were decided Episcopalians and wished to enjoy their faith and forms in peace, which they knew they could not under the intolerant spirit that prevailed in Massachusetts. At the head of this party were the Reverend Robert Jordan of Spurwink, Henry Josselyn of Black Point, and Arthur Macworth of Casco, all firm in their faith and determined to resist while there was hope of success. Cleeves and others were stimulated in their opposition by the possession of power which they were anxious to maintain. Jordan was imprisoned in Boston for his opposition. He and Henry Josselyn refused when summoned to meet the Massachusetts commissioners at York in 1657. Cleeves had been to Boston two years previous in behalf of the inhabitants of Ligonia to protest against the proceedings of Massachusetts, but without encouragement. In August, 1656, seventy-one persons living between the Piscataqua and Saco rivers addressed a petition to Cromwell praying to be continued under the government of Massachusetts, giving as reasons that they were few in number and not competent to manage weighty affairs. Encouraged by this expression

a new commission was appointed by the Bay province in
1658, to visit the settlements included in their claim, and by
threats and promises the people generally, as far east as Saco,
signed a submission to Massachusetts.

The people east of Saco continued their opposition to the
last. The General Court of Massachusetts had called on
these people to meet the commissioners at York, which they
neglected to do. Then came a summons from the same
body to appear at the General Court at Boston in October,
1657. Cleeves disregarded this order and sent a protest
against the legality of their proceedings, and the resolution
of the inhabitants to deny submission to the court. The
General Assembly at Boston, seeing the determined opposition of the Casco and Scarborough people, resolved to
" surcease for the present from any further prosecution."

Learning of some disorders east of the Piscataqua and
some disaffection among the people for want of a stronger
government, the General Court took advantage of the supposed change in public opinion, as an excuse to again push
their claim, although six months previous they resolved to
" surcease." In May, 1658, they appointed a commission to
proceed to the disputed territory and receive the submission
of the inhabitants, commencing at Black Point, and continuing on to Richmond's Island and Casco. It is evident that
the sturdy supporters and adherents of the English Church
in these three districts had become weary of the controversy,
as they consented to confer with the Massachusetts commissioners. Reverend Robert Jordan and his adherents met
them by appointment at his house at Spurwink in Falmouth,
in July, 1658, where a majority of the people of Casco and
Black Point attended. In the commissioners' report they
say, " After some serious debate of matters betwixt us, the

removal of some doubts, and our tendering some acts of favor and privilege to them, the good hand of God guiding therein, by a joint consent we mutually accorded in a free and comfortable close." Cleeves was not a churchman, but his interest was then with the Episcopalians against Puritan Massachusetts. The form of the submission was as follows: " We, the inhabitants of Black Point, Blue Point, Spurwink and Casco Bay, with all the islands thereunto belonging, do own and acknowledge ourselves to be subject to the government of Massachusetts bay in New England, as appears by our particular subscriptions in refference of those articles formerly granted to Dover Kittery and York which are now granted and confirmed unto us, together with some additions as upon record doth appear." This was signed by twenty-nine persons, of whom the thirteen following lived in Falmouth, viz.: Francis Small, Nichols White, Thomas Standford, Robert Corbin, Nathaniel Wallis, George Lewis, John Philips, George Cleeves, Robert Jordan, Francis Neale, Michael Mitton, Richard Martin. The remainder, with the exception of John Bonighton who lived in Saco, were inhabitants of Black and Blue Points. One of the articles of agreement between the inhabitants and the commissioners, was that " the obligations entered into were to be void if the jurisdiction of Massachusetts was not allowed by the government of England." The sixth article was that " their civil privileges not to be forfeited for differences in religion." The eighth article was, " Those places formerly called Spurwink and Casco bay from the east side of Spurwink river to the Clapboard islands in Casco bay, shall run back eight miles into the country and *henceforth shall be called Falmouth.*" Tenth, " The towns of Scarborough shall have commission courts to try causes as high as fifty

pounds." Eleventh, The same towns "are to send one
deputy yearly to the court of election, and have the right to
send two if they see cause." The name Yorkshire was
given to so much of the former province of Maine as fell
under the jurisdiction of Massachusetts. "Right trusty
Henry Josselyn, Esq., Mr. Robert Jordan, Mr. George
Cleeves, Mr. Henry Watts, and Mr. Flavius Neale" were
appointed commissioners with the consent of the inhabitants
of Scarborough and Falmouth to hold the local court for
petty causes without a jury. Any of these could solemnize
marriages. Thus the government of Massachusetts came
into possession of the ancient province of Maine as far east
as the bounds of North Yarmouth, which, with the exception
of two or three years, she held until the separation of 1820.

George Cleeves did not live to be sold with his lands to
Massachusetts. In a deed executed in 1671 by Anthony
Brackett, of land formerly owned by Cleeves, he is referred
to as "deceased." In his memorial to the court against
Jordan in 1662, he says, "my wife being four score and
seven years of age." From this we must infer that he lived
to a great age as well as his wife; the date of the death of
either of them is not known. They probably were buried
in the oldest part of the old burial ground. Cleeves left
but one child, Elizabeth. It is not known that he ever had
any other. His daughter married Michael Mitton whose
posterity are numerous. She died in 1682, and undoubtedly
her dust rests near her parents. Elizabeth Clark, a daughter
of Michael Mitton who lived to a great age, testified in 1728
that her "grandfather, Mr. George Cleeves, lived on his
estate at Falmouth many years after the death of her father,
Michael Mitton." Cleeves came from Plymouth, England.
In 1883 an elegant granite monument was erected to the

memory of George Cleeves on the eastern slope of Munjoy's Hill, at the eastern terminus of Congress street. It was the gift of Payson Tucker, Esq.

Folsom says: "A sense of the injustice of the Massachusetts' claim and a deep-rooted aversion to the principles of the colony operated strongly on many of the inhabitants and led them to express an open contempt of its assumed jurisdiction." John Bonython of Saco, together with Mr. Josselyn of Black Point, and Reverend Mr. Jordan of Spurwink, were so active in their opposition that an order was issued for their arrest. The two latter were required to give bonds for their appearance before the General Court. Bonython escaped, whereupon a decree of outlawry was published against him in 1658, of which this is the closing sentence: "And further this court doth impower any person that hath submitted to this government after the first of August, to apprehend the said Bonython by force and bring him alive or dead to Boston declaring and proclaiming, that whosoever shall so do shall have twenty pounds paid him for his service to the country, out of the common treasury which may be levied with other charges upon the said Bonythons estate." The next year Bonython appeared before the commissioners and "yielded and subscribed his subjection to this government." Willis thus describes the situation in Maine:

Although the inhabitants had now generally submitted to her jurisdiction, there were many who carried in their bosoms a spirit of determined hostility to the power of Massachusetts. We believe this to have been founded chiefly in a difference of religious sentiments. Massachusetts at that time could hardly allow a neutrality of this subject; none but church members could be freemen, and those who did not "after the most straitest sect of our religion" live puritans were not tolerated. Many of our early settlers were Episcopalians; Jordan was a priest of that persuasion and had been the minister to the people here for many years. Although new settlers crowded into our plantations from Massachusetts bringing the religious doctrines and feelings which prevailed there, still the attachment of many to the mode of worship under which they had been educated was not nor could not be eradicated. On this subject Massachusetts exercised her power with no little severity, and notwithstanding her guaranty in the sixth article before mentioned "that civil privileges should not be forfeited for religious differences," she did proceed to enforce her own doctrines, regardless of the religious principles which prevailed here. Reverend Robert Jordan was frequently censured for exercising his ministerial office in marriages, baptisms, etc. In 1660, only two years later he was summoned by the general court to appear before them to answer for his "irregular practices" in baptizing the children of Nathaniel Wallis "after the exercises were ended on the Lord's day in the house of Mrs. Macworth in the town of Falmouth" and was requested "to desist from any such practices for the future."

The limits of Falmouth were described in general terms in the compact with Massachusetts of 1658; they were to be particularly marked out by the inhabitants themselves, or, in case of their neglect, the next county court was to appoint commissioners for that purpose. This duty not having been performed, the General Court at their session in May, 1659, appointed "Captain Nicholas Shapleigh, Mr. Abraham Preble, Mr. Edward Rishworth, and Lieutenant John Saunders to run the dividing lines," not only of Falmouth, but of Saco and Scarborough. This committee attended to the service and reported "that the dividing line between Scarborough and Falmouth shall be the first dividing branches of Spurwink river, from thence to run up into the country upon a due northwest line, until eight miles be extended; and that the easterly bounds of Falmouth shall extend to the Clapboard Islands, and from thence shall run upon a west line into the country till eight miles be expired." * These boundaries are the same as at the present time, with the exception of the eastern line which now runs northwest from the white rock opposite Clapboard Island referred to in the survey of the eastern line of the province by Massachusetts. The two side lines of the tract are now parallel, now running north forty-five degrees west, a distance of over eight miles from the sea. The rear line is a few rods over ten miles long.

The name given to the town was borrowed from that of an ancient town in England, standing at the mouth of the river *Fal* in Cornwall, and hence called Falmouth. The river after passing through a part of Cornwall, discharges itself into the British Channel, forming at its mouth a spacious harbor. Several of the early settlers came from that neighborhood, and adopted the name in compliance with a natural and prevailing custom in the first age of our history, of applying the names which were familiar to them in the mother country, to places which they occupied in this. Previous to this time the plantation upon the neck, and, indeed, all others in the bay, were called by the general name of Casco, or Casco Bay; but when a particular spot was intended to be designated, the local terms borrowed principally from the Indians were used, as Machegonne, Purpooduck, Capisic, Spurwink, Westcustogo, and others. The term Machegonne is used in the deed from Gorges to Cleeves but was never in general use among the white settlers. The most of these names continued to prevail for many years, and some of them remain in familiar use to the present day.

On the restoration of Charles II., in 1660, Ferdinando Gorges, a grandson of the old lord proprietor, sent over

* Return of the committee.

his agent with letters from the King to the governor of
Massachusetts Bay, requiring either a restitution of his
lawful inheritance, or that they should show reasons for the
occupation of the province of Maine.   The next step was
the appointment of commissioners by the crown to visit
New England and inquire into all the existing grievances.
They came into Maine in the summer of 1665, and issued
their proclamation, in which they charge the Massachusetts
colony with having " refused by sound of trumpet to submit
to his majesty's authority, looking upon themselves as the
supreme power in those parts, contrary to their allegiance and
derogatory to his majesty's sovereignty."   They then proceeded to appoint a number of gentlemen in the province,
known to be friendly to the claims of Gorges, as magistrates
to exercise authority there until his majesty's pleasure be
further known.   These were Messrs. Champernoon and Cutts
of Kittery; Rishworth and Johnson of York; Wheelwright
of Wells; Hook and Phillips of Saco; Josselyn of Black
Point; Jordan of Richmond's Island; Munjoy of Casco;
and Wincoll of Newichawannock, now Berwick.

Massachusetts did not long acquiesce in this arrangement,
for in July, 1668, four commissioners, escorted by a military
force, entered the province and proceeded to hold a court at
York.   The king's magistrates were present and remon-
strated, but to no purpose.   The account of the matter
given by John Josselyn, who was then residing with his
brother at Black Point, is that " as soon as the commissioners returned for England the Massachusetts men entered the
province in a hostile manner with a troop of horse and foot,
and turned the judge and his assistants off the bench,
imprisoned the mayor or commander of militia, and threatened the judge and some others that were faithful to Mr.

Gorges' interest." At length both parties to this exciting controversy appeared by their agents at the palace of White-hall, and his majesty, upon a fair hearing of their respective claims, "decided that the Province of Maine was the rightful property of the heirs of Sir Ferdinando Gorges, both as to sale and government." As soon as this decision was known, an agent of Massachusetts made overtures to Mr. Gorges for the purchase of his title, which he finally sold to that colony in March, 1677, for twelve hundred and fifty pounds sterling, or about six thousand dollars. This transaction gave great offence to the friends of Gorges in the province, who sent a remonstrance to England, but it was too late. Such, however, was the continued opposition to Massachu-setts on the part of the inhabitants, that it became necessary to send an armed force into the province to awe the people into submission and prevent disturbance.

Maine was now fairly annexed to Massachusetts, not in accordance with the wishes of the people, but by a legal transfer of the soil and government for a valuable consider-ation; and in the act of taking possession by the colony, the title of Gorges was duly recited; nothing further was heard of its being embraced in their own patent. After the purchase of Maine, many persons in Massachusetts were desirous of selling the province with all the inhabitants, in whom they had expressed so much interest, to defray the expense of defending it during the late war, which was estimated at eight thousand pounds. A committee of the General Court was appointed for this purpose, but the vote was reconsidered before any further action was taken on the subject.

The British government took offence at the sale and pur-chase of Maine, and contended that the jurisdiction over a

colony or province was inalienable, and that by the conveyance, although Massachusetts might have acquired a right
to the soil, she acquired none to the government, which
consequently reverted to the crown, and required an assignment of the province on being paid the purchase money.
The subject was continually agitated until it was finally
settled by the charter of 1691, which not only included the
province of Maine, but the more remote provinces of Sagadahoc and Nova Scotia.

A separate government was now organized for the province, at the head of which, Thomas Danforth, Esq., of
Cambridge, was placed, with the title of President of the
Province of Maine. Beside being at the head of the separate government for Maine, President Danforth held the
office of Deputy Governor of Massachusetts Colony.*

One of the reasons why the Episcopalians of Maine
objected to coming under the jurisdiction of Puritan Massachusetts, was that "none should be admitted to the body
politic but such as were church members," and, of course,
could not vote for civil officers. The provincial churches
and ministers were the power in the land.

In 1639, Hugh Peters, in the name of the church at
Salem, wrote to the church in Dorchester as follows:
"Reverend and dearly beloved in the Lord, — We thought
it our bounden duty to acquaint you with the names of such
persons as have had the great censure past upon them in
this our church, with the reasons thereof, beseeching you in
the Lord, not only to read their names in public to yours,
but also to give us the like notice of any dealt with in like
manner by you; that so we may walk toward them accord-

* He held these offices from 1678 to the arrival of Andross in 1686. He
died in 1699, aged 77.

ingly, for some of us here, have had communion ignorantly with some of other churches. We can do no less than have such noted who disobey the truth." Then follow the names of twelve delinquents, one of whom was "William James, for pride and divers other evils in which he remained obstinate." These delinquents were to have their names "read in public," with their offences, in all the neighboring towns.* William Blackstone, whom the Winthrop colony found in possession of Shawmut, told them that he came from England because he did not like the Lord's bishops, but he could not join with them, because he did not like the Lord's brethren.

The egotism of the leading Massachusetts people was exemplified by a member of the council at the time of the retirement of Governor Shute, in 1722, which made Lieutenant-Governor Dummer acting governor. He had made a conciliatory speech to the two houses, when Councilor Sewall said: "With the leave of your Honor, and this honorable Board, I would speak a word or two on this solemn occasion. Although the unerring providence of God has brought your Honor to the chair of government in a cloudy and tempestuous season, yet you have this for your encouragement, that the people you have to do with are a part of the Israel of God, and you may expect to have the prudence and patience of Moses communicated to you for your conduct." Ten years previous to this, the same councilor was sitting as one of the witch judges; one of his acts is given by Hutchison. Rebecca Nurse was on trial for witchcraft. Hutchison says: "She was a member of the church and of good character, and the jury brought in a verdict of 'not guilty,' upon which the court expressed their dissatis-

* Hutchison's History of Massachusetts.

faction with the verdict, which caused some of the jury to desire to go out again, and then they brought her in 'guilty.'"

It seems that the puritan churches had no established customs or forms for worship, but each minister, who had sufficient independence, introduced customs into his own meetings to suit himself. Mr. Davenport of New Haven, who afterward removed to Boston, required all his congregation to stand up while he named his text. The reason given was that it was the word of God and deserved peculiar honor. Mr. Williams, of Salem, required all the women of his congregation to wear veils. In his Plain Dealing, published in London in 1642, Thomas Letchford, who had been in New England, says of the contributions in the meeting-houses of Massachusetts: "The magistrates and chief gentlemen first and then the elders and all the congregation of men, and most of them that are not of the church, all single persons, widows, and women in the absence of their husbands, come up one after another one way and bring their offerings to the deacon at his seat, and put it into a box of wood for the purpose if it be money or papers; if it be any other chattel they set it, or lay it down before the deacons, and so pass another way to their seats again."

That everything approaching to an acknowledgement of the authority of Episcopacy might be avoided, the Puritans never used the additional word saint when speaking of the apostles and ancient fathers of the christian church, and even the names of places were made to conform. The island of St. Christophers was always written "Christophers," and by the same rule all other places to which saint had been prefixed. If any surprise was manifested, this answer was ready: Abraham, Isaac, and Jacob had as good a right to this appellation as the apostles. The Bay people began their sabbath the last day of the week at sunset. This was not settled until 1640, and then not without a controversy. From a sacred regard for the christian sabbath, a scruple arose of the lawfulness of calling the first day of the week Sunday, and they always on any occasion, whether in a civil or religious relation to it, styled it either the Lord's day or the Sabbath. As the exception to the name Sunday was its idolatrous origin, the same scruple naturally followed with respect to the names of the other days of the week, and of most of the months, which had the same origin. Accordingly Monday, Tuesday, and so on, were changed to the second and third days of the week; and instead of March, which was then the first month of the year, it was called the first month; instead of the third Tuesday in May, the style was, the third third day of the third month. This custom originated in England but did not last many years.

The Massachusetts Puritans expressed a bitter feeling against the Episcopalians on account of their observance of the feasts and fasts of the Church. Judge Samuel Sewall, of Boston, notes in his diary for several years, with much apparent satisfaction, the non-observance of Christmas by the people of Boston. In 1685, December 25, he says: "Friday, carts come to town, and shops open as usual. Some somehow observe the day; but are vexed I believe that the body of the people prophane it, and blessed be God no authority yet to compell them to keep it." In 1697 Sewall thus notices the day: "Shops are open, and carts and sleds come to town with wood and fagots as formerly. I took occasion to dehort my family from Christmas keeping, and charged them to forbear."

8

This bitter feeling against the Church of England, her ordinances and customs, was the growth of the few preceding years. It was not cherished by the fathers of the Winthrop colony. While they were on their passage to Massachusetts Bay, (April 7th, 1630,) Governor Winthrop and divers others on board signed a paper headed, "The humble request of his majesties loyal subjects, the governor and the company late gone to New England; to the rest of the brethren in and of the Church of England, Reverend fathers and brethren." In this paper are many expressions of love for the church at home. Among them is this: "We desire you would be pleased to take notice of the principals, and body of our company, as those who esteem it an honor to call the Church of England from which we rise, our dear mother." Signed by John Winthrop and many others.

The appropriation by the "society for the propagation of the gospel among the Indians," an English institution, amounted to six or seven hundred pounds sterling, per annum. This was intrusted to a commission composed of some of the old magistrates and ministers in New England. They would not suffer Aaron, an Indian preacher who could read English, to have a bible with the common prayer in it, but took it away from him.

The cod-fishery first drew the attention of the English merchants to our state. Captain John Smith, who was here in 1714, wrote a glowing account of the country. He says he arrived at "Menhegan." "Had the fishing for whale proved as I expected I had stayed in the country . . . . I was contented having taken by hooks and lines with fifteen or eighteen men at most, more than sixty thousand cod in less than a month; whilst myself with eight others of them, in three months ranging the coast in a small boat, got for trifles, eleven hundred beaver skins, besides otters and martins; all amounting to the value of fifteen hundred pounds, and arrived in England with all my men in health in six or seven months." Captain Smith made a map of the coast and called it New England. On it he calls Casco Bay "Harrington Bay," Black Strap Hill is named "Schooters Hill." He says, "The most remarqueable parts thus named by the high and mighty Prince Charles, Prince of Great Britain." His account of his several voyages to America, published in 1631, drew public attention in Europe to this profitable trade. He says that in 1622 there were thirty-seven sail of ships from England on the New England coast, and all made good voyages.

In the "New English Canaan" published in Amsterdam in 1637 by Thomas Morton, who gave the Pilgrims so much trouble, he says, "The coast of New England aboundeth with such multitudes of cod that the inhabitants do dung their grounds with cod; and it is as a comodity better than the golden mines of the Spanish Indies, for without dried cod the Spaniards, Portuguese would not be able to victual a ship for the sea.* I have seen in one harbor next to Richmond's Island, fifteen sail of ships at one time, that have taken in dried cod for Spain, and the straights."

The "harbor next to Richmond's Island" could have been no other than the harbor of Falmouth. The Pool at the mouth of the Saco is the next harbor on the west of the island, and of this Levett says, "Where two good ships may ride, being moored head and stern." Falmouth alone had

---

* Fisher Ames once said that "every cod-fish drawn up had a pistareen in its mouth."

room for fifteen ships to ride at anchor. Winter mentions having fished at Casco before he took charge of Richmond's Island.

Fishing was a principal industry pursued by the first settlers of Falmouth, but they were not the kind mentioned by Talleyrand. He says, "All the qualities, all the virtues which are attached to agriculture, are wanting in the man who lives by fishing." The Falmouth fishermen were most of them agriculturists also.

CHAPTER V.

AT the beginning of the first Indian, or Philip's war, Falmouth, which then included a large territory, was having a thrifty trade in fish, masts, spars, ton-timber, oar-rafters, and sawed lumber, as mills had been built at Capisic, at Long Creek, and at some other places. In the vicinity of each were settled active and enterprising men with families. The Purpooduck side of the harbor, from Simonton's cove to Stroudwater, was fringed with farms and settlers. From the mouth of every creek went shallops and fishing boats, and some had their "bylanders" or coasting sloops, carrying cord wood and fish to the Isles of Shoals and ports beyond. Fishing ships harbored here, from which they sent out their boats to take and cure the much valued cod for their home cargoes. The same year of the breaking out of the war, John Josselyn, "gentleman," who spent eight years with his brother at Black Point, published his "Two voyages into New England." In his book he described all the settlements on the coast from the Piscataqua to Sagadahock. He says, "Casco Bay is the largest in the province and full of islands. Nine miles east of Black point lyeth scatteringly the town of Casco, upon a large bay, stored with cattle, sheep, swine, abundance of marsh, and arable land, a corn-mill or two, with stages for fishermen." Of Richmond's Island Josselyn says, "It is three miles in circumference and hath a passable and gravely ford on the north side, between the main and the sea at low water. Here are found excellent whetstones, and here likewise are stages for fishermen."

At this time Robert Jordan and his sons occupied the "ould plantation" at Spurwink, and one son, John, lived on Richmond's Island. In 1680 he was appointed, by Governor Andross, judge for the county of Cornwall at Pemaquid. The letter containing his commission was directed "to Justice Jordan, at Richmond's Island, near Casco Bay." There was also a hamlet at the mouth of the Presumpscot river, the principal man of which was Arthur Macworth, and there were scattering settlers along the shore from there westward to Capisic and Stroudwater where was a landing for the unloading of masts and spars. Here also was a settlement, and another at Long creek, with a saw-mill. Casco contained at this time about four hundred inhabitants. Josselyn says, "The people of the province [Maine] feed generally upon as good flesh, beef, pork, mutton, fowl, and fish, as any in the world beside." On the neck, at a point now included in the property of the Portland Company, was a meeting-house, of which Reverend George Burroughs, who was executed in 1692, at Salem, for witchcraft, was the minister. This apparently well established town was doomed to destruction.

Immediately after the outbreak in Massachusetts, means were taken at Falmouth to ascertain the feeling of the eastern Indians toward the English. The fear and jealousy of the savages were aroused and they began to suspect that it was the object of the English (who had tried in vain to get them to give up their arms), to deprive them of their means of obtaining subsistence, and finally to drive them from the soil. In September the buildings of Thomas Purchase were robbed by the Indians while he was absent. An armed party of twenty-five settlers was sent out to gather corn in the same vicinity. They discovered three Indians, one of whom they killed, and wounded a second. The third escaped and informed his friends who were in the neighborhood; they rallied and drove the English to their vessel with the loss of two boats laden with corn. This was the first blood spilled in Maine in Philip's war, and was shed without justification on the part of the English; it naturally excited in the Indians a spirit of revenge. Opportunities for retaliation were not wanting, the settlers being unprotected along the whole frontier.

In their lamentations they could with propriety and truth adopt the language of the scripture book of Lamentations, in the fifth chapter, "We gat our bread with the peril of our lives, because of the sword of the wilderness." "In those times there was no peace to him that went out nor to him that came in, but great vexations were upon all the inhabitants of the country."

A Massachusetts order of court in 1674, compelled "every man to take to meeting on Lord's days his arms with him with at least five charges of powder and shot." Also, "that whosoever shall shoot of a gun except at an Indian or a wolf shall forfeit five s."

Of the order to take arms to meeting, McFingal wrote —

> " So once for fear of Indian beating
> Our grandsires bore their guns to meeting;
> Each man equipped on Sunday morn
> With psalm-book, shot, and powder horn,

And looked, in form, as all must grant
Like th' ancient true church militant,
Or fierce, like modern deep divines,
Who fight with quills like porcupines.''

The first attack in this neighborhood was on the family of
Thomas Wakely of Falmouth. who lived on the east side of
Presumpscot River below the falls. They killed Wakely
and his wife, his eldest son John and his wife, with three
of their children, and carried one daughter eleven years old
into captivity. After taking all they wanted from the house,
they set fire to it, and it was consumed. Lieutenant George
Ingersoll, who had seen the smoke, visited the place the next
morning with an armed party to learn the cause, when they
came upon a scene too horrible to describe. The daughter
was carried by a Saco sachem to Major Waldron of Dover,
where she remained and was subsequently married to Richard Scammon of that town. The Indians went off in a
westerly direction. They burnt several houses at Saco, and
afterward killed several persons at Blue Point. In October
they killed the brothers Arthur and Andrew Alger, at
Scarborough, and burnt their houses. About the same time
the enemy killed a son of George Ingersoll and another
man at Falmouth, and attacked the Jordan settlement at
Spurwink. The father, Robert Jordan, left his house and
fled, when his house (the one in which George Cleeves
formerly lived), was destroyed with all its contents, except
what could be taken away by the inmates in haste. The old
minister fled to Great Island, now New Castle, at the mouth
of the Piscataqua, where he lived until his death in 1679.
After these outrages by the Indians, many inhabitants left
their homes and sought safety with their friends in the
vicinity of the Piscataqua and in Massachusetts. The with-

drawal of so many from the vicinity of Casco Bay, weakened those remaining for their own defence, but fewer were exposed to the tomahawk of the Indians.

The most authentic, and, therefore, the most satisfactory account of the Indian attack upon the settlement of Casco, is a letter from Thaddeus Clark, a prominent inhabitant, to Mrs. Harvey, his wife's mother, who was the only child of George Cleeves, and first married Michael Mitton and second a Harvey. This letter with an introduction was communicated to the Historic Genealogical Register by Dr. Fogg, of South Boston, in 1877.

The following letter, written from " Casco " by Thaddeus Clark, three days after the Indian attack upon that place in August, 1676, differs somewhat from the various accounts of that affair which are on record.

A reference to Willis' "Portland," pages 204 and 205, will make this more apparent. George Lewis is there stated to have escaped to the island in safety; in the letter he and his wife are said to be killed or captured. In " Willis " the Wakely killed is *Isaac;* in the letter it is plainly *Daniel.* Hubbard says there were thirty-four persons killed and made captive — agreeing exactly with Clark's statement, viz.: " Of men slain eleven, of women and children twenty-three killed and taken." Willis says, page 206, " To what extent the buildings were destroyed we have no means of ascertaining." Hubbard states " that the homes of those killed and taken prisoners were burned," while Clark's letter says, " G^m Wallis his dwelling house and *none besides his* is burnt."

On the twentieth of August George Munjoy was sent to Falmouth from Boston with fifteen hundred pounds of bread for the relief of persons there. This was probably immediately upon the receipt of Clark's letter to Mrs. Harvey, written on the fourteenth of August.

Willis says, page 200, that in the beginning of 1675 Elizabeth Harvey, the mother of Thaddeus Clark's wife, was a member of Thomas Brackett's family in Falmouth. She must have gone, subsequently, to Boston, as Clark's letter is addressed to her there. She probably went with James Andrews, her son-in-law, who removed from Falmouth to Boston in 1675. Andrews died in Boston, 1704. Mrs. Harvey was a daughter of George Cleeves, was married to Michael Mitton (prominent in the early history of Maine), who was the father of all her children. Subsequently she married a Harvey, and died a widow in 1682.

Mr. Willis, in his "Portland," page 292, is in error as to the education of Clark. He says "he was not much educated; his signature to instruments was made by a mark." The letter which follows is unusual for that period, in its expression and in its chirography, especially from one occupying no official position.

Honoured Mother

After my duty & my wifes presented to your selfe these may inform you of our present health, of our present being when other of our friends are by the barbarous heathen cut off from having a being in this World. The Lord of late hath renewed his witnesses against vs, & hath dealt very bitterly with vs in that we are deprived of the Societie of our nearest friends by the breaking in of the adversarie against us: On Friday last in the morning your own Son with your two Sons in Law, Anthony & Thomas Bracket & their whole families were Killed & taken by the Indians, we Know not how, tis certainly known by us that Thomas is slain & his wife & children carried away captiue, & of Anthony & his familie we haue no tidings & therefore think that they might be captivated the night before because of the remoteness of their habitation from neighbourhood. G^m Corban & all his family G^m Lewis & his wife, James Ross & all his family, G^m Durham, John Munjoy, & Daniel Wakely, Benjamin Hadwell & all his family are lost, all slain by Sun an hour high in the Morning & after. G^m Wallis his dwelling house & none besides his is burnt. there are of men slain 11, of women & children 23 killed & taken; we that are aliue are forced upon Mr Andrewes his Island to Secure our own & the liues of our families. we haue but little prouision & are so few in number that we are not able to bury the dead till more strength come to us, the desire of the people to your Selfe is that you would be pleased to Speak to Mr Munjoy & Deacon Philips that they would entreat the Governour that forthwith aid might be Sent to us either to fight the enemie out of our borders that our English Corn may be inned in wherby we may comfortably liue or remoue vs out of danger that we may prouide for our Selues elswhere, hauing no more at present but desiring your prayers to God for his preservation of vs in these times of danger, I rest

Your dutifull Son

from Casco-bay   THADDEUS CLARK.
14. 6. 76.*
remember my Loue to my sister &c.

[Addressed: "These | ffor his honoured Mother | Mrs Elizabeth Harvy, living | in Boston."]

* Which being interpreted means the fourteenth of the sixth month (August), 1676.

Thaddeus Clark, whose letter about the sacking of the town has been preserved for two hundred years and more, was an Irishman, so says Alden, and as Dr. Fogg testifies, was of good education. In 1663 he received an assignment of the one hundred acres of land formerly deeded to Michael Mitton, his father-in-law, by Cleeves. The assignment is on the York records in these words: " These presents witness that I Elizabeth Mitton, late wife of Michael Mitton, deceased, in consideration that Thaddeus Clark married my daughter Elizabeth, I do by these presents grant give and make over all my right, title, and interest in the lands within mentioned, unto the said Thaddeus Clark, his heirs," etc. Clark could not have been long married, as his wife was then only eighteen years old. This gift from the Widow Mitton became Clark's home farm, reaching from the foot of High street to a point above the gas works, which now occupy " Clark's Point " where his house was. His cellar was to be seen in 1831. Clark subsequently conveyed to Edward Tyng, who married his daughter Elizabeth, forty-four acres of this tract, which extended from the river northwesterly, where Congress street now is. Tyng had this lot surveyed in 1687 and then had three houses upon it, in one of which he lived. Clark was lieutenant of a company of soldiers here in 1690, and was killed at the head of his detachment in the Indian attack that year. Two prominent families at least claim their descent from him.

In writing of Thaddeus Clark it came to my mind that I had not, in its proper place, written a proper notice of his father-in-law Michael Mitton. He came from England with Cleeves when he returned in 1637, and subsequently married Cleeves' only child. Cleeves made large grants to him as Rigby's deputy, notably Peaks Island. Mitton lived near the Cape Elizabeth landing of Portland bridge, on a lot deeded to him by Cleeves in Rigby's name in 1650. That he had lived there before the conveyance, is proved by the wording of the instrument, which says to "butt against the dwelling house of him the said Michael Mitton." Willis locates his house on the city side. According to Josselyn, Mitton was a great fowler when he first arrived here. He says (1639): "One Mr. Mitton related of a triton, or mereman which 'he saw in Casco bay. The gentleman was a great fowler, and used to go out with a small boat or canoe, and fetching a compass about a small Island for the advantage of a shot, was encountered with a triton, who laying his hands upon the side of the canoe, had one of them chopped off with a hatchet by Mr. Mitton, which was in all respects like the hand of a man. The triton presently sunk, dying the water with his purple blood, and was no more seen." That Mitton "was a great fowler," is proved by Winter's accounts of disbursements at Richmond's Island. He wrote, 1639, "foull from Myhell Myttinge of Casko, geese at 1 s. pece, 4 d. a pece for ducks, & 2 d a pece for taill, [teel] which amounted to 8-13-0." Morton in his New English Canaan, says, "I have fed my dogs with as fat geese as I ever fed upon myself in England," and this makes it probable.*

*Up to the beginning of this century, wild swans were among the waterfowl frequenting the small ponds of Cumberland county. At the time mentioned Richard Knight, of the present town of Falmouth, shot a white swan; one of a pair which came to the Duck pond in Westbrook every season. None have been seen there since. About the same time William McGill, of Standish, killed one of the same species while flying from one pond to another. John Josselyn says in his time in Maine, 1670, "The waterfowl are these Hookers or wild swans, cranes, geese of three sorts gray, white, and the brant goose — the first and last are the best meat. The white are lean and tough and live a long time." Now there are only the gray remaining in Maine, with occasionally a brant.

There is one indelible blot on the character of Mitton. In 1640, Winter wrote to Trelawney from Richmond's Island this: " Mr. Francis Martin is here with us, and is not settled in any place as yet to remain. This next week I shall go up to Casco with him to seat him in some place there. I know not how he will live here well, except he have brought money with him. He hath never a servant, and he cannot work himself, and here is nothing to be gotten without hard labor." Martin was evidently a decayed gentleman, or he would not have been styled Mister by Winter. This was an honorable title then. Two years later Winter again mentions Martin to his principal: " Also herein goes a bill upon Mr. John Martin for his uncle Francis Martin. Also he was with us five months and spent upon our provision, and cannot pay for anything. He is in a bad way of living here with his two children. He plants a little Indian corn and that is all he hath to live upon. He hath neither goat nor pig, nor any thing else. He is old and cannot labor, and his children are not brought up to work, so I know not what shift he will make to live."

These " two children" were daughters. The fate of the eldest is given by Willis, being the substance of her history as written in Winthrop's journal. Willis says: " Martin, an early inhabitant of Casco, was the father of two daughters, whom, being about to return to England to arrange his affairs, he left in the family of Michael Mitton. During their residence of several months with him in 1646, he insinuated himself into the favor of the eldest, named Mary, whom he seduced. She afterwards went to Boston and was delivered of a bastard child, of which she confessed Mitton to be the father. Overcome with shame, she endeavored to conceal her first crime by the commission of a more heinous one in the murder of her infant; for this she perished on the scaffold at the early age of twenty-two years, in March, 1647." Cotton Mather says of her trial: "When she touched the face of the child before the jury, the blood came fresh into it, so she confessed the whole truth concerning it." He also says: "Her carriage in her imprisonment and at her execution was very penitent. But there was this remarkable at her execution. She acknowledged her twice essaying to kill the child, and now through the unskilfulness of the executioner she was turned off the ladder twice, before she died."

The York records give the date of Mitton's death to be in 1660.

A noted Indian of Philip's tribe, named Simon, had escaped to Maine and was the instigator of the outrages at Falmouth. Just before the attack Simon had made himself familiar at the house of Anthony Brackett, who lived near where the Deering house now is at the head of Back Cove. Brackett had lost a cow, and had accused Simon of the theft. Simon went away but soon returned with other Indians, whom he introduced to Brackett as "the fellows who killed your cow." They immediately seized all the weapons in sight and made prisoners of Brackett, his wife, their five children, and a negro servant. The brother of Mrs. Brackett, Nathaniel Mitton, in resisting the binding was instantly killed. They next day dispatched with their tomahawks Brackett's neighbors, Robert Corbin, Humphrey Durham, and Benjamin Atwell, at Presumpscot, and hurried away their wives and families to the shore. One woman escaped with one of the canoes. Some townsmen, who were coming to reap grain for Brackett, saw the Indians and made their escape. The remaining inhabitants fled to

Munjoy's garrison on the hill and from there to Andrews, now Bang's Island. In the night some of them returned and secured some powder left in their houses when they fled.

The Indians having the Bracketts in charge went up the bay, probably to New Meadows, where they learned of the success of the Indians who went to Arrowsic, and leaving their prisoners on the shore, they went to meet their friends. Brackett and his wife found a leaky canoe which she mended with a needle and thread, which she found in a deserted house. In this frail canoe they crossed the bay, Hubbard says eight or nine miles wide, and finally reached Black Point, where they found a vessel bound to Piscataqua in which they took passage to that place.

Thomas Brackett, who was one of those killed at Falmouth, married Mary, a daughter of Michael Mitton, and granddaughter of George Cleeves. She was carried by the Indians to Canada and died in the first year of her captivity. None of her children returned to Falmouth, but two of her grandchildren, Anthony and Thomas Brackett, who owned a large tract of land reaching across the neck above High street, came here when the town was resettled.

Two days after the escape of the Falmouth people to Bang's Island, Bryan Pendleton, of Winter Harbor, wrote a letter from there to Governor Leverett, of which this is an extract:

Honored Governor together with the council

    I am sorry my pen must be the messenger of so great a tragedy. On the 11th of this instant, we heard of many killed of our neighbors in Falmouth, or Casco Bay, and on the 12th instant, Mr. Josselyn sent me a brief letter written from under the hand of Mr. Burras [Burroughs] the minister. He gives an account of thirty two killed and carried away by the Indians. Himself escaped to an island — but I hope Black Point

men have fetched him off by this time — ten men, six women sixteen children. Anthony and Thomas Brackett, Mr. Munjoy his son only are named. BRYAN PENDLETON.
Winter Harbor at night the 13th of August 1676.

A few years ago there was, (and it is probable there is yet), on the north slope of Bang's Island, opposite Peaks Island, a few rods from the high bank, the remains of a wall of stone among the trees. It was evidently hastily laid up of the loose surface blocks of the slate stone. It showed great age and rude construction. I first examined it half a century ago, when it was more perfect than at my last visit. I have since repeatedly examined it, and imagined it to be the breastwork behind which Reverend George Burroughs sheltered his fugitive flock while they were hiding from the Indians on the island in 1676. He was just the man for a leader, fearless, and of reputed great strength, which would serve to nerve his men in rolling those large blocks of stone up the steep slope.

Not many rods from the ruined wall, is the well-known natural spring of water, from which thousands of visitors now drink every season. This spring probably drew the fugitives to the spot to make a stand. Below the bank, at the sheltered cove, and on the rocky beach, is an artificial pool, evidently made by throwing out in a circle the small beach-stones and pebbles, to a considerable depth. Probably at the time it was made it was much deeper than now, reaching below the low tide-mark. The sea-water flows and ebbs through the surrounding ridge of cobble-stones, making a pool of the clearest water. It requires no great stretch of imagination to suppose this to be the enclosure where the imprisoned people, in 1676, kept their fish and lobsters alive for use in bad weather. In good weather the fish could be taken from the rocks at White Head. This commanding bluff would also be a fine lookout for the picket sentinel who watched for the expected enemy. An aged gentleman tells me that the pool was there when he was a boy, and its construction and use could not then be accounted for.

George Munjoy sailed from Boston by the order of Governor Leverett on the twentieth of August, with fifteen hundred pounds of bread for the people, and then they had been on the island nine days, with no other food but fish and the berries of the island. There is no record of the time of their relief. George Munjoy did arrive with his stores; evidence of which is furnished by the records of the general court of 1679, showing that not having received compensation for his service, he petitioned that body to pay his bill.

1680 — no month named — Sewall's diary says, "Sylvanus Davis went out [of Boston] on Saturday to carry corn and other necessaries to the fort at Casco, is driven on the sand; essaying to put to sea again in the sabbath day storm. So the corn lost and the soldiers disappointed."

Many of the inhabitants of the shores of the bay fled to Jewell's Island, trusting in its distance from the main for their security. There was a fortified house on the island but no sufficient guard was kept. A party of Indians came upon them suddenly, but the small number of English at home defended themselves bravely. Those who were absent returned and fought their way to the garrison house and prevented its capture. Seven men were also slain on Munjoy's Island, where they had gone for some sheep for food. One of them was George Felt, a useful man in the

9

settlement. They retreated to the stone house so often mentioned, but it was in ruins and could not be defended.

The party of Indians who left those that came to Falmouth, at Merrymeeting Bay, and proceeded down to Arrowsic Island, reconnoitered for a day or two. Richard Hammond had a fortified house there which was attacked and its owner killed. Clark and Lake of Boston also had a fort and trading house at the lower end of the island, of which Sylvanus Davis was commander and agent. On the fourteenth of August the Indians watched for the opportunity and followed the sentinel into the fort. The garrison defended the fort as long as there was any hope of holding it and then fled. Captain Lake, who was then at the fort, and his agent Davis, attempted to reach another island in a canoe, but were overtaken just as they were stepping on shore. Davis was disabled by a gunshot wound, and crept unperceived to a cleft of the rocks, where he remained undiscovered two days. He finally reached a canoe and escaped across the river. Captain Thomas Lake was killed outright because he would not surrender, but presented his pistol in defence. His fate was not known to his friends. His body lay all winter exposed on the island, until March, 1677, when it was recovered and carried to his home in Boston.

Judge Sewall in his diary records, " March 13th, Capt. Lake, the remainder of his corpse, was honorably buried. Captains and Commissoners carried. No magistrate save Major Clark there." Captain Lake was buried on Copp's Hill where his headstone may now be seen. He was the ancestor of Sir Biby Lake.

On the receipt of the advices from Falmouth, giving an

account of the Indian hostilities, the government of Massachusetts began to gather a force to protect the inhabitants of Maine. One hundred and seventy English and friendly Indians were dispatched to Falmouth, where they arrived on the twentieth of September. The Indians had learned of their arrival and drew off, although they had felt safe to stop about Falmouth and had been thrashing out the grain in Captain Brackett's barn. The Massachusetts officers could find no Indians, but occasionally there would be a bloody raid made on some unprotected settlement. The troops left Casco Bay in October, when immediately an attack was made upon Black Point, where the people had gathered in the garrison of Henry Josselyn, who went out of his palisade to negotiate terms for a surrender, and when he returned the people had fled to their boats and escaped. Josselyn was compelled to surrender without terms. The war was continued until April, 1678, when at their request commissioners were appointed to treat with the Indians. They met at Falmouth and signed a treaty of peace. By this treaty each family, who returned to their homes, were to pay to the Indians one peck of corn annually except Major Philips, of Saco, who from his wealth was required to pay a bushel. The captives were now restored, and the people generally returned to their habitations after two years' absence. Reverend Robert Jordan, of Spurwink, one of the most wealthy landholders of the town, never returned. After his flight from his burning dwelling in 1676, he lived at Great Island, now New Castle, New Hampshire, until his death in 1679, in the sixty-eighth year of his age. He had given to his children each a farm, and by will he divided the remainder between his wife and children. Some of the descendants yet retain a share of the paternal acres.

After the treaty of peace was concluded, Captain Sylvanus Davis, who had so narrow an escape when Captain Lake was killed at Arrowsic, came to Falmouth and obtained, by grant and purchase, some of the best mill-sites in the township. In 1680, he received from President Danforth a home lot between what is now India and Hancock streets. Here he lived and had a store of goods, probably on a breastwork of logs, to serve customers coming by land or water. Here in 1687 he had the only store in the town. He was licensed by the court to retail liquors out of doors. Richard Seacomb, who had held a license to keep an ordinary years before, had moved to what is now East Deering. Seacomb's was probably the first fully equipped tavern in the settlement.

Reverend George Burroughs, the minister, returned to his charge in 1683. He had been preaching in Salem. That year he relinquished a large part of his former town grant of land, for the convenience of his townsmen. In their application they offered him land further off in exchange but he replied that "as for the land already taken we were welcome to it, and if twenty acres of the fifty above expressed would pleasure us, he freely gave it to us, not desiring any land anywhere else, nor anything else in consideration thereof." In the items of indebtedness for which the assessment of 1683 was made by the town, was this : " Richard Powsland for money lent the town to go for Mr. Burroughs 1 p 10 0 To anthony Brackett to pay part of Mr. Burroughs passage 5 s." It is not known when Mr. Burroughs first came to Falmouth, nor when he finally left. He was at Black Point in 1686 and must have stood high among the ministers of the province. The court records for that year contain the following : " March 30th It is ordered by this court yt the

Re cor, do give notice to Mr Burrows, minister of Bla Poynt to preach before the next General Assembly at Yorke." This was nine years after the purchase by Massachusetts.

In his diary for 1685, Judge Sewall, of Boston, records, " Nov 18 Mr. G. Burroughs dined with us." Seven years later, Sewall sat in judgment on his guest and assisted in his condemnation for witchcraft. During the excitement about witchcraft, Mr. Burroughs was complained of for practicing that undefined power. He was carried to Boston and imprisoned two months, previous to the sitting of the court of Oyer and Terminer at Salem, where he was returned for trial. The evidence against him was of the most ridiculous character. His well-known great strength and activity were enlisted against him, as something supernatural. In all the trivial and unsupported testimony there was nothing half as reasonable offered to show a disordered mind, as was his act at Falmouth in giving away his valuable land without compensation. Of course he was condemned. His execution took place with that of several others at Salem, on the ninth of August, 1692.

This same Judge Sewall notes the execution in these words under the head of " Doleful witchcraft " : " This day George Burroughs, John Willard, John Proctor, Martha Carrier, and John Jacobs were executed at Salem, a very great number of spectators being present. Mr. Cotton Mather was there, Mr. Sims, Hale, Noyes, Chiever, &c. All of them said they were innocent, Carrier and all. Mr. Mather says. they all died by a righteous sentence. Mr. Burroughs by his speech, prayer, protestation of his innocence, did much move unthinking persons, which occasions their speaking hardly concerning his being executed." Mr. Burroughs left a wife and children, some of whom have

descendants here. In the witch delusion in New England
the sad fate of Reverend George Burroughs stands out as
prominently as does the burning of John Rogers among the
martyrs of the time of bloody Mary. No victim's unjust
death ever excited so much sympathy in the colonies as his.

All those men mentioned as being present at the execution
were ministers. Judge Sewall was probably there himself—
if he was not there, how should he know and make a record
of all the particulars the same day? He commences with
" This day." Parson Hale, of Beverly, one of those mentioned as present, wrote a book which was published in 1697,
entitled, " A modest enquiry into the nature of witchcraft,
and how persons guilty of that crime may be convicted."
It is now a rare book. My extracts are from a copy loaned
to me by Mr. Lewis, of South Berwick. In this work the
author relates the only known instance in which any one
was suspected of witchcraft in Falmouth, although all
Europe, as well as New England, entertained and suffered by
the delusion. Mr. Hale has a word of caution as follows: .

We must be very circumspect lest we be deceived by human
knavery as happened in a case nigh Richmond's Island Anno, 1659.
One Thorpe a drunken preacher was gotten in to preach at Black
Point under the appearance and profession of a minister of the
gospel, and boarded at the house of Goodman Bailey, and Baileys
wife observed his conversation to be contrary to his calling, gravely
told him his way was contrary to the gospel of Christ, and desired
him to reform his life, or leave her house. So he departed from her
house and turned her enemy, and found an opportunity to do her an
injury. It so fell out that Mr. Jordan of Spurwink had a cow died,
and about that time Goody Bailey had said she intended such a day
to travel to Casco-Bay. Mr. Thorpe goes to Mr. Jordans man or men,
and saith the cow was bewitched to death, and if they would lay the
carcass in a place he should appoint, he would burn it and bring the
witch; and accordingly the cow is laid by the path that led from

Black Point to Casco, and set on fire that day Goody Bailey was to travel that way, and so she came by, while the carcass was burning, and Thorpe had her questioned for a witch: But Mr. Jordan interposed in her behalf; and said his cow died by his servants negligence, and to cover their own fault they were willing to have it imputed to witchcraft. Mr. Thorpe knew of Goody Bailey's intended journey, and orders my servants (said he) without my approbation to burn my cow in the way where Bailey is to come; and so unriddled the navery and delivered the innocent.

Robert Jordan was not that kind of a man to be looking for something supernatural in every uncommon occurrence, but weighed matters of that kind by the standard of common sense. This transaction at Spurwink was thirty years before the execution of George Burroughs.

The first person executed for witchcraft in Massachusetts was Margaret Jones, of Charlestown. Her execution took place in June, 1648. From this time until the spring of 1692, the colonies, especially Massachusetts, were exercised and deluded with the idea that the Devil was let loose upon them. When Sir William Phips arrived with the charter and a commission as governor, the prisons were full of those condemned, or suspected to be guilty of the undefined crime of witchcraft. A court of Oyer had been formed especially to try this species of offenders, and the people were dissatisfied if any were let off. On the nineteenth of September, 1692, Giles Corey was pressed to death at Salem " for standing mute." The editor of Sewall's diary in a note thus explains the case :

The poor victim was eighty-one years of age. At first, apparently a firm believer in the witchcraft delusion, even to the extent of mistrusting his saintly wife, who was executed three days after his torturous death, his was the most tragic of all the fearful offerings. He had made a will, while confined in Ipswitch jail, conveying his

property, according to his own prefferences, among his heirs; and, in
the belief that his will would be invalidated and his estate confiscated if he were condemned by a jury after pleading to the indictment, he resolutely preserved silence, knowing that an acquittance
was an imposibility. He therefore bore with unflintching nerve and
spirit, the penalty of English law for standing " mute " and refused to
plead to an indictment — the *peine forte et dure* of being pressed to
death.

Of those accused over fifty had confessed that they were
guilty of what was charged upon them. The inducement
was, confession insured immunity from trial or imprisonment
or execution. How noble to us appears the calm firmness
of George Burroughs. When deliverance by confession was
so readily offered him, he refused to purchase it by a false
statement; although it would injure none but himself, it
would encourage the persecutions, and leave an indelible
stain on his memory.

Governor Phips, who was a native of Maine, arrived from
England with the new charter and a commission to execute
it, in May, 1692. Then as I have said the prisons were full.
To oppose the delusion violently would endanger his popularity and the success of his purpose to save those condemned and accused. Cotton Mather says of him :

Therefore when he had well canvassed a cause, which perhaps
would have puzzled the wisdom of the wisest men on earth to have
managed without an error in their administrations, he thought if it
would be an error at all, it would certainly be safest to put a stop to
all future prosecutions, as far as it lay in him to do it. Now upon a
deliberate view of these things, his Excellency first reprieved and
then pardoned many of them condemned; and there fell out several
strange things that caused the spirit of the country to run as vehe-
mently upon the acquitting of all the accused, as it by mistake ran at
first upon the condemning of them.

Judge Sewall in his diary notices a session of the Governor and council which shows Governor Phips' opinion of the witch court. He says: " October 29 1692, Mr. Russel asked whether the Court of Oyer and Terminer should sit, expressing some fear of inconvenience by its fall. Governor said *it must fall.*"

At the session of the general court in 1696, the fourteenth of January, 1697, was appointed to be observed as a fast day on account of what might have been done amiss " in the late tragedy raised among us by Satan and his instruments through the awful judgments of God." At the afternoon service at the south meeting-house on fast day, Judge Sewall acknowledged his errors at the witch trials. In his diary he gives a copy of his confession, headed as follows: " Copy of a bill I put up on the fast day; giving it to Mr. Willard [the pastor] as he passed by and standing up at the reading of it, and bowing when finished." Governor Hutchinson in his History of Massachusetts says: " The great noise which the New England witchcrafts made throughout the English dominions, proceeded more from the general panic with which all sorts of persons were seized, and an expectation that the contagion would spread to all parts of the country, than from the number of persons who were executed; more having been put death in a single county in England, in a short space of time than have suffered in all New England from the first settlement to the present time."

T. W. Higginson says Cotton Mather was popularly identified beyond any one with these prosecutions, yet he used these words: " If a drop of innocent blood should be shed in the prosecution of the witchcrafts among us, how unhappy are we!" The eminent English judge, Sir Matthew Hale, giving his charge at the trial for witchcraft of Rose

Cullender and Anne Duny in 1668 — a trial which had great weight with the American judges — said that he "made no doubt there were such Creatures as Witches, for the Scriptures affirmed it, and the Wisdom of all Nations had provided Laws against such Persons." The devout Bishop Hall wrote in England: "Satan's prevalency in this Age is most clear, in the marvellous numbers of Witches abiding in all places. Now hundreds are discovered in one Shire." To see the delusion in its most frightful form we must go beyond the Atlantic and far beyond the limits of English Puritanism. During its course thirty thousand victims were put to death in Great Britain, seventy-five thousand in France, one hundred thousand in Germany, beside those executed in Italy, Switzerland, and Sweden, many of them being burned. In all, there were nineteen persons hanged at Salem.

I have devoted more space to witchcraft in Massachusetts than would seem appropriate in a work on local history, but it should be kept in mind that George Burroughs suffered death by the delusion, and that final relief from the mania, came by Governor Phips, a native of Maine. Further, Falmouth was then a part of the Bay Province.

CHAPTER VI.

IMMEDIATELY after the peace of April 12, 1678, concluded at Falmouth, the exiled people of the town began to return. Their farms had been tenantless two years, their interests were here, and the township's natural advantages were unsurpassed. A fort was built at the foot of "Broad street" and named Fort Loyal. This fort was probably built with the assistance of the province, as President Danforth held a court there in September, 1680. He came to lay out a compact settlement which would be defensible. The record of this court is preserved in York County. In the history of Portland, this document is given entire. Lots were confirmed or granted to some thirty persons. Some exchanges and restitutions were made with the consent of President Danforth. The record is dated "Fort Loyal 23 of September 1680. These the within and above written orders being read to the selectmen of the town of Falmouth, they manifested jointly their full and free consent thereto." Present, Lieutenant Anthony Brackett, Mr. John Wallis, Lieutenant George Ingerson, Ensign Thaddeus Clark. These constituted the first board of selectmen of the town, of whom we have any authentic record; and this was preserved by being deposited with the records of the county.

One item of the doings of Danforth's court was this: "It is ordered that there shall be an highway three rods wide left against the water side towards the meeting house." This shows that the meeting-house, at the point below, had not been destroyed during the time the town lay desolate, and the mention of selectmen shows a town government had been organized previous to the visit of President Danforth or while he was here. The fort was built on a rocky bluff about fifteen feet above the level of highwater and a rod or two east of the present India street. The first lot on the westerly side of India street was assigned to Captain Edward Tyng, who was in command of the fort. He was the son of Edward Tyng, of Boston, who came there about the time of its first settlement.

A second Indian war commenced in 1688, before the people of Falmouth had expected it. The menaces and occasionally hostile attacks on the remote inhabitants by small parties of Indians, created alarm through the eastern settlements. To bring the Indians to a conference Captain Blackman seized about twenty Indians at Saco, among them were several chiefs; the most noted was Hopegood. These were brought under a strong guard to Fort Loyal, where they were confined. This seizure did not have the desired effect, but caused the Indians to make reprisals. In September Captain Tyng wrote from Falmouth that he feared that Casco would be the center of trouble. Troops were sent from Boston accompanied by Councillor Stoughton seeking a reconciliation with the Indians without further hostilities. Governor Andros sought further to conciliate the Indians and ordered the release of those confined at Fort Loyal. On the twentieth of October he issued a proclamation requiring the release of the prisoners held by the enemy, and Indian murderers to be given up for trial. He soon discovered that proclamations were of little effect on savages.

In November the Governor raised a force of seven hundred men with whom he marched through by land to Falmouth, leaving a force at each principal town on the way. At Fort Loyal he left a garrison of sixty men under Captain George Lockhart. The Governor continued his laborious winter march to Pemaquid, where he left two companies of sixty men each, one of which was under the command of Captain Tyng, of Falmouth.. This force was independent of the ordinary garrison under Captain Lockhart. The whole number of troops left by Governor Andros on his way and at Pemaquid, was more than five hundred; enough to have insured the safety of every fortified place if they had remained. In April of the next year Andros was seized in Boston and imprisoned. This was on account of the reception in Boston of the news of the landing in England of the Prince of Orange. The people of Massachusetts revolted and the revolt became contagious. The military officers in the garrisons, who were commissioned by Andros, lost control of their men, and many of them abandoned their posts at the eastward and came to Falmouth.

In the first volume of Hutchinson's History of Massachusetts is a note copied from a manuscript letter. It is in these words: "In August 1680, the deputy governor, Mr. Saltonstall, Nowell, &c. sailed from Boston with 60 soldiers, in a ship and sloop, to still the people of Casco Bay, and prevent governor Andros's usurpation." This can only be explained by supposing that the date of the visit of this force to Casco Bay is a misprint, and should read 1689; as Andros did not arrive in Boston until the twentieth of

December, 1686. True, there was some agitation here in
1680, but nothing caused by the fear of " Andros's usurpation," nor was it sufficient to warrant the sending of an
armed ship with sixty soldiers.

Probably the French and Indians learned of the subver-
sion of the authority of Andros, and that of the officers who
held commissions under him, which was the cause of renewed
hostilities. At least their raids commenced immediately
after the revolt.

The capture of Pemaquid fort caused the whole population of the east to abandon their settlements and retreat to
Falmouth which was their first stopping-place. Notwithstanding the importance of Fort Loyal, it was neglected by
the Provincial government. In June, 1689, the officers of
the fort and some other leading men of the town represented
to the authorities in Boston the weakness of its garrison and
the lack of ammunition in its magazine; having only three
and a half pounds of powder, and no muskets. Its provisions had been supplied by Sylvanus Davis, the commander,
from his store of goods.*

Those in power after the seizure of the Governor finally
awakened to the danger of Falmouth. Major Swain was
dispatched by land from Boston with a large force to garrison the eastern towns. Two companies of soldiers under
the command of Captains Hall and Willard were distributed
among the garrisons of the town and the fort. In September the renowned Major Benjamin Church, of Plymouth, who
had shown so much valor in destroying Philip's Indian army

---

* "Falmouth, Province of Maine, August 1689. Received of Georg
Bremhall for the supply of forte Loyal one quarter of Booll Beef waight
seventy tow pouns I say receved by me Sylvanus Davis Capt." — George
Bramhall's Papers.

ten years before, was engaged to lead a force through Maine.
President Danforth who had been restored to his former
presidency of the province, gave to Church the following
instructions: " You are with all possible speed to take care
that the Plymouth forces both English and Indians be fixed
and ready, and the first opportunity of wind and weather,
to go on board such vessels as are provided to transport you
and them to Casco, where if it shall please God you arrive,
you are to take under your care and command the companies of Capt. N. Hall and Capt. S. Willard. . . . . we
have ordered two men-of-war sloops and other small vessels
for transportation to attend you." It was agreed that the
soldiers should " have the benefit of the captives and all
lawful plunder and the reward of eight pounds per head for
every fighting Indian man slain by them over and above
their stated wages." Major Church was further instructed
to consult with Captain Davis, of Falmouth, who "is a
prudent man and well acquainted with the affairs of those
parts and is writ unto to advise and inform you all he can."

At the time of the alarm expressed for the safety of Falmouth the neck was a small settlement clustered around the
fort near the junction of Fore and Broad (now India)
streets. A short lane led from the foot of Broad street to
the ferry way, which was at a point of land at the eastern
entrance to Clay Cove, and was known as " Ferry point."
This ferry was a part of the highway to all the western
towns. It followed the shore round Cape Elizabeth, to
Spurwink, which river like all others west of it, was crossed
by a ferry. Fort Loyal was depended upon in case of an
attack, but we have seen that it was not in a condition for
defence. The following order copied from the records of
the general court shows the estimation in which the fort was

held by those in authority: "The surveyor General is ordered to deliver unto Capt. Edward Tyng for the support of Fort Loyal, one barrell of powder *the meanest* of the countries store or waste, and the value to be repaid by the treasurer as soon as the quit-rents come in." We have seen that the officers in command of the fort thought *bull-beef* good enough for the garrison.

In the summer of 1688, Governor Andros in the frigate Rose had robbed Baron Castin's residence at Bagaduce of everything valuable, which exasperated him, and caused him to get up the expedition to take Pemaquid fort. This did not satisfy the Indians and they determined to attack Falmouth also.

On the seventeenth of September, 1689, Joseph Prout, of Falmouth, wrote to Boston that two hundred Indians were then on "Palmers" (Peaks) Island. These were probably the Norridgewock and Canada Indians who were waiting for the arrival of those from the Penobscot. On the twentieth another large party joined them at the island and in the darkness of that night the whole Indian army moved up by the entrance to Back Cove, to Anthony Brackett's farm, now the Deering estate. The house according to tradition was a few rods south of the present mansion. The cellar was to be seen when Mr. Deering came into possession, about the beginning of this century.

The account says the Indian camp was discovered by Brackett's sons "by virtue of twelve firings." This has been considered to mean twelve musket shots. This seems to be ridiculous. The Indians were hiding, there were no English there to fire at, and why proclaim their coming by a salute? "The alarm was given by the Bracketts." They had seen the smoke of twelve separate camp-fires where the enemy had prepared their morning meal of fish which they had brought with them from the island.

I give Major Church's own account of his battle, thinking it preferable to one rewritten two hundred years after the transactions, without access to any new facts:

Being ready, Major Church embarked with his forces on board the vessels provided to transport them for Casco, having a brave gale at S. W. and on Friday about 3 o'clock, they got in sight of Casco harbour; and discovering two or three small ships there, not knowing whether they were friends or enemies; whereupon the said Commander, Major Church, gave orders that every man that was able should make ready, and all lie close, giving orders how they should act in case they were enemies. He going in the Mary sloop, together with the Resolution, went in first, being both well fitted with guns and men; coming to the first hailed them, who said they were friends, presently mann'd their boat, brought to, and so came along the side of them; who gave the said Church an account, that yesterday there was a very great army of Indians and French with them upon the island, at the going out of the harbour, and that they were come on purpose to take Casco fort and town; likewise inform'd him that they had got a captive woman aboard (Major Walden's daughter of Piscataqua) that could give him a full account of their number and intentions: He bid them give his service to their Captain, and tell him, he would wait upon him after he had been on shore and given some orders and directions. Being come pretty near he ordered all the men still to keep close, giving an account of the news he had received, and then went ashore, where were several of the chief men of the town who met him, being glad that he came so happily to their relief; told him the news Mrs. Lee had given them, being the woman aforesaid. He going to Captain Davis's to get some refreshment, having not eat a morsel since he came by Boston castle; and now having inquired into the state of the town, found them in a poor condition to defend themselves against such a number of enemies: He gave them an account of his orders and instructions, and told them what forces he had brought, and that when it was dark they should all land, and not before, lest the enemy should discover

10

them. And then he went on board the privateer, who were Dutch-
men; but as he went call'd aboard every vessel, and ordered the
Officers to take care that their men might be all fitted and provided
to fight, for the people of the town expected the enemy to fall upon
them every minute, but withal charging them to keep undiscovered;
and coming on board said privateer was kindly treated, discoursed
Mrs. Lee, who informed him that the company she came with had
fourscore canoes, and that there were more of them whom she had
not seen, which came from other places, and that they told her when
they came all together, should make up 700 men. He asked her
whether Casteen was with them? She answered, that there were
several French men with them, but did not know whether Casteen
was there or not. He then having got what intelligence she could
give him, went ashore and viewed the fort and town, discoursing
with the Gentlemen there according to his instructions; and when it
began to grow dark, he ordered the vessels to come as near the fort
as might be, and land the soldiers with as little noise as possible;
ordering them as they landed to go into the fort and houses that
stood near, that so they might be ready upon occasion; having
ordered provisions for them, went to every company and ordering
them to get every thing ready; they that had no powder-horns or
shot-bags, should immediately make them; ordering the officers to
take special care that they were ready to march into the woods an
hour before day: And also directing the watch to call him two hours
before day: so he hastened to bed to get some rest.

At the time prefixed he was called, and presently ordering the
companies to make ready, and about half an hour before day they
moved. Several of the town people went with them into a thick
place of brush, about half a mile from the town; now ordering them
to send out their scouts, as they used to do, and seeing them all
settled at their work, he went into town by sunrise again, and
desired the inhabitants to take care of themselves, till his men had
fitted themselves with some necessaries: For his Indians most of
them wanted both bags and horns; so he ordered them to make bags
like wallets, to put powder in one end, and shot in the other. So
most of them were ready for action, (viz.) the Seconet Indians, but
the Cape Indians were very bare, lying so long at Boston before they
embarked, that they had sold every thing they could make a penny

of; some tying shot and powder in the corners of their blankets. He being in town, just going to breakfast, there was an alarm, so he ordered all the soldiers in town to move away as fast as they could, where the firing was; and he, with what men more were with him of his soldiers, moved immediately, and meeting with Captain Bracket's sons, who told him their father was taken, and that they saw a great army of Indians in their father's orchard, &c. By this time our Indians that wanted bags and horns were fitted, but wanted more ammunition. Presently came a messenger to him from the town and inform'd him, that they had knock'd out the heads of several casks of bullets, and they were all too big, being musket bullets,* and would not fit their guns, and that if he did not go back himself a great part of the army would be kept back from service for want of suitable bullets.

He run back and ordered every vessel to send ashore all their casks of bullets; being brought, knock'd out their heads, and turn'd them all out upon the green by the fort, and set all the people in the town, that were able, to make slugs [by hammering the bullets]; being most of them too large for their use, which had like to have been the over-throw of their whole army: He finding some small bullets, and what slugs were made, and three knapsacks of powder, went immediately to the army, who were very hotly engaged; but coming to the river the tide was up; he call'd to his men that were engaged, encouraging them, and told them he had brought more ammunition for them. An Indian call'd Captain Lightfoot, laid down his gun, and came over the river, taking the powder upon his head, and a kettle of bullets in each hand, and got safe to his fellow soldiers. He perceiving great firing upon that

* This extract from Major Church's narrative is not intelligible unless we consider that this was about the time of the transition from "*match-locks* to *firelocks*." It seems that the old matchlocks were then the only arm known as "muskets." They were long heavy pieces intended to be aimed over a rest which was carried with them. They carried a larger bullet than the improved arm with a flint-lock, which was to be used without a rest. Undoubtedly both kinds of arms were used by the soldiers of this expedition, hence the different sizes of the bullets. He says, "Presently a messenger came to him from the town and informed him that they had knocked out the heads of several casks of bullets and they were all too big, being *musket bullets* and would not fit their guns."

side he was of, went to see who they were, and found them to be two of
Major Church's companies, one of English and the other of Indians,
being in all about fourscore men, that had not got over the river, but
lay firing over our men's heads at the enemy; he presently order'd
them to rally, and come all together; and gave the word for a Casco
man: So one Swarton, a Jersey man, appearing, who he could hardly
understand; he ask'd him how far it was to the head of the river, or
whether there was any place to get over?   He said there was a
bridge about three quarters of a mile up, where they might get over:
So he calling to his soldiers engaged on the other side, that he would
soon be with them over the bridge, and come upon the backs of the
enemy; which put new courage into them; so they immediately
moved up towards the bridge, marching very thin, being willing to
make what shew they could, shouting as they marched: They saw
the enemy running from the river-side, where they had made stands
with wood to prevent any body from coming over the river; and
coming to the bridge, they saw on the other side that the enemy had
laid logs and stuck birch brush along to hide themselves from our
view.

He ordered the company to come altogether, bidding them all to
run after him, who would go first, and that as soon as they got over
the bridge to scatter, that so they might not be all shot down
together, expecting the enemy to be at their stands; so running up
to the stands, found none there, but were just gone, the ground
being much tumbled with them behind the said stands.   He ordered
the Captain with his company of English to march down to our men
engaged, and that they should keep along upon the edge of the
marsh, and himself with his Indian soldiers would march down
through the brush: And coming to a parcel of low ground, which
had been formerly burnt, the old brush being fallen down lay very
thick, and the young brush being grown up made it bad travelling;
but coming near the back of the enemy, one of his men called unto
him, their commander, and said, that the enemy run westward to get
between us and the bridge, and he looking that way saw men
running, and making a small stop, heard no firing, but a great chop-
ing with hatchets; so concluding the fight was over, made the best of
their way to the bridge again, lest the enemy should get over the
bridge into the town.   The men being most of them out (our ammu-

nition lay exposed) coming to the bridge where he left six Indians for an ambuscade on the other side of the river, that if any enemy offered to come over, they should fire at them, which would give him notice, so would come to their assistance; (but in the way having heard no firing nor shouting, concluded the enemy were drawn off) he asked the ambuscade, whether they saw any Indians? They said yes, abundance. He asked them where? They answered, that they ran over the head of the river by the cedar swamp, and were running into the neck towards the town.

There being but one Englishman with him, he bid his Indian soldiers scatter, run very thin to preserve themselves, and be the better able to make a discovery of the enemy; and soon coming to Lieutenant Clark's field, on the south side of the neck, and seeing the cattle feeding quietly, and perceiving no track, concluded the ambuscade had told them a falsehood; they hastily returned back to the said bridge, perceiving there was no noise of the enemy. He hearing several great guns fire at the town, concluded that they were either assaulted, or that they had discovered the enemy: He having ordered that in case such should be, that they should fire some of their great guns to give him notice; he being a stranger to the country, concluded the enemy had by some other way got to the town; whereupon he sent his men to the town, and himself going to the river, near where the fight had been, asked them how they did, and what was become of the enemy? Who informed him that the enemy drew off in less than an hour after he left them, and had not fired a gun at them since. He told them he had been within little more than a gun shot of the back of the enemy, and had been upon them had it not been for thick brushy ground, &c. Now some of his men returning from the town gave him the account, that they went while they saw the colours standing and men walking about as not molested. He presently ordered that all his army should pursue the enemy; but they told him that most of them had spent their ammunition, and that if the enemy had engaged them a little longer they might have come and knock'd them on the head; and that some of their bullets were so unsizable that some of them were forced to make slugs while they were engaged. He then ordered them to get over all the wounded and dead men, and to leave none behind; which was done by some canoes they had got. Captain Hall and his men being first engaged did great service, and suffered the greatest loss in his men; but Captain Southworth with his company, and Capt. Numposh with the Seconet Indians, and the most of the men belonging to the town all coming suddenly to his relief, prevented him & his whole company from being cut off, &c.

By this time the day was far spent, and marching into town about sunset, carrying in all their wounded and dead men, being all sensible of God's goodness to them, in giving them the victory, & causing the enemy to fly with shame, who never gave one shout at their drawing off. The poor inhabitants wonderfully rejoiced that the Almighty had favored them so much; saying, That if Maj. Church, with his forces had not come at that juncture, they had been all cut off; and said further, That it was the first time that ever the eastward Indians had been put to flight, and the said Church with his volunteers were wonderfully preserved, having never a man killed outright, and but one Indian mortally wounded, who died, several more being badly wounded, but recovered.

The place of this battle was probably on the site of the present sloping lawn in front of the Deering mansion. Here was Brackett's orchard. In that field are now several apple trees, the remains of an orchard, but these cannot be the original trees, they cannot be two centuries old. The place where the Indian "Lightfoot" crossed was so deep that he was compelled to carry the powder on his head. It must have been nearly down to the present Deering's bridge. The creek has filled up perceptibly within the last sixty-five years, since I first sounded its depths, very, very thinly clad. At the time of the battle it must have been much wider and deeper than now.

In the Massachusetts archives is a letter written by Major Church dated on the day of the battle. "september 21 1689. A liste of the men that was slain in a fite at Falmouth and also how many was wounded in said fite; of Capt. Hall's soldiers six slain — Thomas Burton, Edward

Ebens, Thomas Thaxter, Thomas Berry, John Mason, David Homes — Of Capt. Davis' company two, Giles Row, Andrew Alger, belonging to the fort of the town. An Indian a negro of Col. Tyngs Capt. Brackett carried away or slain eleven in all — wounded six friend Indians — of Capt. Davis' company two, James Freeze, Mr. Bramhall, Thomas Brown, Mr. Palmer, inhabitants total twenty one slain and wounded."

Of those wounded, Freeze and Bramhall died of their wounds, and one friendly Indian; making fourteen deaths on the side of the English. Of the enemy's loss nothing definite was known, as they carried off their dead and wounded.

Mr. Willis in his history gives an extract from B. York's deposition given in 1759, which furnishes some additional particulars:

I well remember that said George Bramhall was shot by the Indians about ye same time in ye fight over on Capt. Bracketts farm, and said Brackett was also killed at the same time at his own house on Back Cove, and said Bramhall was brought over after ye fight to the Neck near Fort Loyal, and put into Capt. Tyngs house to the best of my remembrance, and died the next day of his wounds: and his son and other help they got, brought a number of hides from ye house and tan pits to said neck: and I remember said George Bramhall left three sons, Joseph, George and Joshua, and I think one daughter, who all moved away to the westward with their mother soon after.

The history continues:

The timely arrival of this succor saved the whole population from the merciless hands of their savage enemy; had Church arrived a day later, he probably would have been called to bury the bodies of his slaughtered countrymen and to mourn over the ruins of their settlement.

The people of Casco felt perfectly safe while Major Church was within marching distance, but as winter approached, and

he was about to return to Plymouth, their courage failed.
He says:

The poor people, the inhabitants of Casco and places adjacent,
when they saw he was going away from them, lamented sadly, and
begged earnestly that he would suffer them to come away in the
transports; saying, that if he left them there, that in the spring of the
year the enemy would come and destroy their families. So by their
earnest request, the said Major Church promised them that if the
governments that had now sent him, would send him the next spring,
he would certainly come with his volunteers and Indians to their
relief.

Falmouth, the 13 November [1689], at a council of war held in
pursuance of what is above written, by Major Benjamin Church and
the officers aforesaid. Added Captain Nathaniel Hall, Lieutenant
Thaddeus Clark, Lieutenant Elisha Andrews, Mr. Elisha Gallison,
Lieutenant George Ingersoll, Lieutenant Ambrose Davis, Mr. Robert
Lawrence, Mr. John Palmer, and others. It is ordered that sixty
soldiers be quartered in Falmouth besides the inhabitants, and the
soldiers that shall belong to the fort, which shall be fifteen soldiers
besides the commander, and the remainder to be sent to Boston, to
be ready to return according to order. It is ordered that there be a
sufficient garrison erected about Mr. Gallison's house for a main court
of guard, together with Mr. Robert Lawrence, his garrison, which two
garrisons are to be supplied with sixty soldiers, left to guard the said
town.

After stationing soldiers at Black Point, Blue Point, Spurwink, Scarborough, and Saco, Major Church bought a horse
and in company with Captain Scottow of Scarborough, rode
to Boston. There he remained several weeks before leaving
for Plymouth, pleading with those in authority to send
relief in the spring to the people of Casco and vicinity.
The people of Boston were about sending Governor Andros home a prisoner, and made that an excuse for neglect-
ing Church's importunities. Church went home without a
hearing, but returned in February to Boston. He presented

a written statement to the council of the state of Falmouth and its dangers. He said, " Moreover in thus doing he had complied with his promise to the poor people of Casco, and should be *quit of the guilt of their blood.* The Governor thanked him for his pains taken and he took his leave."

The catastrophe foreseen by Major Church, which must fall on the people of Falmouth if not protected by the province, and the guilt of whose blood he was anxious to be quit of, was not long in coming.

As early as the next March, Salmon Falls was destroyed by a body of Indians commanded by a French officer. In order to punish the enemy for a raid after cattle, Captain Willard was ordered to pursue the enemy to their strongholds. The command of the fort then devolved upon Captain Sylvanus Davis, the officer whom President Danforth ordered Church to advise with as " a prudent man, and well acquainted with the affairs of those parts." Rev. Richard Mather, agent of Massachusetts in London, also considered him a prudent man, and the next year nominated him to the king and council, as one of the councilors under the new charter. He was re-elected in 1693.

The attention of the Boston provincial government was taken up by a plan of aggression, instead of providing for the defence of the people on the frontier. Sir William Phipps was put in command of an expedition to Nova Scotia for the capture of Port Royal, which sailed from Boston on the twenty-eighth of April. During the winter or early in the spring a concerted plan was perfected between the French authorities at Quebec and Castin of Penobscot, with their Indian allies, to take Fort Loyal and to destroy Falmouth. Belknap says that Hartel, the Canadian commander, who had led the party that destroyed Newichawannock (Berwick) a month previous, acknowledged that the Indians were paid the same as were the French soldiers — ten livres per month. For more than a century the French pursued without intermission a regular design of exterminating the British colonists.

Early in April a rendezvous was established by the French commanders, probably at some sheltered cove at the east end of Casco Bay. From their hiding-place they sent a foraging party to the vicinity of Falmouth and drove off twenty head of cattle to their headquarters. They were probably waiting for Castin and his father-in-law, Madocawando, with their Penobscot forces, and were securing provisions for a feast on their arrival. Captain Willard, the experienced commander of Fort Loyal, had been ordered to pursue the enemy to their strongholds and had gone into the interior with all the soldiers which could be spared from the fort and fortified houses, not expecting that the enemy had formed a camp within reach of Falmouth by water. Sometime in the first days of May a fleet of canoes was seen stealthily crossing the bay inland. They had probably been hiding at Jewell's Island and catching fish and seals. Undoubtedly they had discovered the passing squadron of Sir William Phips led by a frigate and a sloop-of-war, bound to Port Royal, Nova Scotia. He sailed from Boston on the 28th of April. He was a Maine man and a good pilot, and of course coasted along shore.*

Probably a sight of this squadron frightened the fishing

---

* Cotton Mather, in his life of Sir William Phips, says of him: "He would, particularly when sailing in sight of Kennebec, with armies under his command, call the young soldiers on deck, and speak to them after this fashion. 'Young men, it was on that hill that I kept sheep a few years ago; and since you see that Almighty God has brought me to something, do you learn to fear God, and be honest, and mind your business, and follow no bad courses, and you don't know what you may come to.'"

party and caused them to hurry in to their headquarters with the news, and in their haste exposed their flotilla to the sight of the English.

Williamson, without citing his authority, says, "There were at that time on the peninsula three fortifications besides Fort Loyal. One near the burying ground ; another on the rocky elevation southerly of the new court-house, almost indefensible; and a third in a better condition further westward near the water side." Where Elihu Gallison's house, which Church's council of war constituted a "main court of guard," was situated is unknown. The fortified house "near the burying ground," mentioned by Williamson, was probably Lawrence's house, which Cotton Mather in his account of the attack calls a "block house." It stood on the highest ground opposite the head of Mountfort street, and this street was "the outlet from the town to the wood" which Mather in his account of the ambuscade says "was through a lane that had a fence on each side, and a block house at the end of it." On the fifteenth of May, Lieutenant Thaddeus Clark and about thirty of the stoutest young men, Mather says,

Went out to the top of the hill, and the English were suspicious when they entered the lane that the Indians were lying behind the fence, because the cattle stood staring that way, and would not pass into the wood as they used to do. This mettlesome company then ran up to the fence with an huzza ! thinking thereby to discourage the enemy, if they should be lurking there; but the enemy were so well prepared for them that they answered them with a horrible vengeance, which killed the Lieutenant and thirteen more on the spot, and the rest escaped with much ado unto one of the garrisons. The enemy then coming into town, beset all the garrisons at once except the fort; which were manfully defended so long as their ammunition lasted, but that being spent without a prospect of a recruit, they quitted all the four garrisons, and by the advantage of the night got into the fort. Upon this the enemy set the town on fire, bent their whole force against the fort, which had hard by it a deep gully that contributed not a little to the ruin of it, for the besiegers getting into that gully lay below the danger of our guns. Here the enemy began their mine which was carried so near the walls that the English, who by fighting five days and four nights, had the greater part of their men killed and wounded, (Captain Lawrence mortally among the rest,) began a parley with them. Articles were agreed, that they should have liberty to march unto the next English town, and have a guard for their safety in their march, and the French commander, lifting up his hand, swore by the everlasting God for the performance of these articles. But the agreement was kept as those that are made with Huguenots used to be. The English being first admonished by the French that they were all rebels for proclaiming the Prince of Orange their king, were captived, and many of them cruelly murdered by the Indians; only some of them (and particularly Major Davis) were carried into Canada, where the gentry very civilly treated them. The garrisons at Purpooduck, Spurwink, Black Point, and Blue Point were so disanimated at these disasters that without orders they drew off immediately to Saco, twenty miles within Casco, and in a few days also they drew off to Wells, twenty miles within said Saco.

When the Indians were got into the woods, they made one Goody Stockford their messenger to her neighbors, whose charity she so well solicited that she got a shallopfull of it unto Casco, where the Indians permitted us to redeem several of the prisoners.

This account by Mather, of the destruction of our town, is given in his Magnalia, first published in London in 1702. It was probably written within ten years of the occurrences narrated, and, of course, is correct. It is more minute than that of Captain Davis, the commander of the fort, which follows.

Account of the attack on, and surrender of Fort Loyal by Captain Sylvanus Davis the commander of the fort. The original paper is preserved in the Massachusetts Archives.

Myself having command of a garrison in Falmouth for the defence of the same, a party of French from Canada joined with a party of Indians to the number of betwixt four and five hundred French and Indians, set upon our fort. The 16th of May 1690 about dawning began our fight. The 20th about three oclock, afternoon, we were taken. They fought us five days and four nights in which time they killed and wounded the greatest part of our men, burned all the houses, and at last we were forced to have a parley in order for a surrender. We not knowing that there was any French among them, we set up a flag of truce in order for a parley. We demanded if there were any French among them, and if they would give us quarter. They answered that they were Frenchmen, and would give us good quarter. Upon this answer we sent out to them again to know from whence they came, and if they would give us good quarter, both for our men and women, and children, both wounded and sound, and that we should have liberty to march to the next English town and have a guard for our defence, and safety unto the next English town — then we would surrender; and also that the governor of the French should hold up his hand and swear by the ever living God, that the several articles should be performed. All which he did solemnly swear to perform; but as soon as they had us in their custody, they brake their articles, suffered our women and children, and our men to be made captives in the hands of the heathen, to be cruelly murdered and destroyed many of them, and especially our wounded men; only the French kept myself and three or four more, and carried us over land to Canada. . . . . About twenty four days we were marching through the country for Quebec in Canada, by land and water, carrying our canoes with us. The chief of the Indians that came against us was those Indians that we had in hold that Sir Edmond Andros ordered to be cleared,* and Sieur Castine

---

* It will be recollected that in September, 1688, Squire Blackman of Saco issued a warrant to Captain John Sargent by whom twenty Indians, especially those who were the known ringleaders in the last war, were arrested and all were sent under a strong guard to Fort Loyal. As a conciliatory measure, on his arrival in Boston from New York, Sir Edmund Andros ordered their release and the restoration of their arms. Their participation in, or rather their leading the party who besieged and destroyed Falmouth, as Davis says, showed the folly of the course pursued by the governor. Their imprisonment simply gave them a knowledge of the means of defence of the fort and town and encouraged the siege.

and Madocawando, with their eastern forces. The French that took us come from Canada, in February last past designed for the destruction of Falmouth, by order of the Governor there, the Earl of Frontenac. The commanders name was Mons Burniffe; his Lieut's name was Mons Corte de March who was at the taking of Schenectade. They brought several Indians from Canada, and made up the rest of their forces as they marched through the woods from Canada, but I must say, they were kind to me in my travels through the country. Our provisions was very short — Indian corn and acorns — hunger made it very good and God gave it strength to nourish. I arrived at Quebec the 14 of June 1690. . . . . I was at Quebec four months and was exchanged for a Frenchman Sir Wm Phips had taken, the 15th of October 1690.

Captain Davis returned with Governor Phips on his return from his expedition against Quebec.

It seems by a note in Sewall's journal, written in Boston, that Captain Willard has returned from his expedition after the enemy. He was at Fort Loyal on the ninth of May. The journal says: "April 15. Capt. Willards letter comes to town of the 9th instant, giving an account of the danger they were in at Casco of an assault from the enemy 30 Indian canoes being seen and several fires on the land." When Judge Sewall received the news of the fall of Falmouth, he wrote to a friend in Plymouth under date " Boston, May 21. Exceeding bad news from the eastward. 'T is believed that Casco garrison and fort are burnt and the inhabitants destroyed; so that we do not understand that there is one escaped or shut up or left. . . . . This disaster fell out on Friday and saturday last." On the twenty-third the journal mentions, " Casteen is said to head about 70. French, and Indians about two hundred." Captain Davis' estimate of " betwixt four and five hundred," is probably correct.

In the general Court files in Boston are two letters written at Portsmouth — one on the nineteenth of May, 1690, saying, that two men at Spurwink garrison hearing the firing went to see what caused it, when they " saw only two houses standing, the fort on fire, and the enemy very numerous there about." The second letter was written on the twenty-second of May. Vessels had been sent from Portsmouth, which reported that they were fired upon from the fort at Casco, and that the enemy, three or four hundred strong, had possession there. In October, the General Court ordered the payment of the wages to the wives or other relatives of soldiers who were slain or taken at Casco. Very few of the names of the slain, or of those captured at Falmouth at its destruction, have been preserved. Everything combustible and not worth carrying off, was destroyed. The town records have never since been accounted for. They were probably burnt in the house of their custodian.

In the fall of 1690, Major Church was sent with several vessels to the eastern extremity of Casco Bay, " to visit the enemy at their headquarters at 'Amerascogen, Pejepscot, or any other Plat.' " In his account of this expedition, Church says, the vessels anchored for a night at Purpooduck, and says, " the vesssels being much crowded, the Major ordered three companies should go on shore and no more. Himself and capt Converse went with them to order their lodging, and finding just housing convenient for them, viz two barns, and a house." This force was attacked by the enemy at daybreak and a sharp skirmish ensued ; the English drove the Indians through a swamp, which was probably the marshy land between Cushing's Point and Spring Point. The vessels were probably anchored inside of Spring Point, and the buildings used to shelter the soldiers were near the site of Fort Preble.

In a letter to the governor, Church gives the sequel of this fight. He says, "We went on board, sent away two vessels with the captives [which he had ransomed or exchanged for] . the sick and wounded men and buried our dead, which was 3 English and 4 Indians [friendly, of his force]. The wounded were 17 English and 7 Indians." It does not appear that Church came up to the ruins of Fort Loyal, but sailed for Boston.

The bodies of the slain at Falmouth must have remained where they died; Lieutenant Clark's and the remains of his thirteen "of the stoutest young men," who fell by the fatal ambush, could not have been recovered before the fall of the fort, but, like those killed in the town, lay exposed to the wild beasts and birds for two years. There were no white inhabitants east of Wells during that time. Holmes' Annals says the killed numbered over one hundred. No more cruel massacre was ever committed by the savages in New England. The commander of the fort, Captain Davis, says in his official report, "They [the French] suffered our women and children, and our men to be made captives in the hands of the heathen to be cruelly murdered and destroyed many of them, and especially our wounded men."

When Sir William Phips received the new charter in London, from William and Mary, in October, 1691, with his commission as governor of the united provinces, he also received instructions to build a strong fort at Pemaquid. In August, 1692, the Governor took with him Major Church and sailed for Falmouth to take away the eighteen-pounder guns, to be placed in the new fort of Pemaquid.

In his "third expedition" Major Church gives this brief account of the melancholy duty performed, without a reflection or casual remark: "Coming to Boston (from Plymouth), His Excellency having got things in readiness, they embarked on board their Transports, his Excellency going in person with them being bound to Pemaquid, but in their way stopped at Casco and buried the bones of the dead people there."

The skeletons of those killed in and around the fort were probably buried in one pit somewhere about the foot of India street. Some indication of the spot may yet be discovered in excavating for other purposes.

The war was continued six years after the sacking of Falmouth, but there were no inhabitants in the town for the savages to prey upon. Probably vessels occasionally sailed into the harbor, as did Sir William Phips and Major Church in 1692, or passing vessels took refuge in Hog Island roads to be safe from a coming storm. The contending nations, England and France, which involved the American colonies of both belligerents and the savage allies of the French, concluded a treaty of peace at Ryswick, in the Netherlands, in 1697. All these Indian wars were commenced by the savages in New England, as soon as there was a reasonable prospect of a war between England and France, and were continued a year after the cessation of hostilities at home. It was so in this case. The war was continued in America until 1699, when articles of agreement were entered into in October. This involved a meeting of the chief men of the several Indian tribes and commissioners from the English colonies somewhere in Maine to ratify it; often at Falmouth, but now there was not a roof in the town to shelter them, so they met at Mare Point at the head of the bay, and ratified the treaty. Between 1675 and 1760, there were six Indian wars; during which there were thirty-five years of war.

It is a subject of interest to know what kind of fire-arms were used in these French and Indian wars. The first portable fire-arms were served by two men, one to aim over

11

a rest, and the other to handle a match; the touch-hole was on top of the barrel. The Harquebuse, the prototype of the modern firelock, having the touch-hole on the right side, with a pan for priming, a trigger to move the match to the powder, and nippers to hold the match which moved on a slide, was invented in Spain about 1530 to 1540. This style of fire-arm, with some improvements, one of which was a rest that went with it to stick in the ground, was the matchlock of the Pilgrims in 1620. Flintlocks were invented in France about 1630, but were long in coming into general use in this country. In the inventory of property at Richmond's Island, in 1635, was " one arquebus — 1 musket, both with firelocks." In Plymouth colony, in 1638, thirty men were ordered to be raised, each " to be provided with *musket, firelock* or *matchlock*, a pair of bandoleers or pouches for powder or bullets, a sword and belt, a worm and scourer, a rest, and knapsack." This order shows that there were then three different kinds of fire-arms in use.

In August, 1680, a major's warrant in Boston directed him to impress from the eight companies of militia " twenty able soldiers, two of them carpenters, all well armed *with fixed firelock arms* — one pound of powder, three pounds of shot, for service of the country at Casco Bay." The firelock had now come into general use, but of very imperfect operation, as will be seen by the following.

Major Church, in his night skirmish with the Indians, while a part of his forces were encamped on Spring Point, Cape Elizabeth, in September, 1690, relates this incident:

Philip, an Indian of ours, who was out on the watch, heard a man cough, and the sticks crack; who gave the next an account that he saw Indians, which they would not believe, but said to him you are afraid; his answer was that they might see them come creeping; they laughed and said they were hogs. Ay (said he) and they will bite you by 'nd by. So presently they did fire upon our men; but the morning being misty *their guns did not go off quick, so that our men had all time to fall down before their guns went off*, and saved themselves from that volley, except one man who was killed.

The Indians did not use fire-arms until the firelocks came into use. When the Pequots were destroyed by the New England colonists in 1637, "they had no arms but bows, tomahawks, and English hatchets," says Hutchinson.

Bradford, in his history, says, in 1628 Morton, at Merrymount, sold guns to the Indians. He says further, " Those Indians to ye east parts which had commerce with the French got pieces of them, and made a common trade of it." Josselyn says, 1673, " He is a poor Indian who is not master of 2 guns which they obtain from the French." These French guns, which the Indians of Maine obtained, were very light ; some of the barrels are yet in use by sportsmen, and are much valued. They are of a peculiar brown color and do not corrode. They all bear· the fleur-de-lis of the Bourbons. I have one which was used by my grandfather a century ago.

In 1807, Alexander Forsyth, a Scottish clergyman, took out a patent for a percussion gunlock, but the flintlock held its place through the first quarter of the present century. Samuel Pepys, in his diary, says he saw in London in 1662, " a gun to discharge seven times ; the best of all devices that ever I saw, and very serviceable and not a bawble."

The bayonet, which the books say was invented at Bayonne, in France, in 1640, was not known in New England until 1687. That year Judge Sewall, of Boston, wrote : " Oct. 26, His Excellency [Gov. Andros] with sundry of the Council Justices and other gentlemen, four Blue coats, two trumpeters, 15 or 20 Red Coats with small guns, and *short lances in the tops of them*, set forth for Woodcocks (in Attleborough) in order to go to Connecticut to assume the government of that place."

This anecdote of an incident at " deserted Casco," is related in the Magnalia by Mather.   He evidently enjoyed the story.

The Indians (as the captives inform us) passed through deserted Casco, where they spied several horses in Capt. Bracketts orchard. Their famished squa's begged them to shoot the horses, that they might be revived with a little roast-meat, but the young men were for having a little sport before their supper.   Driving the horses into a pond they took one of them, and furnished him with an halter, suddenly made of the mane and tail of the animal, which they cut off. A son of the famous Hegon was ambitious to mount this Pegasean stead; but being a pitiful horseman, he ordered them for fear of his falling, to tie his legs fast under the horses belly.   No sooner was this " beggar set on horseback," and the spark, in his own opinion, thoroughly equipped, but the nettlesome horse furiously and presently ran with him out of sight.   Neither man nor horse were ever seen any more.   The astonished Tannies howled after one of their nobility, disappearing by such an unexpected accident.   A few days after they found one of his legs (and that was all) which they buried in Capt. Bracketts cellar with abundance of lamentation.

CHAPTER VII.

A PLEASANTER path now lies before us than that by which
we have come, from the beginning of Falmouth to the re-
peopling of the town after its desertion the second time.

Notwithstanding the naked chimneys, monuments of the
catastrophe of eight years previous, and the encroachments
of the natural shrubs and bushes on the once fair fields, there
were attractions enough to draw many exiles back to the
sites of their former homes. As soon as the sachems had
put their ugly hieroglyphics to the articles of peace, the
broken families began to return; some led by a manly son,
some by an energetic mother, who first sought out the common
pit where Governor Phips had buried husbands and fathers,
then surveyed, with blinding tears, the remains of their once
pleasant homes. Some few families returned unbroken, with
good courage to begin life anew. The waters, as ever, teemed
with fish, and the beaches yielded "the treasures hid in the
sands" for immediate sustenance.

Spurwink, the first place to be settled in the town, originally was, also now, the first neighborhood to be repeopled.
The energetic Jordans, sons and grandsons of the old minister,
were the first to venture. Penhallow says of the war of 1703:

"Spurwink, which was principally inhabited by the Jordans, had no less than twenty-two of that family killed and taken." Purpooduck Point, where Fort Preble now stands, was next occupied by the Loveitts, Whites, and others, whose descendants yet hold places in the town.

Then the fugitives began to gather at the mouth of the Presumpscot, and near the lower falls. Old Casco remained desolate, and the Presumpscot settlement was called "New Casco," claiming to be the new center of the revived town. In 1700, a fort was erected near the shore on the eastern side. It was intended for a fortified truck-house in fulfillment of treaty stipulations. The Provincial government agreed to maintain trading-houses at certain points, stocked with supplies for the Indians, and to keep an armorer at each of these truck-houses to repair the Indians' guns, in exchange for their furs.

This fortification had no other name than "Casco fort." Its official description was as follows: "Casco Fort, being an oblong square of 250 foot in length, and a hundred and ninety foot in breadth—the bastions not included. The covert-way to the Block-house, 230 foot in length." A plan of the fort in my possession represents small bastions, or watch-boxes at the two rear corners, and at the corners facing the water large bastions of diamond form. "The covert way" ran from the fort proper to the shore where there was a block-house. There were several buildings inclosed, and a magazine in the south bastion. There is no mark, nor mention of a palisade enclosure, but the plan shows that the whole exterior walls were of timber, and more than one thousand feet in circuit. The site of this extensive fortification is well known and is worth a visit.

On the breaking out of the war between England and

France in 1702, apprehensions were entertained by the Massachusetts government, that the eastern Indians would again commence hostilities. To prevent this calamity, Governor Dudley, in the summer of 1703, visited the coast as far east as Pemaquid and held conferences with the Indians. On the 20th of June, a grand council was assembled at the fort in New Casco, attended by the chiefs of the Norridgewock, Penobscot, Penacook, Amerescoggin and Pequakett tribes. The two chiefs from Amerescoggin came with two hundred and fifty men in sixty-five canoes, all armed and in their war paint. A large tent was put up, large enough to accommodate both English and Indians. A peace was concluded, promises made and accepted on both sides, and presents to the Indians made by the Governor, the whole ending with volleys. At this conference the Governor and his party had a narrow escape from death by treachery.

Captain Samuel Penhallow, who was in the service of Massachusetts and New Hampshire in the war which ensued, gives this account of the intended treachery:

But I should have taken notice of two instances in the late treaty, wherein the matchless perfidity of these bloody infidels did notoriously appear. First, as the treaty was concluded by volleys on both sides, the Indians desired the English to fire first, which they readily did; concluding it no other than a compliment; but so soon as the Indians fired, it was observed that their guns were charged with bullets; having contrived (as it was afterwards confirmed) to make the English the victims of that day. But Providence so ordered it, as to place their chief councillors, and sachems in the tent where ours were seated, by which means they could not destroy one without endanger the other. Second, as the English waited some days for Watanummon, (the Pigwacket sachem) to complete their council, it was afterwards discovered, that they only tarried for a reinforcement of 200 French and Indians, who in three days after we returned, came among them; having resolved to seize the Governor and Council and Gentlemen, and then to sacrifice the inhabitants at pleasure; which probably they might have done had they not been prevented by an over ruling power.

Captain Penhallow continues:

Purpooduck [Point] was of all places (for number) the greatest sufferers [1703], being but nine families, and no garrison to retire unto; neither any men at home, where they took eight, and inhumanly butchered twenty-five; among whom was the wife of Michael Webber, who being big with child, they knocked her on the head and ript open her womb, a spectacle of horid barbarity.

Major March was at this time in command of New Casco fort, which was besieged by the enemy. Its brave defence and final relief is described by Penhallow.

Casco, which was the utmost frontier, commanded by Major March,* who was all this while insensible of the spoil that the Indians had done, was saluted by Mauxis, Wannugorset, and Assacombuit, three of their most valiant and puissant Sachems. They gradually advanced with a flag of truce and sent one before them, to signify that they had matter of moment to impart to him. At first he slighted the message, but on second thoughts went out to meet them; they seemed to him but few in number, and unarmed: however he ordered two or three sentinels to be ready in case of danger.

No sooner had they saluted him, but with hatchets under their mantles they violently assaulted him; having a number that lay in ambush near them, who shot down one of his guards: but being a person of uncommon strength, as well as courage, he soon wrested a hatchet from one of them with which he did good execution: Yet if sergeant Hook (with a file of ten from the fort), had not speedily succored him, they would have overpowered him. Mr. Phippeny and Mr. Kent, who accompanied him, were attacked by others and soon

---

* Sewall says, " 1703, Aug. 2. Thomas the governors coachman having offended him, he sends him on board Capt. Southacs in order to make him a sentinel under Major March at Casco fort. I moved the governor to try him a little longer, but would not." The governor was Joseph Dudley. A month previous he had been to the conference at Casco fort.

fell by their fury; for being advanced in years, they were so infirm, that I might say of them as Juvenal did of Priam, they scarce had blood enough left to tinge the knife of the sacrifice. The enemy being defeated in their design fell upon the several cottages which lay around, and destroyed all they could. But the Major on rallying his men together, seeing nothing but fire and smoke, divided them into three parts, which were twelve in each, and interchanged them every two hours, who thus continued six days and nights without the least intermission; by which time the whole body of Indians came together being upwards of five hundred, besides French commanded by Monsieur Babasser, who had laid waste the several settlements before mentioned, and being flushed with success, having taken one sloop, two shallops, and much plunder, attempted to undermine the fort from the waterside, in which they proceeded two days and nights, and probably would have effected their design if they had not been prevented by the arrival of Capt. Southack who raised the siege, retook the shallop and shattered their navy, which was upwards of two hundred canoes.*

Captain Moody, who succeeded Major March in the command of New Casco fort, was the organ of Governor Dudley in the correspondence with Father Rasle, the Jesuit missionary at Norridgewock.† The following letter, in its origi-

* Captain Cyprian Southack, whose arrival was as opportune as was that of Major Church at Old Casco in 1686, was a noted Bostonian and long in command of the Massachusetts Galley, a man-of-war belonging to the Province. A long service on the sea-board of the Provinces induced him to prepare a chart of the coast from Cape Canso to "sandy point" (Sandy Hook,) about one thousand miles. It was published in 1718, and was the only chart of that coast until De Barres' chart was completed in 1764. Captain Southack was the father of Commodore Edward Tyng's first wife; she died in London. Sir Hovenden Walker, while fitting out his fleet at Boston for Quebec in 1711, was the guest of Captain Southack.

† In a postscript to a letter from Captain Samuel Moody to Governor Dudley, dated "Casco, 10th Decemb," 1712, he says, "The Indians have made us three visits in my absence and brought several letters from the Friar, which are enclosed."

nal language, is printed in the third volume of Massachusetts
Historical Collections.   Until now no English translation of
it has been published.   It does not indicate the savage nature
which has been attributed to its author.

Addressed to Mr. Moody, Captain and Governor of the fort.
Letter from Father Rasle to Captain Moody.

NARRANTSOAK [NORRIDGEWOCK], 18, Nov. 1712.

Sir : — The Governor General of Canada lets me know by his letter,
brought to me some days ago, that the last vessel of the King which
arrived at Quebec the 30th of September reports that peace is not yet
concluded between the two crowns of France and England; it is true
that they talk much of it.   This is what he told me about it.

And other letters which I have received, inform me that the *Commissary
of stores,* who arrived in this vessel, said that being on the point of
embarking at Rochelle, they received there a letter from Monsieur de
Tallard which declared that peace was made and that it would be made
public at the end of October.

Now, they cannot know it in Canada but they may know it at Boston
where vessels can arrive at all seasons.   If you know anything about it,
I beg you to inform me, that I may send immediately to Quebec over the
ice to inform the Governor General of it that he may prevent the savages
from committing any act of hostility.   I am

Your very humble and
very obedient servant,

SEB. RASLE, *Sy.*

New Casco fort continued to be maintained during the
war, but in 1704 Colonel Church recommended its abandonment.   In 1710, the House of Representatives passed a
resolve to demolish the works, but the Council non-concurred.
Several subsequent attempts were made to induce the Governor and Council to abandon the fort as an unnecessary
public burden, but they would not consent to it.   A controversy was carried on between Governor Dudley and the
House.   The Governor said, "I shall give orders to draw
out nineteen men and an ensign from Casco fort for Arrowsic,

and also raise fifteen men for Brunswick, but cannot see reason at present to demolish Casco fort until his Majesty's pleasure be known." The House adhered to their resolution and " voted that no more money be drawn from the public treasury to pay officers or soldiers at the fort of Casco after September first next."

Major Samuel Moody, of Falmouth, succeeded Major March, in 1707, in command of the fort, and was the organ of correspondence between the Indians and the government, which resulted in a treaty at Portsmouth in July, 1713.

Governor Dudley having been superseded, the House of Representatives succeeded in the demolishing of the fort in 1716. It " Resolved that his Honor, the Lieut.-Governor, be desired to direct a full performance of the votes of this Court and order the removing of the stores to Boston and the entire demolishing of the fort and the houses therein without delay." A sloop was immediately sent from Boston to remove the stores belonging to the government to that place. This left no fort from Fort George, at Brunswick, to Saco river.*

In July, 1713, a treaty of peace was concluded at Utrecht, in Holland, between France and England ; when hostilities ceased in Maine.

The spiteful votes in the House of Representatives, relating to the dismantling of New Casco fort, were in the same spirit with the neglect which caused the destruction of the town in 1690, and the death of one hundred people. The foundations of New Casco fort are yet to be seen and also the well.

* Williamson, in his History of Maine, says, "A strong garrison was maintained through the last war [1703 to 1713] at Fort Loyal." This fort had not been rebuilt after its destruction in 1690. He mistakes New Casco fort for Fort Loyal.

After the demolishing of the fort, Major Moody and Benjamin Larrabee, the lieutenant, took up their residence on the Neck and became leading citizens in its resettlement. The following order was passed by the Massachusetts Council July 2, 1716 :

A memorial presented by Capt. Samuel Moody, late commander of his Majesty's fort at Casco Bay, praying that he might have liberty to build a small fortification with stockades at the town of Falmouth, commonly called Old Casco, about his own house, upon his own land in the said town, and that he may furnish the same with arms and amunition at his own charges, for himself and the inhabitants there, being in number fifteen men besides women and children. Ordered, that the prayer of said petition be granted.

Major Moody's house was at the foot of the present Hancock street.

In 1707, Falmouth was made a recruiting station for a retreating squadron, and what was called in the dispatches an army. In 1707, Governor Dudley, of the Massachusetts Province, prevailed upon the House of Assembly to furnish the means for an expedition against Port Royal, Nova Scotia. Sir William Phips took the fort with ease in 1690, and obtained plunder enough to pay the cost of the expedition. This success encouraged the Governor to insist upon its being again reduced. The expedition was hastily fitted out. The naval force consisted of the Deptford man-of-war, Captain Stukely, and the Shirley Galley, Captain Southack, belonging to the province. The land force consisted of one thousand men from Massachusetts and a goodly number from Rhode Island and New Hampshire. The command of the troops was given to Colonel March, who had successfully defended the fort at New Casco, in 1703, but had not had any previous large command. The fleet of transports with the naval convoy sailed from Boston on the thirteenth of May, and arrived at Port Royal on the twenty-sixth. After some skirmishes without loss, the land force disgracefully retreated and re-embarked on the seventh day of June. Colonel Redknap, the engineer, and Colonel Appleton, in a fast vessel, arrived in Boston in advance of the fleet.

Governor Dudley was chagrined at the failure, and sent out a dispatch vessel to intercept the fleet and order them to Casco Bay which was successfully accomplished. Of what occurred at Falmouth we have no home record.* There was a very bitter feeling cherished at the time by a small party in the province against the Governor, at the head of which was Dr. Increase Mather and his son, Rev. Cotton Mather.

Quincy, in his History of Harvard College, says:

The election of Leverett [as president of the college] was insupportably grievous to Increase Mather and his son. They had anticipated that the choice would have fallen on one or the other of them. Between them there was no rivalry, but for the disappointment of both they were not prepared. Their indignation was excited against Dudley (the Governor) who, as they thought, had buoyed up their hopes until he had arranged measures and agents to insure their defeat.

The elder Mather had served as president of the college from 1685 to 1701.

In July, 1707, there appeared in London a pamphlet setting forth in bitter terms the short-comings of Governor Dudley. It pretended to be published in Boston. It was supposed that Cotton Mather was at least the inciter of this pamphlet. It was entitled "A memorial of the deplorable state of New England."

* Sewall's Diary, says, "1707, July 1st. A rainbow is seen just before night, which comforts our distresses as to the affairs of the expedition, and the unquietness of the soldiers at Casco, of which Gideon Lowell brings word, who come thence yesterday."

The "memorial" provoked a fitting reply from the Governor's party, and then followed a rejoinder pamphlet, to which was added "an account of the shameful miscarriage of the late expedition against Port Royal. London, printed in the year 1708."

The pamphlet says Colonel Church was the commander of the expedition; that there was an army of volunteers "of as likely men as can be imagined; the best part of 2,000; they were mostly good livers at home." Then follows a ludicrous account of the attack.

It was the universal opinion (in Boston) that if the army had only stayed and played at quoits in their camp (far enough from the fort) at Portroyal, the fort would have been within a few days surrendered to them; but, like men afraid of having the fort fall into their hands, they ran back to New England as fast as their canvas sails would carry them. In the midst of their dispersion there came orders to stop as many of them as were together at Casco Bay.

Another ship of war was fitted out and recruits of soldiers were sent unto the fleet, which now lay at Casco Bay. Which, after tedious and expensive delays of many weeks, set sail again to Portroyal. Our fleet, arriving there a second time, found that in the time of their withdrawal to Casco, the Portroyalers had much recruited themselves; and had taken and carried in some English vessels laden with provisions, and had despatched away their galley for France. Therefore, after a little skirmish on the opposite shore and some follies not to be mentioned, away they come for Boston. So the second expedition was as bad or worse than the first.

Governor Hutchinson's history says, that three of the Council, Colonel Hutchinson, Colonel Townsend, and Leverett, were sent in charge of the second expedition with Colonel March in the immediate command. He does not mention Colonel Church. Colonel Hutchinson was the father of Thomas, the governor and historian.

The soldiers at Falmouth seem to have been in a state of mutiny. Governor Hutchinson says in his history:

I find a round robin among Colonel Hutchinson's papers, signed by a great number, peremptorily refusing to go to Portroyal, but the ringleaders being discovered and secured, whilst their sentence was under consideration, the next humbled themselves and submitted, and the the ships of war and transports sailed.

Colonel Hutchinson wrote to Governor Dudley from Falmouth on the twenty-sixth of July, as follows:

We have so little prospect of any service from the marine, after we have taken the ground, that for the keeping of it we must have dependence upon our other force, being only seven hundred and forty-three officers and soldiers, sick and well; and they are so extremely dispirited that we cannot look upon them equal to three hundred effective men.   How ever, we have your Excellency's commands, which we yield an absolute obedience to, and shall proceed.

The expedition harbored at Passamaquoddy for a few days and on the tenth of August sailed for Port Royal. I have already quoted an account of the entire failure of the expedition.

The first expedition sailed from Port Royal on their return, on the seventh of June, and probably arrived at Falmouth about the fifteenth, and remained here until about the first of August, when the second expedition sailed, — about seven weeks. During that time a court-martial was held to try mutineers, and the Neck must have been a complete camp.

This fortress of Port Royal, the citadel of a town, and, in fact, the stronghold of Acadia and all Nova Scotia, had been several times taken by the English and as many times restored to the French nation by treaty. In 1710, an expedition was fitted out at Boston for another siege of the famous fortress. It was commanded by Colonel Nicholson, of the British army, and was composed of one regiment of marines and four New England regiments. The naval force consisted of seven men-of-war, which, with the transports from four New England provinces, numbered thirty-six sail. After a siege of seven days, Suberease, the French commander, capitulated.

Nicholson's "last traverse," a ditch fifteen feet deep and perhaps forty feet wide at the top, is yet very perfect. It is diagonal to the ramparts and within one hundred yards of them. In this trench were placed three batteries of cannon and twenty-four Cohorn mortars. In the south corner of the fort is the old magazine. From its construction it is an interesting relic of French dominion in the province. It is built of Tufa stone, of a drab color, cut in France, consisting of a single arch with an air space all round to prevent the communication of dampness from the ground. It is a very perfect piece of stone-work. After the capture of Port Royal, in 1710, it was named by the English Annapolis Royal, and has been held by them ever since.

Without the fort at New Casco, the little hamlet which had sprung up under its timber walls and protected by its guns, was not tenable. The inhabitants took the general court's order to dismantle the fort, as meaning that they must henceforth care for themselves. Therefore, " westward the course of empire took its way."

The little meeting-house on the Point where George Burroughs, who had spent four years at Harvard under President Chauncy, preached the word in its purity, and where the settlers on the shores of the bay had been wont to come in their boats and to hitch them on the beach as they would their horses, had disappeared. So earnest had the reverend pastor been in his work, that he, with the consent of his people, exchanged the house the town had built for him a mile away, for one near the meeting-house, so as to always be prompt in his attendance on the Sabbath and on "lecture-days." At the time of which I commenced to write, the church, the minister and the people had disappeared, and cellars with rude old chimneys were the principal memorials of a former village. The people of New Casco came in a body to old Old Casco, and restored its waste places.

Major Moody, the commander of the fort of New Casco, was a graduate of Harvard College in 1689, and had formerly been a minister at Newcastle, New Hampshire. He was well qualified to be, as he was, the leader of the little colony. It was he who built and armed a garrison house at his own expense for their protection.

Although there were but fifteen men on the Neck in 1716, two years later the town was incorporated by the name of Falmouth, and, after the demolishing of the fort at New Casco, the Neck became the business center. On March 10, 1719, the first town meeting was held. The general court had authorized the resettlement in 1714. There was no defensive work except Moody's garrison, which was on the Neck at the east corner of Hancock street, and perhaps one or two others in different parts of the town.

In 1739, the town "voted that the representative [Phineas Jones] apply to the general court for the erection of a fort." In 1741, that body granted the town four hundred pounds for that purpose. In 1743, the town received a further grant of thirty-three pounds to build a platform for guns and a breast-work, and two half barrels of powder. The first sum had probably been expended in a timber tower with ports, called a block-house, which was the common fashion of fortifications at that time. The breast-work was probably projected for defence against armed vessels, as there was then expec-

12

tation of war which took place the next year. Spain and
France joined against England. A town meeting was held and
adjourned to the battery, and from there "to the loft over
Captain Bangs' warehouse." His wharf and warehouse were
where the Galt block on Commercial street now is. In 1754,
a town meeting voted " to repair the breast-work of the fort."

This fort, which never received any distinctive name, was
built on the same site as Fort Loyal, which was destroyed in
the sack of the town in 1690. Some idea of the new fort
may be obtained from the report of a committee consisting of
Charles Strout, John Wait, and James Lunt, who, in 1754,
were chosen by the town to confer with the owner of the
land on which the fort stood.

The committee to confer with Samuel Cobb, Jr., about compensation for the land the fort stands on are of the opinion that he have
liberty to pull down the back part of the wall from the guardhouse to
the bastion and have the improvement of said guardhouse and land
as far as the platform during the time of peace, and he to keep said
guardhouse in repair, and in case of war to deliver the same to the use
of the town immediately on their demanding.

This report was accepted September 10, 1744. It seems
by this report that there was a guard-house and bastion with
a wall between. These were probably the flankers of one
side of a square, with the main block-house at another corner,
and the platform for guns occupying another side of the
square. By removing one side wall the interior of the square
would be opened for cultivation.

During the Indian war of 1745, there was some kind of a
watch-tower on the Neck. It was probably on top of the high
block-house of the fort, as all forts for protection against
Indians had such a timber tower. In his account book, March
5, 1745, Ephraim Jones, of Falmouth, credited Deacon James

Milk with "twenty shillings paid for me at *ye watch-tower*." The following entry in Parson Smith's journal, probably refers to the same precautionary lookout: "Sept 8 1750. There was an alarm in the night at *the tower* occasioned by an express from Richmond [fort on the Kennebec] that an Indian had told them that in forty eight hours the Indians would break upon us, and that the Canada Indians were come to reinforce them."

One of the most energetic and useful men of New England during the first half of the last century was Thomas Westbrook. Colonel Westbrook's services in the wars with the Indians, and as a leading inhabitant and business man of old Falmouth, render everything with which he was connected of interest to the present residents of the towns whose territory once formed a part of that ancient jurisdiction. He was the foremost public man of the town. His daring expedition to Norridgewock in winter, for the capture of Father Rasle and the private papers of the priest, which were brought off, has been the theme of all writers of the annals of his time. He was a native of New Hampshire and early came into public life as a councilor. Mr. Willis supposed that Thomas Westbrook, the councilor, was his father.

New Hampshire was then under the same government with Massachusetts, with Colonel Samuel Shute as governor, who was commander-in-chief of all the forces of the province. A conference was held at Arrowsic, in 1721, with the eastern Indians. To this conference Thomas Westbrook was a delegate for New Hampshire. This conference was attended by the Jesuit missionary of Norridgewock, Father Rasle,*

---

* In a letter to his brother, written October 18, 1723, Rasle describes his interview with the Governor. He says: "The Governor took me aside.

M. Crozier from Canada, and the young Baron de St. Castin, of Penobscot, whose mother was an Indian.

Exasperated by what they deemed the insolent attitude of the Kennebec Indians and their French allies, Castin was soon after seized and imprisoned at Boston. The provincial government of Massachusetts, having succeeded in confining De St. Castin, thought that Rasle could also be seized at Norridgewock and brought to Boston. They believed that he planned all the Indian raids to the sea-coast. He was in constant correspondence with several of the ministers of Boston, and ridiculed their Latin. Governor Hutchinson says that "his Latin was pure, classical, and elegant."

This seems to be the proper place for a description of Norridgewock. Captain Joseph Heath had been much in the employ of the province as an interpreter. He made a measurement and plan of the Kennebec river to Norridgewock, and described the Indian village, as follows:

Norridgewock the fort is built of round logs nine feet long — one end set in the ground; is one hundred and sixty feet square with four gates, but no bastions; within it are twenty six houses built much after the English manner. The streets regular — that from the west gate to the east is thirty feet wide. Their church stands four perch without the east gate.* Their men able to bear arms are about three score. From Sagadahoc to Norridgewock as the river runs, is one hundred and eleven miles. Brunswick in the late Province of Maine in New England,

May 16 1719.   JOSEPH HEATH.

'I pray you, Monsieur,' said he, 'do not induce the Indians to make war on us.' I replied to him that my religion, and my character as a priest, engaged me to give them only councils of peace." Rasle says there were more than two hundred Indian canoes in number at the conference.

*The church at Norridgewock was built by English Mechanics, some of them captives, in 1698. — *Pejepscot Papers, Vol. V., p. 271.*

In " Early Jesuit Missions," translated from the French by Rev. W. J. Kip, are letters written by Father Rasle. The first letter is addressed to his nephew, and is dated at " Narrantsouac," the Indian name for Norridgewock and that part of the river. It was written " Oct. 15, 1722," only three months before Colonel Westbrook's visit to the place.

The valley in which I live is called Narrantsouac and is situated on the banks of the river which empties into the sea at the distance of thirty leagues below.   I have erected a church which is neat and elegantly ornamented.   I have indeed thought it my duty to spare nothing either in the decoration of the building itself, or in the beauty of those articles which are used in our holy ceremonies.   Vestments, chasubles, copes, and holy vessels are highly appropriate, and would be esteemed so even in our churches in Europe.   I have also formed a little choir of about forty young Indians, who assist at Divine service in cassocks and surplices.   They have each their appropriate functions, as much to serve in the holy sacrifice of mass, as to chant the Divine offices for the consecration of the Holy Sacrament, and for the procession which they make with great crowds of Indians, who often come from a long distance to engage in these exercises; and you would be edified by the beautiful order they observe, and the devotion they show.

They have built two chapels at three hundred paces distance from the village; the one, which is dedicated to the Holy Virgin, and where can be seen her image in relief, is above on the river; the other, which is dedicated to the Guardian Angel, is below on the same river.   As they are both on the road which leads either into the woods, or into the fields, the Indians can never pass without offering up their prayers.   There is a holy emulation among the females of the village as to who shall most ornament the chapel of which they have the care; when the procession is to take place there, all who have any jewelry, or pieces of silk or calico, or other things of that kind, employ them to adorn it.

The great blaze of light contributes not a little to the beauty of the church and chapels; it is not necessary for me to be saving of the wax, for the country itself furnishes it abundantly.   The islands of the sea are bordered by a kind of wild laurel [the bayberry] which in autumn produces a berry a little like those borne by the juniper. They fill their kettles with these and boil them with water. In proportion as the water thickens the green wax rises to the surface where it remains. From a measure of about three bushels of this berry, can be made almost four pounds of wax.

It is very pure and beautiful, but neither sweet nor pliable. After several trials, I have found, that by mingling with it an equal quantity of fat, either of beef or mutton, or of the elk, beautiful tapers can be made, firm and excellent for use. With twenty four pounds of wax, and as much of fat, can be made two hundred tapers of more than a foot in length. A vast quantity of these laurels are found on the islands and on the borders of the sea; so that one person in a day can easily gather four measures, or twelve bushels of the berry. It hangs down like grapes from the branches of the tree. I have sent one branch of it to Quebec, together with a cake of the wax, and it has been found to be excellent.

None of my neophytes fail to repair twice in each day to the church, early in the morning to hear mass, and in the evening to assist at the prayers which I offer up at sunset. As it is necessary to fix the imagination of these Indians, which is too easily distracted, I have composed some appropriate prayers for them to make, to enable them to enter into the spirit of the august sacrifice of our altars. They chant them, or else recite them, in a loud voice during mass. Besides the sermons which I deliver before them on Sundays and festival-days, I scarcely pass a week-day without making a short exhortation to inspire them with a horror of those vices to which they are most addicted, or to strengthen them in the practice of some virtue.

After the mass, I teach the catechism to the children and young persons, while a large number of aged people who are present assist and answer with perfect docility the questions I put to them. The rest of the morning even to midday, is set apart for seeing those who wish to speak with me. They come to me in crowds, to make me a participator in their pains and inquietudes, or to communicate to me causes of complaint against their countrymen, or to consult me on their marriages and other affairs of importance. It is therefore necessary for me to instruct some, to console others, to re-establish peace in families at variance, to calm troubled consciences, to correct others by reprimands mingled with softness of charity; in fine, as far as possible to render them all contented. After midday I visit the sick and go round among the cabins of those who require more particular instructions. If they hold a council, which is often the case with these Indians, they depute one of their principal men to ask me to assist in their deliberations. I accordingly repair to the place where the council is held. If I think they are pursuing a wise course I approve of it; if on the contrary, I have anything to say in opposition to their decision, I declare my sentiments, supporting them with weighty reasons, to which they conform. My advice always fixes their resolutions. They do not even hold their feasts without inviting me. Those who have been asked carry each one a dish of wood or bark, to the place of entertainment; I give the benediction on the food, and they place in each dish the portion which has been prepared. After this distribution has been made, I say grace and each one retires; for such is the order and usages of their feasts.

In the midst of such continued occupations, you cannot imagine with what rapidity the days pass by. There have been seasons when I scarcely had time to recite my office, or to take a little repose during the night; for discretion is not a virtue which particularly belongs to the Indians. But for some years I have made it a rule, not to speak with any person from the prayers in the evening until the time of mass on the next morning. I have therefore forbidden them to interrupt me during this period, except for some very important reason, as for example to assist a person who is dying, or some other affair of the kind, which it is impossible to put off. I set apart this time to spend in prayer, or to repose myself from the fatigues of the day.

When the Indians repair to the sea-shore, where they pass some months, in hunting the ducks and other birds, which are found there*

---

* In giving an account of Governor Shute's conference with the Indians at Arrowsic, in August, 1717, Captain Penhallow, who was present, says, "One thing I cannot here omit: three days after our departure, a number of Indians went a duck-hunting, which was a season of the year that the old ones generally shed their feathers in, and the young ones are not so well flushed as to be able to fly; they drove them like a flock of sheep before them into the creeks, where without powder or shot they killed at one time four thousand and six hundred; for they followed them so close that they knocked them down with billets and paddles, and sold a great number of them to the English for a penny a dozen, which is their practice yearly, though they seldom make so great a slaughter at once.'

in large numbers, they build on an island a church which they cover with bark, and near it they erect a little cabin for my residence. I take care to transport thither a part of our ornaments, and the service is performed with the same decency and the same crowds of people as at the village.

You see then, my dear nephew, what are my occupations. For that which relates to me personally, I will say to you, that I neither hear nor see, nor speak to any but the Indians. My food is very simple and light. I have never been able to conform my taste to the meat or smoked fish of the savages, and my nourishment is only composed of corn which they pound, and of which I make each day a kind of hominy, which I boil in water. The only luxury in which I indulge, is a little sugar which I mix with it to correct its insipidity. This is not wanting in the forest. In the spring the maple trees contain a liquor very similar to that which is found in the sugar-canes of the southern islands. The women employ themselves in collecting this in vessels of bark as it is distilled from the trees. They then boil it and draw off from it a very good sugar. That which is drawn off first is the most beautiful.

The whole nation of Abnakis is Christian and very zealous to preserve their religion. This attachment to the Catholic faith has induced them, even to this time, to prefer our alliance, to advantages which might be derived from an alliance with the English, who are their neighbors. These advantages, too, of very great importance to the Indians. The facility of trading with the English from whom they are distant but one or two days journey; the ease with which the journey can be made; the admirable market they would find there for the purchase of the merchandise that suits them; these things certainly hold out very great inducements. In place of which in going to Quebec, it is necessary to take more than a fortnight to reach there; they have to furnish themselves with provision for the journey, they have different rivers to pass and frequent portages to make. They are aware of these inconveniencies, and are by no means indifferent to their interests, but their faith is infinitely more dear to them; and they believe if they detach themselves from our alliance, they will shortly find themselves without a missionary, without a sacrifice, with scarcely any exercise of their religion, and in manifest danger of being plunged into their former heathenism. This is the bond that unites them to the French.

Hutchinson says of Rasle :

He was ranked by the English among the most infamous villains and his scalp would have been worth an hundred scalps of the Indians. His intrepid courage and fervent zeal to promote the religion he professed. and to secure his converts to the interest of his sovereign were the principal causes of these prejudices. The French, for the same reason, rank him with saints and heroes. He had been nearly forty years a missionary among Indians commencing in 1690, and their manner of life had become quite easy and agreeable to him. They loved and idolized him and were always ready to hazard their own lives to preserve his. His letters on various subjects discover him to have been a man of superior natural powers, which had been improved by an education in a college of Jesuits. He had taught many of his converts, male and female, to write, and corresponded with them in their own language, and made some attempts in Indian poetry. When he was young he learned to speak Dutch, and so came more easily to a smattering of English, enough to be understood by traders and tradesmen, who had been employed in building a church and other work at Norridgewock.

This description was written by Governor Hutchinson while some of the public men were living who had known the missionary personally, or had held correspondence with him. His own father was one of them.

During the session of the general court in December, 1621, the governor was requested to send an expedition to Norridgewock and seize Rasle, the missionary, and bring him to Boston. An order was issued to Colonel Thomas Westbrook, then in the military service of the province under Colonel Walton, at Falmouth, to enlist, if possible, if not to impress, two hundred and fifty men for the expedition. The force was raised with much difficulty, and fell some short of the authorized number. This hastily organized expedition was led to Norridgewock in January, 1722, by Colonel Westbrook, traveling more than one hundred miles on snow-shoes and carrying all their provisions, ammunition, tools, and blankets on their backs; in addition, of course, each man must carry his musket. The Indians learned of the march of the expedition and left their village.* In "The Early Jesuit Missions in North America," is the following copy of a letter from Father Rasle, which describes Colonel Westbrook's arrival and his proceedings at Norridgewock, as follows:

I had remained alone in the village, with only a small number of old men and infirm persons, while the rest of the Indians were at the hunting grounds. The opportunity seemed to them a favorable one to surprise me, and with this view they sent out a detachment of two hundred men. Two young Abnakis, who were engaged in the chase along the sea-shore, learned that the English had entered the river, and they immediately turned their steps in that direction to observe their progress. Having perceived them at ten leagues distance from

* "Col. Harmon was intended for Norridgewock with about 120 men at the same time with Col. Westbrook and set out on the 6 of Feb. but the rivers were so open, and the ground so full of water that they could neither pass on land or ice and having with great difficulty reached the upper falls of Androscoggin [Lewiston] they divided into scouting parties and returned without seeing any of the enemy."—*Pejepscot Papers, Vol. V.,* *page 289.*

This expedition of Harmon's was by order of Colonel Westbrook, as the certificate of Joseph Bane, the pilot, shows. Williamson says this was in 1723, but the following document fixes the date to be 1722:

"ANDROSCOGGIN UPPER FALLS [LEWISTON] Feb 14 1722

"I Joseph Bane having been appointed pilot to a party of the forces detached by Col Westbrook to march up Androscoggin river to near Narriegook, but finding the freshet high, the lowlands full of water, this river open not only below but even to these falls, thirty miles above Pejepscot, I am therefore of opinion that the proposed march can not be performed at this time by the reason of the great thaws that broke up the rivers.

"Witness my hand,

"JOSEPH BANE."

Pejepscot Papers, Vol. V., page 107.

This detachment was probably intended to strike Sandy river and follow it to Norridgewock.

the village, they outstripped them in traversing the country to give me warning and to cause the old men, females, and infants, to retire in haste. I had barely time to swallow the consecrated wafers, to crowd the sacred vessels into a little chest* and to save myself in the woods. The English arrived at the village in the evening, and not having found me, came the following morning to search for me, even in the very place to which we had retreated. They were scarcely a gunshot distant when we perceived them, and all I could do was to hide myself with precipitation in the depths of the forest. But as I had not time to take my snow-shoes, and besides had considerable weakness remaining from a fall which took place some years before, when my thigh and leg were broken, it was not possible to fly very far. The only resource which remained to me was to conceal myself behind a tree. They began immediately to examine the different paths worn by the Indians when they went to collect wood, and they penetrated even to within eight paces of the tree which concealed me. From this spot it would seem as if they must inevitably discover me; for the trees were stripped of their leaves; but, as if they had been restrained by an invisible hand, they immediately retraced their steps and repaired again to the village.† It is thus through the particular protection of God, I escaped from their hands. They pillaged my church and humble dwelling, and thus reduced me almost to death by famine

* This "little chest" was probably the "strong box" which has been preserved to this time, of which a cut, engraved from a photograph, is given. The "sacred vessels" must have been small. In a letter to his brother the priest describes his journeys with the Indians. He says, "I carry with me my plate and everything which is necessary to ornament the choir, and Divine service is performed there as at the village."

† "Boston February 12, 1722.
"Last week, his Excellency received a letter from the forces at the Eastward giving an account that they were marching to seize Father Ralle, he made his escape out of the house with so much haste, that (being then writing) he left his papers on the table, among which was found a letter from the governor of Canada directing the Indians to use their utmost force to keep the English from settling at the eastward, and promising to supply them with powder and ball for that end; at the same time charging the Jesuit to keep the matter private. Tis said that his excellency has wrote to England of this affair."—*New England Courant.*

in the midst of the woods. It is true that as soon as they learned of my adventure in Quebec, they immediately sent me provisions; but these could not arrive until very late, and during all that time I was obliged to live destitute of all succor.

The "little chest," into which Father Rasle "crowded the sacred vessels" of his church, was probably the same which held his papers and writing materials, and which Colonel Westbrook brought away. In a compartment, of which it was hard to discover the entrance, were Rasle's letters from the French Governor of Quebec, confirming the conjectures of the Massachusetts Province officers, that the French officers in Canada were the instigators of the Indian raids on the settlements of the northern provinces, hoping, finally, to discourage and drive off the settlers north and east of Casco Bay and leave the territory to the French, who claimed it as a part of Acadia. Rasle was a "Jesuit of the four vows," the fourth of which is to undertake any mission to which they may be ordered. A part of the Jesuit creed is that *the end justifies the means*, hence the encouragement of the Indians to drive off the settlers.

In this little chest was also a manuscript dictionary of Abnaki language, prepared with great labor by the Jesuit missionary. It contains five hundred quarto pages of manuscript. At the commencement, in Rasle's own handwriting, is this memorandum in French: "1691. Having been a year among the savages, I begin to arrange in the form of a dictionary the words which I learn." The manuscript, in a strong binding, is now in the library of Harvard College, to which it was presented by Middlecott Cook. It was published under the supervision of the learned John Pickering, LL. D., in 1833, and is the best authority for the Abnaki langugage.

Another relic of much interest, which was a part of the con-

FATHER RASLE'S STRONG BOX.

BELL OF THE INDIAN CHAPEL, NORRIDGEWOCK, MAINE.

Burnt 1722.

tents of the priest's box, is a hand-book for Catholic worship. Its title is "*Medulla Theologia Moralis.*" This well-worn book, showing the thumb marks of the devoted missionary, is now in the Willis room of the Portland Public Library. The box was brought more than one hundred miles by men on snow-shoes. Its own weight is twelve pounds, and its contents must have weighed as much more.

The "little chest," into which the missionary "crowded" what he knew to be his most valuable treasures, was the means of preserving a knowledge of the man, and of his great labors in the wilderness. The chest, with its contents, was brought to Falmouth, and remained here while Colonel Westbrook lived. Its contents were carried to Boston and were turned over to the governor and council. The captured letters of the Marquis de Vaudreuel, governor of Canada, were considered valuable by the Massachusetts government, and in some measure atoned for the failure to capture Father Rasle, for a hostage, with De Castin of the Penobscots. These letters were ·the subject of an angry correspondence between the Massachusetts and the Canadian governors, and was the cause of much confusion to the latter, refuting, as they did, his assertion that he had nothing to do with the raids of the Indians.

The "little chest" is now a relic of much interest. It is ten by fifteen inches in size, and eight inches deep, divided into ten compartments, two of which are filled by a square inkstand, and a sand-box. These are of metal and fitted into wooden boxes which have sliding covers overlaid with leather and gilt. The entire outer surface of the box is covered with sheet-brass, embossed. There are riveted iron straps on all the edges, and a similar strap of iron encircles the chest at each end of the iron handle in the middle of the top.

The lock is double and protected by a broad plate of iron, having two key-holes, the principal one of which is covered by a long hinged drop, which is secured by a second key below the first one. This "little chest" is well entitled to the name "The Jesuit's strong box," which was undoubtedly given to it by Colonel Westbrook, at the time of its removal from the cabin of its owner, and by which it has been known by historical writers for more than a century and a half.

The box seems to have been carefully and strongly made by the direction of its owner, probably in France, to be carried in the hand in all his wanderings. He was for a time stationed with the Algonquins on the Mississippi, and also for a time with the Hurons and Iroquois. He embarked at Rochelle, France, for Quebec, in July, 1689, and came to Norridgewock in 1690. It adds to the interest of the strong box to read his letter to his nephew, from which we learn that in the visits of the Indians to the sea-shore in summer, a chapel was erected and an altar set up. He says: "I take care to transport thither a part of our ornaments, and the service is performed with the same decency, and the same crowds of people as at the village. . . . I always carry with me a beautiful board of cedar, about four feet in length with the necessary supports, and this serves for an altar, while above it they place an appropriate canopy." From these letters we learn that the removal of the "consecrated wafers" and the crowding of the "sacred vessels" that held them, into this little chest, at the time of his flight, was not the first time the same thing had been done by the missionary. There is no mention of the final fate of these altar vessels, which were probably of silver, and made to fit into each other. A Puritan soldiery would not hold them in high veneration.

Historians disagree as to the custodians of the strong box.

Some assert that it is in the library of the Massachusetts Historical Society. The History of Portland said, in 1865, it was in the library of the Maine Historical Society, but all were in error. It was for a few years intrusted to the custody of the Massachusetts Historical Society, but, by the agreement of the Waldron family, it became the property of one member. In 1871, the writer was commissioned by the Maine Historical Society to make an effort to obtain that valuable relic of the military service of Colonel Westbrook. Professor Packard recollected that it was sent to Brunswick from its owner in Portsmouth, at the request of President Allen, for his examination, and returned. From Portsmouth it was traced to the possession of Rev. E. Q. S. Waldron, priest of the Catholic church of St. Charles Bonares, at Pikesville, Maryland. The head of the Order of Jesuits of the United States claimed that the box should finally go to their Order, but, after twelve years' correspondence, the box was, by its owner, presented to the Maine Historical Society, and is now in the custody of their committee. We give a very correct cut of the Jesuit's strong box.

Colonel Westbrook's raid upon Norridgewock fort and village roused in the Indians the savage spirit of revenge, which soon burst forth in a similar raid on the settlements of the whites. The planting and hoeing of their corn, on which they largely depended for subsistence, must be attended to in the season for it, which, with their rude tools, was accomplished with great labor. Their fertilizer was alewives, which were caught at the mouth of the Sandy river, near their planting ground, in immense numbers.*

* Bradford's History of Plymouth, page 100, is good authority concerning the Indian mode of planting corn. He says: "Afterwards they [the Pilgrims] began to plant their corn, in which service Squanto stood them

In the letter to his brother written from Norridgewock, October 18, 1723, Rasle describes at much length the Indian habits of life. He says:

Our Indians have so entirely destroyed the game in this part of the country that during ten years they have scarcely found either elk or roebuck. The bears and beavers have also become very rare. They have scarcely anything on which to live but Indian corn, beans, and pumpkins. . . . . At a particular season of the year, they repair to a river not far distant, where during one month the fish ascend in such great numbers that a person could fill fifty thousand barrels in a day if he could endure the labor. They are a kind of large herrings very agreeable to the taste when fresh, crowding one upon another to the depth of a foot. They are drawn out as if they were water. The Indians dry them for eight or ten days and live on them during all the time they are planting their fields. It is only in the spring that they plant their corn, and they do not give it their last tillage until Corpus Christi day (12 of June). After this they deliberate as to what spot on the sea-shore they shall go to find something to live on until harvest.

These annual summer visits to the sea-coast, of the entire tribes of Indians, account for the great extent of clam and oyster shell heaps along the coast of Maine. They had no other means of opening oysters but by heat, hence the frequently occurring circles of shell heaps at Damariscotta.

In 1722, immediately after finishing the cultivation of their corn, of course the Indians were short of provisions, and were also desirous for revenge for Colonel Westbrook's raid on their village. It was the time for their annual visit to the sea-coast. They made a war party to attack Brunswick and obtain present supplies. In the fifth volume of the Pejepscot

in great stead, showing them both ye manner and how to set it, and after how to dress and tend it. Also he told them that except they got fish and set with it (in those old grounds) it would come to nothing and he showed them that in the middle of April they should have store enough come up ye brook."

Papers, (page 277,) is an account of this attack and the punishment of a party of the Indians therefor. It is in the handwriting of John McKeen, taken partly from Penhallow and partly from tradition in McKeen's time, who lived at Brunswick. He says:

In July 1722, Col. Harmon was stationed at Arrowsic with a number of men and whaleboats. He discovered that the settlement of Brunswick was on fire, and at once concluded that the Indians had made an attack upon it. He immediately manned two whaleboats and with Major Moody proceeded up the river to the relief of Brunswick. It was night when he entered Merrymeeting bay and he soon discovered the fires kindled by the Indians on Somerset Point. They quietly landed and found the Indians asleep. Knowing that they were returning fatigued from the destruction of Brunswick, Harmon and his party fired upon them but did not wait to see how many were killed.

The destruction of their village, fort, and church, and a large number of the Norridgewock tribe, was cruelly accomplished in August, 1724, but I am pleased to be able to say that our townsman, Colonel Westbrook, was not in command, nor was he one of the party. It was done by four companies, consisting, in the whole, of two hundred and eight men, under Captains Harmon, Moulton, Bourne, and Bean. The Indians were surprised in their houses and fired upon as they came out, killing indiscriminately men, women, and children. Their minister was the last one killed, but it was done contrary to the orders of the commanding officer. He, with the Indian dead, old and young, male and female, were scalped, and these bloody trophies were paraded in the streets of Boston with much triumph, as the following from the diary of Councilor Sewall shows:

SATURDAY August 22 1724.

The Sheerness (man-of-war) comes up, and Capt Harmon with his Norridgewock scalps, at which there is great shouting and triumph. The Lord help us to rejoice with trembling.

13

The manuscript journal of Rev. William Holmes, of Chilmark, Cape Cod, under date August 30, 1724, gives an account of Harmon and Moulton's attack on the Norridgewock village. He says, " The scalps of twenty-eight of them were brought to Boston, of which their priest's and Bomazeen's were two."

There is an order recorded on the province records, December 24, 1724, in these words :

The Indian scalps, now in keeping of the treasurer, to be buried in some private place, so as not to be discovered or produced again.

After shooting and scalping the Indians, and with two children as prisoners, Harmon and Moulton, with their whole force, " lodged in the wigwams, keeping a guard of forty men." They started early on their return march, leaving the chapel and wigwams standing. " Christian," a Mohawk Indian of Harmon's force, was sent, or went back of his own accord, and set fire to the wigwams and to the church in the turret of which hung a bell. Of course all these buildings were destroyed and the village and the cornfields were left desolate.

[Massachusetts Archives, Vol. 52, page 34.]

FALMOUTH Augt 18th 1724.

May it please your Honour

Cap^{tn} Harmon arrivd this day with the Fryars and Twenty Six Scalps more from Norridgewock and brought Bombazees Squaw and three more Indian Captive's retook three English boys, he Informes a great number of Indians are comeing on our fronteir Sundry from Canada and Two Hundred from Penobscutt for a more account I refer to him; They have taken Leiu^t. Kenadys Coat at Norridgewock who resided at Saint Georges which makes us doubt they have taken the garrison, I am Sending Cap^{tn} Sanders in his Sloop strongly guarded to that place and am likewise dispatching orders to all the fronteirs to be strict on their guard.

Cap! Harmon and the officers Judge, that by the modestes Computation besides the Scalps and Captives they brought in, what they killd and drownded there could not be less than thirty or forty, God has now been pleasd to Crown your Honours unwearied Endeavours with success, which I desire to rejoyce at   I hope y^r Honour will smile on Cap^{tn} Harmon and favour him with a Commission for a field Officer

I am your Honours most Dutiful
Humble Servant
THO^s WESTBROOK

I have Imprest Mr Dokes Scooner
to convey Cap! Harmon to Boston.

It will be noticed that Colonel Westbrook's letter from Falmouth to Governor Dummer, announcing Captain Harmon's arrival here, is dated August 18th; he must have occupied several days in his return. The account in the Massachusetts Historical Collections, published in 1819, says Father Rasle was killed August 23d, and the monument erected to his memory at Norridgewock, in 1834, has the same date. Governor Hutchinson, in his History of Massachusetts, published in 1795, says he was killed on the twelfth, which is probably the correct date. This probability is strengthened, not only by Colonel Westbrook's letter but by Sewall's Diary, which says Captain Harmon arrived in Boston with his scalps on the twenty-second of August.

The bell of the chapel disappeared to be brought to light eighty-four years later. This bell was very necessary to proclaim the hour of worship in a village without time-keepers of any kind. It was probably brought by the Indians from Quebec, through the woods and over the ponds and rivers. Rasle, in his letter, says, " In going to Quebec it is necessary to take more than a fortnight to reach there. The Indians have to furnish themselves with provisions for the journey; they have different rivers to pass, and frequent portages to make." There is a possibility that the bell might have been sent by Castin from Penobscot, by the way of the Kennebec. This would require a vessel, which would have to ascend the river in time of peace. The bell is thirteen inches high, eleven inches across the mouth, and weighs thirty-one and a half pounds.

The Maine Historical Society also holds this other relic of the Indian community at Norridgewock, a reminder of Father Rasle and his little church. In his letter to his nephew, written in 1722, he says: "None of my neophytes fail to repair twice in each day to the church; early in the morning to hear mass, and in the evening to assist in the prayers I offer up at sunset." This is the bell which called the Indians to the matins and vespers in this church of the forest. It was presented to the society by Mr. John Ware. The following is his statement at the presentation in about 1822. It is copied from the society's records:

An ancient bell found at Norridgewock in 1808. It was found about a mile from the Indian chapel, on the western side of the Kennebec. Here are falls around which canoes, etc., were carried, and by the side of the path the bell was found, under a decayed hemlock. Probably it was either placed near the tree, which was afterwards blown down over it, or it might have been placed under the trunk after it had fallen. The tree had so decayed that the bell was discovered in the midst of the rotten wood, standing a little on one side, and sunk about eight inches into the ground.

The surviving Indians probably took it across the river and secreted it, intending to carry it back to Quebec, but never could raise force enough.

Another memento of Father Rasle was found in the summer of 1885, by a young man named Hitchcock. With others he was digging on the site of the Indian village of

Norridgewock, and, when about six inches below the surface, he came upon a silver crucifix about five inches long. The figure of the Saviour is surmounted by a crown, and beneath the feet is a skull with cross-bones. The metal is gray with age. It was undoubtedly the property of Father Rasle, and was lost at the time of his death. It is said that the owner intends to present the crucifix to the Maine Historical Society, to be placed in their cabinet with the other relics of the missionary.

Everything relating to these relics is interesting to the people of this vicinity, because Colonel Westbrook, who was sent by the provincial government to arrest Father Rasle, lived and died in old Falmouth; also for the fact that many of the soldiers, who made that long march with him on snow-shoes, were Falmouth men.

In May, in the year 1700, " The Great and General Court of Assembly of His Majesty's Province of the Massachusetts Bay, in New England," passed an act that any Catholic priest or missionary " who shall say any Popish prayers by celebrating masses, or who shall abide or come into this Province after the tenth day of September next, shall be adjudged to suffer perpetual imprisonment. And if any person being so imprisoned, shall break prison and be afterwards retaken, he shall be punished with death. Any one who harbors a Romish Priest shall be fined two hundred pounds, and shall be further punished by being set in the pillory on three several days, and be bound to good behavior."

Yet these descendants of the Pilgrims and Governor Winthrop's colony let no opportunity pass without proclaiming that their ancestors came here to escape from intolerance. Judge Sewall said to Lieutenant-Governor Dummer in council, " You have this for your encouragement, that the people you have to do with are a part of the Israel of God, and you may expect to have the prudence and patience of Moses communicated to you for your conduct."

This law shows the sentiment that prevailed in the New England colonies at that time against Romish priests, aside from the influence they exerted upon the Indians. It is not a matter of wonder that there " was great shouting and triumph," (as Sewall says,) in the streets of Boston at the exhibition of Father Rasle's bloody scalp.

A bounty of fifteen pounds was offered by the province for every scalp taken from a male Indian twelve years old and upward, and eight pounds for every captive woman or child. Afterward the government offered to every volunteer who would enter into the service, without pay or rations, one hundred pounds for a scalp; and if he had rations and found his own arms, sixty pounds, and promised pensions to all who should be wounded. This was the immediate cause of the activity in hunting Indians. They were put upon the same footing with other wild game. In 1675, the general court ordered, " That whosoever shall shoot off a gun on any unnecessary occasion except at an Indian or a wolf shall forfeit five shillings for every such offence."

The large bounty offered by the government for scalps, caused the formation of numerous private hunting parties after Indians, for years, when a war broke out. Many of these were stock companies, which were supplied by individuals on shares. There were several organized in Falmouth. Parson Smith records, " May 11th 1756, Capt. Milk with forty men; Capt. Ilsley with a company, and Capt. Skillin with another went out in pursuit of the Indians." Parson Smith had a share in a hunting party for Indians. He says:

1757 April 20; Jos. Cox, Baily and otheres sailed on a cruise for six weeks after the Penobscot Indians.

June 2nd. Cox and Bailey returned from their cruise after the Indians, bringing with them the scalps of two men whom they killed; two canoes and a quantity of feathers.

June 18, I received 165 pounds–3-3, of Cox of my part of *scalp money.*

Shakespeare, in The Tempest, makes Trinculo say of the English, " When they will not give a doit to relieve a lame beggar, they will lay out ten to see a dead Indian."

Stimulated by the bounty for Indian scalps and prisoners, Captain John Lovell, of Dunstable, made three expeditions against the Pequaket Indians. In his first expedition, undertaken in December, 1724, with thirty men, they killed and scalped one Indian man and carried an Indian boy to Boston ; for both they received the bounty promised by the province and likewise a liberal present. In February following, with a party of seventy, he went again to the same vicinity and came upon a camp of ten Indians lying round a fire asleep, nine of whom were killed and the tenth was badly wounded. He was chased and held by a dog until he was also dispatched. The party received for these ten scalps one thousand pounds and much applause. On his third excursion, Captain Lovell was joined by forty-six others, and left Dunstable on the fifteenth of April. On the eighth of May, on the shore of a pond in the present town of Fryeburg, a large party of Indians was encountered and a desperate battle was fought, with the loss of more than half of the number of the whites including Captain Lovell.

From the activity of this commander the war has been designated as "Lovell's war." It was terminated in 1725. The treaty was ratified and signed at Falmouth, December 15th of that year, and was known as Dummer's treaty.

Massachusetts Records, Vol. 52, p. 205, gives this letter to the Lieutenant-Governor :

FALMOUTH, 22 of June 1725.

I am surprized the Indians are so still at this juncture. I omited to inform your Honor of Capt. Moultons return on the 15 of this instant from Pigwocket. He made little or no discovery of the enemy, saving where Capt. Lovewell had his fight; there he found the places where the bodies of twelve of our men and four of the enemy were buried. As they went up by the side of the Osaby river they found a dead body and judged it to be Capt Lovewells Lieut. . . . . .

If your Honor should think fit, I believe it would be best that all the officers return to their posts as soon as their affairs will admit of it; so that we may be in the best posture we can in all our frontiers to receive the enemy they should make their attempts on us.

I am your Honors most dutiful serv't

THOS. WESTBROOK.

In 1725, after a protracted conference at St. Georges' fort, between the commissioners of the province and the Indians of the Kennebec and Penobscot tribes, a further conference was agreed upon to be held forty days after, at Boston. This meeting was attended by the chiefs of all the tribes of Maine and Nova Scotia. It was begun November 10th, and lasted until December 15th, when a treaty of peace was signed by both parties, and has been known as Dummer's treaty.

After some negotiation Falmouth was fixed upon as the place of meeting for the ratification of the treaty, and a vessel was sent to Penobscot, to transport the Indians to the place of meeting. On the fifteenth of July, the New Hampshire officials arrived by water with Rev. William Shurtleff, of Portsmouth, as chaplain. On the sixteenth, Lieutenant-Governor Dummer with the majority of the council of Massachusetts arrived.

At this time there were, according to a memorandum made

by Rev. Mr. Smith, but fifty-six families on the Neck. The meeting-house was roughly covered, but no window-sashes. Governor Wentworth, of New Hampshire, seeing its forlorn look, gave the glass for the windows, and with some other assistance the outside was finished that season. This meeting-house stood near the west corner of Middle and India streets.

We can imagine the excitement in the village caused by the arrival of the two governors with their chaplains and retinues, and Colonel Mascarene, of Nova Scotia. We get the most authentic history of the proceedings from the journal of Parson Smith, who had been settled here only one year. He records as follows :

July 17. (Sunday,) Mr. Shurtleff preached here A.M. Mr. Fitch P.M. The gentlemen all at meeting. In the morning the gentlemen came on shore and made considerable appearance with their drums and guns. The governor guarded in pomp to meeting.

20. The gentlemen spent this week entirely idle waiting for the Indians.

23. The Indians came here from Penobscot on a message to the government, and were sent away in the afternoon.

24. (Sunday,) I preached here A. M. Mr. Tappan P. M. Mr. Fitch baptized the children twenty-two in all, besides one grown person. Mr. White preached over to Purpooduck A.M. The Lieut.-Governor with the gentlemen sailed up the bay, [to cross the land to Winnegance creek and to Arrowsic].

29. This morning the gentlemen returned from Arrowsic. The Indians to the number of forty, all of the Penobscot tribe, came in here. In the afternoon the Congress opened.

Aug. 1. There was a public dinner at which I dined. Several days were spent in private treaties to pave the way for the private ratifications.

4. All private conferences were finished this day.

5. The ratification of the peace was publicly done this day in the meeting-house.

Aug. 6. Some affairs relating to the ratification that were left
        unsettled yesterday were this day finished and all con-
        cluded with a public dinner.
      8. The New Hampshire gentlemen sailed.
     10. This week spent in interpreting to the Indians the journal
        of all their actions — and in settling some other matters.
     12. The governor and other gentlemen sailed this day for
        Boston. Capt. Franklin carried the Indians to St. Georges.

Colonel Westbrook was one of the "thirty associates,"
proprietors of the Muscongus patent and called the Lincolnshire Company. At a meeting held at the Star Tavern, in
Boston, October 9, 1721, he and seventeen other partners
were present. He was there styled "Captain." Colonel
Samuel Waldo, who afterward became proprietor of this
patent, was first admitted a partner in about 1750. His
interest was valued at about three hundred pounds.

The Lincolnshire Company built a fort at St. Georges' river,
in what is now Thomaston, in 1720, and armed it at their
own expense. Captain Westbrook was made military commander. This was previous to his appointment as commander-in-chief of the province troops. The government afterward
accepted it as a public work and garrisoned it with province
troops. Williamson gives this account of Colonel Westbrook raising a siege at this fort:

The last attack of the Indians this season, (1723,) was December
25, upon the fort at St. Georges' river. Being fortunate enough to
take two prisoners, who gave them intelligence concerning the indefensible condition of the garrison, the assailants, about sixty in number, were encouraged to prosecute the siege for thirty days with a
resolution, or rather madness, that was desperate. They seemed to
be flushed with the absolute certainty of compelling a surrender of
the fort. But Captain Kennedy, the commanding officer, being a man
of intrepid courage held out until Colonel Westbrook arrived and put
the enemy to flight.

Douglass describes the Pejepscot purchase as follows:

Mr. Wharton, a merchant of Boston, purchased of six sagamores about 500,000 acres called the Pejepscot purchase; bounded five miles west of Pejepscot (Androscoggin) river by a line running at five miles distance, parallel with the river, to a certain fall in said river and thence northeast in a straight line to Kennebec river. . . . . . Wharton, dying insolvent, the administrator sold, in 1714, this purchase for not much exceeding one hundred pounds New England currency to eight or nine proprietors, viz.: Adam Winthrop, Thomas Hutchinson, John Wentworth, John Watts, David Jeffries, Stephen Minot, Oliver Noyes, John Rusk, in equal eighths.

These were all of Boston but Wentworth, who was of New Hampshire.

It was bounded on the southwest by North Yarmouth, which takes in a small part of this grant. Georgetown, Brunswick, and Topsham, are in this grant. The title to a part of the territory was disputed by the Plymouth Company. A paper war between the wealthy companies was carried on for years, by newspaper advertisements and pamphlets, with much personal abuse. It was carried to the courts, and a trial was had at Falmouth, in July, 1754. Parson Smith says:

Oct. 5. I have spent a good deal of time at Court to hear the case between the Plymouth and Pejepscot proprietors. Gridley for the former, Otis for the latter.

Gridley was attorney-general of Massachusetts, and James Otis was the distinguished advocate of the rights of the colonies. The controversy was ended by compromise in 1766.

Beside the eight original purchasers, several other active men became interested in the company, and received power to act as agents. Edmond Mountfort and Benjamin Larrabee were agents, and afterward became prominent citizens of Falmouth.

Colonel Westbrook's last military service was rendered at the conference in Falmouth, which ended in the Dummer treaty. He was made agent for the Pejepscot Company, and was a partner. The following letter, one of many similar ones on the records, shows his energy and how he stood in relation to his Boston partners:

HARROW HOUSE IN FALMOUTH, June 27, 1734.

Captain Larrabee is with me to sign his power for acting for Brunswick company. I assure you I will not do it till the account of my disbursement is adjusted. I have your note to pay it sometime or other. I am well pleased that you improve captain.* I long to wait on you at Boston, or at Harrow House, and am sir,

Your most obedient servant at command,

THOS. WESTBROOK.

Col. Ad. Winthrop, Esq.

One of Arnold's field officers, in his expedition to Quebec in 1775, was Major Return J. Meigs. He kept a journal on their way up the Kennebec. He says: "At Norridgewock are to be seen the vestiges of an Indian fort and chapel, and a priest's grave. There seems to have been some entrenchment and a covered way through the bank to the river for the convenience of getting water." This was more than fifty years after the fort was destroyed.

In 1833, Bishop Fenwick, of Boston, having purchased an acre of land at Indian Old Point, where the church formerly stood, raised a monument in memory of Father Rasle on the twenty-third of August, supposing that to be the anniver-

---

* Adam Winthrop was captain of Castle William. His grandfather was a son of governor John Winthrop; Adam was born in 1694, — Harvard College 1724, — lived in Boston and died in 1743. He had a son Adam a merchant in Boston, and also a son John, Harvard College, 1732, LL. D. and F.R.S. Was a professor of mathematics at Harvard College, and was sent by the province to Newfoundland with a party from the college to observe the transit of Venus in 1761. He published a pamphlet account of it.

sary of the destruction of the church and village. The monument consists of a granite obelisk, three feet square at the base and eleven feet high, placed on a granite base five feet high. On the top of the obelisk is an iron cross two feet high, making the whole height to the top of the cross eighteen feet. There is a lengthy inscription in Latin on the south side of the base. Two years after its erection the monument was thrown down, but was immediately rebuilt by the citizens of Norridgewock. It was intended to be placed over the burial place of the missionary, as near as it could be ascertained.

While in command of the military forces of the province in Maine, Colonel Westbrook's headquarters were at Falmouth, as were those of his predecessor. Parson Smith says, "In June, 1725, I, Thomas Smith, came here and found one Mr. Pierpont (who was chaplain to the army, *whose headquarters was on this Neck*) preaching to the people." The army headquarters were here in 1724, and Colonel Westbrook received Captain Harmon here when he returned from Norridgewock with the scalps and "pressed" a vessel to take him to Boston, as the Colonel's letter shows. This was at the fort at the foot of India street. New Casco fort was demolished eight years previous to this.

It was at New Casco that Colonel Shadrack Walton, of Somersworth, New Hampshire, who was in command before Colonel Westbrook, had his headquarters. At New Casco fort stood the "two brothers," pillars of stones built by the two contracting parties at a treaty, and added to at each subsequent conference. Captain Samuel Penhallow, who represented New Hampshire at the conference at New Casco fort, in June, 1703, which ended in a treaty, thus mentions these stone pillars:

The Indians said they aimed at nothing more than peace; and as high as the sun was above the earth, so far distant should their designs

be of making the least breach between each other. And as a testimony thereof they presented him a belt of wampum, and invited him
to the two pillars of stones which at a former treaty were erected and
called by the significant name of the *two brothers.*

These "two pillars of stones" are mentioned as a place of
burial in a letter to Governor Dudley from Captain Cyprian
Southack, dated "Casco Bay, May the 17: 1703 from on
board the Maj'tys ship Province Galley." Captain Newman
with some of his men belonging to a sloop, were on shore on
Cousins' Island at work, when the Indians shot one of the
men. Captain Southack took the dead man on board of his
ship for burial. This is his account of it:

Sir on the 11 of May at 2 oclock afternoon we got off the dead man
from Cousins' Island, and no sign of any French or Indians about the
bay.   At 7 oclock afternoon came down to the fort (New Casco) and
the next morning we buried the man at *our heap of stones.*

This occurrence was a month before the treaty when the
Indian sagamores invited Governor Dudley to "the two
pillars of stones," as sacred monuments to good faith. The
stones of these "two brothers" perhaps yet remain near the
site of the old fort.

Southgate, in his History of Scarborough, says:

Colonel Thomas Westbrook was residing here as early as 1719, at
which time he, with his lumbermen, and John Milliken jr., were
the only persons living at Dunstan. Mr. Westbrook was then a
shipper of masts, and continued here a long while in the successful
pursuit of that business.

I am of the opinion that Mr. Westbrook only had a lum-
bering establishment and house for his men at Dunstan.
Brewster, in his "Rambles about Portsmouth," says that in
1727 Thomas Westbrook was the thirteenth in the order of
the principal tax-payers in Portsmouth, New Hampshire.
He bought into the Muscongus or Waldo Patent in 1719.

He was admitted an inhabitant by paying twelve pounds by the Falmouth proprietors in 1727; that year the king's mast business was transferred from Portsmouth to Falmouth, and Thomas Westbrook was appointed mast agent. The transfer was probably made by the recommendation of Mr. Westbrook, who had been shipping masts from here on private account.

The New England Weekly Journal of May 8, 1727, printed in Boston, says:

We have an account that the mast business, which has for some time been of so much benefit of the neighbor province of New Hampshire is removed farther eastward, where it has been carried on the last winter with such success as could hardly have been expected, considering the very little seasonable weather for it. Capt. Farles, in one of the mastships now lies in Casco Bay, who, we hear, is not a little pleased with the peculiar commodiousness of that fine harbor to carry on the said business. And as this must tend very much to encourage the settlements of those parts of the country, especially the flourishing bay that will be the center of it; so there is no reason to fear but that our government will in their wisdom, look upon it very much to their interest to protect and encourage it.

In February, 1726, the Scarborough people voted that " the meeting for divine worship shall be held one Sabbath day at the house of Colonel Westbrook at Dunstan, and another at the house of Samuel Libby at Black Point." Colonel Westbrook also assisted at the organization of the Black Point church in 1728, but he did not live there then, nor was his house, where the meetings were held, occupied by him at the time, but was probably an unoccupied loghouse owned by him. While collecting the masts at Scarborough, Colonel Westbrook probably hauled them to the waters of Long creek, to be floated down to Fore river for shipment. There is no mention of mast ships coming to Black Point.

In Trelawney Papers, page 64, in John Winters "Bounds of the Trelawney Patent," this paragraph occurs:

There is a Creeke after you are 1 Mile & ½ within the Barre of the Riuer Spurrwinke which lyes awaye nearest N° : W: & B: N° : yt a little Boate att highe Water may goe into itt ½ a Mile, & extends neare about a Mile to the first Arme of the Baye of Caskoe yt lyes awaye to the West-ward, which Arme lyes awaye W: S: W: & as neare as (I Can iudge).

It seems, by Winter's description, that the Spurwink and Fore river waters nearly meet at the head of Long creek. These creeks would make an easy and short winter road between Scarborough and Falmouth.

In the under sheriff's return of his levy on the estate of Thomas Westbrook in 1743, he mentions the "Mast Road" in these words: "Also a tract of land on the eastermost side of the *Mast Road* that leads from Stroudwater to Dunstan containing ten acres." The name indicates that this road was made through which to haul masts to Stroudwater in the early years of the last century.

The procuring of masts for the English navy was early a matter of anxiety to the officers of the crown. New England furnished a share of them. In the diary of Samuel Pepys, who held an office in the navy board, is the following:

1666, December third. There is also the very good news come of four New England ships come home safe to Falmouth with masts for the King; which is a blessing mighty unexpected, and without which (if nothing else) we must have fallen next year.

The same year, 1666, October 10, the Massachusetts general court agreed to send to his Majesty, Charles II., "two large masts aboard of Captain Pierce, thirty-four yards (one hundred and two feet) long, and one thirty-six and the other thirty-seven inches diameter." This generous gift was intended as a sop to prevent the king from taking away their charter, which was nevertheless done eighteen years later.

Again, December 24, 1666, Pepys writes: "No news yet of our Gottenberg fleet, which makes us have some fears, it being of mighty concernment to have one's supply of masts safe." The Gottenberg fleet arrived on the twenty-ninth safe, with the supply of masts, and, yet, within a year, the Dutch fleet broke the chain that guarded the river at Chatham, and burnt several English men-of-war in the Thames.

The Massachusetts charter of 1691 contained this restriction:

And lastly, for the better providing and furnishing of masts for our Royal Navy, we do hereby reserve to us, our heirs and successors, all trees [no species named] of the diameter of twenty-four inches, and upwards, twelve inches from the ground, growing upon any soil or tract of land within our said Province or Territory of Massachusetts Bay, not heretofore granted to any private person. And we do restrain and forbid all persons whatsoever from felling, cutting or destroying any such trees without the royal license first had and obtained; upon penalty of forfeiting one hundred pounds sterling for every such tree so felled.

A surveyor general of woods was commissioned for the province. At the period of which I am writing, John Bridges held the office. Like many public officers since, he was accused of selling indulgences for private gain, and the territory of western Maine was kept in a turmoil about the mast trees. Near the coast the woods were surveyed and the king's mark cut on such white pines as were suitable for masts or bowsprits. The mark put upon the trees was called the "broad arrow" — like the barbed head of an arrow — three cuts through the bark with an ax, like a crow's track. The mast agent granted permits to cut the trees as they were wanted for shipping to England. Within my recollection

14

some pine trees bearing this mark were standing and were pointed out as curiosities. Long after the Revolution had obliterated the royal authority, men, who had been taught in boyhood to respect the king's mark, hesitated to cut these trees.

In felling a mast tree it was necessary to "bed it," to prevent its breaking in its fall. This was done by cutting the small growth, and placing the small trees across the hollows so that, when the monster pine struck the ground in its fall, there should be no strain on one section more than another, causing a break. The hauling of a mast was an event of much interest to the people within walking distance, and all attended. Masts were hauled on one strong sled out of the woods, winter or summer. A long team of oxen were required for the purpose, and often the hind ones were choked in crossing a hollow by being hung up in their yoke, by those forward. The masts were drawn to the nearest navigable water, and in the spring rolled in and floated to the mast landing above Clark's Point, where the British government had a "mast house" for the hewing the mast to the proper taper. The measure that fixed the price was taken at the butt-end after the hewing.

The carrying of masts required the largest ships of the time; from four to six hundred tons, and some were even larger. Bowsprits and yards were shipped with masts. A mast one hundred feet long and three feet in diameter required a powerful purchase to draw it on board and put it in place. The masts were drawn in through a port in the stern of the ship. In time of war "the mast fleet" was convoyed by men-of-war. Parson Smith, in his journal, makes frequent mention of the arrival and departure of the mast ships, and the news they brought from "home." In May, 1766, Captain

Samuel Tate, in a mast ship, brought the news of the repeal of the stamp act.

The crown paid a bounty of one pound a ton on masts and bowsprits, and the commissioners of the navy, by a law, had a right of pre-emption on them for twenty days after they were landed in England. The regulation was that the mast must be as many yards in length as it was inches in diameter at the butt, after it had been hewed to the proper dimensions. In 1770, the price fixed in England for a mast thirty-six inches in diameter was one hundred and ten pounds. Two years before that the price for the same was one hundred and thirty-three pounds.

Colonel Westbrook, of whose active career I have been writing, was the government mast agent for New England until his death in 1744. In about 1750, George Tate, of London, was sent over as his successor.

After Colonel Westbrook gave up the military command in Maine, he went extensively into the land and lumber business with Colonel, afterward Brigadier, Waldo, both here and on the Georges river. He bought into the Muscongus patent in 1719, I think before Colonel Waldo did. The oldest conveyance to Thomas Westbrook on the York County records, is from Thomas Hutchinson, of Boston, of his one-eighth interest "in a large tract of land bordering on Kennebec, Pejepscot, and Androscoggin rivers," for one thousand ounces of silver. This was the Pejepscot purchase. The deed is dated January 1, 1729, and Westbrook is named resident of Falmouth. On the York records he appears as grantor alone and with another eighty-one times, and as grantee alone and with another sixty times. His partner in these transactions was, in most instances, Samuel Waldo. The same year Westbrook and Waldo purchased of the heirs the Ingersoll estate at Capisic, "the mile square." The first mention I find of Colonel Westbrook's residence here with his family, is in Smith's journal. He records, "1732, July 28. The Governor did not meet the Indians to day, he being with all the other gentlemen, up to Col. Westbrook's, at dinner." The governor was Jonathan Belcher. He came here in the armed ship Scarborough to meet the Indians. Colonel Westbrook's residence was on the south side of Stroudwater river near where it falls into Fore river. He seems to have had a large fortified establishment. In the return of the sheriff's levy, in June 1743, on execution in favor of Samuel Waldo, his former partner, it is thus described: "Also part of a triangular piece of land on the south side of the river Stroudwater, containing 69 acres and 55 rods, with the house called *Harrow House*, and sundry out houses and garrisons round the same, and three small cottages."

Colonel Westbrook and Samuel Waldo were the first that dammed Presumpscot river, at the lower falls, for milling purposes. In a petition of Richard Frye for writ of review, on record in Boston, we get some idea of the first movement there. Frye was then held in Boston jail on execution in favor of Waldo and Westbrook. These are his words in part:

Your petitioner indented with Mr. Samuel Waldo in the year 1731 in London, to have built within ten months after my arrival in New-England a papermill. Your petioner arrived in New-England in the year 1731 and waited four years wholy at his own expense, till such time as the said mills were built, (and there is no member of this Honourable House but must know the keeping a family in a pretty genteel manner four years must amount to a large sum). Your petioner willing to promote the good of his country, drew a plan for sundry sorts of mills to be built, which was across Presumscot river in Falmouth; which scheme the said Waldo and Westbrook came into and built the said mills. And your petioner sent for one Mr. John

Collier from England, which took the lease of the said mills at two hundred pounds sterling per annum for twenty-one years. Your petitioner was to pay sixty-four pounds sterling per ann. for twenty one years for the papermills. And the said Samuel Waldo and Thomas Westbrook confessed before Capt. Greenwood, Mr. George Craddock, and Mr. Brandon, merchants of Boston, that they held and owned in the township of Falmouth, fifteen thousand acres of land, and that one acre with an other was three pounds more in value for these mills. But the said Waldo and Westbrook not content with their improvement of two hundred and sixty-four pounds sterling per ann. and the vast improvements of their land they coveted the improvement of all the mills, and paid Mr. John Collier six hundred pounds for his lease.

About the same time that the Presumpscot mill was built, Colonel Westbrook built another paper-mill at Stroudwater. According to tradition this was on his own account and stood on Stroudwater river, a small stream running through his own farm and near his residence, which, after the English custom, he called " Harrow House." In the diary kept by the Rev. Thomas Smith, then the only minister in the town, under the date September 5, 1733, is the following entry : " We all rode in the Colonel's new road to see where the papermill is to be set."

This extract is all the written history relating to this paper mill; but it is an undoubted fact, well known in the village, that Colonel Westbrook did have a paper-mill there, and marks of the dam are still to be seen, a few rods above the present grist-mill, at a narrow place where the stream could be easily and safely dammed. Both banks are ledge rock, and on the south bank there is a gap blasted out to receive the cap sill, and on the other side there is a large iron rod standing in the rock, probably to secure the other end of the cap sill. It is said that when the mill pond below is drawn off the foundation timbers of the paper-mill are yet to be seen.

Whether Richard Frye had any connection with this Stroud-water mill, we have no means of knowing, but there is a tradition that there grew up a dissatisfaction among the English workmen about their wages, and that they stole and secreted some important parts of the machinery to prevent the running of the mill, and that duplicates were procured from England. This tradition was singularly verified more than a century after the occurrence. In plowing on the neighboring farm, now occupied by the state reform school, in 1845, Mr. Carter, the owner, turned up an iron press plate, formerly used in the old-fashioned paper machinery, and answering to the description of some of the lost pieces. There can be but little doubt that this casting is a part of the machinery of this ancient mill, the first in Maine (except, perhaps, that on the Presumpscot which was built at about the same time), and these were the only ones for seventy years later.

Waldo and Westbrook must have purchased the right to manufacture paper of Henchman, and his associates.

An act to encourage the manufacture of paper in New England was passed by the general court of Massachusetts, on the thirteenth of September, 1728, and a patent was granted to Daniel Henchman, Gillam Phillips, Benjamin Faneuil, Thomas Hancock, and Henry "Dering," for the sole manufacture of paper for ten years. In modern phraseology this would be called a "respectable firm," well connected. I have taken some pains to ascertain who they were, and find that they were nearly all of one family connection. Daniel Henchman, the head of the firm, was a bookbinder, and the leading bookseller of Boston at that time. Thomas Hancock, served his time with Colonel Henchman as a bookbinder, and married his daughter. He was the builder and owner of the historic Hancock mansion on Beacon street, taken down in

1863. Before his death, in 1764, he bequeathed the bulk of his large fortune to his nephew, John Hancock. These rich possessions, perhaps, inspired John, the governor, with the confidence which is manifest in his bold signature to the Declaration of Independence. General Henry Knox, President Washington's secretary of war, also served his time at bookbinding in Henchman's shop on State street. Benjamin Faneuil was the father of Peter, of Faneuil Hall memory.

In order to carry out their design and to make their exclusive charter profitable, and to enable them to comply with its terms, they built a small mill adjoining Neponset river, then in the town of Dorchester, now Milton, near the lower bridge, where the tide prevented the running of the mill six hours of the twenty-four. The terms of the charter were, that they should within the first fifteen months make one hundred and forty reams of brown paper, and sixty reams of printing paper. The second year they were to make fifty reams of writing paper in addition to the first mentioned quantity. The third year, and afterward yearly, they bound themselves, in accepting the act, to make twenty-five reams of a superior quality of writing paper, in addition to the afore-mentioned, so that the total annual produce of the various qualities should not be less than five hundred reams.

Daniel Henchman appears to have been the managing partner of the company. It is recorded that he produced to the general court of 1731, a sample of the paper made at his mill.

The industrious and observing journalist, Parson Smith, records in June, 1743, ten years after, alluding to the preparation for the paper-mill, " Mr. Waldo came to town with an execution against Colonel Westbrook for ten thousand five hundred pounds and charges." Mr. Smith mentions Colonel

Westbrook's death in February, 1744. Judge Freeman, the compiler of the journal, whose father administered on Colonel Westbrook's estate, says in a foot-note, "He died of a broken heart caused by Waldo's acts who led him into large land speculations and then struck upon him in an unfortunate time."

Waldo's execution swept off all of Colonel Westbrook's large property, including his splendid seat, which with all his other lands were set off to Waldo, and were held by his sons for many years after.

The levy on Colonel Westbrook's real estate, mills, etc., was made by "Joshua Bangs, an under-sheriff," June 25, 1743. The levy included "the mile square" at Capisic, containing five hundred and seventy-nine acres of upland, saw-mill, grist-mill, three dwelling-houses, two barns. Also the estate of Harrow House already described. The privilege of the stream called Stroudwater, with the browse and timber, with four acres of land on the north side of the river, with a paper-mill, two dwelling-houses, and one cottage thereon. Two hundred acres of land on the northeast side of Presump-scot river with a house, two cottages, and two barns. One hundred and nine acres of land on the southwest side of Presumpscot river with a garrison house, one other house and cottage, and a large frame thereon, together with the sole privilege of the stream of water, or river, called Presumpscot, and the lower falls for building mills on both sides of the river; with privilege of timber, with a triple saw-mill, grist-mill, and fulling mill; part of a double frame of a saw-mill, as also the dam.

The officer's return of the levy, beside what has already been copied, names "Great Chebeague" Island, "except 65 acres claimed by the Old Church in Boston." Also twenty nine eightieth parts of Little Chebeague Island. In addition to the property already described, there were twelve other tracts of land, large and small, seized on the two executions in favor of Samuel Waldo.

Colonel Westbrook died February 11, 1743. Enoch Freeman administered on his estate, the remnant of which he sold in 1758, for seven thousand three hundred and two pounds, " old tenor."

The damming of Presumpscot river, at the lower falls, was a more extensive work of the kind than had been before attempted in Maine. This was done in about 1738. Previous to this enterprise, sites for mills were chosen more with regard to the facilities for damming than for the constant supply of water.

In 1741, the General Court passed an act that "all the owners or occupants of any mill-dam heretofore erected and made across such river or stream where the fish can't conveniently pass over, shall make a sufficient way either round or through such dam for the passage of such fish." In 1739, at a town meeting, it was " voted, that John Wait go to make answer to the presentment against the great dam across Presumpscot river." This was for the want of a fishway in the dam.

In Colonel Westbrook's time there was a road made from Stroudwater to Presumpscot Falls. In 1748, it was altered. The termini named in the vote was "from the paper-mill (at Stroudwater) to Presumpscot Falls." This is the road now traveled by the way of Stevens' Plains. " The papermill," or " Harrow House," were named in all the records of new roads near. In 1741, a road was laid out from " Harrow House to Scarborough by Beech ridge." In 1752, a road was surveyed "from Stroudwater falls to Harrow House."

Colonel Westbrook was a liberal man, and helped along every good work. In a letter to one of his associates of the Pejepscot Company, he thus addresses him:

HARROW HOUSE FALMOUTH, June 30 1735.

Sir.— In my return from St. Georges, I called at Kennebec, and went up to Col. Nobles farm. He told me that they had desire to build a meeting-house on his farm near his garrison, on which I readily gave him my note for ten pounds towards it, and to give the minister that belongs to it fifty acres of land, which I hope will be agreeable to you, your farm being so nigh.

The deed was given in October, 1736. The consideration named in it is, "In consideration of the love and affection I bear my well beloved friend Wm. McLenichon, now minister on Kennebec river."

In 1731, Colonel Westbrook proposed to his associates of the land company to go to Europe to obtain settlers, but there is no documentary evidence that he made the voyage. The town of Falmouth had long been entitled to two representatives in the General Court, but, as the towns were compelled to pay their own representatives, only one had been sent, and some years none. In 1737, Colonel Westbrook gave a written obligation that if the town would send two representatives, he would pay one-half of their regular pay, consequently Moses Pearson and Phineas Jones were chosen, and accordingly he paid nineteen pounds and ten shillings.

Thomas Westbrook was selectman and town treasurer in 1736, and re-elected the next year. He was much respected in Boston. Chief-Justice Sewall, who was also one of the governor's council, on the occasion of Lieutenant-Governor Dummer assuming the government, on the retirement of Governor Shute, recorded in his diary the following:

1723. January, 11th. The L! governor dines at the Green Dragon upon the councils invitation. Dr. Mather prayed excellently in the council for the governor, L. Govr, council, Representatives, upon the change of government. Dined with us, Mr. Secretary, Mr. Samuel Dummer, *Col. Westbrook.*

This was at the time that Colonel Westbrook was made commander-in-chief of the forces in the eastern country. In writing to him his associates of the Pejepscot Company always addressed him as "The Honorable Colonel Westbrook, Esquire."

The burial place of Colonel Westbrook is not known. There is a tradition that, fearing a seizure of the body for debt, his family had him privately buried by night, in the Stroudwater burial ground. I think the place named at least is an error, as that spot was then the property of the Waldos whom they suspected of an intent to arrest the body.

In a deed of the surrounding land, in 1786, Sarah Waldo, administratrix, reserves the burying ground by this sentence: "Reserving nevertheless out of the same piece of land, a reasonable and convenient quantity thereof for a burial ground for the use of the parish." Yet there may have been burials on the spot previous to the release of title.

The fear of the arrest of the body of an insolvent debtor was a bugbear that drew the last dollar from many a bereaved widow and her personal friends. It was done in cases where pride and tender sorrow prevented a legal test of the question.

The St. Louis Law Journal has the following:

But this property in coffin and shroud can not be taken for debt. In 1784, the funeral of Sir Barned Turner proceeding from London to Hertfordshire, was stopped by an arrest of his body until his friends entered into an agreement for his debts. But whether this could be done legally may well be doubted. Such attempts have been made in modern times, but such extreme diligence in collecting debts generally comes so near bringing Shylock within the jurisdiction of Judge Lynch, that it is seldom attempted.

Lord Ellenborough in discussing the sufficiency of a consideration to support a promise, says: As to the case there cited by him of a mother who promised to pay on forbearance of the plaintiff to arrest the dead body of her son, which she feared he was about to do, it is contrary to every principle of law and moral feeling — such an act is revolting to humanity and illegal.

Colonel Westbrook's wife was Mary, a daughter of John Sherburne, of Portsmouth. He left no son. His daughter Elizabeth married Richard Waldron, of Portsmouth, long secretary of New Hampshire, a grandson of Major Waldron who was killed by the Indians at Dover, in 1689. Elizabeth Westbrook Waldron was the only child of Colonel Thomas Westbrook. She was born November 26, 1701, and married December 31, 1718. She had a son, Thomas Westbrook Waldron, who was a captain in the Louisburg expedition, and died in 1785. She has descendants yet living by the name of Waldron.

On the fourteenth of February, 1814, an act was passed by the General Court, dividing the town of Falmouth and incorporating the western part as the town of "Stroudwater." The inhabitants were dissatisfied with the local name, and two months later petitioned to have the name changed to "Westbrook," which was done; thereby honoring the name of their former most distinguished citizen.

CHAPTER VIII.

As we have seen, a treaty was signed with the Indians by
Governor Andross, at Casco, in 1678. A similar one was
confirmed at Mare Point, Casco Bay, in 1699. A conference
with the Indians was held by Governor Dudley at New Casco
Fort in 1703, which resulted in a treaty. Governor Dudley
and his council executed a treaty with the Indians at Falmouth Neck, in July, 1718. Lieutenant-Governor Dummer
concluded a treaty with the Indians at Boston, which was
ratified at Falmouth in July, 1726.

We have now come to the time of the industrious journalist,
Rev. Thomas Smith. We get from his journal accurate and
full descriptions of most of the gatherings at Falmouth of
the royal governors, the provincial councillors, province
officers, and the Indian sagamores with their retinues, who,
after a year or two of fighting, gathered at Falmouth to proclaim their peaceful disposition. Both belligerents seem to
have appreciated the importance of making an imposing
demonstration on these occasions. The governors of Massachusetts, New Hampshire, and Nova Scotia usually attended
with one or more men-of-war ships, an official staff, private
secretary, and chaplain. The Indians came with all the savage
show of paint, feathers, and clothing made of the skin of the
fur-bearing animals, and of the choicest specimens. A dressed

otter skin of the darkest kind, with the head, tail, and legs in place, was considered the proper protection, when in full dress, for the arm that wielded the weapon. Before the erection of the meeting-house of 1740, a large tent was usually constructed on the southerly slope of " The Hill," for these gatherings.

In his account of the treaty of 1713, begun at Portsmouth and finished at Casco, Captain Penhallow, one of the New Hampshire councilors, says :

For a further ratification of this treaty, several gentlemen of both governments (Massachusetts and New Hampshire) went from Portsmouth to Casco, where a great body of Indians were assembled to know the result of matters: it being a custom among them on all such occasions, to have the whole of their tribes present; having no other record of conveying to posterity, but what they communicate from father to son, and so to the son's son. . . . In their council they observe a very excellent decorum; not suffering any to speak but one at a time, which is delivered with such a remarkable pathos and surprising gravity, that there is neither smile nor whisper to be observed until he that speaks has finished his discourse, who then sits down and another rises up.

This conference, of 1713, was held of necessity at New Casco fort, as the Neck since 1690 had been really a " valley of dry bones."

In 1741, William Shirley succeeded William Burnet as governor of Massachusetts Province.* His first visit to

---

* Benjamin, brother of Peter Faneuil, returned from a visit to Europe, in August, 1741. The following note from Peter to his brother, who was disinherited by their uncle, explains itself. Peter was then forty years old and a bachelor, and his brother Benjamin was eighteen months his junior. The ease and intimacy of their friendship will be perceived by the note.

"BOSTON Tuesday, the 18 August, 1741.

" *Dear Cockey :* The occasion of my not sending my Chase for you was on account of Mr. Shirleys receiving of his majties commission last

Falmouth was in August, 1742. On petition of the representative of the town, Phineas Jones, the general court, in 1741, made an appropriation of four hundred pounds to build a fort on the Neck, which was in progress when Governor Shirley was here. He had a large number of both branches of the legislature with him. In his communication to the council, after his return, he approved of the site chosen for the battery, where formerly stood Fort Loyal, and recommended an appropriation for a platform for heavy guns, which induced the general court to grant thirty-three pounds for that purpose and provided two half barrels of powder.

Parson Smith does not mention the visit of the Governor; he was then engaged with a great revival of religion; nor does Willis in his history mention it. In May the Parson records: "The people voted to receive the money"; but the compiler of the journal marvels that he did not mention "what the money was for"; this was the money for the fort.

Tuesday appointing him Govr of this Province wh. was read the next day, upon which occasion he ask't me to Loane my charrot wh. I granted him till Last night, so that I presume will plead my excuse. I now send you up the chaise to bring you home, and have delivered ye Coachman Some Boild Beef, a dozen of brown biskett 6 bottles of Madera and 2 of Frontenac with a dozen of Lemmons. Your relations and friends are all well, and desire their love and service may be made acceptable to you. Pray my Compliments to the Gentn and Ladys with you — and give me Leave to assure you that I am, Dear Cockey,   Your Affectionate Brother,

PETER FANEUIL."

Shirley was but a poor practicing lawyer in Boston at the time of his appointment as governor, and probably had no chariot, which was essential to have when he rode to the town-house to have his commission proclaimed with sound of trumpet, as the custom was. By counting the days it will be found that the governor borrowed the chariot to be kept until after Sunday, when he probably rode to King's Chapel in state, and returned the chaise to its owner on Monday. From that day forward Governor Shirley was gorgeous on all public occasions.

The Governor went from here to Pemaquid and St. Georges (Thomaston), taking a particular view of the eastern country. On his return, he represented to the legislature that "The inexhaustible supplies of wood and lumber, and the several kinds and great quantities of naval stores, which this region is capable of producing, no less than the navigable rivers, the numerous harbors and good soil it possesses, render it highly deserving the encouragement and protection of the government." Shirley was the first governor to appreciate the capabilities of Maine. A few years later he became a proprietor in the "Kennebec Purchase." By his representation to the legislature on his return, seven hundred pounds were appropriated to complete the works at Fort Frederic (Pemaquid), St. Georges, and Saco, and a chaplain furnished for Pemaquid and the vicinity.

While at St. Georges, the Governor and his retinue met, by appointment, a large number of Indians in a conference, and promised them presents and supplies, if they would continue peaceable, which they agreed to. But their memory of their own promises was very short.

In 1749, Governor Shirley was appointed by the crown a commissioner to France to settle the western boundary of Acadia, and was absent four years, returning in August, 1753.

In 1754, the Plymouth Company, who owned an immense tract of land, fifteen miles wide on each side of the Kennebec, conceived the project to induce the province to build a strong fortress at their most remote northern boundary to facilitate the settlement of their lands. The Plymouth Company at this time consisted of some thirty members, who owned a large or small number of shares. Several of them were the most wealthy and influential men of the province, some were officially connected with the government, others were judges, merchants, and baronets. In fact, this corporation might, with almost as much truth, exclaim as did Louis XIV., "I am the state." Sullivan, in his History of Maine (1795), says of the Plymouth Company: "They had great influence with the government; to them Governor Shirley was very attentive."

In compliance with a vote of the assembly, the Governor decided to visit the Kennebec and send a force up the river to the "great carrying place," to see if the French were fortifying there as was reported. Fearing a rupture with the Indians, he invited the Norridgewocks and Penobscots to meet him and the commissioners of New Hampshire, at Falmouth, in June, for a conference and a renewal of treaties. The real object was to obtain their consent to the erection of the proposed fort. For the march up the river and for the building of the fort, it was decided to enlist eight hundred men and to put them under the command of General John Winslow, of Marshfield. The second officer in command was Colonel Jedediah Preble, of Falmouth; afterward the noted brigadier.

He descended from the Preble family of old York. He was in Waldo's regiment, under General Pepperell, at the siege of Louisburg in 1746. He was probably a subaltern, as he was commissioned as captain in the same regiment while there. He was commissioned as lieutenant-colonel for the Kennebec expedition. He removed to Falmouth about 1748. He acted as major under Moncton at the taking of the French forts in Nova Scotia, and in the removal of the Acadians, in 1755, in which service he was slightly wounded at Chignecto.

Colonel Preble was again with General Winslow in the expedition against Ticonderoga. He was next in command.

15

under Governor Pownal in the building of Fort Pownal, on
the Penobscot, in 1759, and took command of its garrison
when the fort was completed, and remained there until 1763,
when he resigned the command. He was representative to
the general court and counselor of the province. In 1774,
he was elected commander-in-chief of the Massachusetts forces,
but declined the office on account of age and infirmities,
when General Ward was promoted to that office.

In 1778, General Preble was appointed justice of the Court
of Common Pleas for Cumberland, and in 1783, he was
appointed judge of the Inferior Court under the new constitution. He died in 1784, aged seventy-seven years.

General Preble was the father of ten children, one of whom
was Commodore Edward Preble, and grandfather of Admiral
George H. Preble, of the United States Navy.

Willis' History of portland says, that General Preble commanded a company of provincial troops under General Wolf,
on the Plains of Abraham, and "was near General Wolf
when he was killed," September 13, 1759. This is a mistake.
General Preble was with Governor Pownal in his Penobscot
expedition to build Fort Pownal, which was completed in
July, 1759, and was left there in command of its garrison,
where he remained until 1763.

General Winslow was popular as an officer, and of course
was not long in enlisting the required force of eight hundred
men for the expedition. They embarked at Boston in transports for Falmouth. The Governor, with a quorum of the
council, the speaker of the house, with several of its members,
and several other gentlemen connected with the colonial government, also Colonel Mascarene, commissioner from Nova
Scotia, all embarked at Boston, on board the province frigate
Massachusetts, of twenty guns, for the same place. Parson

Smith recorded their arrival and every day's movements while here, and his own preparations to receive them. Of course it was quite an event in the little town of not over one hundred and fifty families. The reverend gentleman's first mention is :

June 18. We have been painting and fitting up our house for the treaty which is approaching.

June 21. The Norridgewock Indians came here — forty-two in all, and twenty-five men.

June 24. Several transports that have the soldiers for Kennebeck got in to-day.

June 25. Eight hundred soldiers got in and encamped on Bangs' Island.

June 26. The Governor got in this morning. P.M. Came on shore and lodged at Mr. Foxes.*

June 27. The government dined at the Court Chamber.

June 28. Yesterday and to-day we had a vast concourse dined with us at our expense.

June 29. The gentlemen yesterday met the Norridgewock Indians, and to-day proposed to them the building of a fort at Teuconic.

June 30. Sunday, Parson Brockwell preached in the forenoon and carried on in the church form. †

July 1. The Norridgewock Indians gave their answer and refused the fort's being built at Teuconic.

July 2. The treaty was signed between the Governor and the Norridgewock Indians.

* Jabez Fox, who had been one of the Governor's council three years. He was the son of Rev. John Fox, of Woburn, whose wife inherited an interest in the Plymouth Company from her father, Edward Tyng, one of the four purchasers of 1661. Jabez Fox had been employed by the Company as a land surveyor. He was sick at the time of the Governor's arrival and died April 7, 1755, aged fifty. He occupied one of the best houses in the town, on the west side of Exchange street.

† Rev. Charles Brockwell, assistant minister of King's Chapel, Boston, where Governor Shirley worshiped. He came as chaplain to the Governor and council.

July 3.   The Indians had their dance; three of the Indians went to Boston and the rest returned home.

July 5.   The Penobscot Indians came — fifteen men, and the government met them in the meeting house.

July 6.   The treaty was finished; seven gentlemen went up the bay and the others to Boston.*

* These treaties are preserved in the archives at Boston. They were drawn on very large sheets of parchment, elaborately ornamented, and colored, probably to impress the Indians with their sanctity. All the gentlemen connected with the government, and the Commissioners from New Hampshire and Nova Scotia signed them. The Indian signatures are hieroglyphics, effigies of some bird, beast or fish, with their Indian name annexed, written probably by the secretary of the province, who was a clerk of the council. Sacred as these treaties were considered, they were soon broken.

The seven gentlemen who went up the bay, as mentioned by Mr. Smith, were probably Gen. Winslow and the committee of the Plymouth Company, to build Fort Western. They undoubtedly went up New Meadows river, and walked across to the Androscoggin, where a boat was waiting to take them to Cushenoc, by the way of Merrymeeting bay. It was by this route that the express was established the next year.

"Articles of agreement indented and made the sixth day of July, A.D. 1754, between Capt. Isaac Ilsley, of Falmouth, in Casco Bay, in the Province of Massachusetts Bay, carpenter, on the one part, and his Excellency, Wm. Shirley, Esq., Governor of said Province, of the other part, as follows, vizt: The said Capt. Isaac Ilsley covenants, promises, and agrees to and with the said Wm. Shirley, that he will, on the ninth day of July instant, proceed with twelve other persons, all carpenters, whom he hath engaged for that purpose, to Kennebec River in a schooner, or other vessel, to be hired by the said government, and there continue with the aforesaid twelve other persons, for the space of two months, to be employed in helping to build a fort, to be erected at or near Taconnet Falls, or such other place upon, or near said river, as shall be judged most convenient by Maj. General Winslow. The said Ilsley and his four apprentices, being five of the twelve, at the rate of 9 pounds old "tenour" per day. Six others, 30 shillings old tenor each, and John Tomes at the rate of forty-five shillings, together with the Province's ordinary allowance

July 8th, Rev. Mr. Smith mentions, "The ship sailed with Mr. Danforth, Oliver, Bourn, and Hubbard from us, and the whole body of representatives." The ship referred to was the frigate Massachusetts. Mr. Hubbard was speaker of the house. The following letter by Governor Shirley to the secretary of state, explains why the ship returned to Boston. It is dated at

FALMOUTH, CASCO BAY, July 8, 1754.

SIR: — The Speaker, to whom I am much obliged for his assistance in the public business here, and the pleasure of his company, both of which I shall miss upon his leaving me, doth me the favor to be the bearer of this.

As he is able to give you a perfect account of the issue of the conference with the Indians who met me here, and the result of the interview, I refer you to him for it. It hath been, I think, favorable beyond even our expectations, and may, I hope, have good consequencys for the tranquillity of the Province, and the general service. It certainly will if Indian faith may be in the least depended upon. Mr. Danforth, Mr. Oliver, and Col. Bourn, are to embark this day with the Speaker, and some other gentlemen of the House, for Boston. Mr. Fox is extremely ill, so that there will be wanting four gentlemen of the Council to make up a quorum upon any emergency of public business. I must therefore desire you to let Mr. Wheelwright, Mr. Chever, Cols. Minot, Weston and Lincoln know that their attendance upon it here will be requisite, and that I hope they will not fail of letting us see them here as soon as may be. They will have an

of provisions and drink. To commence on the ninth of July, to continue until they return to Falmouth.*

"(Signed,)   WM. SHIRLEY,
PAUL MASCARENE.
JOSEPH CALEF."

Ilsley's bill, which is on file, is dated the twenty-eighth of September, being 82 days each for himself and twelve men, amounting to 1660 pounds, 10 shillings.

---

* Mr. Ilsley was often employed as captain of scouting parties. He was the ancestor of all of the name in Portland and vicinity. He was at the taking of Louisburg, in 1745. He died in 1781, aged 78.

opportunity of coming in the ship which I have ordered to wait upon the gentlemen of the Council and Mr. Speaker, and the gentlemen of the House who go up to Boston, and to attend upon Mr. Wheelwright and the other three gentlemen, to bring them hither.

I hope you will transmit to me what public letters or accounts of public affairs you shall judge proper to be communicated to me here, from time to time, how matters go on, and to revive your letters upon any subject.

I am with truth, sir, your faithful friend and humble servant,

W. SHIRLEY.

To Hon. Secretary WILLARD.

July 14th, being Sunday, Parson Smith mentions:

Mr. Brockwell preached; he gave great offence as to his doctrine. Our fishermen have all fled home, allarmed with the news of a French war proclaimed at Halifax.

Parson Smith continues:

July 19th. The ships returned. Mr. Wheelwright, Lincoln and Minot of the Council, Hancock and others.

This was Thomas Hancock, chairman of the committee of the Plymouth Company for the construction of the fort at Cushenoc.

The journal continues:

July 23d. The Governor dined at Col. Cushing's — the rain prevented me.

28th. Capt. Osborn sailed for Boston, having paid me near one hundred pounds for my house.

August 30th. The Governor and the gentlemen with him sailed in Saunders* for Kennebec.

* This Capt. Saunders deserves a special notice. His name appears on all occasions where there is any freighting to be done for the province. He commanded the armed sloop Massachusetts, which was constantly in commission. Thos. Saunders was an inhabitant of Gloucester, Cape Ann. His name appears in the province service in 1725. At the siege of Louisburg, in 1745, he commanded the province sloop of war, and received

Parson Smith records: "Sept. 3d. The Governor returned from Kennebec." It will be well to note that Mr. Smith mentioned on the thirtieth of August that the Governor, and gentlemen with him, sailed for Kennebec. The date of his return shows that he had been absent only four days.

The Governor wrote the same day from Falmouth, to Secretary Willard, "I finished my business at the two places, Cushenoc and Taconett, and arrived at this place last night, having, for the sake of expedition, proceeded from Taconett to Falmouth in the Castle pinnace* and left the sloop to follow me with several of the gentlemen."

a special letter of thanks from Commodore Warren. In 1761, he was sent by Governor Barnard to convey Prof. Winthrop, of Harvard College, to New Foundland, to observe the transit of Venus. He died in 1774, aged 70. Thomas Saunders, son of the captain, married Lucy, daughter of Parson Smith.

* The only "castle" within the Governor's jurisdiction was Castle William, Boston harbor, now Fort Independence, and the "Castle pinnace," in which the Governor came from Kennebec, was probably the small vessel used by the officers of the garrison to go up to town. She would now be called a yacht. How the pinnace came to be at Kennebec, is, I think, explained by the following circumstance: The council records mention the sending of a dispatch by express to Governor Shirley, while he was in the eastern country. Accompanying it was an order to Enoch Freeman, captain of the fort at Falmouth, saying that, if the Governor was gone to Kennebec, to forward the dispatch to him there. The Castle pinnace was probably a fast vessel, and as nearly all communication with Maine was then by water, she was sent as a dispatch vessel. On her arrival at Falmouth, Captain Freeman undoubtedly thought the most expeditious way to convey the dispatch, was to send the same vessel to Kennebec with it. We have seen that the letter from Sir Thomas Robinson, secretary of state, to the Governor, was dated at London, July 5th, and it will also be recollected that the Governor, in his letter of July 8th, directed Secretary Willard to forward to him all dispatches of a public nature while he was absent. Probably Sir Thomas Robinson's dispatch to the Governor was brought by the Castle pinnace to Kennebec.

In the Governor's letter to Secretary Willard he referred him to the Governor's son,* who had accompanied the expedition to the head waters of the Kennebec, and was the bearer of his father's letter. On his arrival in Boston, young Shirley communicated the result of the march to the newspaper, by which it is preserved for us.

From the Boston *Gazette* of Tuesday, September 8, 1754:

On Saturday last, John Shirley, Esq., son of His Excellency, our Governor, arrived here from Falmouth in Casco Bay, by whom we have the following account, viz: That the forces under General Winslow set out from Teconnett with something more than 500 men and 15 battoes, on the eighth of August past, but after proceeding two days up the river, the General was taken so ill that he was obliged to return, leaving the command, with the instructions to him, with Col. Preble, who on the 10th, at nine in the morning, proceeded with thirteen battoes, one-half the men on one side, and the other half on the other side of the river, and on Tuesday, the thirteenth, arrived at Norridgewalk, which is thirty-one miles above Teconnet, beautifully situated, near 400 acres of clear land, on which the grass is generally five or six feet high. Here they found six Indian men, three squaws and several children, who appeared at first surprised to see such a number of men and battoes so far advanced into their country, but after they were told by Col. Preble that they had nothing to fear from him, that none of his men should hurt the least thing they had, nor go into their houses, and that Governor Shirley had ordered they should be treated with civility and kindness, they appeared well satisfied and were kind and friendly; and Passequeant, one of their chiefs, presented him with two fine salmon, and some squashes of their own pro-

* From Council records, page 281:

" FALMOUTH, August 29, 1754.

"The forces being returned from their march to the Kennebec River, the result of which you will hear from my son, I shall be at Boston in less than a fortnight.

"JOSEPH WILLARD, ESQ.   WM. SHIRLEY.

"If there is any necessity for issuing papers I will send power of attorney."

duce, and were all very free in drinking King George's and Governor Shirley's health, and told him he was welcome there. They camped that night half a mile above the town, and the next day, leaving the battoes there with a detachment sufficient to guard them, they proceeded on their march to the great carrying place between Kennebec and the river Chaudiere, where the French were said to be building a fort, and arrived there on the eighteenth, which is thirty-eight miles and three-quarters above Norridgewalk, a few miles below which they met three birch canoes with eight Indians in them, who had lately come over the carrying place, and as they supposed from Canada. The Indians were much surprised on discovering the party, and endeavored to return up the river with their canoes, but the rapidity of the stream prevented their speedy flight, on which they run the canoes on shore, on the opposite side of the river, catched one of them up and ran off into the woods, leaving the other two on the spot, and made their escape to the carrying place, and so returned to Canada, to carry intelligence, as Col. Preble supposed, for he tracked them in his march across the said carrying place; the course of which from the head of the Kennebec River is due west, and the distance three miles, three-quarters and twenty-two rods, to a pond about two miles long and one and a half miles wide; beyond that there is another carrying place of about one mile, which leads to another pond, that runs into the Chaudiere.

They returned from the first mentioned pond the same day, and came to Norridgewalk the twenty-first of August, early in the day, where they found Capt. Wright and the detachment under his command all well, and thirty-five Indians, old and young, who, upon the knowledge of Colonel Preble's return, dressed themselves up in their way very fine, *by putting on clean shirts and painting and decorating themselves with wampum.* They saluted him with a number of guns and three cheers, and then a number of them waited on him at the camp, welcomed him back, and seemed to express a good deal of satisfaction at his return.

After drinking King George's and Governor Shirley's health, they invited him to their houses, and ten or twelve of their chiefs desired a short conference with him; and after having cleared the house of young men, who diverted themselves, meanwhile, playing ball, &c.,

told him that he had passed and re-passed through their country, they were glad to see him come back, and he was heartily welcome; and they had told him, before he went, there was no French settlement at the carrying place, and since he had been there and found it so, hoped he would now look upon them as true men; and that we were now all one brothers; and if their young men should get in liquor and affront any of the English, hoped we should take no notice of it, that they were determined to live in friendship with us; and if the Canada Indians had any design to do any mischief on our frontiers, they would certainly let us know it; and if any disputes arose betwixt the French and us, they were determined for the future to sit still and smoke their pipes.

The Colonel told them the resolution they had taken would be very pleasing to Governor Shirley, and as long as they kept their faith with us they might depend on being treated as friends and brethren, and be supplied with all the necessaries at Teconnet, which would be much more convenient than at Richmond; all of which they told they liked very well; and were sorry they had no liquor to treat them with, but desired he would see their young men dance and they ours, which they said was a token of friendship, and was accordingly performed.

Next morning, on the Colonel's taking his leave of them, they wished him safe to Teconnet, and saluted him with thirty or forty small arms, as fast as they could load and discharge.

The army arrived at Teconnet on Friday, the twenty-third of August, at five o'clock in the afternoon, having been sixteen days on the march [History of Augusta says ten]. As to the course of the river into the country, it must be referred until a plan of the same, which has been taken by a skillful surveyor, shall appear. The soil, for the most part, is extremely good and appears to be fertile. There are many beautiful islands in the river, some of which contain near a thousand acres of intervale; but the land is not plentifully supplied with timber.

The navigation to Norridgewalk is considerably difficult by reason of the rapidity of the stream and rippling falls, but 't is likely will be much easier when the water is higher. There is but one fall above Teconnet Falls that is necessary to carry the battoes around before we come to Norridgewalk, betwixt which and the carrying place the navigation is vastly better than below, there being only two falls to carry round, one of which, notwithstanding it is a mile in length, there is a plain beaten path; the other is not above thirty or forty rods.

Later historians all concur in the erroneous assertion that Governor Shirley accompanied the exploring expedition to the head waters of the Kennebec. It was brought about a little at a time, in this way.

Minot, 1803, II., p. 186, says:

The Governor then (that is, after the treaty) proceeded to the building of the fort at Taconett Falls, and explored the river up to the great carrying place between the Kennebec and Chaudiere.

Holmes, II., p. 202, three years later, says:

The Governor proceeded to explore the Kennebec about forty miles above Norridgewog.

Williamson's history, 1832, II., p. 300, says:

He [Gov. Shirley] proceeded to Taconnet and ascended the river as far as Norridgewock.

Parson Smith, in his journal, notes: "Aug. 30th. The Governor sailed for Kennebec." In his revised edition of the journal, 1849, p. 229, Mr. Willis distrusts Mr. Smith's accuracy, and, to make the journal harmonize with later historians, says: "This date should be July 30."

In the History of Portland, 1865, p. 249, Mr. Willis still doubts the accuracy of Parson Smith, and asserts that "The Governor continued in this neighborhood until *July* 30th, when he sailed for the Kennebec, and proceeded to Teconnet and marked out the site of a fort."

The "Materials for a history of Fort Halifax," in Vol. VII., of Maine Historical Collections, contains an extract from Governor Shirley's message to the house, October 18th, which is correctly copied, until it comes to the Governor's account of his visit to the forts on the last days of August, when, like Mr. Willis, the editor seems to distrust the Governor's language and substitutes his own. He says, p. 176 :

The Governor also states that with five hundred men he went up the river seventy-five miles to the great carrying-place, and explored both sides; that the time occupied was ten days.

To set all this right, and make it tally with the facts, it is only necessary to note the Governor's letter to Secretary Willard on his return, the vote of the council advising his stay at Falmouth, and his message to the house, on the eighteenth of October ; of all of which copies are here given :

FALMOUTH, CASCO BAY,* Sept. 3, 1754.

Finding it necessary, too, for the public service upon which I came down here that I should visit the two forts at Cushenoc and Taconnet before I returned to Boston, I sent for Capt. Saunders and embarked on board the Province sloop, on Friday, thirtieth of August, about five in the afternoon; finished my business at those two places and arrived at this place (where I likewise have some business to settle) about ten o'clock last night.

Yours,

Mr. Sec. WILLARD.   W. SHIRLEY.

Council records, 25th July, 1754 :

COUNCIL AT FALMOUTH, COUNTY OF YORK, 27th July.

Resolved unanimously, That His Excellency stay in Falmouth until Major General Winslow's return from his march up to the head of Kennebeck River, and as long afterwards as His Excellency shall judge proper *upon the advice he shall receive from the march to the head of Kennebeck River*.

In Governor Shirley's message to the House of Representatives, October 18, 1754, he says :

As to the nine days which the troops remained encamped on Bang's Island, from the time of their arrival at Casco Bay to the day of their

*In the provincial documents, when Falmouth, Maine, was mentioned, " Casco Bay " was annexed, to distinguish it from Falmouth, a seaport in Barnstable County.

embarcation for Kennebeck, I did not think it proper that they should proceed to execute any part of the intended service before I had finished the conference with Norridgewock Indians, though I had determined to have the march made to the head of Kennebeck River and half way over the carrying-place, and to have the forts erected at Taconnett and Cushenoc, whether they gave their consent or not; yet that might have given them or the French too much colour to have taxed us with stealing an opportunity to march through the country of the Norridgewocks and build forts upon the Kennebeck, whilst we had drawn them to Falmouth and engaged them in a treaty with us there.   Such a reproach would have ill suited the honor of this government; wherefore, now we have obtained a formal treaty, not only to our doing this, but to make new settlements upon the river, to all of which they were ever before, and even at the beginning of the late conference, greatly averse.   And besides, I am persuaded that this appearance of the troops at Casco contributed not a little to our gaining this consent from them. . . . . . Though the troops, gentlemen, found no French settlement to be removed, yet by their late march on both sides of the river Kennebeck to the head of it, and to the first pond on the carrying-place, you have probably prevented them from attempts to make one there. . . . . .

We see that the Governor remained at Falmouth during the time occupied by General Winslow and his troops in the building of a part of the fort, the march to the portage, and the making of eighteen miles of wheel road between the two new forts, being fifty-six days.   With him was a quorum of the council.   The frigate Massachusetts was running as a dispatch and passenger vessel between Falmouth and Boston, for the accommodation of the council and the other gentlemen connected with the government.

Governor Shirley also arranged an express route to Fort Halifax by whale boats, by which dispatches could be transmitted in twenty-four hours and return in twenty hours.   This was probably by the way of Casco bay and New Meadows river to Brunswick, thence through Merrymeeting bay to the Kennebec. This became necessary, as the announcement was daily expected of war between England and France, which Parson Smith mentions as being already known at Halifax.

The Governor remained at Falmouth from the third to the eighth of September, when he sailed for Boston. His embarkation is thus recorded by Parson Smith: "September 8th. The Governor sailed with Col. Mascarene, Mr. Brockwell, Mr. Wheelwright, Richmond, Gerrish, Minot and Price. Thus ends a summer scene of as much bluster as a Cambridge Commencement, and now comes on a vacation when our house and the town seem quite solitary." We can readily imagine the change. The town had, for ten weeks, been the headquarters of a large number of the dignitaries of the provincial government, with the commissioners from New Hampshire and Nova Scotia ; these officials were then invested by the people with much more dignity and splendor than now. The representatives of two dreaded Indian tribes swelled the pageant, who closed the treaty with a dance, in all their paint and feathers. All this bustle and parade in the little town of one thousand inhabitants, unused to such scenes ! A man-of-war was anchored in front of the town, which, with the fort, announced every movement of the Governor, as the custom then was, with guns and flags.

Those royal governors were not like the modest, unostentatious chief magistrates of our time. When they arrived at Boston, from any distant official service, they first landed at the castle and waited for an enthusiastic reception to be arranged for the next day, when they embarked under a salute of the castle guns and the men-of-war in the harbor, and landed at Long wharf under another salute, where the " Governor's company of Cadets " received and escorted them to the Province house. Governor Shirley arrived at the castle on the ninth of September, and after all this parade took charge of the government the next day.

We must now take leave of Governor Shirley in connection with the eastern country. The subsequent career of this remarkable man claims our notice. He had weightier matters on his hands than the defences of Maine. He had, since November, been in correspondence with the home government, and Governor Lawrence of Nova Scotia, concerning an intended expedition to reduce the French fort at Chignecto, Nova Scotia, the building of which the English claimed was an encroachment.

In a letter to Governor Lawrence, at Halifax, dated December 14th, he wrote : " I have for several days had an inevitable load on my hands. It is now eleven at night, and I have been writing ever since seven in the morning to dispatch a London ship waiting for my letters, and can scarce hold my pen in my hand."

During the winter, Governor Shirley, with Colonel Moncton, of the British army, and Provincial General Winslow, raised two thousand New England troops for, and fitted out the Bay of Fundy expedition against the French forts, which sailed from Boston on the twenty-second of May. The Governor was also raising and fitting out another expedition for Oswego, of which he took command, after being commissioned a major-general. He left Boston for that place on the twenty-eighth of June. General Braddock was killed and his army defeated on the Monongahela, on the ninth of July. Among the officers killed in that action was William Shirley, son of the Governor, who was Braddock's secretary. By the death of Braddock, General Shirley. became commander-in-chief of the army in America. He was

an officer of great energy and perseverance, but, having failed
in an expedition against Crown Point, in 1756, he was superseded by Abercrombie, and was ordered to England.   However, he was finally cleared of the charges against him.

Governor Shirley's first wife (to whose family influence it
is said he owed his first advancement) was Frances Barker,
born in London, in 1692, and died in Dorchester, Massachusetts, in 1746.   She was the mother of the Governor's four
sons and five daughters.   She has a mural tablet in King's
Chapel, with her family arms and a lengthy Latin inscription.

In 1749, Governor Shirley was appointed by the Crown,
commissioner to France, to settle the boundary of Acadia.
While he was in Paris, on the commission, he secretly married
a young Roman Catholic, the daughter of his landlord.
This injudicious alliance subsequently caused him much
mortification and regret.   In 1759, he was made lieutenant-
general, and, after long solicitation, was appointed governor
of the Bahama Islands, in which he was succeeded by his son
Thomas.   He was the author of several pamphlets on the
French Wars, and, in 1748, devised the scheme of establishing a British colony in Nova Scotia (the inhabitants were
then all French), which was carried out the next year by the
founding of the city of Halifax.   Governor Shirley was born
in England, in 1693, where he practiced law, came to Boston
in 1735, and pursued his profession until his appointment as
governor of the Massachusetts Province, in 1741.   At the
appointment of his son to succeed him in the government of
the Bahamas, he returned to Massachusetts, and died at
Roxbury, in 1771, aged seventy-eight.   He was buried with
military honors in his family vault, under King's Chapel, in
Boston.   This church was rebuilt mainly by his exertions.
The corner-stone was laid by him in 1752.

Minot says of Governor Shirley, "Although he held some of the most lucrative offices within the gift of the Crown in America, he left nothing to his posterity but a reputation, in which his virtues greatly outweighed his faults."

The Suffolk Probate Court records show that he died intestate.

Governor Shirley's residence, erected in about 1748, was in Roxbury, and was called Shirley place.

F. A. Drake says, " It became, in 1764, the property of Judge Eliakim Hutchinson, Shirley's son-in-law. Long afterwards it became the home of Governor Eustis. Washington, Franklin, Lafayette, Webster, Clay, Calhoun and Burr were numbered among its distinguished guests."

It is now (1885) rented in several tenements. It is of wood, two stories, with windows on the roof, and a cupola and vane. It rests on a high basement of dressed granite. The wide veranda at the rear remains, but that formerly on the front has been removed. The main entrance is reached by a long and wide flight of freestone steps. The parlors have been divided by partitions, but the elaborate finish and original ample size can be seen. The spacious entrance hall is the grandest of the old suburban houses of Boston. The stair-case is of easy circular ascent; the stair-rail, with a generous scroll at the bottom, is of the richest St. Domingo mahogany, inlaid with various colored woods, and the balusters are artistically carved.

The extract below shows that Governor Shirley had a fatherly care for the interest of his children. It is from the Nova Scotia Archives.

Extract from a letter from Governor Shirley to Governor Lawrence, of Nova Scotia, relating to the expedition to drive the French out of that Province. It is dated Boston, January 6, 1755:

16

"Your Honor hath, I perceive, given Colonel Moncton (who was enlisting men, ordering supplies and transports in Boston,) unlimited credit upon Messrs. Apthorp and Hancock, and he looks upon himself confined by that to those gentleman for every article to be provided for this expedition. . . . . . My kindness still remains for them, and we are upon exceedingly good terms; but as I have a daughter lately married to a merchant here, who is a young gentleman of extreme good character, and for whose fidelity and honor in his dealing I can be answerable, of some capital, and eldest son to a merchant of the largest fortune of any one in Boston, I think I shall not do anything unreasonable by Mr. Apthorp and Hancock, if I request your Honour to let my son-in-law, Mr. John Erving, be joined with them in furnishing money and stores for this expedition upon the same terms they do."

The register of King's Chapel shows that Robert Temple, son of the elder Robert, who had deceased, was married to Harriet Shirley, daughter of the Governor, one month after the movement in the House of Representatives to build Fort Halifax. Young Robert Temple was by inheritance a large proprietor in the Plymouth Company.

The John Erving, who married Shirley's daughter, Maria Catherina, was the father of Dr. Shirley Erving, a practicing physician, who came to Portland in 1789. He connected an apothecary shop with his practice, which was large. He was the architect of old St. Paul's brick church, built in 1802. He returned to Boston in 1811, and died there in 1813.

From the following document on file at the Boston State House, we must conclude that a large quantity of powder was burnt in honor of the Governor during the ten weeks of his stay at Falmouth. Major Enoch Freeman "captain of the battery in Falmouth Casco bay," petitioned Governor Shirley and the council for repairs and supplies in these words :

The following things at this juncture are necessary and wanting for the said battery viz. more guns, shot and powder. The walls and guardhouse to be clapboarded. The flanker door to be repaired. A new gate at the entrance. The watch box wants repairing. New gun carriages all but one. Windows for the guardroom chamber, and cartridge paper, and a new flag thirty one feet long and seventeen feet deep.

The store of powder having been expended on the occasion of your excellencys late visit.

The Governor entered his approval of Major Freeman's petition on the back of it, and recommended to the council to grant the stores and repairs asked for, which was done.

From all these documents we learn that what Major Freeman called a "battery" simply, was an extensive work with all the necessary buildings for a permanent garrison, and that he had a laudable pride in his large English flag.

We can learn very little of the subsequent history of the fort without a name, except that Parson Smith, says, "Oct. 16, 1759. The cannon were fired at the fort yesterday and to day." This was rejoicing for the surrender of Quebec to the English. A great event for the frontier District of Maine. When Mowatt threatened to burn the town in October, 1775, in reply to a committee, he proposed to grant a respite if the four pieces of cannon then in the town were surrendered to him. Two of these were, probably, all that remained of the armament of the fort. The other two undoubtedly were those that belonged to Captain Pearson. My reason for this conclusion is the assertion of Governor Sullivan, who wrote, in 1795, that on the arrival of another armed ship in the harbor, after the burning, that "the people fitted two six pounders in a battery, which were all they had."

The most considerable event of the administration of Governor Shirley, and, indeed, the greatest achievement of the colonies in the wars with France, was the siege and capture of Louisburg, on the Island of Cape Breton, in 1745. The expedition was projected by a Maine man, Captain William Vaughan, of Damariscotta, and the chief command was given to another man of Maine, Colonel William Pepperell, of Kittery, who was knighted on the occasion of the success. Moses Pearson, of Falmouth, was in command of a company, of whom about fifty were enlisted here. Parson Smith says, "February 22, 1745, all the talk is about the expedition to Louisburg. There is a marvelous zeal and concurrence through the whole country with respect to it: such as the like was never seen in this part of the country."

Beside being honored with knighthood, General Pepperell was presented by the corporation of London with a dinner service of silver and a silver side table on which to display it. To my knowledge, there is no published description of this numerous table service, or the table which was made to bear it. At the time of its arrival at Kittery Point, there was, probably, no set of plate in New England approaching it in extent or elegance. It descended with the title, by will, to Sir William's grandson, young Sparhawk, on condition that he assumed the name of his grandfather. By the confiscation act of 1777, this plate was allowed to be taken from the Pepperell mansion at Kittery, and transported by land to Boston, whence it was shipped to England to its owner, who was a refugee. Colonel Moulton with six mounted soldiers was ordered to guard its conveyance to Boston for shipment. Two or three pieces of the Pepperell plate were presented to individuals and are still preserved. I have recently obtained from Baltimore, a manuscript written in 1846, by a lady of York, formerly a resident of Portland, describing the Pepperell mansion at Kittery Point, as she knew it in her girlhood, when it contained the plate and portraits. She was born in 1759, and consequently was eighteen years old when the plate was taken from the Pepperell house. This lady was a granddaughter of Judge Sayward, of York, and was intimate with the residents of the Pepperell mansion from childhood to womanhood. She was eighty-two years of age when she wrote. The manuscript was preserved at the Wentworth house, Little Harbor, by Mrs. Charles Cushing, for whom it was written at her request. The writer of the manuscript died in 1855, aged ninety-five years.

At the death of Mrs. Cushing, the manuscript, which is very valuable, passed to other hands. Beside the description of the Pepperell home, as she knew it one hundred and ten years ago, there is much other matter of interest which I hope to make public in another connection. The description of the London plate and silver table on which it was displayed, though brief, is of interest, as it is the only authentic one extant. It is in these few lines :

The City of London presented him [General Pepperell] with a service of plate, and a table of solid silver. *I have seen them;* the table was very narrow, but long, and the articles were very numerous, but of small dimensions. The tureen did hold more than three pints.

Then follows an account of the transportation to Boston by Sheriff Moulton. While in London, George II. honored Sir William with a commission of lieutenant-general in the royal army, bearing date February 20, 1759 ; an honor never before conferred on a native of America. Previous to this, the Duke of Newcastle and Lord Halifax had twice sent him the king's commission of a colonel in the royal army, and in 1756 that of a major-general.

Before he achieved the victory of Louisburg, Colonel Pepperell long held the highest office in the gift of the people, that of president of the governor's council. The colonial council of that day was not a mere executive council like those which exist in Massachusetts and Maine, under their present constitutions, but a co-ordinate and independent branch of the colonial legislature. It was composed of twenty-eight members, a larger number than the senate of the United States contained at the adoption of the Constitution, and was analogous to the senates of our own day.

In May, 1759, Governor Pownal, of Massachusetts, visited Sir William Pepperell at his residence in Kittery, on the occasion of his dangerous illness. The Governor was escorted across New Hampshire, by order of its governor, by a "troop of horse." Sir William died on the sixth of July, 1759. The manuscript from which I have been quoting gives this description of the funeral:

I have said so much of Sir William that I must mention his death. I cannot say what year that event took place, but I know the funeral was such as had never been witnessed in the country. The body lay in state a week. The house was hung with black — every picture in the mansion of Mrs. Sparhawk (his daughter,) was wound with crape, and all of a sable hue.* A sermon was delivered at the meeting-house. The pews were covered with black; the procession was the largest ever known — two oxen were roasted but not whole; bread, beer, and spirits were given to all the common people; while rich wines, with

* Usher Parsons, the biographer of Pepperell, says of the house of Sparhawk, near that of his father-in-law, Sir William: "The large hall of this mansion was lined with some fifty portraits of the Pepperell and Sparhawk families, and of the friends and companions-in-arms of Sir William."

In the manuscript so largely quoted from, written by the aged lady, is a poetical description of the Sparhawk house. It contains these lines:

> "Where rows of pictures set in goodly frames,
> Of squires and belted knights and stately dames,
> Hung on the walls now desolate and bare,
> Or patched with paper fluttering in the air."

richer viands covered the costly table in the house that had been the dwelling place of him who should know it no more.*

I have written this of Sir William Pepperell because, at the time of Louisburg, he was the foremost citizen of Maine, and, while he commanded the " Yorkshire regiment," the only one in Maine, he was frequently in Falmouth. He was here in 1744, then on his way with other commissioners to meet the Indians in a conference at St. Georges.

In 1718, William Pepperell, of Kittery, father of Sir William, purchased of Dominicus Jordan, one-half of Hog Island, which is thus described in the deed :

One half of an Island Called hogg Island lying & being in Casco Bay in y⁰ town of falmouth in y⁰ County Afores⁴ & lycth on

*Among Sir William's papers, in 1850, was found a bill for funeral expenses. One item is in these words: " Five gallons of rum, ten pounds of sugar, and half a pound of allspice, to make spiced rum." At that time and for a century later, rum was used at funerals as an assuager of grief. It was also offered as a refreshing drink to all visitors.

In September, 1746, Sir William was with Admiral Knowles returning from Louisburg, whither he had been with Governor Shirley to quiet the troops, who complained of detention. The squadron met a great storm, in which some ships were dismasted and others lost their guns. The Admiral was so long in repairing his ships in Boston that many of his men deserted. He obtained from the governor a warrant to fill up his crews by impressment. He took seamen from the merchant ships, and swept the wharves, taking mechanics and laborers. This caused a great riot. Pepperell, by his popularity and as president of the council, relieved Knowles from his dilemma, by promising the mob, in the name of the governor, that the inhabitants should be released. The Admiral felt very grateful to Pepperell for his service, and his gratitude found expression in the offer of the sovereign balm. He thus wrote from Jamaica to Sir William :

"I have sent you by Captain Andrews a box of sweetmeats, and desired Governor Shirley to send you a part of some good old rum I have sent him. You soon shall have a hogshead yourself, but I am nice, and therefore until I can meet with what is old, and choice, and good, I have deferred it for the present, but my friends have promised to get me some."

This shows the value set on choice spirits in those days.

y⁰ Northeast Side of y⁰ *Coming in to Portland* & Lyeth over against old Casco.

At that time the Neck had not been called "Portland." The sentence "coming into Portland" meant coming into "Portland sound." The earliest English name by which the island now called Bangs and the main-land opposite were known was "Portland," as was also the main channel between them and the anchorage at Hog Island called "Portland sound." The headland on which the lighthouse stands has ever been and is yet called "Portland head." From these localities was the name of the town adopted at its incorporation.

In 1743, although Nova Scotia had no English inhabitants, except the garrisons at Annapolis Royal and at a fort at Canso, which was a harbor of much resort by fishing vessels, the territory was the property of the Crown of Great Britain, and was in the care of the government of Massachusetts Province, to which it was joined by the charter of 1691. It was guarded with zealous care by the province, as the safety of their fishing vessels depended upon its possession. March 15, 1744, war was declared by France against England, and before the news could reach Boston, an armament was fitted out at Louisburg, Cape Breton, which assailed the fort at Canso. The garrison, consisting of ninety men, surrendered, and were carried to Louisburg, where they were held a short time as prisoners, until they were exchanged and arrived at Boston. Their arrival caused much resentment against the French. The Canso garrison, while at Louisburg, lost no opportunity to examine the defensive works of that stronghold of the French, as it was the key to the river St. Lawrence. Captain Vaughan was at Boston when the Canso men arrived, or he immediately went there, where he met them and learned that, in their opinion, the place might be taken.

Hutchinson's history (1795) says, "Mr. Vaughan, *who had been a trader at Louisburg*, was very sanguine that the place might be taken by surprise."

In his History of New Hampshire Dr. Belknap said, in 1784:

Vaughan had not been to Louisburg, but had learned, from fishermen and others, something of the strength of the place, and nothing being in his view impracticable, which he had a mind to accomplish, he conceived a design to take the city by surprise, and even proposed going over the walls in winter on drifts of snow. This idea of a surprisal forcibly struck the mind of Shirley, and prevailed with him to hasten his preparations, before he could have an answer or order from England. Governor Shirley laid his matured plan before the House in secret session. At the first deliberation the proposal was rejected, but by the address of the Governor, and the invincible perseverance of Vaughan, a petition of the merchants concerned in the fisheries was brought into court, which revived the affair, and it was carried in the affirmative by one voice, in the absence of several members who were known to be against it. Circular letters were immediately sent to all the colonies, as far as Pennsylvania, requesting their assistance, and an embargo on their ports. With one of these letters Vaughan rode express to Portsmouth, where the assembly was sitting. Governor Wentworth immediately laid the matter before them, and proposed a conference of the two houses, to be held the next day. The House of Representatives, having caught the enthusiasm of Vaughan, were impatient of delay, and desired that it might be held immediately. It was accordingly held and the committee reported in favor of the expedition.

In the army Vaughan was commissioned a lieutenant-colonel, but refused to have a regular command. He was appointed one of the council of war, and was ready for any service which the general might think suited to his genius. He conducted the first column through the woods in sight of the city, and saluted it with three cheers. He headed a detachment, and marched to the northeast part of the harbor, where they burnt the warehouses containing a large quantity of wine and brandy, and the naval stores. The smoke of this fire being driven by the wind into the Grand Battery so terrified the French that they abandoned it and retired to the city, after having spiked the guns and cut the halyards of the flagstaff.

The next morning, as Vaughan was returning with thirteen men only, he crept up the hill which overlooked the battery, and observed that the chimneys of the barracks were without smoke, and the staff without a flag. With a bottle of brandy, which he had in his pocket (though he never drank spirituous liquors), he hired one of his party, a Cape Cod Indian, to crawl in at an embrasure and open the gate. He then wrote to the General these words:

"May it please your honor to be informed, that by the grace of God and the courage of thirteen men, I entered the Royal Battery about nine o'clock, and am waiting for a reinforcement and a flag."

Before either could arrive, one of the men climbed up the staff with a red coat in his teeth, which he fastened by a nail to the top. This piece of triumphant vanity alarmed the city, and immediately an hundred men were dispatched in boats to retake the battery; but Vaughan with his small party on the naked beach, and in the face of a smart fire from the city and the boats, kept them from landing till the reinforcement arrived.

In every duty of fatigue and sanguine adventure he was always ready, and the New Hampshire troops, animated by his enthusiastic ardor, partook of all the labors and dangers of the siege.

Such is Belknap's account of Colonel Vaughan's services in the siege and its inception. Colonel Vaughan opened the fight, and fixed the standard of gallantry by his fearless resistance to the landing of the enemy, who were ten times his own number, and under a brisk fire from the city upon his little band standing on the open beach. This fearless exploit of "holding the fort," was the first success at Louisburg. It encouraged the troops in landing their siege guns through a dangerous surf, and in dragging them through a morass on timber sleds to prevent their sinking. In this service the troops were engaged fourteen successive nights in mud and water.

In the grand battery were found twenty-eight forty-two pound cannon, two eighteens and two hundred and eighty shells, with cannon balls and other munitions of war. This acquisition weakened the means of defence on the part of the French, and transferred to the English a powerful means of protection in the erection of their advanced batteries. This was an annoying, offensive work, all built and armed, to their hands. The French fired briskly on this battery from the citadel, with cannon and mortars, but Colonel Vaughan continued to drill the spikes from his guns, and, as fast as they were freed, he turned them on the city wall with success. And the Maine fisherman, millman, and merchant, who first conceived the plan to take Louisburg, captured the first guns, and was the first to batter its walls and gates.

This expedition was tinged with religious romance — in fact it had the air of a crusade. It was Protestant against Papist. It is said that a very zealous clergyman carried on his shoulder a hatchet for the purpose of destroying the images in the French churches. Deacon John Gray, of Biddeford, wrote thus to General Pepperell: "O that I could be with you and dear Parson Moody in that church, to destroy the images there set up, and hear the true gospel of our Lord and Saviour there preached." *

The Roman Catholic religion was viewed by New England as the leading element of the almost continual strife in which they had been involved with the natives. In the history of Wells and Kennebunk, Judge Bourne, the author, says, that the ministers of York County were assembled together at York, on the day of the capitulation, for prayer, that a blessing might attend the expedition. The Rev. Joseph Moody, of York Upper Parish, son of the chaplain with the army,

* After the surrender of the city, the Provincials held a Thanksgiving service in a French church within the walls. From this church a metallic cross was taken, which has been placed over the entrance to the library of Harvard College.

led the supplications in a prayer of two hours in length, for the speedy reduction of the city. In the midst of his prayer he exclaimed, "It is done. It is delivered into our hands," and went on blessing God for his mercies. On the return of the troops, it was verified that this remarkable exclamation was uttered at the same hour with the signing of the capitulation. Judge B. says: "Of the facts stated, there can be no doubt."

All are familiar with the result of this siege. The city capitulated on the sixteenth of June, after a siege of forty-seven days, which gave the captors two thousand French troops as prisoners, seventy-six cannon and mortars, six months' provisions, and an immense amount of other property. The loss to the besiegers was one hundred and thirty, and of the French three hundred were killed within the walls. General Pepperell threw into the city and batteries nine thousand cannon-balls and six hundred bombs, which made a complete wreck of the fortifications and city walls, which were thirty-five feet high on the land side. On entering the city, the extent and strength of its defences made it apparent that Vaughan misjudged in his plan to take the city by surprise, although many of the besiegers were of the opinion that, if the entire army had been landed and ready to follow Colonel Vaughan in the first movement, the city might have been taken at that time by storm.*

---

* A serious annoyance to Pepperell's soldiers in the batteries was the bursting of the old honeycombed guns. They were like the fowling gun described by Butler: "When aimed at duck or plover was wont to kick the owner over." These guns had "thundered at Quebec" in the expedition of Sir William Phips, in 1690.

Cotton Mather thus describes his bombardment: "He lay within pistol-shot of the enemy's cannon and beat them from thence, and very much battered the town, having his own ship shot through in almost a

The news of the surrender was received throughout New England with great enthusiasm. Rev. Mr. Smith's journal is the only source of information as to how the news was received on Falmouth Neck. He records as follows:

July 6. We had news today that Cape Breton was taken the 27th of last month. There is great rejoicing through the country. We fired our cannon five times and spent the afternoon at the fort rejoicing.

The next day was the Sabbath but the jubilee feeling could not be suppressed. The journalist records the facts with no word of censure for the desecration of the Sabbath day.

7th. Sunday. Our people on the Neck were again all day rejoicing, and extravagantly blew off a vast quantity of powder.

18th. Public thanksgiving on account of the success at Cape Breton.

In 1749, Captain Pearson, and forty-five others of his company, petitioned the general court for the grant of a township of land. In their petition they say, "Some of us were detained there for the defense of Louisburg, until relieved

hundred places with four-and-twenty-pounders, and yet not one man was killed on board him in this hot engagement, which continued the greatest part of that night and several hours of the day ensuing." This same William Phips was a Maine man. His attack on Quebec was the first regular bombardment attempted by the provincials. He had been in command of a British frigate where he had learned gunnery.

Josselyn says, "In 1631 Dr. Wilson gave 1000 pounds to New England with which they stored themselves with great guns." Among the Pyncheon papers is a document with this heading: "An account of certain ammunition etc. being a part of Mr. Wilsons gifts to public use, being shipped in the Griffin July 7 1634, and by order of general court, was appointed to be received by William Pyncheon." It is a fair supposition that many of Pepperell's guns dated back to Dr. Wilson's gift. Nearly every letter from Pepperell to Governor Shirley contained mention of bursted guns.

by his majesty's troops from Gibralter, being about sixteen months from the time of entrance into said service." Their petition was granted in 1750. The township was called " Pearsontown," and now is included in the town of Standish.

Soon after the peace concluded at Casco, in April, 1678, the former inhabitants began to return to their desolate farms, and many wished to have the resettlement made under some authority that would secure stability and quietness, although there was not a general unity of feeling. Massachusetts had purchased the territory of Maine and claimed the right of jurisdiction. Thomas Danforth, deputy-governor of the Bay Province, was appointed president of Maine, under the purchased Gorges' charter. The first general assembly at York, in 1680, appointed Anthony Brackett lieutenant of Falmouth, and Thaddeus Clark, ensign.

Fort Loyal had been hurriedly erected, and President Danforth came, like William the Conqueror to England, to grant and lot out the lands anew. With him came, by direction of the general court, Nathaniel Saltonstall and Edward Tyng as advisers; the latter to act as magistrate and military commander. He, like the old nobility of England, " came in with the Conqueror" and came to stay, and soon after he married a great-granddaughter of the first settler, which would seem to make their children, born here, legitimate Casconians.

Captain Edward Tyng's command of Fort Loyal has been alluded to in the account of Colonel Church's battle at Deering's Oaks,* in September, 1689. He had a lot and house at the south corner of what are now India and Com-

---

* To perpetuate the remembrance of the site of this well fought battle, the city, when it comes to need it, should obtain the Deering field in front of the mansion, and adjoining the creek, and name it *Battle Park.*

COMMODORE EDWARD TYNG.

By Blackburn.—1683-1755.

mercial streets. Benjamin York, in his deposition given in 1759, — seventy-eight years after the occurrence, — says, "George Bramhall was brought over after ye fight on Captain Bracketts farm, to the Neck near Fort Loyal, and put into Capt. Tyngs house, to the best of my remembrance, and died the next day of his wounds."

Beside his house near the fort, Captain Tying had two other houses in 1687, when his lands were re-surveyed by order of Governor Andross. At that time he lived on York above State street, on a lot of forty-four acres, which included what is now Park and State streets, their entire length. He, with Sylvanus Davis and Thaddeus Clark, were supporters of the administration of Andross, but the majority of the citizens were against him. Captain Tyng still held his office as councilor under Andross, who gave him a lieutenant-colonel's commission and a supervision of the fort at Pemaquid. At the abandonment of the eastern country, in 1690, he returned to Boston. After the conquest of Nova Scotia by Sir William Phips, in 1690, Colonel Tyng was appointed governor of Port Royal. Before his arrival there, the vessel was captured by a French frigate and the prisoners carried to Quebec, from there Colonel Tyng was carried to France where he died.

Edward, the third son of Colonel Edward, was born in Falmouth in 1683. He early went to sea. Preble's "Early Ship Building" says he commanded the ship Massachusetts, of twenty guns, in the Port Royal expedition of 1707. He was then only twenty-seven years old. In the summer of 1744, Captain Tyng was in command of the snow "Prince of Orange," of sixteen guns, for the protection of the provincial trade and fisheries. He fell in with a French privateer, the "De la Brotze," of eighteen guns and ninety-four men. A force every way superior to the snow.* After a sharp engagement the privateer struck his colors and Captain Tyng brought his prize into Boston, where his victory was much applauded. Several of the merchants of Boston presented to Captain Tyng a "silver cup" of the weight of about "one hundred ounces." It is yet an elegant piece of plate and bears this inscription: "To Edward Tyng Esq. commander of ye snow Prince of Orange; as an acknowledgement of his good service done the Trade, in taking ye first French Privateer, on this coast, the 24th of June, 1744; this plate is presented by several of ye merchants of Boston in New England."

This "plate," or "cup," would now be called a vase. It is thirteen inches high and nine broad at the brim. It is of hammered silver, and shows that the bottom was soldered in. The maker's name was Jacob Hurd. The vase is elegantly engraved with naval emblems, and the British flag. This piece of rich plate descended to Captain Tyng's son, Colonel William Tyng, of Falmouth, and was taken from his house by the country soldiery in 1775, who were assembled here and very disorderly on account of the presence in the harbor of Captain Mowatt in his ship.

In an account of these riotous proceedings against the Loyalists, written at Falmouth, on the twelfth of May, by Enoch Freeman to his son Samuel, who was secretary of the continental Congress, then sitting at Watertown, he says: "They have this day carried off Mr. Tyng's Bishop, a piece of plate said to be worth 500 pounds Old Tenor, and his laced hat, but they say they have only taken these things as

---

* A "snow" was brig rigged with a try-sail-mast abaft the mainmast and close to it, for the hoops of the try-sail to run up on in hoisting the sail, and to hold the strain when the sail was set.

SILVER VASE PRESENTED TO COMMODORE TYNG,

By Boston Merchants in 1744.

pawns to make the owner behave better." Why this vase was called "Tyng's Bishop," I have never heard explained. The present owners know nothing of that name, but say this was the piece of plate that was taken, which was notorious in the Tyng family. The vase was restored to Mrs. Ross, mother of Mrs. Tyng, by order of the provincial Congress.

Captain Tyng's family may have lived in Boston, but he was in partnership, and owned vessels and their cargoes with Phineas Jones, of Falmouth. His private account book shows charges to " Edward Tyng, Esq. To sundries supplied the snow Prince of Orange," showing that she was frequently at Falmouth. Also, 1744 (the year of the presentation of the vase), Captain Tyng is charged with "supplies for the schooners Falmouth, Little Hannah, and Spry." In 1743, Jones credited Tyng with "balance due pr. adjustment, 2200 pounds, 16, 6." In 1750, Jones charged Tyng with " Half the bad debts out standing this day *while in Partner-ship*, which you promised to allow, Old Tenor 2100 pounds, Lawful 1050."

Commodore Tyng was born in Falmouth, and these books show conclusively that he continued a citizen here until 1750. He held the westerly half of the forty-four acres inherited from his father. It descended to his heirs, who sold it to Joseph H. Ingraham, who opened State street through it in 1799, ninety-nine feet wide, and built the first house on that street, now standing near the east corner of Danforth street.

Captain Tyng's bravery and skill shown in the capture of the French privateer of superior force to his own, brought him into notice as a commander. When the conquest of Louisburg was resolved on the next year, public opinion was as unanimous in favor of him for commander of the naval

17

force, as it was in favor of Pepperell to command the army. He was made commodore, and Governor Shirley directed him to look up and purchase the largest vessel in the provinces for his flagship. He found one on the stocks nearly ready for launching, which, by additional strengthening, he made suitable to carry an armament of twenty-six guns. She was named the "Massachusetts Frigate." There was no difficulty in obtaining what the province afforded, which was necessary for this expedition. The act of the general court authorizing the project, also authorized its committee to enter store-houses and cellars and take provisions.

After the arrival of Commodore Tyng and his fleet of small vessels before the doomed city, Commodore Warren, of the royal navy, unexpectedly arrived with his Atlantic squadron, when Shirley ordered Tyng to take his orders from Warren. The loss of the principal naval command did not sour Commodore Tyng; he was foremost where any fighting was to be done.

On the thirtieth day of the siege and blockade of the city, a French sixty-four gun ship, having six hundred men and laden with military stores, attempted to run the blockade and enter the harbor, which, if she had been successful, would have very much relieved the garrison and prolonged the siege; perhaps into the long spell of bad weather which ensued, which would have compelled Pepperell's unsheltered troops to raise the siege. But fortune favored the provincials from the beginning. The French ship, the "Vigilant," was engaged by two of Warren's ships of the navy, whom she could outsail. She then was attacked by Commodore Tyng in his little hastily got up frigate. He, by his pluck and dash in the dark, gave the Frenchman the impression that

ANN WALDO,

Second wife of Commodore Edward Tyng.

By Blackburn.

the Massachusetts was a vessel of much more force than she really was, and he struck to her.

This feat of Tyng's gave him prestige with Warren, who offered him a commission of post captain in the British navy and the command of the Vigilant; which he declined, offering his age as the reason of his declining.

The Vigilant was manned with seamen from Pepperell's transports and army, and put into commission under Captain Douglas. A view of the Vigilant under sail, with the British flag at her stern, appears in Blackburn's portrait of Commodore Tyng, an engraving of which is here inserted. The smooth wooden cased spyglass without a joint, which he holds in his hand, and the sword which appears at his side are yet preserved by his heirs. The Vigilant was of superior force to any one of the besieging fleet.

The capture of the Vigilant produced a burst of joy in the army, and animated them with fresh courage to persevere. The loss of their supplies of ammunition and reinforcement produced a corresponding depression on the garrison of the city. On the fifteenth of June, after a siege of forty-six days, the city capitulated.

Commodore Tyng's first wife was the daughter of the noted Captain Cyprian Southack. She died in London without issue. In 1731, when nearly fifty, the Commodore married Ann, a daughter of Jonathan Waldo, of Boston, and sister of Brigadier Samuel Waldo. By her he had seven children. The mother died in 1754. She has a fine portrait by Blackburn, in the dress of her time, in the Tyng collection, a representation of which is presented.* Commodore Tyng died in Boston, of apoplexy, September 8, 1755, aged seventy-two.

* Before sun pictures came in, portrait painters' services were sought by most families, who had the means, far back in colonial times. Their

Three only of the Commodore's seven children lived to maturity. Ann died in 1756, a month only after her marriage to a British officer. Her portrait, in the character of a shepherdess, with crook and lamb, painted by Copley, hangs by that of her father and mother in a similar frame. Edward Tyng, son of Edward, died in England, in 1776, an officer in the British army and a bachelor.

The youngest of the three adult children of Commodore Edward Tyng was William. What Cotton Mather says of Sir William Phips and his twenty-one brothers, would, with equal propriety, apply to the children of Commodore Tyng. Mather says, " But equivalent to them all was William, the youngest." William Tyng, son of Edward, was born in Boston, August 17, 1739, and was eighteen years old at the death of his father. When he arrived at a proper age he opened a book store in Corn Hill. It is probable that he was frequently in Falmouth, to look after the twenty-two acres of valuable land left by his father, which had at least one house on it. It is now the most beautiful part of the city,

house furnishings were not considered complete without portraits of the family. There were fashionable and favorite painters of portraiture in capital towns. Boston was the metropolis of New England, and her artists, of course, were considered to be at the head of the profession.

Smybert was the first portrait painter of note in Boston. He was a Scotchman and came to Boston after traveling through Europe. There are thirty of his portraits there yet. He died in 1751. A year before that there had come to Boston a young artist, Jonathan B. Blackburn, whose father had been a traveling portrait painter in Connecticut. Young Blackburn, from his skill, succeeded Smybert as the painter of the quality. So similar are their styles that it is hard to distinguish them except by the date.

There are more than fifty portraits by Blackburn now known in and near Boston, all painted within fifteen years. He suddenly left Boston in 1765; Copley's friends said on account of young Copley's increasing success. Of him I shall speak further on.

ELIZABETH ROSS,

At the Age of Sixteen.

By Copley.—1751-1831.

having State street through its entire length. Jabez Fox and both the Bracketts, Thomas and Anthony, were his relatives; so he was not without kinsmen here. Although his parents lived in Boston at the time of his birth, William Tyng was to the manor born; being a descendant in the fifth generation from George Cleeves, the first settler of Falmouth.

In June, 1767, Moses Pearson, the first sheriff of Cumberland County, died, and in December of that year William Tyng was appointed his successor. His large land property here probably prompted him to apply for the office.

In 1769, Mr. Tyng married Elizabeth, the only child of Captain Alexander Ross, a ship master and merchant, who came here from Long-hope, Island of Orkney. His ancestors originally came from Rosshire, Scotland, in the time of the rebellion.

Captain Ross had died a few months previous to the marriage of his daughter. He opposed the match while living, having in view a more satisfactory one in the person of a rich Bostonian. The only person present, except Mrs. Ross and the minister,* was Elizabeth Tate, then in the protection of Madam Ross, whose name she bore, being only seven years old. She became the wife of Joseph H. Ingraham and died in Portland. I had the facts from her daughter now dead.

At the time of their marriage, Mr. Tyng was thirty-two and Miss Ross was eighteen. Her portrait by Copley painted in 1767, when she was but sixteen, is one of the Tyng por-

* Parson Smith records, November 3, 1769: "I married Tyng to Elizabeth Ross." Rev. Mr. Wiswall, minister of St. Paul's church, must have been sick or absent at the time, or he would have been called to officiate, as both the bride and her mother, and the bridegroom were prominent members of St. Paul's parish.

traits. It is in a very elaborate and richly carved frame.
She has a falcon on her finger, after the style of portraits in
the days when hawking was a sport of both sexes. The
frame suffered by exposure for three days in a field in the
rain storm that followed Mowatt's burning of the town, in
1775, but it is elegant yet. This is said by her heirs to have
been Copley's third portrait; but this must be a mistake, as
he began to paint portraits in 1752, when only fifteen years
old. Lieutenant-Colonel, afterward General, George Washington, while in Boston, in 1756, sat to Copley for a miniature.
The history of one of his early portraits will bear repeating
here.

Arthur Dexter tells the story in "The Artists of Boston,"
and gives an engraving of the picture.

In 1774, Copley took a step which changed the whole course of his
life. Some time previous he had painted a portrait of his half brother,
Henry Pelham, "The boy and squirrel." The painter sent it to England, to be exhibited at Somerset House. A letter which should have
accompanied it did not arrive; and West, to whom it was consigned,
could only guess it was an American picture from the wood of the
stretching frame, and because the flying-squirrel is an American
animal. In his enthusiasm he declared the coloring worthy of Titian.
The rule excluding anonymous works was waived and the picture was
received. The praise of the best judges reached his friends in
America; they urged him to go to London. It was a bold step, and
he hesitated long before taking it, but finally he went and never
returned.

Copley's success in London is a matter of history. He
painted the portraits of the nobility including three prin-
cesses, daughters of George III., and several very large
historical pictures, one of which now hangs in Boston Public
Library. He had a son, Lord Lyndhurst, who was thrice
lord chancellor of England. Copley died in 1815.

COL. WILLIAM TYNG,

(In Gold Locket).

The hands of his subjects are well shaped and delicately molded. His draperies are admirable. His pictures show the faces and forms of the aristocrats of Boston and of New England. Almost every great man of his day is found in the list of his sitters, so that some one has said that one of these ancestral pictures is a New Englander's best title of nobility. I am pleased to be able to insert here engravings of some of his portraits, of undoubted authenticity; particularly as they represent a prominent family of old Falmouth. The owners of the miniature portrait of Colonel William Tyng, in a gold locket, are not sure that it is by Copley; but he was the only known painter of miniatures in Boston at the time it was executed. The sitting of Colonel Washington to him in 1756, for a miniature, is good evidence that he had an established reputation as a painter of that style of pictures.

This is the only existing likeness of Colonel Tyng. On its reverse side, under glass, is a lock of his hair bound with a string of pearls. The picture is painted on ivory, and was probably a present to Elizabeth Ross before marriage. The gold loop at the top of the locket shows that it was intended to be worn suspended from the neck by a chain or ribbon, and sometimes placed in the lady's belt with her watch. This was the fashion in their time and after, until the sun pictures became so common as to supersede the expensive and elegantly mounted miniatures.

Colonel Tyng was the first "master" of Portland Lodge of Freemasons, then Falmouth Lodge 1769, and afterward of the Ancient Landmark Lodge. His life size portrait, in oil, hung in the lodge room until it was consumed in the great fire. It had no merit as a work of art.

While Colonel Tyng was sheriff of the county he was also in business as a merchant. Smith's journal has this entry:

"1771, Oct. 28. We are in a great toss by the seizure of Tyng's schooner by a tender."

The collector of revenue, Francis Waldo, was absent in Europe, and Arthur Savage, controller and naval officer, next in authority, ordered an armed revenue vessel to seize Mr. Tyng's schooner for a breach of the revenue laws. These laws were odious to the people, and they mobbed the controller for the act. Dr. Deane says in his diary, "Dec. 11. Warrant from Judge Lynde to bind over Stone, Armstrong, and Sanford for riot." This was Benjamin Lynde, of Salem, judge of the superior court, who held one term annually in Falmouth. Four years later, Colonel Tyng was the obnoxious man seized by the mob, although he had been elected representative to the general court in 1771 and 1772.

Colonel Tyng lived with his wife's mother, Madam Ross, who had a house on the south corner of Middle and what is now Franklin street. In October, 1769, Dr. Deane mentions the raising of Colonel Tyng's house adjoining above on Middle street. It was a well built wooden house of two stories, without exterior ornament. Here Colonel Tyng lived until his loyalty to the crown made it unpleasant, if not unsafe, for him to remain here. He had accepted a commission of colonel from Governor Gage, in 1774.

Because Colonel Tyng held a commission as colonel from Governor Gage, and had taken the usual oath to uphold the Crown, he was looked upon with suspicion by the popular party. We have learned, within the last quarter of a century, to place a higher value on men who have dared to keep their oaths of allegiance. It was not to be expected that one who had taken repeated oaths of allegiance to the king and government of Great Britain, and who, for years, had in the prayers of his church acknowledged that allegiance and

REVERSE OF THE TYNG LOCKET.

(Hair and Pearls.)

besought for blessings on the reigning monarch, should easily swerve to the popular side.

The result of the vote of the town of Falmouth in February, inviting other towns to choose delegates to meet theirs, was that a county convention was held at Mrs. Greele's little one story tavern, in Falmouth, on the twenty-first day of September, 1774.

This was the first political county convention held in Cumberland, of which the record has been preserved. It was composed of thirty-three delegates from the nine old towns of the county. Although a hundred and eleven years have intervened since it was held, there has been no improvement on the course then adopted to secure a true expression of the popular will. The people of the country towns chose their delegates who attended, and they then went themselves to see that their delegates obeyed their instructions, as the record shows. After organizing, by the choice of the Hon. Enoch Freeman, for chairman, and his son, Samuel Freeman, for clerk, the record says, "A committee from the body of the people, who were assembled at the entrance to the town, waited on this convention to see if they would choose a committee of one out of each town, to wait on Mr. Sheriff Tyng, to see whether he would act in his office under the late acts of Parliament for regulating the government." By these acts the appointment of all civil officers was taken from the people and vested in the Crown.

Sheriff Tyng was summoned before the convention and attended, and subscribed to a written declaration "that he would not, as sheriff of the county or otherwise, act in conformity to, or by virtue of, said acts, unless by the general consent of said county." This declaration was voted to be satisfactory to the convention.

While these proceedings were going on in the convention, the people from the country had marched to the town house. The record continues: " The convention then formed themselves into a committee to accompany Mr. Sheriff Tyng to the body of the people, to present the declaration." The people " voted it satisfactory, and, after refreshing themselves, returned peaceably to their own homes," after a brief session.

The convention met again in the afternoon, and a committee, of whom Samuel Freeman was chairman, reported a long and spirited preamble and resolutions, which were adopted. The second resolution would, if carried out now, be a public benefit. It was as follows: " That every one would do his utmost to discourage lawsuits, and likewise compromise disputes as much as possible." " Each member was interrogated separately, and pledged himself not to accept any commission under the late acts of parliament."

From the time of the county convention, the excitement against the home government increased and men were compelled to take sides. Excitable men engaged in personal rencontres. Colonel Tyng became involved in such a one, in 1775, with his friend Brigadier Preble, who was also passionate. Dr. Deane gives an account of it, but does not give all the facts as they have been related to me by old men who were familiar with the history of the quarrel. Parson Smith does not mention it, probably from family reasons. There are now no susceptibilities to be wounded by giving all the facts.

It was a casual meeting in the street. From political matters the controversy became personal. Preble called Tyng hard names, and, in resentment, Tyng accused Preble of being the father of Sarah Smith's first child, who was born too soon after her marriage to be the legitimate son of Deacon Codman, her husband, who so declared, but he condoned her offence. Mr. Willis, in a pencil note in his interleaved volume of his own publication, in the public library, mentioned the popular belief of the parentage. After threats by both combatants, Colonel Tyng asked pardon for his rashness, which General Preble granted, and they shook hands.

Soon after the difficulty with Preble, Tyng went to Boston, leaving his wife with her mother. In June he came back in Captain Coulsen's ship and took his wife away, by permission of the committee of safety. In March, 1776, when General Howe with his forces left Boston, Colonel Tyng went to New York, which was then occupied by the British forces. Here he remained until the evacuation of the city by Lord Howe in November, 1783.

At New York, Colonel Tyng had the opportunity to display those traits of Christian charity and benevolence which pertained to his amiable disposition. He administered to the sick and wounded prisoners of the American army. Unlike some other loyalists and refugees, his kind heart was in sympathy with his countrymen, and he found many opportunities of assisting them, especially the soldiers from Falmouth, to whom he furnished, from his own private means, food and clothing, when they were in a state of destitution. Edward Preble, afterward the distinguished commodore, the son of his old friend and townsman, General Preble, with whom he had the quarrel, was brought to New York, a prisoner of war, and was confined on board the infamous prison ship, the Jersey.

While a prisoner there Brigadier Preble wrote to his son in these words. The letter is taken from Admiral George H. Preble's " Preble Family ":

FALMOUTH, *July* 11, 1781.

DEAR CHILD. — I received your favor with great pleasure and satisfaction to find that you have met with so much kindness and friendship from Col. Tyng and lady. I have written him my acknowledgements on the subject, and hope that your future conduct will be such as to render you, in some measure, worthy their future notice. As you are admitted on shore, a favor denied all the officers of the ship, never stain your honor by attempting to escape. I shall do everything, and pursue every measure that affords the least prospect of success, to get you exchanged in a justifiable way. Present your mamma's and my best compliments to Col. Tyng and lady, and let them know Madam Ross was in good health yesterday. Be always on your guard against temptations, or giving the least occasion to any that has shown you favors to charge you with a breach of trust. Be kind and obliging to all; for no man ever does a designed injury to another, without doing a greater to himself. Let reason ever govern your thoughts and actions. Be sure and write me at all opportunities. Your mamma, brothers and sisters join me in presenting their love to you, and wishing you a speedy exchange. I am your ready friend and affectionate father,

JEDIDIAH PREBLE.

Colonel Tyng obtained young Preble's release, took him to his own house, ministered to his necessities in sickness and restored him to his friends.

If we can judge anything from Colonel Tyng's conduct throughout the war, it is that during these events he never became alienated from his affection for his country, and at all times kept up the lingering hope that peace would be concluded, and that he might again return to his home in Falmouth. The surrender of Yorktown and the evacuation of New York were the destruction of the last hopes of the "American Loyalists." He, with others like him in misfortune, left the soil of his native land to seek a new home in the wilds of New Brunswick.

He received a grant of land in what is now Queen's county and settled at White's cove on the St. John river.* Immediately after his arrival in the province, he became a mediator between the large number of Loyalists there and the home government, for the obtaining and settling of the wild lands, and had the confidence of both parties. He was appointed chief justice and held other offices in the province.

Notwithstanding all the emoluments which were bestowed upon him, and the high position occupied by him in the affairs of the province, his attachment for his home remained. After residing in the province a few years, he resigned the offices of trust held by him, and, in 1793, he returned with his wife to Portland, his former home.

* A writer of the vicinity thus describes the locality in 1879: "The situation which he chose for his home on this beautiful river, cannot be surpassed by any in the province, either in fertility or in scenery. In front of it flows the river, whose surface, in those days, was scarcely ever disturbed by anything but the bark canoe of the Indian, though now traversed by vessels of all descriptions. The house that he built, which is large and square, built after the old fashion, occupies the summit of a knoll, and faces the river. It must have presented a great contrast to the log habitations, which were generally built in this province during those days, as sawed lumber was not obtainable here then. The lumber for it was imported from the United States. It still remains in good preservation, being now, as for many years, occupied by Mr. Fox, the proprietor of the farm. Could Colonel Tyng now behold the surrounding country, the changes which have taken place within the last century would astonish him. Instead of a vast wilderness, unbroken by the advances of civilization, he would see many villages, surrounded by broad fields, comfortable farm houses, and well filled barns. The bridle paths, which connected the detached settlements, having given way to turnpike roads, and railroads which intersect the country in all directions. The country owes a great deal to such men as Colonel Tyng, who braved every danger, and overcame every hardship, in order to establish for themselves and their children a home.   w."

White's Cove, New Brunswick.

The manner in which he was received by his former friends, associates, and townsmen, indicated that their respect for, and confidence in him was not shaken by political differences, and he was restored at once to the social position formerly held by him. The independence of this country as a free nation, had obliterated all the prejudices that existed toward those, who, from conscientious views of duty, had adhered to the Crown.

Not long after his return, he went to reside with Madam Ross, who, soon after Mowatt's burning, built a large house at Gorham, about two miles from Saccarappa, and continued to live there. Although Colonel Tyng's lands in Portland had been sold under the absentee act, he recovered the title for a nominal sum.

Mrs. Ross bequeathed her property to her daughter, Mrs. Tyng. Her residence at Gorham Colonel Tyng and his lady continued to occupy, going to town on Saturdays to attend church at St. Paul's and returning after the afternoon service, in a genteel carriage and pair.*

Colonel Tyng died of apoplexy, December 11, 1807. His funeral service was held at St. Paul's church. His widow erected a large and handsome monument of freestone over

---

* The following is an extract from Rev. Dr. Deane's poem, "Pitchwood Hill"; so named for a hill on his own farm, and near that of the Ross-Tyng homestead. "Eliza" was for Madam Ross. The poem was written by Dr. Deane in 1780.

> "Lo! hard by, toward the west,
> Green Hill rears his lofty crest,
> By Rosses tenants half is till'd;
> Half remains a wooded wild.
> See the mansion, large and fair!
> Eliza dwells in quiet there,
> Dispensing good to all around;
> Pouring balm for every wound."

his grave in the eastern cemetery. He had no descendants, and he was the last of the family bearing the family name.

After his death, the Ross-Tyng residence was destroyed by fire, and was by Madam Tyng rebuilt in the original style, and is yet standing. Mrs. Tyng had a niece who lived in her family and married Rev. Timothy Hilliard, who was a graduate of Harvard College of the class of 1793. He was minister of St. Paul's seven years, and resigned in 1808. Madam Tyng died October 25, 1831, aged eighty years. She was buried at Gorham.

The Tyng relics are of much interest to Portland people, not only as works of art but from the fact that they were long parts of the rich furnishings of the residence of Sheriff Tyng, who, soon after the death of Captain Alexander Ross, married his only child Elizabeth, as we have seen, and with her mother occupied the house on the south corner of Middle and Franklin streets; the last was then called Fiddle lane, afterward Essex street.

Colonel William Tyng inherited the oldest of them from his father, Commodore Edward Tyng, son of the second Edward, who came from Boston, and married Elizabeth, daughter of Lieutenant Thaddeus Clark, granddaughter of Michael Mitton and his wife, Elizabeth, who was the only child of George Cleeves.

At the bombardment by Mowatt in October, 1775, these portraits, with all the household furniture, were taken from the house to a field in the rear of the town for safety, where they remained exposed to the pelting rain, which Dr. Deane's diary says lasted three days. This long exposure to wet, loosened the glue at the corners of the frames of the portraits, which caused them to seem loose and rickety. In taking them from the parlors to the open air for the purpose of having them photographed, the artist was compelled to have help and to handle them very carefully. The finely carved frame of the portrait of Elizabeth Ross is very rich, with most of the original gilding remaining; but the projecting carved ornaments at the top and bottom are missing, from the softening of the glue in that " awful rain storm," which the old people in my boyhood never tired describing. These valuable works are now the property of the heirs of Rev. Timothy Hilliard, who married the niece of Mrs. Elizabeth Ross Tyng, and who was adopted by Mrs. Tyng and became her heir.

Another active officer in the Louisburg siege from Falmouth was Brigadier-General Samuel Waldo, who was third in rank and command. The second was Deputy Governor Roger Walcot, Esquire, of Connecticut, who was then sixty-six years old. Maine historians invariably say that Waldo held the second place, but Usher Parsons sets it right. Waldo was a son of Jonathan Waldo, a merchant of Boston, but the son was born in England in 1696. Mr. Willis does not mention him as ever a resident of Falmouth. He did reside in Boston until about 1742. That year he was appointed one of a committee to thank Peter Faneuil for his gift of the hall. He was then a large land and mill owner in Falmouth and had a residence in both towns.

Williamson says the Yorkshire regiment was divided and Samuel Waldo appointed colonel in 1740. The appointment could hardly have been so early. Parson Smith records in August, 1744, " Mr. Waldo came here with a colonel's commission." He must have had a nominal residence here to hold the commission. The regiment included all between the Saco and the Kennebec. He had, with Colonel Westbrook, been building and running mills here for several years previous. He also had two sons here. Samuel, junior, was chosen representative to the general court for Falmouth in 1744. The history of Warren says the father removed to Falmouth in 1740. He probably did not entirely give up his residence in Boston until after the death of Mrs. Waldo, which occurred August 7, 1741. He is named in deeds as a resident of Boston after that; he had lodgings in both towns and could claim a residence in either. The conveyancers hardly knew which town to insert as his residence.

If an ambitious New Englander in those days could, with any show of consistency, claim Boston as his home, he was sure to do it; as in the ownership of a vessel, if a New Yorker owns one-sixteenth the ship hails from there, as that port is known and her ships have a good reputation abroad.

As the History of Portland does not mention Brigadier Waldo as a resident of Falmouth, I have searched with some care and have found undoubted evidence that he did have a legal residence here. The Waldo house and lot was the next one east and adjoining the house of Enoch Freeman, afterward occupied by his son, Judge Samuel Freeman. After the death of General Waldo, and probably before, the house was occupied by his own son, Francis. In Cumberland Records, volume VIII., page 360, is a deed from Thomas Fluker and wife to her brother, Francis Waldo, in 1775, of

One-fifth part of a certain lot of land containing about two acres, and the dwelling house and other buildings called the *homestead of the late Brigadier General Samuel Waldo, of Falmouth, in the county of Cumberland*, which is bounded as follows, viz., Beginning at the south east corner of Samuel Freemans Esq's dwellinghouse on Middle street; thence north east 220 feet to Fiddle Lane [Franklin street,] thence North West five hundred and ten feet to E. Gustins lot [easterly corner of Lincoln park and round to first mentioned bounds] be-

18

ing in common and undivided and in the said Francis Waldo's actual possession.

Francis Waldo and all the family adhered to the home government, fled the country, were proscribed, and their property was sold under the confiscation act.

In 1783, three-fifths of the Waldo homestead was sold by "the commissioners for the estates of absentees," with the same description, to Thomas Child who came here from Boston, as did the Waldos. He held successively nearly all the offices of the customs, and afterward was postmaster. He married a daughter of Judge Freeman, which probably prevented him from being a Tory as most of his relatives were in Boston. The house he built on the Waldo lot stood on a court which was laid out through the two acres. The house was burnt in 1866. When the province, afterward the district, of Maine could be made to support one more officer of the Crown, or of the province government, he was sure to be sent ready-made, with his commission in his pocket, from Boston.

I think the land conveyance, copied above, establishes the fact that Brigadier Waldo did have a legal residence in Falmouth. If anything further is needed we have it in the Suffolk probate records.

In the inventory of General Waldo's real estate is:

"A house on Falmouth Neck and about two acres of
  flats and a wharf,"   350 pounds.
Presumpcot mills — three saws,   600   "
Stroudwater mill — one saw,   200   "
Interest in the township of Falmouth inclusive of
  several farms under improvement, about 13,000
  acres of land at twenty shillings per acre,   £13,000 sterling.

The inventory of "*personal property at Falmouth*" includes

all the fittings of a well appointed household. Also trunk, portmanteau, blunderbuss and pair of pistols, his wearing apparel, 539¾ ounces of plate, shoe buckles, knee buckles, collar buckles, watch, gold ring, and seal ring. Sundries at Stroudwater farm, including paper-mill utensils. This included Colonel Westbrook's "Harrow House" farm.

"At salt-box farm" (now reform school), all the furnishings of a genteel household, including "knives and forks with silver handles." This was the country residence.

Real estate in County of York,   £41,387, 10s.
   "   "   " Middlesex and Worcester,   £9,783, 11s. 8d.

This was sterling — so marked.

"At Long Creek point" General Waldo had a wharf where considerable business was done in shipping wood and lumber.

Williamson, in his History of Maine, says that at Governor Shirley's first conference with the Indians at Falmouth in 1739 "to render the anticipated conference convenient for all, a spacious tent was spread *upon the hill eastward of Long Creek*, in which were placed rows of seats sufficient for the whole assemblage." At that time, General Waldo was probably staying at the "salt-box farm" and entertained his friend the Governor there. This may account for the fact that Parson Smith did not mention the Governor's visit.

General Waldo's largest interest in Maine was on Georges river in the vicinity of Thomaston. The Muscongus patent was granted by the Council of Plymouth, England, in 1630, to John Beauchamp of London and John Leverett of Boston, England. It embraced a tract thirty miles square. It extended between Muscongus and Penobscot, and was limited on the west and north by the Kennebec patent. It was subsequently divided by the proprietors into thirty shares. Samuel Waldo, by inheritance from his father, and by purchase, came into possession of a large interest in the patent. He was chosen agent, and in 1729 was sent to London in the interest of the patent. On his return the thirty proprietors joined in surrendering to him one-half of the patent, his part being three hundred thousand acres. He finally came to be owner of five-sixths of the whole patent. He went largely into the lumber business and was the first to burn lime at Thomaston. This he shipped in molasses hogsheads to Boston.

Waldo offered large inducements to settlers and succeeded in drawing thirty from Falmouth. In 1740, forty German families settled the present town of Waldoborough. In 1753, General Waldo's son Samuel visited Germany, and induced sixty families from the Rhine country to come over. They suffered everything but death the first winter, and some did freeze to death, neglected by him who had deceived them by his representations of the situation and climate.

In June, 1746, Commodore Warren, General Pepperell, and General Waldo left Louisburg in charge of Admiral Knowles, and took passage for Boston in the Chester man-of-war, Captain Spry. On arrival they were received at Long wharf by the council, house of representatives, the governor's company of cadets, and the Boston regiment, and were escorted to the council chamber, where they were received with formal honors. Sir William Pepperell was elected president of the council, and took his seat at the board.

General Waldo was frequently in attendance on the general court to guard his interests in Maine lands. Sir William Pepperell did not appear at the council board so early in the session as Waldo thought he ought to, and wrote to him in these words: "Your presence in the general court has been always of great service to Maine, and I assure you it never was more necessary than at present."

In September, 1746, Pepperell wrote to Waldo, "I should think it would now be a good time to build a fort at Penobscot; pray think of it, and put it forward if you are of that opinion. I was in hopes you would have called here on your way to Boston" (from Falmouth). The building of a fort at Penobscot was a favorite measure with Pepperell, and of course it would be a great protection to Waldo's St. Georges' settlement. It was delayed until the year of the death of both of these Maine landholders, and when it was accomplished by Governor Pownal, it proved to be of great service to Maine. It was first recommended by Governor Shirley.

The base of operations for the building of this fort was Falmouth Neck, and Brigadier Preble was the agent to superintend the preparations. During the winter, timber was collected for a block-house. The contractor's name was Flag. General Preble was to enlist the men for the expedition. The Governor arrived here May 4th, 1759, to proceed in command of the expedition. In his journal the Governor says he "found the lower story of the block-house finished, and the flooring of the upper story laid." While waiting to have the buildings finished and the troops organized, they were "billeted" on the inhabitants as boarders, without asking leave. Under the Governor, General Preble was the commander of the expedition. There were three hundred soldiers beside mechanics in the expedition. The province man-of-war "King George" was the flag-ship. St. Georges' fort (Thomaston), was the place of rendezvous.

The first officer in his list, the Governor names, " The Hon. Brigadier Waldo, one of his Majesties Council."

Bricks, iron-work, wheelbarrows, and everything, were shipped here. The buildings were put together and taken down before shipping. Now the lumber business is reversed — Penobscot furnishes it.

Forty hogsheads of lime were taken in at Thomaston, for the brick and stone-work; this was from Waldo's lime-kilns, which were first built in 1734. The fort was commenced at what is now " Fort point," Prospect harbor, and while it was building, Governor Pownal with an armed force proceeded up the river above Treat's falls; while there, General Waldo was seized with apoplexy and expired immediately.

Not finding any better site for the fort, the Governor made this entry in his journal: " Determined this to be the place for the fort. Erected the flag-staff, and hoisted the King's colors with all the ceremonies usual on such occasions, adding divine service to beg God's blessing, for unless the Lord builds the house, the laborer worketh but in vain. Treated the troops with a barrel of rum." This odd mingling of " divine service " and rum drinking was held over the dead body of General Waldo. Governor Pownal continues: " At evening buried Brig'r Waldo at the point near the flag-staff, with the honors of war in our power." When finished the fort was named Fort Pownal.

Until within a few years, much interest was expressed by antiquarians and others, in making an effort to ascertain if the body of General Waldo had been removed. There had been talk of a monument to his memory. I personally examined the records of Boston, and the old burying-grounds of the city, to find the Waldo tomb, without satisfactory result. While in an undertaker's room, I casually mentioned my search; the aged father of the undertaker, who had himself followed the same business, came in, when the son mentioned my search. The old man replied that in his old desk somewhere, there was a list of the tombs in the King's Chapel burying-ground, with names of the owners. After a long search, the old discolored list was found, and against No. 21 was written, "The tomb of Samuel Waldo." A visit to the ancient inclosure showed that next to the tomb No. 20, was an unmarked space. It was on the lower side of the inclosure, next to the city hall, and the surface showed that earth from the walks had washed on to the grass. By digging where I supposed the opening to the tomb (if there was one) would be, I came upon a slate stone the size of the entrance, which had been covered six inches deep by the washing. On the stone was this inscription: "The tomb of Brigadier Gen. Samuel Waldo. This stone was erected by Sarah Waldo, August, 1811." There was no other inscription on the stone, so the question of the removal of the body of General Waldo remained unsolved.

Hon. Joseph Williamson of Belfast, with whom I had conferred, had tried to find the original grave at Fort Point, and also to find the burial-place of the Waldos in Boston, without success in either place. Judge Williamson next examined the Knox papers among which are some of Fluker's, Knox's father-in-law, who was one of the administrators of General Waldo's estate. Here was found a bill of expenses at the funeral in Boston, as follows:

1759, July 6.   [Two months after Waldo's death.]

Ralph Inman, 15 1-2 doz. gloves at the funeral,	28. 18. 8.
Clark, the porter, carrying gloves,	8. 0.
William Farfield, repairing the tomb,	6. 0. 0.
To Capt. Sanders' people, the care in removing the remains of the Brigadier from Penobscot,	1. 4. 0.
To Mr. Clark, the sexton,	1. 10. 0.

The Captain Sanders who is mentioned in the bill was long in command of the province sloop "Massachusetts" which made frequent trips from Boston to all the eastern ports and undoubtedly removed the body on a return passage.

Samuel Waldo, jr., was the most active of the two sons of the Brigadier. He was chosen representative for Falmouth in 1744, and several years after. He was married in 1760 to Grizzell Oliver, second daughter of Andrew Oliver, secretary of the province.* She died, and in 1762 Colonel Waldo married Sarah Erving of Boston.

He was judge of probate, and succeeded his father as colonel of the regiment. He was also interested with his father in the Waldo patent, and inherited a large share of it at the death of his father, which occurred only one year before his own. Colonel Waldo, the younger, died April 16, 1770. At that date, Parson Smith records, "Col. Waldo died P.M., at 47 years of age. 20th, Col. Waldo was buried with great parade under the church, with a sermon and under arms."

The son's body was as long in finding a final resting-place as was that of the Brigadier. St. Paul's church, under which he was buried, stood on the west corner of Middle street and what was then Church lane. It was burnt by Mowatt five years after, when the Colonel's body was exhumed and carried to Boston, and undoubtedly rests with that of his father in the family tomb.

Francis Waldo graduated at Harvard College in 1747, and stood second in a class of twenty-eight. Although there was a naval officer and deputy collector resident at Falmouth, there was no collection district here until 1758. That year

---

* Willis, in his history of Portland, transposed her name; he called her "Olive Grizzell."

a custom house was opened and Francis Waldo was appointed collector. The district extended from Cape Porpoise to the Kennebec. Mr. Waldo was elected to the general court in 1762 and re-elected the next year. Soon after the destruction of the town by Mowatt, Waldo went to England and never returned. He died in London in 1784. His property passed to the state under the confiscation act of 1782. Waldo was disappointed in an intended matrimonial alliance, and was never married.

Of the two daughters of General Waldo, Lucy, the eldest, was married to Isaac Winslow of Roxbury. After the death of her mother, and the final removal of her father to Falmouth, Hannah, the youngest, probably lived with her sister, spending much time with her brothers at Falmouth. A love affair and engagement of this young lady has furnished material for several story writers, who have distorted the facts, and added to them fiction without restraint.

Andrew Pepperell was the only son of Sir William Pepperell, and, of course, heir to the most of his father's princely fortune, and the baronetcy. The son's comely person and polished manners were a passport to the best society. Among the young ladies that attracted his admiration was Miss Hannah Waldo. They were betrothed in 1746, much to the gratification of both families. Sir William and Lady Pepperell both expressed their joy at the prospect of receiving Miss Hannah as the wife of their only son. Parsons, in his life of Sir William Pepperell, has culled the facts from the family letters. In the autumn of 1748, Andrew Pepperell and Miss Waldo were published; soon after which he was attacked with a lingering fever, which left him feeble and dispirited, and more so from the loss of property by sea. In 1749, Andrew's father closed a letter to the father of Miss Hannah, in these words: "Mrs. Pepperell joins with me in your wish that the alliance between our son and your daughter were completed, which I do think would be a satisfaction to all their friends, and a means of putting a stop to the talk of their enemies, as there are none without some. As I have often urged him to finish the affair, and he has declined to let me know the time designated, I have no thoughts of mentioning it to him again."

In 1751, two years after the letter just quoted, Sir William again wrote to General Waldo, who had gone to London, that he now had every reason to hope that the long talked of alliance of their two families would soon be completed, much to the joy of himself and family; that the nuptial day was appointed, and that his lady and family connections anticipated the pleasure of joining in the celebration.

Miss Waldo was making preparation in a style becoming the occasion, and of the distinguished guests that were to attend; but, a few days before the one appointed for the wedding arrived, Andrew wrote to her that circumstances had occurred which would make it necessary to defer it to another day, which he named as more convenient for himself. This was too much for her to bear; her mind was from that moment firmly fixed. She returned no answer; the guests assembled at the appointed hour and place, when she enjoyed the sweet revenge of telling Andrew that she would not marry one who had occasioned her so much mortification, and who could not have that love and friendship for her that was necessary for her happiness. Young Pepperell had built an elegant house, near his father's, at Kittery Point, to receive his bride, and had it elegantly furnished. In less than six weeks, the young lady was led to the altar by Thomas Fluker, Esquire, secretary of the province. Their daughter married General Henry Knox of Revolutionary fame.

Within a year, Andrew Pepperell died of typhoid fever. Dr. Deane has this entry in his journal for 1766: " July 25. Col. Powell in town; came to wait on Mr. Fluker and Col. Waldo, who went to Yarmouth to keep Thanksgiving, knowing there would be no preaching there. Great men are not always wise nor always good." Colonel Waldo was an Episcopalian in whom Dr. Deane could see no good.

The loss of Louisburg awakened the French nation to a sense of the danger of losing Canada also, that fortress being the key to the St. Lawrence. The most powerful fleet that had ever been sent to North America sailed from Brest for Cape Breton and Nova Scotia. It consisted of seventy sail, eleven of which were ships of the line, with twenty frigates and three thousand disciplined troops, and immense quantities of ammunition, cannon, and military stores. The whole force was placed under the Duke D'Anville, a nobleman of great experience and ability. He was instructed to retake and dismantle Louisburg; he was then to proceed against Annapolis which he was to take and garrison. He was next to destroy Boston and range along the whole coast of the English colonies and finally visit the West Indies.

News of the sailing of this fleet caused great consternation throughout the coast towns of New England, especially in Boston. The castle was strengthened and new batteries built; one was placed on the end of Long wharf for the defence of the town, while large bodies of militia came from the country for the same purpose. Douglas says six thousand four hundred men, well armed, appeared on Boston Common to oppose D'Anville.

The passage of the French fleet was unprecedently long, and on the first of September they experienced a very severe storm, in which several ships foundered. After a passage of more than ninety days, the fleet arrived at Chebucto (now Halifax), too late to refit and execute any part of the designed conquest that season. The troops had suffered much during the long voyage with sickness, and large numbers had died. The commander of this once powerful armament was so much affected by the disappointment that he died on the fourth day after arrival, of apoplexy; the English said poison. The misfortunes of the fleet and the death of D'Anville so affected the vice-admiral that he was thrown into a delirious fever, and in one of his paroxysms he ran his sword through his body and immediately expired. The fleet and army then went into winter quarters at Bedford Basin, but still suffered by sickness although they were supplied with fresh provisions by the Acadians.

It was decided to abandon the conquest of Louisburg but to attack Annapolis in the spring. A force of French and Indians was sent from Canada to Minas to co-operate with the fleet. Soon after the fleet sailed from Chebucto in the spring for Annapolis it was overtaken by a storm which so much weakened it that the designed attack on Annapolis was abandoned, and the remains of the fleet returned to France.

The failure of this powerful armament was looked upon by the colonies as a peculiar intervention of divine providence in their favor, and a general thanksgiving was proclaimed in Massachusetts.

Hutchinson says Mons. de la Jonquiere, governor of Canada, was on board the Northumberland, and was made third in command, next to the vice-admiral who proposed returning to France. Jonquiere thought they were in condition to recover Annapolis, after which they might winter securely in Casco Bay.

Of this intention, of course, the town knew nothing, but they knew of the sailing of the fleet from France and partook of the general alarm. The people of Falmouth made a laudable effort to defend their harbor. They held a town meeting and directed the selectmen to get four barrels of powder, with balls and flints. Also to apply to Captain Moses Pearson for his two great guns to be placed on Spring Point. That was where Fort Preble now is, and was the first attempt to fortify the point which commands the entrance to the harbor.

These two guns Captain Pearson had taken as a part of his share of the plunder at Louisburg and brought them home. He knew how to mount them in a battery and handle them when mounted. It is probable that the town meeting understood that the " borrowing " of the guns included their owner. How he would have succeeded in driving back D'Anville's "eleven ships of the line and twenty frigates " we can imagine, but the pluck was creditable.

During the whole summer the town had been infested by lurking parties of Indians. Parson Smith says in June, " Our people are more alarmed on account of Indians than ever before." June 6th two soldiers were killed by the Indians in Wescott's field at Long Creek. An Indian was fired at from Frost's garrison at the eastern end of Stroudwater bridge, another one was driven away from Chapman's at Horse tavern ; Joseph Sweat, an inhabitant of the town was killed at New Casco. An Indian was discovered in Brackett's swamp, now in ward seven, and the men of the town spent the afternoon in a thorough search for the Indians with-

out success.   Three days after Mr. Stubs and a soldier with
him were killed by the Indians near his own house.

At midsummer the people of the town commenced a
block-house and stockade for the common defence, on Benjamin Larrabee's land where the old city hall now stands.
This block-house with an addition was made the county jail
on the organization of Cumberland County.   With a timber
block-house and two guns mounted at Spring Point, Parson
Smith and his people seem to have felt more secure.

November 25th the reverend journalist makes this entry:
" Mr. Wait brought news from Boston that a storm cast two
of the transports on shore on the Isle of Sable ; that two of
the large men-of-war (of the Jebucto fleet) had parted with
their masts ; and that a reigning mortal sickness had been
among them."   The storm and the " mortal sickness " saved
Falmouth harbor and town from being occupied several
months by a hostile fleet, and a lawless soldiery.

One cause of the fear of the Indians the same season was
the absence of several of the foremost military men of the
town, who were in the expedition sent to Nova Scotia under
Colonel Noble of Georgetown, to drive off from Minas
De Ramsay and his force, who had been sent from Canada to
co-operate with D'Anville.   While scattered in the houses
of the Acadians, Colonel Noble's force was surprised in the
night, in a violent snow storm, the commander and many of
them killed ; Captain Stephen Jones of Falmouth was among
the slain.   He had been in command of Indian scouts and
other military expeditions.   He was a tailor and had a house
on what is now York street, which was taken away to make
room for the present three story wooden house called the
" Oxnard house."   Captain Jones was a brother to Ephraim

Jones, the merchant who was in partnership with Commodore Edward Tyng.

In September, 1759, the French army and garrison of Quebec surrendered to the British and provincial army, which was led to the attack by General Wolfe. Both the opposing commanders-in-chief fell early in the battle. Several residents of Falmouth were in Wolfe's army. Captain John Wait, afterward sheriff of Cumberland County, was in command of a transport which sailed from Louisburg for Quebec with the fleet. He witnessed the battle from the deck of his schooner. His log-book has been preserved in which is also an account of his voyage to and from the Bay of Fundy in 1755, in which he assisted in the removal of the ill-fated Acadians. This foul blot on English colonial history I wish to avoid. The fall of Quebec caused great rejoicing throughout New England and well it might, as it ended the Indian wars, which had by turns, for nearly a century, been the scourge of the scattering eastern settlements.

CHAPTER IX.

POPULATION OF THE DIFFERENT PARTS OF THE TOWN AT DIFFERENT
PERIODS. STATE OF THE NECK IN 1759, WHEN QUEBEC SURREN-
DERED. EARLY ECCLESIASTICAL AFFAIRS. WHITEFIELD. SHAKERS.

IN 1726, Parson Smith took a retrospective view of the
few years which he had spent as minister of the town. He
says in his journal, "Samuel Cobb came here in 1717 when
there was only one house on Purpoodock side of the water
just built and inhabited by one Doctor Winslow. In 1718
said Cobb moved his family to Falmouth Neck (from Mid-
dleborough, Mass.), when there were fourteen families there
including his."

From the journal we find that in 1749 the population of
the different parts of the town numbered as follows: Cape
Elizabeth, nine hundred; New Casco, three hundred and
fifty; Stroudwater, two hundred and seventy-six; Back
Cove, one hundred and twenty; Neck, now Portland, seven
hundred; slaves, twenty-one; total, two thousand three hundred and sixty-seven. Ten years later, 1759, when Quebec
surrendered, there were on the Neck one hundred and forty
dwelling-houses occupied by one hundred and sixty families,
which would number about one thousand souls. In 1764 a
census gave for the whole town a population of three thousand seven hundred and seventy.

In 1751 the town of Kittery (which then included Eliot),
petitioned the general court to have their valuation reduced.
From this memorial we obtain their estimate of several

towns in the county of York which then included Falmouth. This is their estimate of that town :

Falmouth is four times as big as Kittery for quantity of land, and many more inhabitants. The situation of the place exceeds all others in the county for trading by sea to all parts, and supplys of all sorts of lumber by land; salt and fresh rivers, with profitable mills, timber, wood and every commodity that the land can produce, and fish of all sorts (when and where they please to catch them). It abounds with good farms and cattle; trade and merchandize both by sea and land. The place (as well as the people) is the beauty and riches and strength of the county. Eight military companies in town, besides numbers of gentlemen not liable to military command. A commodious harbor for ships; daily they are increasing in numbers and wealth; which is not possible for Kittery to do, for Kittery produces nothing to trade upon, unless they should sell one another for slaves, as the Africans do.

The memorial says "there is not three rich men in the town." We know there were two, Sir William Pepperell and Nathaniel Sparhawk, his son-in-law, but neither of them signed the memorial, and yet it was signed by eighteen of the foremost men of the town.

After the defences against invasion, and the means to obtain a living, ecclesiastical affairs next claimed attention. In continuation of his retrospect Parson Smith says:

In the year 1725, in June, I (Thomas Smith) came here and found one Mr. Pierpont who was chaplain to army whose headquarters were on this Neck, preaching to the people. There was then forty-five families in the whole town, viz: twenty-seven upon the Neck, one at New Casco, and seventeen at Purpoodock and Spurwink, most of them poor, and some of them miserably so. They had four or five years before erected a meeting house which they had only covered, and the floor of it contained the people, with the fishermen and soldiers and other strangers that used to frequent the place much. The people of Purpoodock had also a log house on the Point, which they

19

built partly for a garrison to the families on the Point, and partly for a meeting house, in which the whole town assembled every third Sabbath."

The log meeting house and garrison was on the rising ground in the rear of Fort Preble. The point was then, and is yet called "Spring Point," from a fine spring of water near high water mark, now inclosed in the defences of the fort. While improving the fort a few years ago an attempt was made to improve the spring also, by blasting, which let the sea water filter in, much to its damage. The graveyard which adjoined the humble meeting-house reaching to the bank is yet used to bury the dead, although many stones have been removed. The southeast side of the burial ground is very much exposed to the open sea, which within my remembrance has encroached some twenty feet or more upon the upland, letting down many graves and lettered stones, where were buried the Simontons, Whites, and others, the first settlers. Parson Smith says here the "whole town assembled every third Sabbath."

In town meeting in 1727 it was voted that "Lieut.* Benjamin Wright shall keep the ferry, and it is understood that the inhabitants on this side of the river as occasion calls for it, shall be carried over to meeting without paying ferriage." The Purpoodockers were not named in the vote; if they wanted to cross to the Neck to meeting it appears they were obliged to pay for it.

---

* It is noticeable that in early records all the minor military officers have their titles perpetuated. This was according to law. In the old colony in 1638 it was " ordered that all military officers elected, shall retain their titles forever after, except they are promoted."

Lord Byron said that military glory consisted in "being shot through the body, and having your name spelt wrong in the gazette," in England, but the colonies made a lasting provision for it.

The meeting-house mentioned by Parson Smith was set some thirty feet southeast of the west corner of what was then King (now India), and Middle streets. It was built in pursuance of a vote of the town passed February, 1720, as follows: "Voted, that a meeting-house be built as soon as possible, thirty-six by twenty-eight, twenty foot stud. Two years after a sum was voted for "boards plank to cover the meeting-house," and in 1723, provision was made for clapboards to cover it. At the same meeting a proposition was made to obtain the services of the Black Point minister half the time, but it met with little favor. There was a feeling that they needed a minister of their own. In August, 1725, it was voted that ninety pounds be raised to finish the outside of the meeting-house, and to pay the town debt. Mr. Smith in his journal certifies that meeting-house was handsomely finished that year. He had received and accepted a call to settle here.

In 1726 the town voted to supply Rev. Mr. Smith with firewood "during his continuance as our minister." He continued their minister sixty-nine years. At the same meeting arrangements were made for Mr. Smith's ordination. At that time town and parish affairs were one and the same thing, and the record of both was kept in the same book. A vote was also passed desiring Major Moody to entertain the ministers and messengers, and that John Sawyer be desired to take care of their horses. Sawyer lived on Purpoodock side, where they were to leave their horses which saved the ferrying over. They all came from the west to the ferry at Purpoodock side. Major Moody was then about the only man on the Neck who had spare rooms suited to the dignity with which the people then invested the clergy. He lived about where the Eagle Sugar House now is. Mr. Smith boarded with Major Moody for which the town voted him ten shillings per week.

At the town meeting to make preparations for Mr. Smith's ordination it was "voted that some persons be appointed to gather and send in what provisions of all sorts that may be had for that purpose, as a freewill offering. Capt. Dominicus Jordan and Lieut. Johnson for Spurwink, Jonathan Cobb for Purpoodock, Thomas Millett and Samuel Proctor for Casco side." The eighth or ninth of March was fixed for the ordination. Mr. Smith records, "March 8, 1726. This day I was ordained minister of the gospel and pastor of the church." A church was organized the same day. The ministers mentioned as present were Moody of York, Wise of Berwick, Newmarch of Kittery, Rogers of Kittery. These with Mr. Jefferds of Wells were then the only settled ministers in Maine. Mr. Smith mentions, "The whole affair was carried on and finished much to the satisfaction and joy of every one concerned." Mr. Smith's salary was fixed by the town at seventy pounds.

In January, 1727, Parson Smith notes, "Today the people met and cut the timber for my house and drew a part of it to the spot." The town had voted to build him a house, at a meeting in October. Two three acre lots adjoining were given to the minister, on which his house was built, on the northwest side of Congress, then called Queen street, and directly opposite to King, now India, street. In 1734 the people of the town built a stockade with watchboxes around the house, and in 1747 "swivel guns" were mounted in the watchboxes. In this house Rev. Mr. Smith lived until its destruction by Mowatt's bombardment in 1775. It was the last house burned, and took fire from a house opposite.

In 1728 the gallery of the meeting-house was finished and a pew built for the minister.

In 1733 the territory now forming the town of Cape Elizabeth was incorporated by the general court as a distinct parish. The frame of the sightly meeting-house now standing on the hill opposite Portland was erected the next year. The frame was of oak and it had no steeple. It was finished in the old style with two tiers of windows and square pews, and so remained within my recollection. I think it is the oldest house of worship in the county, although there are none of its original features remaining.

In 1753 the inhabitants living on the easterly side of Presumpscot river within the Falmouth limits were set off by a vote of the town, to be a separate parish which was known as New Casco parish. They also built a large two story meeting-house, which was standing within my knowledge, with its high partitions between the square pews, and the indispensable sounding-board suspended over the pulpit.

In 1765 the fourth or Stroudwater parish was incorporated and a large meeting-house built true to the regulation style, like all the others of the town. I have a recollection of its interior, but nothing of the house now remains.

The old King street meeting-house served for a house of worship for about fifteen years, but it was cheaply built, and not large enough to accommodate all that attended; then those that remained at home on Sunday were the exceptions. The people of the Neck had begun to move west from the old seat of dominion, but a vote to build a new meeting-house could not be obtained. Some of the most wealthy and enterprising citizens conceived a project to build a meeting-house where they wanted it to stand, and of the then standard style, and trust the generosity of the parish to accept it. The project for a new meeting-house was favored by Parson Smith, who had a large influence, and was a power in the town.

In 1740 the new temple of worship was completed. The cut here inserted is from a correct drawing made at the time of its removal, but to make it represent the house as it was originally, it must be shorn of its tower and steeple, and have one-fourth of its length taken from the center, and then have the two ends drawn together. The porch at the rear was not there originally, it was a bell tower separate from the house for temporary uses and then moved and used for a porch.

The new meeting-house stood on the same spot now occupied by the stone one belonging to the first parish except that it stood with its broadside to the street. The following is a correct description as I knew it in its last years: The pews were square, raised one step above the aisles, which ran crosswise as well as lengthwise. The partitions between the pews were high with an open railing with short balusters on top, showing only the heads of the people above the top rail. The seats were hinged and on all sides of the pew except at the entrance, which was closed by a door as high as the partition adjoining, which gave each pew the appearance of a prisoners' box in a court house of that time. In time of prayer all stood, and turned the board seats up to admit of leaning. At the annual fast in 1750 Mr. Smith says he " had uncommon assistance, was an hour in each of the first prayers." At the "amen" all the seats went down with a loud report as if it was a joyful salute for relief from the long standing.

The pulpit was opposite the front entrance in the middle of the length of the house. It was a formidable looking

MEETING-HOUSE OF THE FIRST PARISH.—1740-1825.

structure painted white, relieved with green, and over the standing place for the minister was the inevitable elaborate sounding board of the time, hanging by a rod from a pineapple at the ceiling and not more than three feet above the minister's head.* In front of the pulpit and facing the audience was the deacon's seat, but within my knowledge Judge Samuel Freeman in long waistcoat and breeches, was the only deacon enjoying that seat. The massive timber of the frame was of white oak and selected with as much care as if it was going into a frigate.

There were galleries on three sides, where many well-to-do people had pews from choice. A wonder to my boyish eyes were the interior braces of hewn oak, showing the axe marks through the limewash. Each cross beam had a brace at each end, which started from the post at the top of the gallery and went boldly out into the audience room and entered the beam at least fifteen feet from the wall. The beams were hidden by the plastering, but the posts showed.

An incident comes to my mind as I write. In October, 1821, Rev. Mr. Payson, (before he was a D.D.,) was invited by the Portland Marine Bible Society to address the seamen. There was no Bethel church then, and the seamen were numerous, and were a much more distinct class than now in dress and manners. They did not often hear a sermon. "The Old Jerusalem," as the memorable church was called, was chosen in which the address was to be delivered. It was a season when there were many sailors in port, and an effort

* At the junction of Free and Congress streets, on the end of the narrow building, are the two fluted pillars which supported the pulpit. They were put there when the building was erected in 1826, by Charles Q. Clapp. The center ornament of the sounding-board is in the cabinet of the Maine Historical Society.

was made to have them fill the lower floor of the church. All sailor boarding-house keepers were invited to go with their boarders. It was a novel occasion and all went. Horatio G. Quincy, a Universalist, kept the largest and best house — it is yet standing on Fore street between Portland Pier and the Custom House. Mr. Quincy marshaled his own men, and all other sailors who would join him, which made a long and remarkable procession. Quincy had a heavy wooden leg and when the procession went through the waiting crowd, cheers could hardly be suppressed, but when the worthy maimed man entered the uncarpeted aisle with his wooden stump, his well-known step awakened the enthusiasm of the audience. They forgot the place and the day, and gave a round of applause. The house was packed as it never had been before.

Mr. Payson's reputation as a pulpit orator was second to none in New England. I have his printed address before me. The incident requires that I should quote from it. The speaker had been describing the final judgment, and used this language: " Then our world driven by the last tempest will strike and be dashed in pieces on the shores of eternity. Hark! what a crash!" At this point an excited sailor jumped to his feet and cried out, "She has struck!" which caused those in the gallery to try to look below, thinking the over-crowded galleries were giving away. A board on which several men were standing broke, which further added to the panic. Some of the lower window sashes were got up, and many jumped to the ground. In the gallery, many climbed into the braces which have been described. A few cool and resolute men succeeded in quieting the excited crowd, who again became seated, and listened to the closing exercises.

The lot on which the meeting-house was built was one

hundred and twenty-two feet on "Back street" and one
hundred and forty feet deep.

The vote whereby the new house was accepted was "that
the new meeting-house on the Neck in the first parish in Falmouth be a parish house forever, reserving to the proprietors
that built said house the pews on the lower floor, and the
privilege of building one tier of pews round the back side of
the galleries. Said pews to be six feet wide. The remainder of said parish to have the privilege of the seats below
and the other seats in the galleries." It is probable that
only a part of the lower floor was then occupied by pews.

The new meeting-house was first occupied by a worshiping
assembly July 20, 1740. In 1758 a bell was procured in
England which weighed eight hundred pounds and cost one
hundred and twenty-three pounds lawful money. It was
imported by Captain Alexander Ross, and was hung on a
frame separate from the meeting-house. In 1759 the opposition against the new order of things had so far subsided
that the parish voted to enlarge the house and build a steeple.
In that year the house was sawed through on both sides of
the pulpit and each end was moved from the pulpit twelve
feet, and the space built up, giving twenty-eight new pews
on the lower floor. In 1760 the tower was built and the
next year the graceful spire seen in the cut was added. The
design was evidently copied from the steeple of the meeting-
house at York which was built in 1727, and stood unaltered
until 1882. The Falmouth spire was its exact counterpart.
I think the front entrance porch was added the same year of
the building of the tower. The western end of the house,
from the town and from the storms, remained without clap_
boards until 1756. In Mowatt's bombardment in 1775 a
cannon shot went through the front wall and lodged inside,

but this was the only injury to the venerable structure. When the present stone church on the same spot was built the shot was used in the suspension of the glass chandelier.

The following letter, with its enclosure, was kindly handed to me by the gentleman to whom it is addressed. As the book in which the draft of the old letter is written once belonged to Moses Pearson, it is probable that he was one of the building committee, and that the draft of the order for the materials for the steeple is in his handwriting. The vane then procured now surmounts the spire of the church on the same spot.

BOSTON, June 8th, 1885.

MR. J. P. BAXTER,

Dear Sir: Your name being the only one known to me as being interested in local history through your late work, I enclose the copy of a draft of a letter I came across on the fly sheet of an old book of Massachusetts Bay Statutes. The book belonged at one time to Moses Pearson. Alex. Ross' name also appears on a front page. Thinking this copy may help to fix some date or be of some interest I send it to you. The draft of the letter was not addressed or signed.

Very Truly,

H. F. HAMILTON,

124 Commonweath Avenue, Boston.

FALMOUTH Sept 9th 1760

Sr. The folowing articols we desire you'l send us as soone as may be, it being late in the year to do the work we are about, viz.

A vane for a Steeple of 120 feet high, to be made of coper or brass as may be thought best and cheepest, As much of the thinest sort of sheet lead as will cover the top of the tower Being 18 feet sq.

100 wt White lead

50 " Spanish white

12 galons Lintseed oyl

14 books of leaf goold

Ye spire is fit for panting and wates for the vane in order to raise. the money for these articols will be collected in a short time which we shall send you and make you reasonable satisfaction for y^r care and trouble in ye affair.

The new spire was the wonder of the eastern country ; there was no other east of York. All will yet admit that its outlines and proportions were graceful. From the order for materials, we find that it was painted white.

From the town records it seems they had bad luck with the bell. The first mention of it after it was hung in the belfry was in June, 1774, when Parson Smith says it " tolled all day as the harbor of Boston is shut up." In 1791 the town " voted to recast the bell provided the expense does not exceed one-half of what it cost to recast it before." In 1792 the town " voted to ring the bell at sunrise, at eleven o'clock, at one o'clock and at nine P.M., and at the usual hours on the Lord's day at the expense of the town." In 1804 a bell weighing eighteen hundred pounds was imported from Liverpool to replace the old one which had long been cracked. At service time on Sunday it was waited for by the sextons of the other churches to give the first note, and in an alarm for fire no bell stopped ringing while the bell of the " Old Jerusalem " could be heard. I think that deference has been accorded to the bell of the first parish until within a few years.

In Mowatt's bombardment in 1775, the meeting-house was an exposed target, with nothing in range to protect it. Only once was it struck, that was by a hot shot which set it on fire but it was extinguished.

A sad accident occurred at the old meeting-house on Christmas day in 1821. Horatio Noyes, aged fourteen years, found the tower door unlocked and went alone up to the belfry. He then attempted to climb to the spire by one of the eight oak posts surrounding the belfry. He lost his hold and fell outside to the ground, a distance of nearly seventy feet. He was taken up alive, but died the next day. He was the son of Jacob Noyes who built the Charles Jones house, Free street.

In 1794 a clock was placed in the tower by the town at a cost of two hundred pounds. In 1802 an additional dial was placed on the eastern side, over the ridge of the roof.*

After standing eighty-five years, the venerable meeting-house became antiquated and unsatisfactory to the younger part of its proprietors, and ungrounded fears were expressed

---

* At the time of which I am writing town clocks were more needed than now. Few people except the rich had time keepers in their houses. All had a mark in the window where the shadow came to at meridian, but this was no use at any other hour. It was common in fixing the sills of a house, especially in the country, to set a compass to have the side or end range north and south for the purpose of showing when it was twelve o'clock. Sun dials were another means resorted to to give the time, but all these means were of no use when the sun was obscured. Judge Sewall in 1687 records, " Have the Lord's supper, got home rather before twelve both by my clock and dial." These sun dials were in use in Falmouth as well. The setting of one made an impression on the memory of a girl of fifteen who mentioned it in a deposition sixty-five years after, which is on record. She says: " When I was in my fifteenth year (1744), I went to service in the family of Stephen Jones in a house which was afterward occupied by Mr. Edward Oxnard [York street]; that while I was there I remember William Pote, then a surveyor, was at said Jones'. The conversation was whether the house stood east and west or not. For the convenience of knowing it was decided to fix up a dial which Jones had in his house. A post was accordingly set, about one rod from the fore-door on toward the water, on which they fixed the dial." This dial was set up a few rods from Gorham's corner, which name, properly, only covers the north corner of Fore and Center streets, where William Gorham had his store. As this locality bears the same

that it was unsafe to ring the bell from the weakness of the spire from decay. The younger men of the parish who wanted a new church, with the aid of Rand, the sexton, had got up the feeling that it was unsafe to ring the bell but no decay could be pointed to. The elderly men from whom the funds were to come, participated in the fright and the fine toned bell hung mute for months. In 1825 the parish decided to pull down the spire and tower, and move the old house back and use it for the regular service until a new church could be built. The pulling over of the spire was a notable event for the boys of the town, among whom the writer was one. This was done early in the spring as it must be the first movement toward the erection of the new house. The contractor for the removal of the ancient building was Charles Frost, senior, the only man of the town who had the necessary appliances for such a job.

In the preparation to pull over the spire, a man was sent up inside above the belfry as far as possible with an axe, and made an opening, and let down a small rope with which he drew up a large one, and made it fast around the spire. While he was doing this, another man was sawing off the oak posts around the belfry.

Frost, the contractor, took his station on the roof of the three story Dr. Deane house, which then stood next above the meeting-house; the long and strong rope was stretched far down Temple street, and manned on both sides by a motley crowd. The word came, " Haul away." It was thought that a gentle pull was all that was needed and the rope was

character of "seven dials," St. Giles, London, and as seven streets open from this square, "seven dials," or perhaps *The Dial*, would be an appropriate name for it.

pulled straight with no movement of the spire. Then came an ill-natured reprimand and emphatic order to "haul," when the rope parted, but the steeple remained in place. The last of the posts was sawn asunder, the rope knotted and another pull given; but not until a piece had been fearlessly chopped out of the near post with an axe could the brave old spire be made to succumb.

The top ball struck the ground first, and within ten feet of the tower. The vane and the iron rod on which it swung, were some twisted, and a few feet of the top woodwork was broken off, but the body of the spire kept its form. Much curiosity was shown in efforts to obtain the documents deposited in the ball, which were found to be as perfect as when placed there. Another object of interest was the vane, to ascertain if there was a bullet hole in it, and true to tradition it was there.

In about 1812 John H. Hall of the town, a boat-builder, completed a breech loading rifle—the first ever known here. To show his success and skill, he stood at the foot of Temple street and put a ball through the vane as he claimed, but many doubted. On examination it was found to be true, and now with a glass the patch can be seen that covers it. In the war of 1812 the United States government purchased Hall's patent, and employed him to superintend the manufacture of his arm at Harper's Ferry.

The removal of the old meeting-house was an event of general interest in the town, whose inhabitants then numbered less than ten thousand. Its memories were associated with those of the venerable ministers Smith and Deane, many of its pew holders having sat under their preaching. The building was no ordinary structure. Its timbers were all of oak or some hard wood.

> " Fivescore years it stood;
> Yes, they built it well,
> Though they built of wood;
> When that house arose,
> For its cross-beams square,
> Oak and walnut fell.
> Little worse for wear,
> Down the old house goes! "

There was a great weight of lime-plaster on the walls and ceiling, nearly an inch thick. Contract plastering had not then come in. The weight of the building far exceeded any estimate. The moving of it only about its own width was found to be a difficult job, and could be accomplished only by the use of the wooden bed screws, then in use, working in pairs through a beam. There were then no iron jack-screws as now. After being moved to the rear, the old house was occupied for worship while the new one was being built, when it was taken down. A two story house, number 22 Parris street, has its walls covered with clapboards from the old meeting-house, and fastened on with the original wrought nails. The house was built in 1826 by a Mr. Millions, a distiller.

In the large closet under the high pulpit were kept the relics commemorative of the bombardment. Two or more cannon shot, one of which went through the wall and pews, the marks of which remained as long as the house stood. There was also a long speaking trumpet made of tin plate, eaten through and through with rust, which was kept in the closet. The trumpet was taken by some of the people of the town from one of a boat's crew who was sent on shore from Mowatt's ship with torches, to set fire to buildings which could not be reached by bombs and hot shot.

Beside its legitimate use for divine service the old meeting-house had been twice used by the authorities of the province for conferences with the Indian tribes, which in both cases resulted in treaties of peace, which were signed within its walls. The first in September, 1749; and again, Governor Shirley and his council, with commissioners from New Hampshire, had a long conference here with the three principal Indian tribes in July, 1754, which ended in the conclusion and signing of a treaty. The two first trials for murder in the county were also held in the meeting-house. First, Goodwin, who was executed in November, 1772. Second, Thomas Bird, in 1790, who was also convicted and executed.

In the spring of 1825, before the removal of the old meeting-house, preparations were made for the erection of the new church on the same spot.* The building committee were Albert Newhall, Joshua Richardson, and John Mussey. The material chosen was granite, from a quarry near the line between Freeport and Yarmouth. The walls are of undressed stone, but laid in regular courses, with door and window arches and all corners cut to dimensions. While the walls were going up a difficulty arose with the contractor for the stone, and that for the most northerly window was obtained at Charlestown state prison; it is Chelmsford stone. Except the jail, built in 1797, this was the first building in the town whose walls were entirely of granite. The interior is eighty-two by sixty-two feet.

* Up to near the middle of this century only the houses of worship of the Episcopalians and Roman Catholics were termed "churches," — all others were from the choice of their owners called "meeting-houses." At the time mentioned, in the city, when "the church" as a building was named, it was understood to mean old St. Paul's on School street.

Although this church was built within the remembrance of many now living, it is the oldest church edifice in the city. Its cost was twenty-three thousand dollars. It is remarkable that after a period of sixty years one of the building committee is yet alive, in the person of Mr. John Mussey who was born in 1790.

Deacon Samuel Freeman, who laid the corner-stone of the new church, then eighty-two years old, had served as deacon and occupied the deacon's seat in front of the pulpit forty-four years. When he was about eighty years old he compiled and published the valuable journal of Rev. Thomas Smith, which is the text-book for the history of the town, remarkable events, and the weather, for nearly seventy years. Deacon Freeman was thirty-two years old at the beginning of the Revolution, and was a member of the Provincial Congress. He died in 1831 at the age of eighty-eight years. His eyesight was good without the assistance of spectacles until his death. He continued to wear breeches and shoes with the broad silver buckles of the olden time. A sight of the cut of the old meeting-house brings to my memory his venerable figure in front of the pulpit. His hand was always open in friendship and in alms-giving.

The removal of the old meeting-house seemed to place the memories of Parson Smith further back in history. His biography has been fully written in connection with the two editions of his journal. He was an able preacher and a laborious and pious pastor, but he never lost sight of this world's interests. He could not have inherited much from his father, who was long a truck-master under the province at Saco and St. Georges forts, with a small salary. After he had been settled here fifteen years over a parish too poor to finish their meeting-house inside, Parson Smith made an

20

inventory which Mr. Willis found among his papers. It bears this heading: "An account of what estate belongs to T. Smith, Oct. 3, 1742." Beside his house and home farm, he enumerates eleven parcels of land, among which were "sixty acres on the Neck; one third part of Peak's Island, and a third part of House Island." He also names his personal estate, farm-stock, and bonds. Also eight hundred pounds due from the parish and town, for which he says he would not have them sued. In a memorandum for his attorney in a case in court, he says, "To look carefully to the jury, etc." He would have shone as a real estate broker in these days.

There was one case of dissatisfaction and ill feeling which he mentions between himself and the childless widow of his son, (they were joint heirs in the son's estate,) the cause of which I think I can explain. The Parson had a son Thomas who was as thrifty as the father. He kept a store (his father calls it a shop), on the north corner of Middle street and Fiddle lane, now Franklin street. This shop and goods escaped Mowatt's burning in 1775, but its owner foresaw the coming storm of the Revolution, and turned his stock into hard cash and put it into a bag. Peter T. Smith, his brother, was then settled minister at Windham, and had a large house yet standing, where the father fled for refuge when his own house on the Neck was burned. The son Thomas, the trader, owned the adjoining farm in Windham, on which stood the first frame house which was built in the town. In July, 1769, Dr. Deane records, "Went to Windham with Judges Oliver and Trowbridge (of Massachusetts), dined at Mr. T. Smith's farm-house."

Thomas Smith, junior, had two negro slaves, a man and a young woman, for whom the father in his complaint said he offered seven hundred pounds — old tenor of course. Fearing more trouble from the armed vessels, Smith junior took his faithful negro man and his money bags into his chaise and drove to Windham, and, unknown to his father, hid the money in the cellar of the farm-house. In the press for soldiers, large bounties were offered, when the negro servant traded with his master for liberty to enlist, they to divide the wages between them. There were two other slaves from Windham in the same — Captain Richard Mayberry's — company. The negro fell sick, and when about to die in the hospital, revealed the secret of the buried treasure to one of the other black soldiers.

In the winter of 1776, Thomas Smith, jr., went to visit his sister Lucy, the wife of Thomas Sanders, of Gloucester, Cape Ann. While there he was seized with what his father calls a pleurisy and fever, and died about the tenth of February. If he retained his reason his wife was not with him, to whom he could confide the secret of the buried money. The father records the starting of his son Peter, with the widow, for Cape Ann, the next day after the receipt of the news of the death.

The father was co-heir with the widow, who administered on the estate. In a paper of minutes, for the consideration of a lawyer as to his rights, Parson Smith says, " She (the administratrix,) never brought in any inventory till a year had past, and then no mention of the cash or monies, though there was in one bag a thousand pounds sterling in hard money." This bag was a part of that hidden in the cellar, unknown to any one but the servant, and for which the innocent administratrix, who knew nothing of it, was blamed. The negro soldier, to whom Smith's servant disclosed the secret on his death bed, came home and hinted to some of the towns-people what he knew of the hidden treasure, but, when he looked for it, it had already been removed. The story became public, and although the house has disappeared, the cellar has many times been dug over during the intervening century, hoping to find some remaining portion of the money. Soon after the negro came home from the war, some of the towns-people became richer than their neighbors, as was supposed from the knowledge of the place of the hidden money bags. Putting these facts and traditions together relieves the careful minister from the imputation of being an unreasonable father-in-law.

The locality where worship according to the Book of Common Prayer was first celebrated on the main-land of Falmouth, although the settlement was subsequently broken up, seems to have retained the seed of the church. Some of the descendants and neighbors of Arthur Macworth still held an interest there. Parson Wiswell of the New Casco Congregational parish, with a portion of his people, declared for the Church of England. This was brought about by the Episcopalians on the Neck, whom the trade by sea had brought here; not for the liberty to worship according to their own faith and forms, for that was denied them, unless they also paid their "rates" to the first parish. The few officers of the crown located here were also favorable to the English church. Occasionally a royal governor from "The Bay" came here to treat with the Indians, and brought his chaplain with him. Governor Shirley brought the courtly Parson Brockwell, of King's Chapel, here in 1754. He was invited to hold service in the meeting-house, which he did. Mr. Smith says, "He carried on in the church form." On the next Sunday he again officiated in the same place. The reverend journalist says, "He gave great offence as to his doctrine."

These occasional services awakened in the Episcopalians memories of the mother-land. When the man of God opened the service, perhaps with the beautiful selection, " The Lord is in His Holy Temple; let all the earth keep silence before Him," how proudly the few church men and women stood up to their full height, and at the conclusion of the service inwardly resolved to make an effort to have a place of worship of their own. This could not be accomplished but by joining hands with those who were dissatisfied with the minister of the parish on other grounds then his faith and forms of worship. In 1757, an effort was made to induce the pastor and people of the New Casco parish to conform to the English church. This was undoubtedly because some of the parishioners were Episcopalians.

Major Benjamin Waite, one of the numerous and influential Waite family of the Neck, owned and occupied the large farm which included Martin's Point. His house was near the site of the present United States Marine Hospital. Although he lived on the opposite side of the river from the meeting-house and was an Episcopalian, he was a prominent member of the New Casco parish. A few individuals of that parish, who possessed the leaven of Episcopacy, came near leavening the whole lump. The Waites were all churchmen and prominent in the movement for a church. Parson Smith, when told of their success, remarked despondingly, " Like a clock, remove the Waites and the old parish will stop." In September, 1763, the Parson wrote, " I have been discouraged about my enemies; they talk of a new meeting-house."

Brigadier Preble favored a new society of the old order. Colonel John Waite, another leader, insisted on a thorough change. At an evening conference of those interested in the

new society, these two prominent men of the two creeds
became excited, and after getting out doors exchanged blows;
giving Parson Smith a text for a cutting observation in his
diary. He noticed the meeting and the quarrel and closed
with this observation, " A foundation for a church was thus
laid, the pillars tremble."

A subscription paper was circulated in November, 1763,
for a house of worship, not naming the denomination, to
which some forty citizens, of different sections of this and
other towns, signed their names and opposite were written
sums varying from forty pounds down to one pound, ten
shillings. During the next eight months the subscribers
settled the important point, — " That the worship carried on
in said house be agreeable to the laws of Great Britain."
Parson Smith's record of events says in July, " The new
meeting men had a meeting and declared for the church.
They have been in a sad toss since the parish meeting (held
a week before) and made great uproar getting to sign for the
church — they began to frame the house." From the parson's
language it would be inferred that some play-house was to be
set up in his parish, instead of a house of worship, and by a
portion of the most respectable people of the town.

In August, Rev. Mr. Hooper, of Trinity Church, Boston,
preached to the churchmen at the town house ; and the next
Sunday, Rev. Mr. Wiswell, who had resigned his charge of
the New Casco parish, and had consented to take charge of
the new society, preached in the town house. Mr. Wiswell
was born in Boston. He graduated at Harvard College in
1749. He had been settled over the New Casco parish eight
years, when he declared the change in his religious views.
With Mr. Wiswell came Major Benjamin Waite, and several
others of his parish; and yet the parish stood firm. Major

Waite's subscription for the building of the church was nearly double that of any other subscriber.

The project to build a church assumed a definite form and a new paper was signed as follows:

FALMOUTH, July 23, 1764.

At a meeting of the Subscribers for building a new Meeting House, a major part being desirous that the Worship carried on in said House be agreeable to the Laws of Great Britain, It is agreed that the said House shall be made fit for, and appropriate to the worship aforesaid — and we the Subscribers oblige ourselves to pay the sums affixed to each of our names, for the purposes aforesaid.

	£ s d		£ s d
James Hope	13 6 8	James Hope, for Capt }	14 0 0
John Waite Jun'r	26 13 4	Haggett, 10 guineas, }	
Wheeler Riggs	13 6 8	Robert McLellan }	6 13 4
Edward Watts	10 0 0	add'nl sub'n }	
William Waterhouse	4 0 0	John Bradbury	3 0 0
James Ross	6 0 0	John Bouten	0 10 0
Robert McLellan	13 6 8	Ann Oulton	4 0 0
Daniel Pettingail	10 0 0	Hannah Oulton	4 0 0
Stephen Waite	13 6 8	Lucy Oulton	4 0 0
Daniel Ilsley	13 6 8	Andrew Patterson	0 18 0
Edmond Mountfort	13 6 8	Christopher Kelley	6 10 0
Isaac Ilsley Jun'r	20 0 0	Richard Sykes	3 0 0
James Purrington	13 6 8	Joseph Dean	1 0 0
John Motley, in work	10 0 0	Jacob Stickney	5 10 0
Ebenezer Hilton	13 6 8	Henry Wallis	4 16 0
John Burnam	5 0 0	Benjamin Weeks	3 0 0
David Wyer	7 0 0	William Boulton, in boards 13 6 8	
Jonathan Craft	7 0 0	Moses Plummer	2 13 4
Benjamin Waite	40 0 0	William McLellan	4 0 0
John Hans	0 12 0	John Hally	0 10 0
John Minot, after his }	13 6 8	Joseph Pollow	13 6 8
return from sea, }		Jona Tyler (New Glou- }	6 10 6
John Thurlo	6 0 0	cester) }	
Joshua Boynton	13 6 8	Floyd Kilpatrick, in }	1 0 0
Abijah Pool	13 6 8	shingles, }	
George Tate	20 0 0	John McDonald	2 0 0
Daniel McCoy	5 0 0	Richard Googins	1 12 0
Floyd Kilpatrick	1 0 0	Moses Merrill, of No.	
Joshua Eldridge	10 0 0	Yarmouth, one	
Thomas Childs	6 0 0	thousand laths	
William Webb	6 13 4	John Dill, one thous'd	
Geo Tate, for his son }		ditto	
Samuel Tate, in }	4 16 0		
clapboards, }			

John McDonald, Sen'r, of Stroudwater, said that he would pay £20 lawful money in cash and £20 in work.

Brigadier Preble's name does not appear on this paper, but in 1769 he was elected senior warden.

September 4, 1764, the Parish of St. Paul's Church, Falmouth, was organized by the choice of officers. The wardens were James Hope and George Tate, both of whom were merchants, born in England. On the same day of their election, the wardens laid the corner-stone of the little church, which was erected at the west corner of Middle and Church streets. It was fifty feet long and twenty-nine feet wide, had three aisles with three doors opening to them, and sixty pews. It also had a tower and bell.

For the want of bishops in the colonies Mr. Wiswell was compelled to go to England for ordination. Mr. Smith's diary, so often quoted, says Oct. 8, " Mr. Wiswell sailed in the mastship Captain Haggett."

The church was ready for occupancy the following spring, when the Rev. Mr. Wiswell, having been duly ordained Deacon and Priest, according to the usages of the Church of England, returned to enter upon his parochial charge. Ere his arrival Mr. Wiswell had addressed to the parish, who were still busied in completing their new church, the following letter, which we give as furnishing some items of interest not to be found elsewhere :

To the Wardens and Vestry of the Church in Falmouth:

GENTLEMEN — Your Petition to the venerable Society for propagating the Gospel was laid before them, by the Secretary at their last meeting, (Dec'r 21), and the members were unanimously of the opin- ion that Falmouth is a very proper place for a Church, they therefore readily agreed to do something towards the support of a Missionary there and the rather because they were well pleased with the good disposition you have discovered in contributing to the support of the Gospel yourselves. I am commanded by the Secretary to acquaint you that they have agreed to allow £20 sterling pr. annum towards the support of the Gospel at Falmouth provided six or more of the principals give bonds to the Society to pay me or whatever minister you shall hereafter choose £75 sterling per annum; and likewise obligate yourselves to secure a Gleab and House to the value £15 or 10 sterling per annum for the use of your Minister — the Societies' Treasurer is not to pay out any moneyes before such a bond is lodg'd with the Secretary, but the sallory commences from the date of the bond. You will therefore send over a bond by the very first opportunity; and therefore provided you bind yourselves to the above, they bind themselves to add to it the £20 per annum. I acquainted him with my determination to build a House myself — in that case he says you must make over a house lot for future ministers, as the condition of your receiving the above mentioned £20 of the Society and that I consent to a remove to some other place provided these conditions are not fulfilled for they will by no means consent that I as their missionary should set down in Falmouth with a less support. Willing to encourage you in your laudable and pious undertaking they on the receit of the bond will furnish your Church with handsome Prayer Books and Bible, a Parochial Library, and from time to time send handsome presents of small Bibles, Prayer Books and other books of devotion to be distributed among the parishoners, as there may be occasion for them.

I shall do all that lays in my power to promote the interest of the Church of England, especially to ease you under your present burden, which I am sensible is great, in going on with your business so far as my abilities will admit of it. I will also improve every opportunity that offers, to intercede with charitable disposed persons, to contribute something towards it. I pray God preserve you in peace and union, and am with great sincerity,

Your most obedient servant,

J. WISWELL.

London, Dec'r the 26, 1764.

You must direct to the Secretary Dr. Burton in Holborn, Bartlett's Buildings, London — To me at Mr. Green's Pen-cutter in Heel street opposite White Fryars — to be left at the New England Coffee House.

P. S. With regard to the Gleeb and House — Gentlemen — as I intend to build, you have my word upon hon'r that I will never exact it for myself being well content with the £75 sterl. But then the

Society (I mentioning this to the Secretary) expect that you appropriate the Land now and acquaint them therewith. The Secretary
proposed 3 acres I convinced him of the impossibility of procuring
that Quantity, and the price of Land in ye Town I informed him
was very high — and satisfyed him that 1-3 of an acre would answer
the purpose. You will I doubt not comply with their demand,
and I will lay myself under obligation never to demand the profits
for my self.

J. WISWELL.

(Outside) — Pray date the Bond March 1.

Yours,   J. WISWELL.

To Mr. CHILDE.

With these requirements from abroad, the members of
the new parish were taxed not only for the support
of worship in the old parish from which they had
seceded, but also for their proportion of the "settlement
money " given to Mr. Deane, the newly chosen colleague of
Mr. Smith. In consequence they found themselves at once
under heavy pecuniary obligations. Mr. Wiswell's salary of
one hundred pounds sterling had commenced from the date
of his ordination. The expense of building the new church
was by no means inconsiderable and the venerable Society
for propagating the Gospel in foreign parts, in England, to
whom they had, as we have seen, applied for assistance in
support of their minister, required of them very properly,
the purchase of a glebe and the erection of a rectory for the
minister, and their entering into a bond to pay the sum of
seventy-five pounds sterling to their rector, ere the additional stipend of twenty pounds from the society funds was
voted them. Consequently in May, 1765, about the time
of Mr. Wiswell's return, the parish addressed a letter to the
Rev. Mr. Hooper, of Boston, asking his good offices in enlisting the sympathy of the churchmen there in behalf of their

oppressed fellow-worshipers in Falmouth. They might well
seek aid from abroad as their respectful petition to the old
parish for relief from payment of debts they had had no
share in contracting had been denied. The result of this
mission to Boston is not recorded but it was the last labor of
love for the church the venerable James Hope, the first senior warden of the parish, was able to render. On his return,
age and infirmities brought his life to a close, and his was
the second burial Mr. Wiswell was called upon to perform.

The church was opened for divine service June 6, 1765.
The subscribers had been warned the previous May to meet
and "draw the pews" as agreed upon in the original articles
of the association and from this opening, recorded on the fly-
leaf of the register of baptisms, etc., with the occasional
exceptions of their rector's absences and sickness, in the
little frame building on the church lot in Falmouth were
heard the same prayers, the same praises, the same doctrines,
that were sounded forth in the proud cathedrals of the
motherland and the same we listen to now.

A year later and the Rev. Mr. Wiswell was able to report
to the Society in London for the propagation of the Gospel
in foreign parts, from whose bounty he received a portion of
his stipend, that his congregation had increased to seventy
families. He noticed the baptism of one adult and twenty-
seven children, of whom two were blacks, slaves, as the
records of the parish inform us. There had been admitted
to the communion twenty-one, and thus everything betok-
ened a year of prosperity to the infant parish.

In April, 1772, the proprietors at a meeting held at the
house of Mr. Moses Shattuck, "voted, that the Rev. Jno.
Wiswell be desired to bring an action against Mr. James
Milk, Treasurer of the first Parish in said Falmouth for

recovery of the rates of every person who attends worship at said church which said Milk has received and refused to pay to said Wiswell, either in whole or in part." This is the first reference the records furnish us, with regard to the struggle going on ever since the church was established, with the old parish from which its members had withdrawn. The churchmen had, as we have seen, petitioned their former associates for relief, but in vain. They had addressed the general court of the province in 1770 for the removal of these heavy obligations, but, owing to the opposition of the first parish, this application had also failed. In January, 1773, a meeting of the proprietors of St. Paul's was held to draft a petition to this effect, a copy of which is as follows:

To his Excellency the Governor, the Hon'ble his Majesty's Council, and the Hon'ble the House of Representatives.

The Petition of a number of Persons, Members of the Church of England usually attending public worship at St. Paul's Church in Falmouth,

Humbly Sheweth,

That in the year of our Lord 1765 your Petitioners at great expense erected a Church, obtained a Missionary from the Venerable Society for Propagating the Gospel in Foreign Parts, which Missionary they laid themselves under an Obligation to support and hitherto have supported said Missionary by laying a Tax upon the pews of said Church, together with a small Tax upon Persons who were not owners of Pews yet usually and frequently attending Public Worship in said Church,

And whereas your Petitioners have lately been put to a great charge and inconvenience on account of their being assessed as Members of the first Parish in said town for the support of the Gospel Ministry and being desirous to avoid such inconvenience in future humbly Pray that your Excellency and Honors would be pleased to provide a remedy for them touching the Premises, by granting them the Privilege of raising, assessing and levying all Ministerial charges independent of any other Denomination of Christians in said Falmouth in such a way as they hitherto have done or as your Excellency and Honors shall judge most expedient.

And your Petitioners as in duty bound shall ever Pray.

J. Preble,	Jno. Armstrong,	J. Bradbury,
Wm. Simmonds,	Jno. Waite,	J. Morse,
D. Wyer, Jr.,	Stephen Waite,	J. Eldridge,
Wm. Campbell,	J. Purington,	S. Lowther,
A. Osgood,	G. Lyde,	P. Fernald,
Cor. Brimhall,	J. Johnson,	T. Oxnard,
Wm. Wiswell,	M. Shattuck,	P. Camet,
Dan. Pettingail,	E. Oxnard,	B. Waite,
B. White, Jr.,	D. Wyer,	J. Minot,
W. Springate,	J. Waterhouse,	J. Kent,
Jno. Thurlo,	J. Minot,	J. Stone,
Thos. Motley,	A. Pool,	Thos. Child.

In March following a committee consisting of "Jedediah Preble and David Wyer, Esq'rs. and Messrs. Wm. Simmons, Stephen and Jno. Waite" were appointed to treat with a committee of the first parish "to settle the dispute respecting the assessing and collecting taxes from the members of the Church of England." The result of this conference and of a further petition to the general court for relief, appears to have been the relinquishment on the part of the first parish of a legal right, the enforcement of which was in opposition to the dictates of equity and religious freedom.

When the dissatisfaction with the mother country began to assume an angry character, there were in Falmouth not over twenty loyalists or tories, as they were styled, of any prominence, but they were nearly all members of St. Paul's parish, and largely the leading men. Many of them were natives of Great Britain. The minister had ten years before taken orders in London which involved an oath of loyalty. He had seen the resources of the mother country, and supposed the estrangement of the colonies was only an ordinary rebellion which would soon be crushed. With these ideas he left his charge to go on board a man-of-war, with several of his parish, whence he wrote to his wardens resigning his charge.

From on board he addressed the following letter to his friend and fellow-churchman, John Waite, then one of the most prominent Whigs, urging him by the memories of an old and tried friendship to cease his opposition to the crown:

My Dear Friend:

The laws of Friendship oblige me to inform you of the reason that inclined me to go on board the Cansaux, the same day that I told you that " I would not preach on board as things there were situated." About noon I had intimations that, at the Library Chamber, it had been agreed on to make every one in town declare their sentiments, and to secure all who would not join in their measures. *This information* when I compared it with what you said to me this morning, " to take care of my self if I tho't my self in danger," did I confess alarm my fears. In the afternoon Mr. Lyde and Simmons called upon me to go on board the Cansaux; said Capt. Mowat had sent for all to come on board who were the declared friends to government. I did not think it prudent for me to tarry on shore, after receiving this information; and I am more and more confirmed in my opinion that the step I took was a prudent one. 'T was the best method to secure the safety of my self and family, and the real Interest of the Church in this Town.

My religious and my political principles are the same now that they were when our friendship first commenced. For months past I foresaw the confusion and disorder which now takes place, and my heart bleeds when I think upon the greater calamities which this poor deluded people may expose themselves to. I love my Country and am willing to sacrifice every thing but a good Conscience to save it from Destruction.

I know that the People are acting a very wrong part, and should they prosper in their machinations, I am determined never to join them in a rebellion.

Now the sword is drawn I must obey God rather than man; and

act agreeable to the dictates of my Conscience, tho' at the hazard of every thing that is dear to me.

Let me ask you my dear friend, when you first joined with Freeman, Preble, &c., did you suspect that they would ever draw the sword against their King? Six months past you would have startled at the tho't, and have said with Hazael, "Is thy Servant a Dog, that he should do this great thing?" By every thing that is tender and sacred in Friendship, let me persuade you to leave the company of these ab — nd men, and meddle not with those who are given to change. Prov. 24, 21. Sure I am that what they aim to accomplish is inconsistant with your principles, and the means they use, with the goodness and integrity of your heart. I am really concerned for you, now is the time to retreat, but should you persevere (which God forbid), I tremble for the consequences which may happen.

Why will you rashly engage in these measures which may (for all you know to the contrary), prove the ruin of your self, family and country when you may retire to your Island with your wife and children, and there in peace and safety, sit under your own Vine and Fig tree; and have nothing to make you afraid. *

How unhappy shall I be if the phrenzy of the times should dissolve that friendship between us, which I have tho't not Death itself would put an end to. Nor shall any thing make me forget you, cease loving you, praying for you, and exerting my best abilities to promote the spiritual and temporal interest of you and yours.

I am your most affectionate Friend,

J. WISWELL.

Nothing but the ardour and sincerity of my friendship would have put me upon writing to you with so much plainness of speech.

Tuesday Evening, May 2d, 1775.

However we may estimate the judgment the letter displays, it certainly does credit to the tory parson's heart.

After Parson Wiswell resigned his charge of the parish, Edward Oxnard, one of the vestry and a graduate of Harvard College, read prayers the two following Sundays. In compliance with an invitation from the parish to officiate

* Waite had inherited his father's farm on Peak's Island.

temporarily, Rev. Jacob Bailey of St. John's church, Pownal-boro (now Dresden), came here and officiated in the church on the sixteenth of October, and baptized two children; one of them was Hannah, an infant child of Captain John Thurlo, who lived a few rods north of the corner of India and Fore streets. Two days after this service by Mr. Bailey the burning of the Neck occurred, when Captain Thurlo's family were removed from their house which was destroyed. Ninety-one years after, this same Miss Hannah Thurlo was removed from the house on the same spot to escape the great fire of July 4, 1866, but this time the house escaped, and a few years after she died on the spot where she was born, and had lived nearly a century. Her mother was one of the Waite family, so prominent in the parish of St. Paul's. Now comes a hiatus in the history of the parish which includes the eight years of the war of the Revolution.

As soon as the war cloud had passed over, the members of St. Paul's parish made efforts for a reorganization. On the fourteenth of August, 1783, there met at the house of Thomas Motley, inn-holder, all those who felt an interest in the parish and elected officers. Mr. Motley then kept the jail where the old city hall now stands and kept a public house with the sign of the Freemasons Arms, in the keeper's house on Middle street; he was a churchman.

The same summer Bishop Bass, of Massachusetts, came to Falmouth and held service in the new three story house then building by Major Lemuel Weeks, which stood where the Grand Trunk passenger station now is. When the land was needed for the station the house was sawn asunder and moved in halves to the east side of Green, below Portland street, and is now kept as the "Portland House." At that service several children of the Thurlo, Motley, and Minot families were baptized. Parson Smith wrote, " April 6, 1785, the church people had a meeting and subscribed ten pounds pr man for a pew in order to build a church." Lay reading on the Sabbath was resorted to to keep the parish together until a church could be built, which was accomplished in 1787. It was a two story frame building with a tower and bell. The same year a vote was passed by the parish " That in consequence of a number of persons in the town of Windham joining the Episcopal church of Portland, the society do consent that their preacher may repair to Windham three Sabbaths in the year for public worship." Abraham Osgood, who was driven from the Neck by the fire, had built a house there, and John Gallison, another Englishman, resided in the town. They obtained liberty to occupy on the Sabbath the Gambo school-house, where these two zealous churchmen took turns in reading the service, with few others except their own families present. A daughter of Mr. Osgood, who died about fifteen years ago, at the age of ninety-four years, described to me these Sunday services when she was a child.

In 1802 Mr. Timothy Hilliard, a graduate of Harvard College of the class of 1793, was engaged as lay reader. In this year the little wooden church became too contracted for the increasing number of worshipers. Colonel William Tyng had returned, whose wealth and zeal were a great assistance to the growing parish.

Stephen Codman, a merchant, came here from Boston and married a daughter of Thomas Robison. Dr. Shirley Erving, a grandson of Governor William Shirley, also came here from Boston. He was a member of a class in Harvard College when the Revolution broke it up. He went to Europe and studied medicine. He came here in 1798, opened an

21

apothecary store at the junction of Middle and Federal streets, practiced his profession, and held the office of inspector of pot and pearlashes, a great article of commerce at that period. Colonel Richard Hunnewell, who afterward succeeded Colonel Waite as sheriff of the county, came here from Hancock County. All these men were zealous church-men, and with their families and friends very much strength-ened the parish which had grown out of their church building.*

To Dr. Erving more than any other one, the parish was indebted for the spacious and elegant church erected in 1802. He had a natural love for architecture, and from his resi-dence in Europe he had opportunities to correct his taste in its study. It was from his designs and drawings that the church of 1802 was built. Except in the small Quaker meet-ing-house of 1795, which stood on the north corner of Fed-eral and Pearl streets, this was the first attempt in the town to use bricks in church architecture. The exterior was with-

---

*The church of 1786 had a steeple, but at first had no bell. In 1787 the second parish built their meeting-house at the corner of Middle and Deer streets, a few rods below St. Paul's. To give notice of the service they erected a flagstaff on which Burns, the sexton, hoisted a flag. There was considerable feeling between the neighboring sextons. Fernald of St. Paul's had been a Tory in the war, and Burns took much pride in flaunting his flag in the Tory sexton's sight. After a while an English sea-captain gave a small bell to St. Paul's, which was the second in the town. It was hung in the belfry and Fernald rang it with much pride and unction. On a Sunday morning after ringing the first bell for ser-vice, Fernald went across the street to see his neighbor Burns, who had his flag proudly flying, and was waiting in the door to meet Fernald. The Tory sexton before entering looked up to Burns' flag and said "What do you hoist that flag for?" That raised the ire of Burns, who angrily but wittily replied, "To let people know when your bell rings." Fernald did not prolong his visit, but returned to ring his bell with increased vigor.

ST. PAUL'S CHURCH.

Built 1802.

out ornament, except a massive tower, the walls of which were three feet thick, with an open arched belfry intended for a chime of bells, and to support a spire if it was wanted. Only one bell was hung, but that corresponded with the tower; it was heavy and of a noble tone. The solidity of this tower and the excellence of the masonry were shown when it was taken down in 1843 to lengthen the church. It required jack-screws to force over the corner piers of the belfry and when they reached the ground they were still a solid mass of many tons weight. The accompanying engraving gives a good view, and the correct proportions of the church as it stood unaltered.

The beauty of old St. Paul's was its interior. There was a gallery on three sides, supported by Doric columns of wood. Over these, on top of the front of the gallery stood eight Ionic columns, which supported a flat central arch in the ceiling. The most elaborate ornamentation was in the chancel. At that time fine wood carving was resorted to to ornament interiors, which brought the art to great perfection. St. Paul's was the first public building in Maine, in which wood carving was extensively used. Ornamental tracery or beading made from a white lead cement or putty was used in connection with carving for interiors. The thick walls of the church admitted of a deep set chancel window, with flaring jambs and a flat arch, which was made to exhibit this kind of work to advantage. Fluted pilasters outside of all, with richly carved capitals, reached above the window arch and supported a pediment with heavy cornice, enclosed crossed branches of oak, with leaves and acorns in carving. This oak symbolized the English parentage of the church. The pulpit was in keeping with the chancel; it was octagonal and stood on a short, single pillar, with flying stairs to reach it. Over the pulpit, suspended by a gilt chain from a pineapple, hung the sounding-board, of so light make that it seemed that if it was loosened it would as readily go up as down. The long reading desk in front of the pulpit was of corresponding workmanship. Like Solomon's temple, " the cedar of the house within was carved with knops and open flowers." All this carved work from the chancel I have preserved to this time.

On the twenty-fourth of May, 1803, Mr. Hilliard was admitted to Deacon's orders in the Trinity Church, Boston, by Bishop Bass, and received Priest's orders at Middletown, Connecticut, from Bishop Jarvis, June 6, 1805. The consecration of the new church was appointed for September, 1803, but the week previous the good old Bishop of Massachusetts, Dr. Bass, whose interest in old St. Paul's dated far back in its history, was called to his reward. The Church cost eleven thousand eight hundred dollars, and the wardens and vestry paid for the land twelve hundred dollars additional. Nearly the whole sum was raised by the sale of pews at the opening of the building. We append the names of the proprietors in this year (1803). Their names will sufficiently attest the prominence of the revived parish.

Richard Hunnewell,	Mary Watts,	Wm. Moody,
James Fosdick,	George Watts,	George Waite,
Wm. C. Weeks,	Thomas Blake,	Wm. Lord,
Stephen Waite,	Samuel Waite,	John Coe,
Nathl F. Fosdick,	John Thurlo,	Peter Warren,
Robt Motley,	Enoch Preble,	Charles Stimpson,
Thomas Minott,	Richard Codman,	Thos. Peck,
Robert Ilsley,	Martha Oxnard,	Aaron Burnham,
John Motley,	John Waite,	James Corry,
Enoch Ilsley,	Eben Mayo,	Anthony Fernald,
Shirley Erving,	Edward Preble,	Arthur McLellan,
H. G. Quincy,	William Tyng,	Saml Gage,

R. Wilkinson,	Edward Oxnard,	Ezra Gibbs,
Jona Ross,	Amos Noyes,	John Wildrage,
Samuel Pearson,	Stephen Codman,	Robert Tate,
Wm. B. Peters,	Abraham Wilson,	Sylvanus Cook,
Wm. Gorham,	Wm. Symmes,	Thos. Webster,
Alex. Motley,	Thos. Motley,	Salmon Chase,
Joshua Waite,	Joseph Cross, Jr.,	G. Lovis.

Mr. Hilliard continued to officiate until 1808. His wife was a niece and an adopted child of Mrs. Colonel Tyng, and that excellent lady bequeathed her large property, with all the family portraits, rare old books, and other relics, to Mrs. Hilliard and her children. Mr. Hilliard, during his ministry, occupied the Tyng house on Middle street, where Colonel and Mrs. Tyng came on Saturday to attend church the next day. Mr. Hilliard died in 1842, at the Tyng residence in Gorham, where he had removed at the close of his ministry.

The new brick church was erected on the west corner of the original church lot fronting on School street, so named for a school-house which stood on one of its Middle street corners; it is mentioned in the original subscription paper of 1764. It was probably the first school-house built on the Neck. It originally stood near the west corner of Middle and India streets, on what was then King street. Dr. Deane records, "May 25th, 1774, town-house, school-house, and engine-house moved." This was to clear the town lot for the new court-house which was built on that spot that year. School street is now a continuation of Pearl street, with a slight alteration.

There was originally a church-yard adjoining the church of 1764, where were many burials. After the church was burned by Mowatt the bodies were removed, but in digging the cellars for the buildings subsequently erected on the lot, the bones of several persons were found.

When the new brick church was ready for occupation the old one was sold to Mr. Enoch Ilsley, who presented it to the increasing society of Methodists, who removed it to the north side of Federal, near Exchange street, and occupied it for worship until 1811.   It was last used for a carriage maker's shop, when it was burned.

Several ministers officiated in the parish of St. Paul's for brief periods, but after Mr. Hilliard Rev. Petrus S. Tenbroeck in 1819 became the first regularly instituted rector of the parish.   Under the ministrations of this amiable man the number of communicants doubled.

A great acquisition to the parish was Simon Greenleaf, a learned lawyer and a zealous Episcopalian, who finally reached the head of his profession. He came here with his family in 1819, and found St. Paul's church closed for the want of a minister. He first attended Dr. Payson's church, but co-operated with the other Episcopalians in obtaining Rev. Mr. Tenbroeck, who was a descendant of the noted Stuyvesant family of New York City, hence his middle name. Mr. Greenleaf became the leading man of the parish, — the Aaron who held up the hands of the rector. He read the service when the minister's absence required it; and in every way helped to strengthen the parish.*   In 1833 he was

* At the beginning of my own attendance at old St. Paul's, which was in 1823, — then a boy of fourteen, — the chancel and its furnishings were standing objects of wonderment to my boyish eyes. Two chairs which stood in front of the reading desk drew my admiration. I learned then, and since, by inquiry, that they once belonged to our Revolutionary ally, Louis XVI., and were parts of the furnishings of the palace of Versailles. When Louis and his amiable queen Marie Antoinette were beheaded in 1793, these chairs were sold, and by some one brought to

appointed Royal professor in the law school of Harvard University. Although he had taken no degree in any college, he was made an LL.D. by Harvard. He died in October, 1853, at the age of seventy years. Mr. Greenleaf was one of the most spiritually minded men of business I ever knew.

Mr. Tenbroeck resigned the rectorship in 1831. Following him in succession as ministers of St. Paul's came several of the leading men of the denomination in New England. More than one afterward became bishops. In 1839 the parish was reorganized under the name of St. Stephen's Parish; injudiciously as several of the oldest members thought, who refused to accept the arrangement, but continued to attend the services. Paul was robbed to pay Stephen. In 1843 the grand old square tower was removed from the church to be replaced by a more modern one; the splendid interior was torn out because it was unique. In the words of the Psalmist who lamented the desecration of the sanctuary, "They brake down the carved work with axes and hammers." By the payment of a considerable sum, the

Washington, where they were obtained by Silas Lee, a member of Congress from Wiscasset. While attending court in that town Mr. Greenleaf boarded with the widow of Mr. Lee, and from her he obtained these chairs, which were immediately placed in the chancel of St. Paul's. They were arm-chairs but of a light and elegant pattern, and richly carved and gilded. The center of the back was filled with a fine network of cane, and the seats were of crimson Lyons velvet. For years these chairs, from their history and elegant pattern, were objects of interest to all. When the other artistic work was taken out of the chancel these chairs were discarded for others more modern. On Mr. Greenleaf's next visit to town he inquired for these chairs, and found them in a lumber room. As he gave them, twenty years before, he obtained leave to take them home. They are now owned by the widow of his son James, of Cambridge. She was Miss Longfellow, of Portland, before marriage.

writer obtained liberty to gather up the carvings of the chancel, and the eight Ionic columns which stood on the front of the gallery to support the central arch, and deposited these relics of correct architecture and good taste in a place of safety, where they have remained forty-three years in obscurity, with a fair prospect of many years to come, "saved as brands from the burning." * And now even the records of the parish of St. Paul's for eighty years have disappeared but its memories remain.

> " Fleet flies his thought over many a field
>   Of stubble and snow and bloom,
> And now it trips through a festival,
>   And now it halts at a tomb."

From this first offshoot from the old parish on the Neck have sprung three Episcopal churches.

For twenty years after the settlement of Dr. Deane as colleague pastor, and the withdrawal of the churchmen from the old parish, it seems to have gone on smoothly, but the support of two ministers was felt to be a burthen. The meeting-house needed repairs which it was estimated would cost two hundred pounds. Mr. Smith was wealthy, he was growing old and had, of course, lost power to please. He was asked to relinquish his salary which he refused to do.

There was no relief for the disaffected parishioners but to withdraw; but if they did, the state law obliged them to pay taxes to the old parish. So deep was the discontent that they felt confident that a separate society, if started, would succeed. After repeated attempts, the disaffected party, in August, 1787, voted, twenty-nine to thirteen, to

---

* Soon after the new church of St. Paul's at north end was built, by the request of the rector one of the eight pillars preserved was given to the new church and was set in the chancel and surmounted with a cross.

separate from the old parish.   Their preliminary meetings
were held at Mrs. Grele's one story tavern, on the east corner of what are now Congress and Hampshire streets.   A
committee was chosen to draw a plan for a meeting-house,
and to "make enquiry about a piece of land to set it on."
This committee was composed of Enoch Ilsley, Thomas Sanford, Abner Lowell, and Joseph H. Ingraham.   At an
adjourned meeting a committee was chosen to confer with
the first parish.   A plan of a meeting-house sixty-five by
fifty-five feet was accepted.

Mr. Elijah Kellogg, of South Hadley, was invited to
preach temporarily to the society, and meetings for worship
were held in a school-house, and Mr. Kellogg was employed
for six months.   The society petitioned the general court
for an act of incorporation, but the court was probably
influenced by the old parish and did not act promptly.   At
a meeting of the society held February 21, 1788, it was
"voted that if the prayer of our petition is not granted at
the next session, but is ordered to be carried over to a
future one, that Mr. Fox be desired to withdraw it.   Second : that in case the petition is withdrawn, this society
will establish the Presbyterian mode of worship."

The act of incorporation passed on the seventeenth of
March, and the petitioners adhered to their original faith.
The act contained the proviso "that the said second society
shall pay to Rev. Thomas Smith one quarter of the sum
that the first parish shall vote annually for his support."
The names contained in the act as corporators were as
follows :

Joseph McLellan,	Stephen Tukey,	Moses Brazier,
Thomas Sanford,	Appollos Cushing,	James Jordan,
John Fox,	Samuel Goodwin,	Isaiah Tucker,

Joseph H. Ingraham,	James Jewett,	Francis Chase,
John Bagley,	Eliphalet Morse, Jr.,	Abraham Beeman,
John Thrasher,	Daniel Cobb,	Daniel Hodgkins,
Abner Lowell,	Alexander Barr,	Joseph McLellan, Jr.,
Joshua Robinson,	Thomas Webster,	William Bond,
Abner Bagley,	Thomas Hopkins,	Stephen Thomas,
Enoch Moody,	John Scott,	Wimond Bradbury,
Abraham Stevens,	Benjamin Moody,	Daniel Mussey,
George Warren,	Charles Hossack,	John Baker,
Abijah Poole,	Lemuel Weeks,	Caleb Aspenwall,
John Dole,	Eliphalet Dean,	William Jenks,
Nathaniel Morse,	John Emmons,	Joseph Jewett,
George Lowther,	Enoch Morse,	Jonathan Swett,
Thomas Cammett,	William McLellan,	William Brown,
Hugh McLellan,	Rowland Davis,	John Lowell,
Daniel Tucker,	James Deering,	Asa Plummer.
William Moody,	Henry Dinsdale,	

Any one familiar with the past and present of Portland
will attest to the respectability of the corporators. Several
of them attended St. Paul's church before the war, but after
the destruction of their church they returned to the old
parish.

Parson Smith mourned over the separation. In October,
1787, he wrote, "One Kellock came here to preach to the
separatists. Poor Portland is plunging into ruinous confusion by the separation."

The overbearing spirit of the first parish may be inferred
from the following vote of the new society. "1789, voted
not to pay any more toward the quarter part of Rev. Mr.
Smith's salary unless the taxes on our pews in his meeting-
house be considered a part."

In 1788 Rev. Mr. Kellogg was called to settle by the new
society, to have one hundred pounds salary and two hundred
and fifty pounds to build him a dwelling-house, which he

accepted. In his letter he said, "In addition to this you and myself are young. I am invited, not by grey-headed fathers who must soon quit the stage, but by youth and those in middle age. Of consequence then our friendship and love must be more warm and lasting." He also stipulated that if he chose to leave the parish, he should have the privilege "to depart in peace without the vexations of references and councils."

The proposed meeting-house was erected in 1789 on the corner of Middle and Deer streets; not of the stately proportions as we recollect it, as it was lengthened twenty-two feet in 1807 by sawing it apart, moving the rear end back, and building up the gap. When first built it had no tower but was a plain two story building with a flagstaff on the front, on which a flag was hoisted at service time. In 1793 the tower was built; and in 1797 a bell was imported from England by Joseph McLellan and son, and hung in the belfry, and the same year the cupola was finished. The town had voted two years before to procure a clock to be placed in the tower " with four dials." The clock was placed above the belfry.*

In 1807 the celebrated preacher, Edward Payson, afterward doctor of divinity, was settled as colleague pastor with Rev. Mr. Kellogg, who had been sole pastor of the second parish for nearly twenty years, and was pleased at the prospect of having assistance. The church had held a meeting on the subject, and at the adjourned meeting a letter was read to the parish from Mr. Kellogg, of which this is an

---

* Soon after the clock was placed in the tower Enoch Lowell, a carpenter, was in the belfry, and, stepping back, he fell into the box in which the weights of the clock ran down to the ground floor. The box grew gradually smaller toward the bottom into which Lowell was wedged and finally stopped, saving his life.

extract: "In case of Mr. Edward Payson's acceptance of your united call and his harmonious settlement among us as colleague pastor with me, I shall and do hereby reduce my legal and other claims of salary to three hundred dollars pr annum." Mr. Payson was settled, but this connection lasted only about four years. In 1811 the senior pastor was dismissed. Several of his friends retired with him and formed a new society called the Chapel Congregational Society, and built the church edifice on Congress street afterward known as the meeting-house of the third parish.

The second parish meeting-house was the first in town to have an organ set up in it. In 1798 a man named Leavitt, a foreigner, who had a shop for some other business, where the old Bethel building at the foot of Exchange street now is, built a pipe organ which was sold to the second church society and set up in their gallery. It was of good size and appearance, having gilt show pipes. In 1799 the parish voted Nicholas Blaisdell twenty-five dollars for his services as organist. Blaisdell was also weigher of hay.

In about 1820 Mr. Payson's people purchased a larger and finer organ, and the old one, of Portland make, was sold to St. Paul's parish, and set up in their church gallery. Here it remained a few years and then gave place to a larger one, built by Calvin Edwards, then of Gorham. The old one ceased to be a church organ, and was set up in the Portland Museum, in Haymarket Row, where it was burned with the museum.

The great fire of July 4, 1866, destroyed all these church buildings of which I have written, except that of the first parish, and came within the breadth of the street of that.

The deaths of these early ministers of the town of whom I have written occurred as follows: Rev. Thomas Smith died on the twenty-fifth of May, 1795, aged ninety-three years, after a ministry of sixty-eight years. Rev. Samuel Deane died on the twelfth of November, 1814, aged eighty-one years, and in the fifty-first year of his ministry. Rev. John Wiswell, minister of St. Paul's, after he left his parish was three years a chaplain in the British naval ship Boyne. He was afterward engaged as a curate for a short time in Suffolk. In 1782 he arrived at Cornwallis, Nova Scotia, having been appointed missionary to that place. Two of his sons were lieutenants in the navy. Mr. Wiswell was afterward missionary at Aylesford. He died at Wilmot, Nova Scotia, in 1812. His son Peleg was appointed judge of the Supreme Court of Nova Scotia in 1816 and died at Annapolis in 1836, aged seventy-four. Rev. Elijah Kellogg died March 9, 1842, aged eighty-one years. Rev. Edward Payson died October 22, 1827, aged forty-four years. Rev. P. S. Tenbroeck died in January, 1849, aged fifty-seven years.

I have not space to even mention the numerous religious societies of the town which have had their origin in the present century. It should be kept in mind that this work was not intended to be a full history.

There are few intelligent people of mature age in New England, who have never heard of Rev. George Whitefield, the famous revival preacher of the last century. In 1738 Whitefield was sent from England to Georgia by the proprietors of that province, to take charge of a parish. He was a minister of the Church of England, and then not twenty years old. He returned to England in a few months to take Priest's orders, and came back the next year, when he visited some of the middle states, and then came to Boston September, 1740. He traveled as far east as York, attracting more hearers than any minister ever had in New England. The President of Harvard College and leading clergy of Massachusetts opposed his preaching, but with little success. The meeting-houses to which he was admitted would not contain all who wished to hear him, and he preached to the multitude on Boston Common and in open fields. Much excitement attended these meetings; silly people committed excesses for which he was not responsible, but for which he was blamed by his enemies. Neither the clergy nor the laity were all agreed about the wisdom of opening their meeting-houses to the eloquent Whitefield, which caused lasting disaffections in many parishes.

Parson Smith believed in Mr. Whitefield and was instrumental in inducing him to visit Falmouth. He mentions him several times in the autumn of 1744. On the thirty-first of October he says, "Mr. Pearson (Moses) this morning came to see me to oppose Mr. Whitefield's coming." Two days later he says, "I am much about with the people to quiet them with respect to Mr. Whitefield." "23, Mr. Whitefield preached in my pulpit." "26, The wonderful providence of God is to be observed with respect to Mr. Whitefield; that Messrs. Loring and Thompson [ministers], should come just as they did, and that Mr. Whitefield should come just as he did, when Messrs. Pearson, Waite, Wheeler, Moody, Freeman and others were all gone out of town, so that there was no uneasiness; but all well and a general reception. Thanks to God." Parson Smith says there was a violent opposition to Whitefield among all the leading men except Mr. Frost. He did not preach in Parson Smith's pulpit on the Sabbath.* A writer in the New England Journal of 1740, thus describes Mr. Whitefield:

* Samuel Lumber of Brunswick, was sent to York by the opposers of Whitefield, to obtain information for the purpose of beginning a controversy in the church. It was March, and the ice on the Saco river gave way and he and his horse were drowned.—*Vol. 5, Pejepscot Papers, p. 368.*

He is a man of middle stature, of a slender body, of a fair complexion, and of a comely appearance. He is of sprightly cheerful temper, acts and moves with great agility and life. The endowments of his mind are very uncommon; his wit is quick and piercing, his imagination lively and florid, and as far as I can discern, both are under the direction of an exact and solid judgment. He has a most ready memory, and I think speaks entirely without notes. He has a clear and musical voice and a wonderful command of it. He uses much gesture, but with great propriety; every accent of his voice, every motion of his body, are both natural and unaffected. If his delivery is the production of art, 't is certainly the perfection of it.

If Whitefield possessed all these gifts, we need look no further for the source of his power. The gift to express unhesitatingly the thoughts of his active mind, without reference notes, was the witchery that attracted and held the attention of the masses.*

While visiting Newburyport, Massachusetts, in 1770, he was seized with sickness and died there. He was buried under the pulpit of a church there, and has a monument to his memory near his burial-place. He was a graduate of Oxford (England) University.

Open air meetings for worship, known as camp-meetings, date back to the beginning of the present century. A camp-meeting was advertised in 1805 to be held at Norton, Massachusetts, "on a similar plan to those at the south." May 8,

* In 1754, November 15, Joseph Gilman, a clerk of sixteen, wrote from Boston to his mother at Exeter, N. H., these lines: "You write you are afraid I do not improve the kind opportunity providence has indulged me with of hearing Mr. Whitefield. I am sure you have no reason to think so. I inform you that I rose at four in the morning to hear him, and the morning he preached his farewell sermon, I rose at half after twelve at midnight for fear of oversleeping myself, and before four in the morning was at the Old South and waited for his coming. The meeting was exceedingly full and were singing when I got there. I missed no opportunity to hear him."

1806, "Joshua Saul, presiding elder of the Methodist societies, of the district of Maine," advertised that a camp-meeting would commence on the sixth of June, in a pleasant
grove a few rods from the Methodist meeting-house in Buxton. The advertisement seems to be intended to convey the
fact that this was to be the first camp-meeting in Maine. In
1822 a camp-meeting was advertised to be held September
third, at "Pejepscot," afterward Danville; "no liquors to
be sold."

Stoves in meeting-houses were introduced first in large
towns in about 1816. Shaw's History of Boston, published
in 1817, says of the first church there: "It has two iron
fire-stoves fixed in it. In this church was introduced the
first organ ever introduced into a Congregational church
in this town. These two accommodations are altogether
novel in New England churches." An organ was placed in
King's Chapel in Boston in 1713. Two years ago it was still
in use in St. John's church, Portsmouth, N. H., having been
sold in 1836 for four hundred and fifty dollars.

About 1820 stoves became common in meeting-houses.
Previous to that "foot stoves" of tin in a wooden frame,
with a sheet iron pan of live coals were used in the long
service-time to warm the feet of the females of the family.
These were filled from the open fire-place at home and carried by a boy, or were filled at a near house.*

* A few years ago, with the sexton, I was examining the heavy timbers of the roof of King's Chapel, Boston, when I observed a black mass
in the dark west corner of the attic. In reply to my question, the sexton
said he did not know what it was. There was no floor by which to reach
it, but by stepping from one timber to another I came to the dusty pile
and found it to be a large mass of old foot stoves of various sizes, for
years used to keep the feet of the former generations from freezing in
service-time. Some of them may have warmed the family of Governor

The first house of worship in Portland that was warmed by a stove was that of the Quakers, which stood on the south corner of the present Lincoln park. I have heard it described as a large box-stove in the middle aisle, and covered with loose bricks, for any one to take to his seat for the warmth they held. This Quaker stove was a subject of much ridicule, and it was several years before any other meeting-house had one; but they all finally came to appreciate the warmth of a stove in church. In their diaries Parson Smith and Dr. Deane several times mention that the water for baptism froze during the service so they could hardly break it.

Within the bounds of ancient Falmouth was once a family or community of Shakers. They occupied several houses within a mile of Duckpond village. The mother of this order of Christians, Ann Lee, with eight of her followers, arrived in New York, in 1774. They embarked in England in a leaky vessel which they believed was saved by the miraculous power, or in answer to the prayers of " Mother Ann." They settled at what is now Watervliet, New York, seven miles west of Albany. Several people of Falmouth soon after became acquainted with their peculiar faith and manner of life, and formed the community at the Duckpond, and there was a similar family gathered at Gorham. At the organization of the Shaker society in New Gloucester in 1794, the Duckpond family joined them with several others from the Neck. The society had been gathering a year or two earlier than the formal organization.

Shirley. Now these people are cold in the tombs in the basement, or in the adjoining burial ground. The wardens and vestry in their wisdom had these comforting warmers carefully preserved, thinking, perhaps, that the new way of warming churches was only a short lived Boston notion, and the little stoves might be wanted again.

22

I am indebted to Elder J. B. Vance for extracts from the New Gloucester Shaker records, showing that the following persons joined that society from Falmouth and Portland as early as 1793. Betty Gibbs, born in Falmouth 1749, died in the Shaker society, 1818. Robert Wilson, born in Falmouth, 1773, died at New Gloucester, 1832. Cynthia Merrill, born in Falmouth, in 1772, died at New Gloucester, 1846. Sarah Lois Coryl, born in Falmouth, 1773, died at New Gloucester, 1857. Jeremiah Wilson, born in Falmouth, 1771, died at New Gloucester, 1859. These were with the society as early as 1793. Nathaniel Waite, born on Hog Island, Falmouth, 1774, went to New Gloucester with his father, Enoch Waite, in 1803, died there, 1849.

At the death of Elder Otis Sawyer, who was at the head of the New Gloucester society, Elder Vance of the Alfred family succeeded him, and kindly furnished to me the facts promised by Elder Sawyer a short time before his death, in 1884. The following letter from Elder Vance, prepared from Elder Sawyer's memoranda, is of interest.

ALFRED, May 23, 1884.

Friend Goold: According to promise I copy from the late Elder Otis Sawyer's papers the following account of the journey from Portland to Albany of a Company of Believers to see Mother Ann Lee. How many of them were from Falmouth you may know better than I.

I leave out such facts as would not apply to your history.

In the month of August, 1784, a Company from Gorham and Sabbath Day Pond (New Gloucester) chartered a small vessel called "The Shark," twenty-eight tons burthen, of Greenfield Pote of Portland, and fitted her out to go to New York and up the Hudson River to visit Mother Ann Lee. Samuel Brown was Commander and Enoch Waite assistant skipper. The following are the names of that Pilgrim band composed of thirteen males and twelve females:

Robert McFarland,	Dora Abigail Thoms,
Barnabas Bangs,	Lydia Freeman,

Nathan Freeman, Sen.,	Barbara Brown,
Samuel Brown,	Nory Hatch,
Moses Hanscome,	Catherine Bangs,
Nathaniel Stevens,	Betty Cotton,
Ezekiel Hatch,	Hannah Whitney,
James Merrill, Sen.,	Betty Stevens,
Nathan Merrill,	Molly Merrill,
Solomon Twombly,	Raichael Merrill,
Gowen Wilson,	Molly Wilson,
Enoch Waite,	Hannah Starbird.
Thomas Bangs,	

It is stated that Mother Ann saw them in vision before they arrived at Niskenna * and told the little family there to prepare for them, which they did, and when the party arrived they were met at the door with the words " Welcome here, we were expecting you. Mother saw you some days ago and told us to prepare for you."

The party on their return left New York the 7th of September encountering a severe storm the next day, but arrived safely in Portland the following Sabbath morning in season for all to go out to Edmund Merrill's house in Falmouth to breakfast, a distance of about three miles.

Believe me your friend,

J. B. VANCE.

* Now Watervliet, Albany County, seven miles west of Albany.

CHAPTER X.

AT the beginning of the troubles with the home government which finally led to the Revolution, Falmouth was
engaged in a profitable trade with Great Britain and the
West India Islands. Regardless of their pecuniary interests, the people on all occasions which required it, expressed
their opinions of the overbearing acts of the government
fearlessly. The revival of the sugar act and its enforcement
by odious officers of the government, caused the first
trouble. The people of the colonies argued that "if our
trade may be taxed, why not our lands and their produce?
This annihilates our charter to govern and tax ourselves."
Before the passage of the sugar act, smuggling had been
winked at by the custom-house officers, but now the odious
law was rigidly enforced and large seizures were made in
Boston and Salem.

On the seventh of August, 1767, the collector of Falmouth seized a quantity of rum and sugar, belonging to
Enoch Ilsley, for breach of the revenue act. In the evening
a mob attacked the house of the comptroller, Arthur

Savage, where the Casco Bank now is. The collector, Francis Waldo, was in the house at the time, and they were prevented from leaving the house until another party broke open the custom-house on India street, and removed the goods to secret places of safety. Governor Barnard issued a proclamation offering a reward of fifty pounds for the discovery of any persons engaged in the removal of the goods from the custom-house. It seems by a Salem paper of the next July, that the prisoners were released from jail by another mob. A communication from Falmouth to the Essex Gazette of August 9, 1768, says: "About thirty men, armed with clubs, axes, and other weapons, attacked the jail in this town (Market square), and rescued two men, John Huston and John Sanborn, who had been convicted of a riot."

The stamp act followed the sugar act in February, 1765, to go into effect in November following. The news of its passage roused the indignation of the people from Maine to Georgia. In August, a mob in Boston completely destroyed the elegant house of Lieutenant-Governor Hutchinson. About the same time the new stamp house was also destroyed by the excited mob.

In Falmouth the mob spirit was awakened, and on the arrival of a brig from Halifax, in January, 1766, with the stamped papers for Cumberland County, they were demanded at the custom-house. On receiving them, the people carried them through the town at the top of a pole to a bonfire prepared for them, where they were burnt in the presence of a large concourse of approving people.

These excited assemblages produced alarm in England. The merchants and manufacturers were earnest in their pleas for the repeal of the obnoxious act, which was accomplished in March, 1766. By the arrival of Captain Samuel Tate in a mast ship May 16, in thirty days from London, the Falmouth people received their earliest news of the repeal of the stamp act. The Boston Evening Post of June 2 gives the following account of the reception of the news from Boston about the same time.

On Sunday noon an express arrived from Portsmouth with a confirmation of the great and glorious news, (for whom a handsome collation was made), which seemed to change the countenances of all ranks of people; on which occasion an anthem was sung after service at church. The morning following was ushered in with every demonstration of loyalty and joy that could be expressed; such as ringing of bells, firing of cannon at the fort and on board the shipping in the harbor. In the evening the houses of the town were beautifully illuminated, fireworks played off, bonfires erected, etc. The whole conducted with so much order and decorum that it did great honor to the town.

On the nineteenth Parson Smith gives about the same account of the rejoicing, except the " order and decorum "; he closes with " and a deluge of drunkenness."

The act of Parliament closing the port of Boston caused a deep feeling of sympathy with that town throughout the colonies, and liberal contributions of provisions and clothing were received from all of them. The act went into effect on the first day of June, 1774, and a month after contributions began to be received. The cash receipts amounted to nearly eight thousand pounds. Of different kinds of grain and corn, over thirty thousand bushels were contributed; and about four thousand barrels of flour. On the day the " Port-bill " took effect, the bell of the Falmouth first parish was muffled and tolled from sunrise until nine o'clock in the evening. In January, 1775, Falmouth sent to the suffering town fifty-one cords of wood, and in March of the same year, a second lot of thirty-one cords. Cape Elizabeth sent forty-four cords. The other towns in Maine which contributed cash and supplies were York, North Yarmouth, Kittery, Berwick, Biddeford, Scarborough, Wells, and Gorhamtown.

At the time of the arrival of the tea ships in Boston the people of Falmouth in town meeting "Resolved that we will not buy nor sell any India tea whatever, after this third day of Feb. until the act that lays a duty on it is repealed." There were then two thousand five hundred pounds of tea in the hands of the dealers in town. Another resolve, passed at this meeting, acknowledges their obligation to "the people of Boston, for their early notice of approaching danger," and for "their intrepid behavior on the late tea-ships' arrival, and trust they will still be our watch-tower, and they may depend on our utmost endeavors to support them at all times, in defence of their rights and liberties." Also, "we rejoice that though surrounded by fleets and armies, you yet remain firm and resolute." At the close of the proceedings the town "voted that a committee be chosen to meet committees of other towns to consult on the alarming state of public affairs."

Mr. Freeman says his notes, after he left Falmouth, were transcribed from the letters of a gentleman in Falmouth to his friend in Watertown. The friend in Watertown was no doubt himself, as he was then in attendance at the provincial congress, and the only delegate from Falmouth. From some circumstances and expressions I am led to believe that the writer of the letters was General Jedediah Preble, a leading merchant of the town, and a member of the committee of inspection.

Captain Samuel Coulson had been for several years

engaged in the mast business between Falmouth and Bristol, England, from whence he came, and had married a daughter of the elder Dr. Coffin, of Falmouth, and resided in the doctor's house on King street. He had built a very large ship for those days at the foot of his street. She was of one thousand tons. To ship masts required large vessels.

Captain Coulson was violently opposed to the popular sentiment of the colonies, and made himself very obnoxious to the people. On the second of May, 1775, a vessel of Coulson's arrived from Bristol, with rigging, sails, and stores, for the new ship. There was a committee of inspection, composed of leading men of the town, one of whom was Samuel Freeman. This committee was called together at the library chamber the same day of the arrival of Coulson's vessel.

There was a compact between the colonies called the "American Association," the provisions of which may be understood from what took place in the committee meetings. Coulson by a vote was desired to attend on the committee. In answer to questions he stated that the vessel was from Bristol, with stores and materials for his new ship. A subcommittee was chosen to go on board and see if there were any other goods there.

At an adjourned meeting of the committee the next day, it was voted that to allow Captain Coulson to land his goods, and appropriate them to fit out his new ship, would be a violation of the "American Association," and directed that they be sent back to England without breaking the packages. This was communicated to Captain Coulson by a sub-committee. Coulson immediately attended, and said the vessel must be repaired before she could go to sea, and in order to do that the freight must be landed; but the vote was adhered to, and the proceedings of the meeting were, by vote, posted up in a public place in the town. Instead of obeying the order to return the goods to England, Coulson left for Boston, under the pretence of asking leave of the provincial congress to rig his ship, and procured the assistance of Captain Mowatt in the sloop-of-war Canceau, to aid and protect him in rigging and loading his ship, and proceeded to land his materials.

During the excitement caused by Coulson's bringing the vessel to assist him in violating the provisions of the Association, on the twenty-first of April news arrived of the battle of Lexington. On the twenty-third a town-meeting was held, and spirited proceedings were adopted, notwithstanding the Canceau was lying in the harbor, whose commander Coulson and others were constantly urging to make some demonstration. The news of the battle of Lexington, set the whole country in a blaze of excitement. At Falmouth a company of sixty soldiers was raised and hurried off to Cambridge.

Next came what Mr. Freeman calls, "Thompson's War." On Tuesday, the ninth of May, Colonel Samuel Thompson, of Brunswick, with about fifty soldiers, came in boats and landed secretly on the north side of the Neck, and encamped in a grove of pines. Each man had a small sprig of spruce in his hat, and a small spruce tree with the lower branches cut off was their standard. They seized and detained several persons who happened to pass that way, in order to conceal their camp from the towns-people. About one o'clock in the afternoon, Captain Mowatt, his surgeon, and the Rev. Mr. Wiswell, of St. Paul's church, were walking for pleasure in the vicinity, when they were seized and made prisoners. As soon as Lieutenant Hogg, then in command of the Canceau, heard of the capture of Captain Mowatt, he sent a threatening letter on shore. General Preble, in a letter to the provincial congress dated on the fourteenth, says, "He clapped springs to his cables and swore if the gentlemen were not released before six o'clock, he would fire on the town. He fired two cannon, and although there were no shot in them, it frightened the women and children to such a degree that some crawled under the wharves, some down cellar, and some out of town."

Some of the prominent men of the town visited Thompson's camp to urge the release of the prisoners. Thompson and his men were inflexible, but night coming on, they concluded to march the prisoners to Marston's tavern for a more sheltered consultation. The soldiers, including a Falmouth company which had assisted in the escort, were paraded in front of the house. Thompson argued that open hostilities between the colonies and the mother-country existed; that Providence had thrown the prisoners in his way, and that they were rightly held. He finally found that the whole town was against him, and at about nine o'clock he concluded to release them, by their giving their parole to come on shore the next morning; General Preble and Colonel Freeman pledging themselves for them. The principal reason given by the Falmouth men for urging their release, was that several vessels were daily expected with corn and flour, of which the town stood very much in need.

Parson Smith, in his journal, under date of the twenty-sixth of June, says: "People are apprehensive of a famine, there being a scarcity of corn and flour." A few days after, he mentions the arrival of three vessels, "with corn and flour." "So we are plentifully relieved from all fears of famine. Blessed be God."

At the appointed hour of nine, on Wednesday morning, Thompson began to look for his prisoners, but none came; whereupon his men became furious, and seized their sureties, Preble and Freeman, and kept them all day without dinner. In the afternoon they sent to Mowatt to know why he did not keep his parole. His reply was, that one of his men whom he had sent on shore to his washerwoman, had overheard several threats from soldiers to shoot him as soon as he made his appearance, and he declined coming. During the afternoon a large force of militia from the country, numbering five or six hundred, arrived, and being greatly enraged on hearing of Mowatt's release, threatened violence to General Preble and Colonel Freeman, the sureties.

All the officers of the militia, including those of Falmouth, next resolved themselves into a board of war, for the examination of tories, and summoned several persons before them. Some came. The Rev. Mr. Wiswell had not gone on board the ship, and attended at the appointed time. In answer to questions, he declared his abhorrence of the doctrine of passive obedience and non-resistance, and was released. Several others were examined, but none were punished. To keep peace and secure his release with Colonel Freeman, General Preble was obliged to furnish the troops with several barrels of bread, a quantity of cheese, and two barrels of rum for each company.

The soldiers entered Captain Coulson's house and took what they wanted, and used the house for a barrack. Some of them became exhilarated by the liquor found in Coulson's cellar, and one, named Calvin Lombard, went down to the shore and fired two balls from a musket, deep into the side of the Canceau. The fire was returned from a "fusee," but no damage was done.

Thursday, the eleventh, was a general fast, which General Preble and Colonel Freeman were not prepared for, as the soldiers had obliged them to fast the day before.

The soldiers seized one of Coulson's boats and dragged it through the streets, to a place of safety, and the next day they seized one of Mowatt's, and hauled it to the same place. Mowatt threatened to fire on the town if they were not returned, but Mr. Freeman's friend writes to him at Watertown, that "he has not fired yet, and here I sit writing at my desk in the old place, being fully convinced that Mowatt never will fire on the town in any case whatever." He also writes: "The soldiers have to-day carried off Mr. Tyng's Bishop, a piece of plate worth five hundred pounds, old tenor, and his laced hat." These were afterward returned to Mrs. Ross, the mother of Mrs. Tyng, by a resolve of the provincial congress. The property destroyed in Coulson's house, and valued at one hundred and forty pounds lawful money, was paid for by authority of the same resolve.

On Friday afternoon, the last of the country soldiers left town, much to the relief of the people. On Saturday, Mowatt made another demand for the boats, but Thompson's men had taken them away when they left. On Monday, Mowatt and Coulson sailed with their ships for Portsmouth and Boston.

On the eighth of June, the Senegal of sixteen guns, Captain Dudington, arrived from Boston, and anchored near the islands, and on the twelfth Coulson arrived again in his new ship, and anchored near the Senegal.* Sheriff Tyng, who had taken refuge with his friends in Boston, was with

* The Senegal was one of the squadron that brought the troops to Boston in September, 1768, in answer to a request from Governor Barnard.

Coulson. In reply to a letter, Captain Dudington of the Senegal wrote the committee that "his orders were to protect the persons and property of his majesty's faithful subjects and not to distress them."

The wives of Sheriff Tyng and Captain Coulson were permitted to go on board the ships; but the committee would not consent that Coulson should have his masts with which he intended to load the ship, as he was a declared enemy of the town. On his arrival, the people had floated them up the harbor out of his reach, the provincial congress having passed a resolve to prevent tories taking their property out of the country.

Coulson next sent an armed boat to the mouth of Presumpscot river, ostensibly for water, but in reality to look out masts and timber for a cargo for his ship. The people seized his boat, guns and men, but finally released his men. Coulson finding he could not get his masts and was losing his boats, sailed without them. These masts were secured in a cove at Cape Elizabeth, near Vaughan bridge, where they remained over sixty years. All left of them in 1835 were built into Sawyer's wharf, at the foot of High street, and they are now covered by Commercial street.

After Captain Coulson had left Boston for Falmouth to take in his masts, Captain Crandall, of Harpswell, was taken by one of Admiral Graves' fleet and carried into Boston, and on his release he reported his interview with the admiral. After the burning of the town, to prove that it was done by order of the admiral, Captain Crandall's sworn statement was procured. I here copy a part of his affidavit from Freeman's notes:

That sometime in the month of June last, I sailed from Harpswell for Salem, and on my passage there I was forcibly taken by an armed

vessel and carried into Boston. And being in the presence of
Admiral Graves, he asked me if such a man-of-war (he named her,
but I have forgotten her name) had arrived at Falmouth. I answered
that I heard she had. He then asked me if I thought she would be
opposed by the people. I answered I could not tell. He then asked
me if Captain Coulson was loading at Falmouth. I replied that I had
heard he met with such opposition from the people as to prevent it.
Upon which the admiral said: " You may tell them that if they will
not let him load, I will send a ship, or ships, and beat the town down
about their ears."

(Signed)   PHILIP CRANDALL.

Sworn to on the 1 of Jan. 1776, before Wm. Sylvester,
of Harpswell, Justice of the Peace.

Dr. Deane says (page 341 of his diary): " Capt. H. Mowatt, of Scotland, obtained, by his most urgent solicitation, an
order from Graves, &c." Mr. Willis, in his History of Portland, page 518, says: " The vessels came here direct from
Boston, and no doubt can be entertained but that the order
proceeded from Admiral Graves, who then commanded on
this station, whose mind had been influenced by the representations of Mowatt, Coulson, and others." In a letter
from Governor Bowdoin to Governor Pownall in London,
dated in Boston in 1783, he says " The town was wantonly
burnt, by order of Admiral Graves."

From the authorities quoted I think all will be convinced
that the bombardment was by Admiral Graves' orders, in
consequence of representations from Mowatt and Coulson.

The following is a condensed sketch of the burning. The
facts are principally taken from the letters of the Hon.
Enoch Freeman, chairman of the committee of safety, to his
son Samuel in Watertown, with the statements of other eye-
witnesses.

On the sixteenth of October, 1775, the people of Falmouth
were surprised by the arrival below of a squadron of four

armed vessels and a store-vessel. The wind being fresh from the northwest the vessels anchored near the islands. When the people learned that Captain Mowatt was in command they supposed he had come for sheep and cattle, for the British forces in Boston. As there were large stocks of cattle on the islands, the enlisted men composing one company and part of another were at dusk sent down quietly to guard the sheep, cattle, and hay.

The next day, Tuesday, the wind being still ahead and very strong, the vessels were warped up the harbor, and anchored in line in front of the town. By a drawing, still preserved, we are enabled to fix the position and rig of each vessel. The Canceau of sixteen guns, the flag-ship, was anchored opposite the foot of India street, next above was a schooner of twelve guns, then the ship Cat, of twenty guns, opposite Union wharf, and a bomb sloop above all. The store-schooner took a station below the armed vessels.

Late in the afternoon, Captain Mowatt sent an officer on shore with the following letter:

CANCEAU, FALMOUTH, OCT. 16th, 1775.

After so many premeditated attacks on the legal prerogative of the best of sovereigns, after the repeated instances you have experienced in Britain's long forbearance of the rod of correction, and the manifest and *paternal* extension of *her* hands to embrace again and again, *have* been regarded as vain and nugatory; and in place of a dutiful and grateful return to your king and parent state, you have been guilty of the most unpardonable rebellion, supported by the ambition of a *set* of designing men, whose insidious views have cruelly imposed on the credulity of their fellow creatures; and at last have brought the whole into the same dilemma; which leads me to feel not a little the woes of the innocent of them in particular, from my having it in orders to execute a just punishment on the town of Falmouth, in the name of which authority, I previously warn you to remove without delay, the human *specie* out of the said town, for which purpose I give you the time of two hours, at the period of which a red pendant will be hoisted at the main top gallant mast head, with a gun. But should your imprudence lead you to shew the least resistance, you will in that case free me of that humanity so strongly pointed out in my orders, as well as in my inclination. I do also observe, that all those who did on a former occasion fly to the king's ship under my command for protection, that the same door is now open to receive them.

The officer who will deliver this letter, I expect to return immediately unmolested.　　　　　　　　I am, &c.

　　　　　　　　　　　　　　　　H. MOWETT.

Dr. Deane says: "Near sunset he made known his errand by a flag (of truce), with a letter full of bad English, and worse spelling."

The Rev. Jacob Bailey, of Pownalborough, who had been officiating at St. Paul's church after Mr. Wiswell had left, says in a letter: "The officer landed at the foot of King street amid a prodigious assembly of people and was conveyed with uncommon parade to the town-house, and silence being commanded, a letter was delivered, and read by Mr. Bradbury, a lawyer; but not without such visible emotion as occasioned a tremor in his voice." After repeating the contents or import of the letter, he says: "It is impossible to describe the amazement which prevailed on the reading of the alarming declaration. A frightful consternation ran through the assembly; a profound silence ensued for several moments. Then a committee of three was chosen, one of whom was Dr. Coffin, brother of the wife of Captain Coulson, to wait on the commodore." This and much more is from the pen of one who received his support from the mother country and was a loyalist. His description of the bombardment, and the fright of the people, makes the scene appear almost ludicrous.

Beside Dr. Coffin, mentioned by Mr. Bailey, General Preble and Robert Pagan were on the committee. It is worthy of remark that this committee were all Episcopalians, and members of St. Paul's parish. The committee immediately went on board the Canceau. In answer to their remonstrance, Captain Mowatt informed them that his orders from the admiral did not authorize him to give any warning to the inhabitants, but they required him to come " opposite the town with all possible expedition, and there burn, sink and destroy," and that he had taken it upon himself to give warning, at the risk of losing his commission.

The committee say, " We expostulated with him upon the severity of such orders, and entreating that if possible some method might be fallen upon to save the town ; or at least to give the inhabitants an opportunity of moving some of their effects; upon which he said, that if the inhabitants would in the morning, by eight o'clock, deliver up four pieces of cannon which were then in the town, with their arms in general, and ammunition, he would in that case do no harm to the town until he had despatched an express to the admiral, who he did not doubt would order him to save the town. And as a token that his demand would be complied with, he required that eight small arms should be delivered up by eight o'clock that evening, which should be the condition of the town's being safe until eight o'clock the next morning."

The committee told him that his demands would not in their opinion be complied with, but that they would inform the town of his conditions. The committee communicated the result of their interview with Captain Mowatt to the people, who were waiting in the town-house. No vote was taken, but it was thought best to send the small-arms that

23

evening, in order to gain time to remove the sick, with the women and children, and what property could be got away that night.

Wednesday morning, the eighteenth, the citizens met at the court-house and "resolved by no means to deliver up the cannon and other arms," and sent the same committee with the answer.

When we consider that Mowatt's four ships with shotted guns already run out, and springs on their cables ready for the bombardment, were anchored in line of battle, within a very short distance of the heart of the town, we must conclude that the decision of the meeting was plucky. No more fearless and patriotic action by a deliberative body of people in such an exposed and helpless condition was taken during the struggle of the colonies, and it should be commemorated on the anniversary of its occurrence. They coolly gave their homes to the flames rather than surrender a principle.

We left the committee on their way to the ship, with the answer of the towns-people to Mowatt's demand. They were directed to spend as long a time on board as possible, to give time to secure more property. They remained on board until half-past eight o'clock, when they were requested by Mowatt to go on shore. He probably felt sore at the refusal of the citizens to be disarmed. The committee obtained half an hour to get out of the way themselves.

Prompt at the moment of nine o'clock, the dreaded signal went up "to the main-top-gallant-mast head with a gun" on board the flag-ship, followed immediately by the blood red pennant on all the other vessels: an appropriate color under which to commit such a dastardly act.

Colonel Enoch Freeman, in his letter to his son, says:

" The firing began from all the vessels with all possible brisk-ness, discharging on all parts of the town, which lay on a regular descent toward the harbor, an horrible shower of balls from three to nine lbs. weight, bombs, carcasses, live shells, grape-shot and musketballs. The firing lasted, with very little cessation, until six o'clock P.M., during which sev-eral parties came on shore to set buildings on fire. Parties of our people and others from the neighboring towns ran down to oppose them, and it is thought killed several."

I am writing this in a house the frame of which was partly raised that morning. The men employed heard the guns ten miles off, and knew what they meant, and they hurried away to the assistance of Falmouth.

Of the parties who landed to set fires, one officer was struck down and disarmed near the present custom-house, according to Dr. Deane.

I saw, years ago, a tin speaking-trumpet, nearly eaten up by rust, which was taken from an officer with a torch in his hand. This, with several cannon-shot, was kept in a closet under the high pulpit of the old meeting-house of the first parish. The shot had pierced the venerable structure, and set it on fire; but the fire was extinguished. This trumpet and the shot were then kept there as mementos of the burn-ing. One shot is still preserved. I have never seen this trumpet alluded to in any account of the bombardment.

None of the towns-people were killed, and only one was wounded. Widow Alice Grele, who kept the fashionable tavern of the town, saved her house by remaining in it, and extinguishing the flames when it caught fire.* The select-

---

* A good story was told which illustrated the coolness and simplicity of Ma'am Grele. It was a well-known fact that she saved her house by remaining in it. A hot shot, after its ricochet, landed in her back yard,

men, in a published statement, say that about three-quarters
of the buildings, including one hundred and thirty dwelling-
houses, St. Paul's (Episcopal) church with the bell, the
town-house, a new fire-engine, and the public library were
consumed.

> He claimed to use the sovereign's rod
> In battering down the house of God.
> And sent men to the lawless siege
> Whose best success was sacrilege.

Only one or two wharves escaped the flames. What vessels
were not consumed were taken away by the enemy, for such
we must now call them.

On Pointer's draught, every house and store and public
building were drawn as they stood before the fire; those
which were destroyed were so marked. This draught was
sent to Dr. Deane to correct, which he did. In a letter to
Mr. Freeman on this subject, he says: "Let barns, &c., be
placed where you can recollect any, and perhaps it would not
be amiss to make some where you *do not* recollect any." It
was then the intention to have it engraved immediately, but
this was not done.*

and fired the chips. She took it up in a pan and threw it into Hampshire street, and said to a man who was passing, "They will have to stop
firing soon, for they have got out of bombs, and are making new balls,
and can't wait for them to cool."

* I have an authentic plan of the Neck with every building and wharf.
The title is this: "A plan of Falmouth now Portland as it appeared the
day before its destruction by Mowatt on the 18th of October 1775; by
Lemuel Moody."

Captain Moody was eight years old when the town was burnt. By the
expression in the title "now Portland" the plan was not drawn until as
late as 1786, eleven years after the burning, and when the draughtsman
was nineteen. Captain Moody was a shipmaster, and was the prime
mover and principal proprietor in the observatory, which was erected in

The following is an extract of Rev. Jacob Bailey's letter, describing the bombardment.

The morning was clear, calm, and pleasant, without a breath of wind, and the town was crowded with people and carts from the country to assist in removing the goods and furniture of the inhabitants; but notwithstanding all this suspension and assistance, many were obliged to leave most of their movables exposed to the fire, and were able to save nothing from the general destruction.

At length the fatal hour arrived! At exactly half an hour after nine the flag was hoisted to the top of the mast and the cannon began to roar with incessant and tremendous fury. The streets were full of people, oxen, and horses. The oxen, terrified at the smoke and report of the guns, ran with precipitation over the rocks, dashing everything to pieces and scattering large quantities of goods about the streets.

And now a scene inexpressibly grand and terrible was exhibited in view of thousands of spectators. Bombs and carcasses, armed with destruction and streaming with fire, blazed dreadfully through the air and descended with flaming vengeance on the defenceless buildings. It was impossible for persons of sensibility and reflection to behold the mingled multitude without emotion; to see the necessitous and the affluent, the gentleman and mechanic, the master and servant, the mistress and maid, reduced to the same undistinguished level. Those ladies who had been educated in all the softness of ease and indulgence, who had been used to the most delicate treatment, and never ventured out of town without an equipage and proper attendants, are now constrained to travel several miles on foot to seek a shelter from the cold and the tempest. About three-quarters of the town was consumed, and between two and three hun-

1807, and of which he had the charge during the remainder of his life, which terminated in 1846.

The plan came into the hands of Mr. York, whose wife was the granddaughter of Captain Moody. By him it was loaned to me to have it restored. It has been elegantly copied by Mr. William S. Edwards, the civil engineer. It adds to the value of the plan to know that it was drawn by one who was born in the town, and was familiar with every street, wharf, and building of the then little town.

dred families, who twenty-four hours before enjoyed in tranquility their commodious habitations, were now in many instances destitute of a hut for themselves and families; and as a tedious winter was approaching, they had before them a most gloomy and distressing prospect.

Much of Bailey's letter giving his Tory view, of course, of the burning, is omitted. He had no word of censure for the wanton burning of the church in which he officiated and baptized two children three days before.

In 1796, Dr. Timothy Dwight, then President of Yale College, visited Portland. In the second of his four volumes of travels he gives a description of the town and people, and its past history. He says: "Among the most respectable inhabitants of this town from whom we received an uninterrupted succession of civilities was Gen. Wadsworth"; from whom he probably obtained the following facts. In his account of Mowatt's bombardment he thus mentions Brigadier Preble, who had then been dead twelve years:

General Preble, whose heart swelled with an indignation which no words can express, at this violation of all faith and decency, this ungrateful return for his own kindness, this outrageous cruelty towards such a number of people, perfectly innocent, and claiming from Captain Mowatt respect and good will for their civilities to him, refused to retire, or to take any measures for the security of his person or property, and spent the whole period while the devastation was going on, upon the ground near the northeastern corner of the town, exposed in the most open manner to the shot and shells, nor could all the solicitations of his friends persuade him to retire. Captain Mowatt has achieved the immortality of Erostratus; and will be remembered by future generations as a fiend and not as a man.

The first tears I ever shed for public misfortunes were, I think, for the suffering women and children of Falmouth.

When a boy I often heard their story repeated by an old lady, who lived near my father's, until I was afraid to go home in the evening for fear of meeting Mowatt, or some of his incendiaries, with a fire-brand. This good woman, at the time of the burning, lived in the town, in "Clay Cove." Her husband had enlisted in the continental army, intending to leave his wife and child in their snug home in Falmouth. On the arrival of the ships he was one of those who went to the islands to guard the cattle and sheep, and could not return until the firing had commenced. His name was Barton, and he was then about twenty-eight and his wife twenty years old. Mrs. Barton remained in her house waiting for her husband, until the hot shot and shell began to fall near, and several of the neighboring buildings were on fire, and her own dwelling had become untenable. She could wait no longer. She tied up her only feather bed with some small articles of clothing in a sheet, and slung it over her shoulder. She then took her little boy on her other arm and fled from the burning town. To reach a place of safety she was obliged to walk nearly a mile through the most thickly settled part of the town, with the ships in full view. Several times bombs with their smoking fuses fell near her, and she quickened her pace to escape the explosion. With many others she took shelter under the high ledges near the Casco street church, which have since been blasted away. The vicinity was then a grove of oaks, which gave Oak street its name. A three pound shot fell near her, which she secured. Here her husband found her on his return from the islands, and here they remained until nearly night. When the firing had slackened they ventured out, and, after depositing their bed in a place of safety, walked to her father's in Windham, eleven miles; one carrying the child, and the other the cannon shot, and occasionally changing.

Their dwelling and household goods were burnt, and they were compelled to begin the world anew. Barton built a small log-house half a mile from the father's, and here he left his wife and joined Captain Richard Mayberry's company as corporal. This was the fifth company of the eleventh regiment of the Massachusetts Bay forces, in the army commanded by General Gates, at the capture of Burgoyne in 1777. This company was also in the battles of Monmouth and Hubbardston. At the end of his term of three years service, Barton left the army, and was paid off in paper money which was almost worthless. He came home and went to work with a will, but was soon after killed by a falling tree. His widow suffered many hardships in her poverty, but a government pension very much relieved her declining years. She died in 1841, aged eighty-six.

On the day set apart for the commemoration of the soldiers' services and sufferings, I am careful that Barton's grave is not forgotten.

> The flag goes up! the cannons' breath
> Wings the far hissing globe of death;
> And there the volleying thunders pour,
> Till waves grow larger to the roar;
> And down come blazing rafters strown
> Around, and many a falling stone,
> Deeply dinted in the clay,
> All blackened there and reeking lay.
> The walls grew weak; and fast and hot
> Against them poured the ceaseless shot,
> With unabated fury sent
> From battery to tenement;
> And thunder-like the pealing din
> Rose from each heated culverin;

And here and there some quiet home
Was fired before the exploding bomb:
And as the fabric sank beneath
The shattering shells' volcanic breath.
In red and wreathing columns flash'd
The flame, as loud the ruin crashed;
Or into countless meteors driven,
Its earth-stars melted into heaven;
Whose clouds that day grew doubly dun,
Impervious to the hidden sun,
With volumed smoke that slowly grew
To one wide sky of sulphurous hue.
The horses from their drivers broke:
The distant steer forsook his yoke,
The nearer steed plunged o'er the plain,
And burst his girth, and tore his rein:
The wolves yelled on the wooded hill,
Where echo rolled in thunder still:
With sudden wing and ruffled breast,
The eagle left his lofty nest,
And mounted nearer to the sun,
The clouds beneath him seemed so dun;
Their smoke assail'd his startled beak,
And made him higher soar and shriek —
" Thus the coward act was done! "

The news of the battles of Lexington and Concord arrived
here on the twenty-first of April, two days after they
occurred, when a town-meeting was called which Dr. Deane
says was fully attended. The Doctor recorded several days
previous that "Some minute men appeared in town, with
extraordinary sort of caps, who were found to be very expert
in the military exercise." Parson Smith says on the twenty-
first, " Our company of soldiers set out for Boston." I have
no means of knowing what company was meant. The
Plymouth men probably belonged to it. They must have

enlisted before the news of the battles, as they left for headquarters on the day of the arrival of the news. Mr. Freeman says in his notes there were three companies raised in Falmouth, Scarborough, and Cape Elizabeth, in the beginning of the war. Captain Brackett, with a company, marched from here for Cambridge on the third of July. On the sixth Dr. Deane preached to Captain David Braddish's company, who Parson Smith says " belong to us." The company were at meeting on the sixteenth, but probably left very soon after.

During the French and Indian wars, commencing with that of 1675, there were many garrison houses in Falmouth, some built for the purpose, but most of them had timber flankers added to the corners with watch-boxes, to houses already built. Nearly all of them were enclosed with a palisade composed of posts set close together in a trench, with strong gates. The principal ones had small short cannon called swivels mounted in the watch-boxes. These private fortified houses will not be included in our history of forts.

There was a timber fort erected in 1746 on the land now occupied by the old City Hall. Parson Smith records in his journal, " June 13, this neighborhood are building a blockhouse near Mr. Larrabee's for the common defence." This building was afterward occupied for a jail. In 1753, in answer to a petition of the selectmen of Falmouth, the court of quarter sessions of the county of York appointed a committee of five persons, all of Falmouth, to let out the building of a new jail, and directed them on certain conditions to " purchase the blockhouse and land thereunto belonging, near Benjamin Larrabee's for a prison-house." The purchase was finally made and this blockhouse was fitted for a prison, and occupied until the building of a stone jail in 1797 on land now occupied by the new city building.

The facts about the fortifications or batteries constructed immediately after the burning must be gleaned from scanty sources. Dr. Deane records: " Nov. 1, 1775. A ship appeared in the offing; arrived at evening; the Cerebus, he sent a letter on shore." Judge Freeman in an account of the war in his notes to Smith's Journal, says: " The purport of the letter was to forbid the people from constructing batteries, or breast-works, which were wholly disregarded; the arrival of this vessel was a signal to summon the militia, who came in large numbers from the neighboring towns and occupied the best of the remaining houses." Judge Freeman was then in his prime, and a delegate to the provincial congress.

Sullivan, in his history, says:

Captain Symonds came into the harbor (of Falmouth) with a ship of more force than all those which had destroyed it. An express was sent to the other towns and a number of volunteers went to the assistance of the remains of Falmouth, and joined the people there. When they arrived, the captain of the ship sent on shore to forbid their throwing up any works; they however proceeded and prepared the materials for a battery, and fitted two six-pounders, which were all the artillery they had. On seeing that they were determined to attack the ship with the means they could command, the captain forgot his threatening and went out of the harbor as soon as he could get away.

Sullivan continues: " The forts which were thrown up hastily before Gen. Frye came are to be seen there now." This was written in 1795. It is good evidence that it was correct that Judge Freeman, who had a personal knowledge of these facts, quotes Sullivan's account in his original edition of Smith's Journal.

These batteries mentioned by Sullivan are also mentioned in Dr. Deane's Journal of that time. He says:

Nov. 4, 1775.　(Sunday), The batteries begun last night. All the people at work to-day and there could be no meeting.

14.　　　　　Mr. Freeman's team at town on the works, and at night brought over my cabbages.

27.　　　　　Snow a foot deep.

Joshua Freeman was Dr. Deane's brother-in-law and lived where Jeremiah Dow now does on Grove street, where he and his wife had taken refuge, relinquishing his own house to General Frye whom General Washington had sent to take command.

At the time of the throwing up of these batteries, in the fall of 1775, Major Daniel Ilsley of Falmouth was in command, and also acted as muster-master for the troops enlisted here. His order book was recently rescued from a dealer in paper stock, and came into my possession by the favor of a friend. This book gives the location of the several batteries.

On the first page of the book, without a date and included in the general orders, is the following : " A convenient place to be looked out within the walls of the fort on the hill for a well and to dig the same." On September 19, 1776, orders are recorded for the posting of sentinels at the several batteries, in which this occurs: " That there be one sentinel placed at the *great fort on the Hill*, to be relieved every two hours."

This "great fort on the hill," I think must have been at the eastern end of Fore street at its junction with the Eastern Promenade. On the south side it was afterward named Fort Allen, probably in honor of Colonel Ethan Allen, who surprised and took the fort at Ticonderoga in May, 1775. This could not have been Fort Sumner, which we recollect, on North street, nor its outlying battery below on Monument street, as these were not begun until 1794 when there was

fear of a war with France. The remains of Fort Allen are
well preserved, showing that its center was a half-moon battery, after the old fashion of military engineering. The
crescent covers about one hundred paces, with two well-
defined embrasures in the center. Probably this is the same
battery mentioned by Sullivan, which was built to drive off
the Cerebus in November, 1775. A vessel of her size as
given by Sullivan would anchor in an enemy's harbor as far
down as that, and this was the favorable site for "two six-
pounders," to annoy her, while her guns could not be ele-
vated sufficiently for shot to reach this battery, and unless
she had mortars she would be compelled to leave, as Sullivan
says she did. If the battery which was hastily constructed
for the two guns had been placed on any other location one
broadside from her would have disabled the whole work.
It is good evidence of the identity of this work that it has
the well-defined depressions for two guns in the center. The
battery was undoubtedly afterward enlarged as it was called
the great fort and had walls enclosing the well, according to
Major Ilsley. The barracks were in one building of, I
think, but one story, of which the cellar only remains.

In May, 1815, the town " voted to authorize the selectmen
to purchase a building standing in Fort Allen, to be used as
a hospital." This building had already been used as a hospital, in one instance at least. In the winter of 1812-1813 a
British cartel-ship, carrying a flag of truce, arrived here from
Quebec with American prisoners of war for exchange. She
came in on account of some unknown sickness among the
soldiers, and a lack of winter clothing. Major Fitz was then
in command here, and the sick, about twenty-five in number,
were landed and taken to Fort Allen.

The Argus, January 7, 1813, says:

Dec. 24, 1812. Arrived cartel ship Regulus seven weeks from Quebec for Boston with 230 prisoners taken at the battle of Queenstown. Col. Scott's regiment, sickly, 26 were too sick to go to Boston in the ship — were carried to the hospital on the hill.

Up to February 4, thirteen had died.

These troops were a part of Lieutenant-Colonel Winfield Scott's regiment, which crossed the river to hold Queenstown Heights, after the death of Brock, in October, 1812, and for want of re-enforcement was obliged to surrender. Of the sick soldiers taken to Fort Allen more than half died, and were buried a little north of Congress street near the Eastern Promenade — a line of granite posts marks the spot. After a long detention the convalescents were taken on board, and the ship sailed for her port of destination.

After the erection of Forts Preble and Scammel, in 1809, and the water batteries in 1812–1814, I think Fort Allen never had any armament. It remained unoccupied until 1824, when it was again used as a hospital. In the spring of that year, the small-pox made its appearance in a small house next above the north corner of Middle and King (now India) streets, then occupied by Levi Rankins and a family named Haskell. This was but a few years after the introduction of vaccination in this country, and the old dread of the disease existed, and with good reason, as the result proved. The street was closed by the authorities, a sentinel was set to enforce the order, and the danger signal was made very conspicuous. Dr. Albus Rea was the attending physician, and the inmates of the house, sick and well, were removed to Fort Allen where eight died and only four recovered. The dead were buried near the graves of Hull's men. A brick pest-house was afterward built near these graves and the old building in Fort Allen was sold to Captain Lemuel Moody and removed.

Fort Allen was never baptized in the blood of battle, but was manned more than a century ago by gallant defenders ready to do or die.

The varied landscape, as seen from the high bluff which it occupied, is now the chief attraction of the spot. Southeast is Castle Gorges with its numerous embrasures and battlements, and further on is Fort Preble, the headquarters of the military defenders of the city, with its starry flag, which is saluted by the morning and evening gun. In full view from the site of the old fort, and in a nearly straight line six or seven miles long, are the white towers of four lighthouses —pillars of cloud by day, and pillars of fire by night, to guide the mariner to our Canaan. Beneath the bluff, hourly, come the thundering trains laden with the products of the far West, to be dumped into the caverns of the immense steamships, which noiselessly glide away to feed the people of Europe.

At this turn in the Eastern Promenade is a very proper site for the proposed soldiers' monument, whose outlines would show against the blue sky to all passers by water, to better advantage than any other spot in the city. This headland is the point from which the description commenced in the first deed of land on the Neck given on the eighth day of June, 1637.

Sir Ferdinando Gorges of Ashton Philips in the county of Somersett, Knight, of the one party, and George Cleeves and Richard Tucker of Casco, in the province of New Somersett in New England, gentlemen, witnesseth. . . . . Beginning at the furthermost point of a neck of land called by the Indians Machigonne, and now and henceforth to be called and known by the name of Stogummor.

This deed to Cleeves and Tucker was not executed until five years after their first occupation of the land described

in the deed.   The name Stogummor never obtained any
hold on the locality.

In Major Ilsley's order book, under the date, September
19, 1776, is this order:

Therefore ordered that there be a main guard composed of one
subaltern, one sergeant, one corporal, and twenty privates, to be
relieved once every twenty-four hours, at eight o'clock in the morning.   That this main guard barrack together while on duty, *in the
old guard-room*, that they keep at all times four sentinels, viz.: One
at the south battery, one at the south fort, one at the county-house,
or magazine, and one at the great fort on the hill.

On the first page is this order without date:

Three guns to be left in the lower battery.   Two others to be
moved to the Haymarket.   Two guns to remain in the upper battery.
Moses Fowler to be chief gunner of the lower battery, with fifteen
men.   Mr. Miller to have the care of the upper battery, with ten
men.   The five guns to be carried to the Haymarket to be in the care
of Mr. (Wheeler) Riggs.   Each gunner to have orders for exercising
the guns every day, and so that each gun be provided with six rounds
of powder and ball, or shot, and other necessaries for said guns.
That Mr. Perkins have four men to go in the boats.   The guns at
Pearsontown (Standish), Gorham, and Windham to be got down to
this town as soon as may be, and fixed with carriages.

There is nothing in the book indicating the size of any of
the guns, but from other sources I know that those obtained
at Windham were one long nine-pounder which had been
mounted in front of the fort at that place to fire as an alarm
gun, and a three pound swivel from a watch-box.   These
two guns were in 1776 put on board the privateer sloop
Retrieve, of Falmouth, Captain Joshua Stone.

From various sources I can determine the location of
nearly all the forts and batteries named in Major Ilsley's
order-book.   " The great fort on the hill " has been already

located and the authority given. The lower battery was undoubtedly on the site of the old fort which was built at the foot of what is now India street, in 1741, and the same on which Fort Loyal was erected in 1678. A strong reason for this conclusion is that the "old guard-room" is named in Major Ilsley's order as a barrack for the main guard. We have seen that twenty years previous Major Enoch Freeman, then in command, obtained the means from the general court to repair the "guard-house" of the fort, and there is no intimation in either Smith or Deane's Journal that it had been destroyed or removed.

The battery and magazine at the Haymarket and that at the county-house were the same. The hay-scales stood where the portico of the old city hall now does, and the county-house was the jailer's house at the other end of that building. The block-house built for the "common defence" in 1746, was then standing there but was used as a jail. Wheeler Riggs, who had charge of this battery was killed in the trenches by a cannon-ball at Bagaduce in 1779. He was "a shipwright," and lived on Plum street, south side, near the head. His widow married James Mitchell, the grandfather of Captain William Mitchell, station-master at the Portland terminus of the Boston railroads. She continued to occupy the Riggs house until her death.

The location of the upper battery is shown beyond a doubt by a deed executed in 1790. The description of the premises ends with the following: "Said lot now conveyed lies on the south side of said Free street, and *is the same upon which the upper fort so called, in said Portland, is partly built.*" This is the site of the present Anderson house which was built by Stevens and Hovey, business partners, in 1803. The breastwork extended over the next lot above on

24

which Ralph Cross built the present three story brick house
in 1792, now the Catholic asylum.   Hon. Neal Dow informed
me that in about 1813 there was in front of this lot a half-bur-
ied cannon projecting from under the fence on to the side-
walk; from his recollection he thinks it was a twelve-
pounder.   This was undoubtedly one of the guns of the
"upper fort" of 1776, and was finally removed to one of the
several batteries constructed during the war of 1812–1815.*

In the winter months of 1776 a fort was erected either of
wood or stone at Spring Point, where Fort Preble now
stands, and also there were some guns mounted at "Portland Point."   This is the point on which the Portland light-
house now stands.   I learn this from the regimental order-
book.   A part of the orders are signed by Colonel Jonathan
Mitchell.   The following order is of the earliest date of any
in the book, but there are others which must have been
written previous to this, but are without date.   The one in

---

* An item in the order-book reads: "Amount of guns fixed in Falmouth brought from Boston by Capt. Cox July 1776." Then follow
several sums paid to Deacon Titcomb, blacksmith, and other mechanics,
for iron-work, etc., for the mounting of these guns. General Washington was much in want of cannon to drive General Howe and his forces
out of Boston. In November, General Knox proposed to transport the
cannon from Ticonderoga and Fort George to Boston, for the purpose.
Washington doubted the feasibility of the enterprise but consented that
he should attempt it. In November, 1775, Knox and his brother started
on the expedition. By great exertions, and the assistance of the people
of Albany, and all along the route, with their teams, Knox brought with
him from Fort George, on forty-two sleds, eight brass mortars, six iron
mortars, two iron howitzers, thirteen brass cannons, twenty-six iron
cannons, two thousand three hundred pounds of lead, and one barrel of
flints.

These guns mounted on Dorchester heights, made Boston untenable
for Howe, and in March he evacuated it. The guns "brought from Boston by Capt. Cox," in July following, were undoubtedly some of those
which General Knox brought from Fort George, and after doing good
service for General Washington, he sent them here.

question purports to be "taken from the little book," and is dated January 14, 1776.

To Capt. Bryant Morton your commission gives you the command at Cape Elizabeth. You will take your post forthwith and keep such guards on the sea coast as the number of men under your command will admit of agreeable to the General courts orders — on the approach of an enemy to fire an alarm with three guns on Spring point.

See that your men are at their barracks at nine o'clock in the evening and at roll call; and obey such orders as may be given from time to time by the officer in command.

DANIEL ILSLEY, Com'd Officer.

FALMOUTH May 7 1776.
General orders for Capt. Bryant Morton's Company at Cape Elizabeth.

That you keep one sergeant or corporal, with seven privates as a guard on Portland Point — on the discovery of a ship, to fire a gun on Portland Point as an alarm, and in case of any number of small vessels more than two, and large enough for armed vessels, to fire

Some extracts from General Knox's diary while on the expedition may be interesting. He left Boston for Albany on the twentieth of November and arrived there December first, and at Ticonderoga on the fifth. The General mentions, January first, while at Ticonderoga, that he wrote letters to General Washington, "and one to my lovely Lucy." This was Lucy Fluker, daughter of the secretary of the province; she was the only Whig in the family. Her mother was Hannah Waldo, who jilted Andrew Pepperell. (See page 274.) Her parents were Loyalists, and early went to England. Miss Lucy became Mrs. Knox, and for years presided at their splendid residence "Montpelier" at Thomaston, Maine. I must claim for General Knox the authorship of the now often used, and expressive phrase "*must go.*" He used it in his journal in this connection. "Fort George Dec. 17, 1775. It is not easy to conceive the difficulties we have had in getting the cannon over the lake, owing to the advanced season of the year, and contrary winds. Three days ago it was very uncertain whether we should have gotten them until next spring; but now *please God they must go.* I have had made 42 exceedingly strong sleds and have provided 80 yoke of oxen to drag them as far as Springfield, where I shall get fresh cattle to carry them to camp." (Cambridge.)

two guns at Spring point, and in case they prove to be enemies to use your best endeavors to annoy them.

You are to keep forty-eight men every day at work on the fort at Spring point with one commissioned officer, one sergeant and two corporals from nine o'clock till six exclusive of one hour and a half for dinner — that your whole company attend roll call each day at sunset, and not absent themselves from their barracks after roll call. That no man leave their station without leave from the commanding officer or whom he may appoint, on pain of being dealt with as deserters.

JONATHAN MITCHELL, Commanding Officer.

Captain Morton was from Gorham. The following orders for a day are samples of the orders for each successive day which are varied.

May 10, 1776. Guards as usual. Countersign York. Officers and privates turn out for fatigue as usual. Capt. Crocker commands for the day.

May 11, 1776. Orders for the day. Countersign Yarmouth. Officers and privates turn out on fatigue as usual. All shovels, spades, and pickaxes to be brought to the county-house, or those that have them in possession will be dealt with as secreting the same.

JONATHAN MITCHELL, Commanding Officer.

Falmouth, May 12, 1776. Orders for the day. Guards as usual. Countersign Boston. The regiment to attend the usual place of parade for public worship. Its fifers to do duty for the day.

May 18. All officers and privates who have been absent from roll-call and parade for public worship will be fined as the law directs when no excuse has been made.

J. M., Com'g Officer.

March 16, 1776. Guards as usual. Countersign Wilks. Whereas several of the inhabitants of this town, who have suffered by the late fire, complain to me that the soldiers stationed in the town have been seen taking their nails and other materials which might be useful to those sufferers had they not been so taken. Ordered, that no soldier take the property of any person in the town, without the leave of the owner, on pain of suffering the penalty of the law.*

D. ILSLEY, Com'g Officer.

The orders to be read in each company at roll-call.

In the order-book is "a memorandum of presents to soldiers," of shoes, clothing, and cash.

May 19 (Sunday). Orders for the day — guards as usual. Countersign York. The whole regiment to parade at the meeting-house Monday, half after three o'clock for review. John Hawkes a soldier to have his trial on Monday at 10 o'clock at Mr. Greenwood's, for misdemeanors as may appear at the trial. Capt. Crocker to relieve Capt. Lord at 8 o'clock. The whole regiment parade for worship at the usual time and place.†

J. M., C. O.

June 22, 1776. At a court martial, Capt. Tobias Lord, President. John Castle, a soldier was found guilty of being asleep on sentry, but being penitent was forgiven by asking the regiment's pardon.‡

*There was, a few years ago, a house in Brunswick, the hinges, doorhandles, and latches of which were taken from the ruins of the Falmouth fire, of October, 1775.

† "Mr. Greenwood's," where the court-martial was to be holden, was a tavern-house on the south corner of Middle and Silver streets. It was a three-story wooden house with brick ends, built in 1774 by John Greenwood, a cabinet maker, son of Professor Isaac Greenwood, of Harvard College. He bought the lot of John Proctor in 1772 for twenty-six pounds lawful money. In 1783 he sold the lot and house, then unfinished, to Joseph Jewett, of Scarborough for five hundred pounds old tenor, equivalent then to one hundred and thirty-six silver dollars. Mr. Jewett finished it and moved into it in 1786. He kept a store and did a large business in the lower eastern room. He died in 1796 leaving a large family of children. The house was removed by John M. Wood to make room for stores.

‡ Courts-martial were held in the last century for the trial of soldiers for very small offences. Titcomb's journal mentions one of this description: "1747, June 23. Brigadier Waldo came to Falmouth escorted by Capt. Perkins, Captain Bean and 24 soldiers. Gen. Waldo and company's visit is to attend a regimental court martial for the trial of one Bolles

A court-martial was ordered to be held at Moses Shattuck's tavern, on the twenty-fifth of June. This was the county-house, or jailer's house, which was always kept as a public house by the keeper of the jail.

September eighteen, a court-martial was ordered to be convened for the trial of Joseph Switcher, on complaint of Captain Crocker, for neglect of duty. This court was to be held at Mrs. Grele's tavern, which was on the east corner of Congress and Hampshire streets. It appears that there were three taverns on the Neck the next summer after the burning.

September 23, 1776. Countersign Newport.
Capt. Hooper is officer of the day.
Capt. Crocker, 32 men on fatigue. Capt. Lithgow, 34 Ditto. Capt. Lord, 26 Ditto. Capt. Hooper, 34 men being agreeable to their weekly returns. DANIEL ILSLEY, Com'g Officer.

September 24, 1776. Ordered that the officers of each company order their men who are not supplied with ammunition, to meet at the county-house at ten o'clock, and apply to Mr. Riggs (Wheeler) for the same, and at two o'clock the regiment meet for exercising at their usual parade. D. ILSLEY, C. O.

I find that the county-house, or fort near it, was the headquarters of the regiment, and there was the magazine in charge of Wheeler Riggs, who was also in charge of the guns at the Haymarket battery.

James Sullivan, afterward governor of Massachusetts, was commissary of supplies for the troops here. He was then a

and Freeman for exchanging guns." Both were found guilty and sentenced to receive ten lashes each. Bolles was pardoned. The journal again mentions, "Aug. 12. Brigadier Waldo set off from this place for Boston. A number of gentleman waited on him as far as Black Point, where an entertainment was made at Mr. Harlow's for the under officers. Rev. Mr. Thompson made a dinner for the Brigadier, the captains and gentlemen."

lawyer of Biddeford. Dr. Deane, in his journal, recorded:
" 1776, Jan. 16. I rented three rooms below and one above
in my house, together with the barn, to Commissary Sullivan
for ten pounds pr month." " May 18. I dined at the Commissary's." General Frye, at the same time, was occupying
another part of the house. The Doctor says: " June 30. I
lodged at my own house with Gen. Frye."

At a meeting of gentlemen from several towns, held in
Falmouth, November 4, 1775, — seventeen days after the
burning, at Colonel Tyng's house, which was probably va-
cant, — Colonel Mitchell, moderator, " Mr. James Sullivan
was chosen commander-in-chief over the militia and the
other companies now in pay in the province. Voted that
four persons be appointed to assist Mr. Sullivan. Voted
that Col. Mitchell be second in command — Col. Fogg
third."

Major Ilsley seems to have had the charge of the province
muskets for distribution. He commenced in March, 1776,
to deliver arms " out of the province store," and took
receipts, which are recorded on several pages of the regimental order-book, the most of which are marked " returned."

The scarcity of men and muskets in Falmouth is shown
by the following letter from Commissary Sullivan to Samuel
Freeman, who was a delegate from Falmouth to the provincial congress then sitting at Watertown.

FALMOUTH 31 Jan. 1776.

Sir: Since I wrote you last I received a resolve of Court, wherein
I find I am directed to assist in raising two hundred and thirty-eight
men in the County of York. I shall obey the orders, and do my
best, and make no doubt but the men may be had, which will leave
the sea-coast of the county entirely without firearms, for our arms
were taken from our people on the last of December by order of Congress; an enlistment for Cambridge will strip us of men for this

winter, and if our guns are again stopped, we shall be in the spring without fire-arms. I venture to affirm as a fact, that more than half the men of Biddeford and Pepperellborough are now in camp at Cambridge. The four hundred men at Falmouth can never be raised, as every one who can leave home is gone or going to Cambridge. The officers appointed here have no commissions,* nor has Gen. Frye any instructions. You might have sent the commissions before now if you had attended to the safety of your own county, and hope you will send them by the first conveyance. If the General should order another reinforcement they must draw upon this part of the province for women instead of men, and for knives and forks instead of arms, otherwise they cannot be obeyed.

I am your humble servant,
JAMES SULLIVAN.

Of the officers of Colonel Mitchell's regiment, no field officers are mentioned except the colonel who was from North Yarmouth, who commanded the regiment from Cumberland County in the Bagaduce expedition, in 1779, and Major Ilsley, who lived at Back Cove, east of fall brook. He was the fourth son of Isaac Ilsley, a joiner, who came from Newbury about 1735, and was the ancestor of most of the name in town. He was an officer in the Louisburg expedition, and a famous Indian hunter. His son Daniel, the major, was born in 1740, and in 1762 he married Mary, the second daughter of Ephraim Jones, by whom he had twelve children. He was a distiller at the time he was doing duty as a military officer, and in 1767 he kept the old timber jail on Market square. He was a delegate to the convention of Massachusetts, which adopted the national constitution, a selectman, representative to the general court in 1793 and 1794, and in 1806 he was chosen a representative to Congress from this district. He left his father's farm

---

* According to the order-book Colonel Mitchell did not receive his commission until May 20.

and spent the last years of his life on Market street. He died in 1813.

The following order for the day gives the names and seniority of the captains of the regiment.

February 27, 1776. Orders for the day. Fifty men to be paraded at Greenwoods at nine o'clock in the morning without arms. No officer or soldier to leave the town till further orders.

Capt. Hooper to be obeyed as first   Captain.
Capt. Lord (Tobias) as   second   "
Capt. Crocker   third   "
Capt. Lithgow (Wm Jr)   fourth   "
Capt. Morton (Bryant) as   fifth   "

till further orders. Guards as usual. Countersign Boston.

DANIEL ILSLEY, Commanding Officer.

William Lithgow jr., the fourth captain, was born at Fort Halifax, now in the town of Winslow, in 1750. His father, afterward Judge Lithgow, of Georgetown, was then in command of the fort. His mother was the only daughter of Colonel Arthur Noble, of Georgetown, who was killed at Grand Pré, Nova Scotia, in 1747, while in command of a body of Massachusetts Colony troops.

Judge Lithgow removed to Colonel Noble's farm at Fiddler's Reach in about 1767, when the son William jr. was seventeen years old. When prepared, he read law with James Sullivan, of Biddeford, who was afterward governor of Massachusetts. Only in the order-book of Colonel Mitchell's regiment at Falmouth as captain is any mention of his military service until he was commissioned as major, and served in an expedition against Canada, where he had his right arm broken at the elbow by a musket-ball. He then retired from the army and commenced the practice of law at Fort Weston, on the Kennebec, having his office in the only plastered room of the principal block-house of the fort, which is yet standing on the east side of the river at Augusta. He was a lawyer of much ability and extensive practice. He was appointed in 1789 the first United States attorney for Maine, and officiated in that capacity at the trial of Thomas Bird and Hans Hanson for murder and piracy in May, 1790, at Portland. He with General Dearborn, the Marshal, came from Georgetown on horseback to attend to their duties at Portland.

Major Lithgow was elected Major-General of militia on the establishment of the eighth division, which embraced the counties of Lincoln, Hancock, and Washington. He was twice elected a senator to the Legislature of Massachusetts. General Lithgow died of a disease of the liver February 16, 1796, at the age of forty-six, never having been married.

In a corner of an open field on the ancient homestead farm of Colonel Noble and Judge Lithgow, at Pleasant Cove, is the private burial-place of the Lithgows. On a broken slate headstone is the following inscription:

IN MEMORY OF
MAJ. GEN. WILLIAM LITHGOW,
Who died Feb. 16, 1796,
Aged 46.

About the time of his death, General Lithgow was to have been married to Miss Mary Deering, who afterward became the wife of Commodore Edward Preble. The intimacy with her family probably commenced while he was serving as captain at Falmouth.

Bryant Morton, the fifth captain, was a prominent citizen of Gorham. He was a delegate from that town to the county convention, which was held at Mrs. Grele's tavern in Falmouth, September 21, 1774. He was one of the earliest members of the committee of safety and correspondence in 1772, and was a delegate to the provincial congress, and was a representative of the town in 1775 and 1776, and was an active man through the Revolution. He died in 1793.

Of the captains Hooper, Lord, and Crocker, I have no knowledge.

Captain Lowell is first mentioned in the following general order of September 19, 1776:

> It is understood that Capt. Lowell with his command is at all times with the cannon and that he keep a sergeant's guard at the lower battery. Their duty is, one sentinel on the platform day and night to hail all vessels coming into the harbor or going out and let no vessel pass the battery without showing a pass signed by order of the committee of the town of Falmouth, in which case they may pass without further orders.
>
> DANIEL ILSLEY, Commanding Officer.

Captain (Abner) Lowell's command was not originally attached to Colonel Mitchell's regiment.

In June the general court ordered a company of fifty soldiers, with ten cannon to be sent to Falmouth for its defence. In the regimental order-book is the following: "Account of guns fixed in Falmouth, brought from Boston by Capt. Cox July 1776." Then follows an account of expenses for mounting them; one item of which is for cash paid Deacon Benjamin Titcomb, who was a blacksmith, for iron work.

The command of the fifty men mentioned was given to Captain Abner Lowell of the town. He had seen considerable military service as had his ancestors. His father came here from Amesbury, Massachusetts. He lived above Clark's point. He and a boy were all that escaped in an attack on Pemaquid fort in 1747, severely wounded. He and his son were joiners. The son, Captain Abner, married

Mercy Paine, a daughter of Jonathan Paine, by whom he had eight children. He died in 1828 at the age of eighty-seven years.

His son John, a mason, was killed by the fall of a staging of a monument, which he was building on Stage Island, at the mouth of Saco river, in 1825, at the age of forty-four. He inherited the military spirit of the family, and was a very efficient commander of the Portland Artillery Company. He was the father of Abner Lowell, the watch-maker.

Major Ilsley was muster-master for Cumberland County, and kept his records in the regimental order-book.

1777, Apr. 2. One man was mustered in for Capt. Keiths company — Col. Jacksons regiment. Thos. Anderson of Falmouth.

April 27. Capt. Israel Davis's company of Boothbay, Col. Wigglesworths reg't. Three men.

June 26. Col. Henry Jacksons regiment. One man.
Capt. Jabez Lanes company. One man.

July 4. Capt. Hills company — Col. Pattersons regiment. Thirty six men offered by Lieuts Stubbs & Gray.
Capt. John Reads com'y — Col. Aldens regiment. Twelve men.

27. Capt. Ellis's company, Col. Bigelows regiment. Twenty two men — two of whom were slaves. Cato Shattuck of Falmouth, and Plato McLelan of Gorham.
Capt. Walkers company, Col. Brewers regiment. Six men who have been mustered and received their bounty given by Congress and by this state, 26 pounds.

1778, July 1. Capt. Norths company, Col. Lee's regim't. Six men — no bountys paid.

March 1, 1777. Capt. Ballards company — Col. Aldens regim't. Twelve men, four of whom were from Falmouth.

Feb. 17. Capt. James Dunnels comp'y, Col. Brewer regiment. Three men.

June 12.   Capt. Nicholas Blaisdels company, Col. Wiggles-worths regim't. Thirty four men. Several from Falmouth, where the captain belonged.

March 21.   Capt. Silas Banks men, Col. Brewers regiment. Thirty one men. Three from Falmouth.

March 21, 1798.   Capt. Richard Mabury's company, Col. Francis' regim't. Seventy four men, five from Falmouth and eleven from Windham, where the captain belonged.

Jan. 25, 1777.   Capt. George Whites company, Col. Francis's regiment. Fifty eight men, eleven from Falmouth.

April 15, 1777.   Capt. Skillings company, Col. Francis's regiment; seventy men; twenty-five of whom are marked from Falmouth, but many others are known to have been from the same town. One, Nathan Noble, was from New Boston, now Gray. He was killed by a musket-ball, which went through his head, while entering the works at the taking of Burgoyne, at Saratoga, in Oct. 1777. He had served in the army that besieged and captured Louisburg in 1745. He was the great-grandfather of the author.

March 13, 1777.   Capt. Josiah Jenkins company, Col. Francis's regim't. Twenty five men — [no mention of their residence.]

Sept. 15.   Capt. George Smiths company, Col. Pattersons regiment. Fifty one men — [no residence given.]

June 10, 1780.   Capt. Lincolns company matrosses (artillery) mustered by Lieut. Ethan More to do duty in the state of Massachusetts Bay for the term of three years agreeable to the General Courts order of May 16 1780. Eleven men.

In all, Major Ilsley records the mustering and paying the bounty at Falmouth of four hundred and twenty-one men previous to July, 1780.

In March, 1777, while Brigadier Preble was in attendance as councilor at the board in Boston, he wrote to Captain John Waite, as follows: "The province of Maine and town of Falmouth in particular, are highly applauded by the general court for being foremost of any part of this state in furnishing their quota of men for the army."

In the war in which the colonies struggled for a separation from Great Britain, the most important event to Maine, and most stirring one for Falmouth, was the Bagaduce expedition. It was projected at their suggestion to drive the invaders from their coast. Every man of spirit in Falmouth felt his blood boil when he learned that the incendiary who had burned his town was the commander of the naval forces who had made a lodgment on the soil of Maine. Mowatt's name was hated here as much as that of Arnold was in Connecticut, and for the same cause, — he had cowardly destroyed their unprotected homes without a reason for it, and laid the blame on his superior, who had consented at his request. The recruiting officer was not compelled to lead his fife and drum through the byways of the town to obtain hesitating recruits; the merchants and the ship-masters, the mechanic and his men left their employments to join the crusade. Major Hugh McLellan, afterward the great ship-owner of the town, enlisted as a private soldier and served as corporal through the disastrous campaign. His father, Joseph McLellan, afterward the senior partner of Joseph McLellan and Son, the great shipping firm, was commissary of supplies. Falmouth and Cape Elizabeth contributed each a company. Of the Falmouth company Captain Peter Warren was commander, a man of much coolness and courage, and Daniel Mussey was first lieutenant; officers worthy to lead such a following.

"Roll of Capt. Peter Warren's Company in the Battalion of militia commanded by Col. Jonathan Mitchell on an expedition against Penobscot. Falmouth, Dec. 25, 1779." (The company were in service two months and twenty-five days. The pay of privates for that time was five pounds and four shillings.)

OFFICERS.	PRIVATES.
Peter Warren, Capt.	Jonathan Sawyer,
Daniel Mussey, 1st Lt.	James Ham or Hans,
Peter Babb, 2d Lt.	John D. Smith,
John Dole, Sergt.	Joseph Radford,
Stephen Tukey, "	Josiah Shaw,
Isaac Minck, "	Joseph Thomas,
Micah Sampson, "	Jeremiah Brackett,
Hugh McLellan, Corp'l	John Small,
John Clough, "	Josiah Walker,
Josiah Bailey, "	John Rowe,
Samuel Knight, "	James Rand,
William Moody, Drummer.	Joseph Johnson,
William Harper, Fifer.	Henry Waite,
PRIVATES.	Lemuel Cox,
Benj Mussey,	Moses Brazier,
Daniel Cobb,	Nath¹ Moody,
David Warren,	Nath¹ Libby,
Daniel Green,	Peter Kelly,
Eben Owen,	Paul Dyer,
Elijah Ward,	Richard Codman,
Ebenʳ Gustin,	Richard Fassett,
Eleazer Whitney,	Robert Poage,
Houchin Tukey,	Somers Shattuck,
Isaac Randall,	Samuel Larrabee,
Isaac Larrabee,	Thomas Gustin,
John Fogg,	Woodbury Storer,
Joˢ Morse,	Wheeler Riggs,
John Ham or Harris,	Wᵐ Maxwell,
John Masury,	Zach Baker.

An entire regiment was raised in this vicinity, the command of which was given to Colonel Mitchell, of North Yarmouth, the same who commanded here during the winter of

1775–1776.   The regiment sailed on the nineteenth of July
in transports which came from Boston to rendezvous at
Townshend.

The cause of this British invasion was this: In 1779, the
British naval and army officers at Halifax became sensible
that they were suffering from American privateers, which
frequented the Penobscot waters, owing to their perfect
knowledge of the numerous coves and harbors which they
could run into at any time to avoid the British cruisers.

The admiral in command foresaw the advantage that
would be gained by establishing a naval and military post in
this quarter for a harbor of refuge for ships and fugitive
loyalists and to command the near coast and harbors, and
from whence they could obtain a supply of some kinds of
ship timber for the royal dockyard at Halifax.   This was
the year after the French king had assumed our quarrel with
the mother country, and had sent a large fleet and army to
our assistance which gave the colonies confidence and made
them more aggressive.

In June, 1779, it was decided at Halifax to send General
McLane with a fleet to occupy Bagaduce, as the harbor best
situated for their purpose.   He arrived on the twelfth of
June with nine hundred troops and eight or nine vessels, all
less than a frigate, under the command of Captain Henry
Mowatt who had become detestable to all Americans by his
cruel burning of old Falmouth four years previous.   The
people of Maine appealed to the general court of Massachusetts for protection, and to have the invaders driven off by
an immediate expedition before they could have time to
complete their works of defence.

Under date June 20, Parson Smith of Falmouth records,
"People are everywhere in this State spiritedly appearing in

the intended expedition to Penobscot in pursuit of the British fleet and army there." This was a state expedition for which Massachusetts advanced fifty thousand pounds.

The Massachusetts Board of War were instructed by the legislature to collect a fleet, state and national, and, if necessary, to impress any private armed vessels in the harbors of the state into their service, under the promise of fair compensation for all losses and detention. The executive department of the province was then composed of the council; there was no state governor until the next year. The council ordered Brigadier-Generals Thompson, of Cumberland, and Cushing, of Lincoln, to detach severally six hundred men from each of their brigades, and form them into two regiments. General Frost, of York, was directed to detail three hundred men from his brigade for a re-enforcement if needed.

The fleet consisted of nineteen armed vessels carrying three hundred and forty-four guns, and convoying twenty-four transports. The flag ship was the new continental frigate Warren. Of the others, nine were ships, six brigs, and three sloops. The command of the fleet was entrusted to Richard Saltonstall of Connecticut, an officer of some naval experience. One hundred Massachusetts artillerists were embarked at Boston under their former commander, Lieutenant-Colonel Paul Revere — he who carried the news to Hancock and Adams at Lexington that the British troops were on the road from Boston, in 1775. The command of the land forces was given to Solomon Lovell of Weymouth, Massachusetts, the brigadier-general of the militia of Suffolk, which then included Norfolk County. He was a man of courage but no war experience. Peleg Wadsworth, then adjutant-general of Massachusetts, was the second in com-

25

mand. He had seen some service on Dorchester heights during the siege of Boston and in other places. The ordnance was entrusted to the command of Colonel Revere.

When the fleet was ready to sail from Townshend, now Boothbay, the place of rendezvous, General Lovell's land forces numbered less than one thousand men, who had been paraded together only once, then at Townshend. They were raw militia who had seen no former service, except perhaps some individuals, who had been in the Continental army for a short time. It was a spirited body of men. Their fathers had been at the siege of Louisburg thirty years before. In one month from the commencement to organize the expedition, it made its appearance in Penobscot bay.

The British commander heard of the American fleet four days before its arrival, and worked night and day to render his fortification defensible, yet it was far from being completed. He at once dispatched a vessel to Halifax, asking for assistance. On July 28, after waiting two days for a calm, our vessels were drawn up in line of battle, and two hundred militia-men and two hundred marines were landed. The best landing-places were exposed to Mowatt's guns, and no landing could be effected except on the western side, which was a precipice one hundred and fifty feet high and very steep. This was guarded by a line of the enemy posted on the summit, who opened a brisk fire as soon as the boats came within gunshot, but the shot from the vessels went over their heads. As soon as the men landed, the boats returned to the fleet, cutting off all means of retreat. No force could reach the summit in the face of such a fire of musketry, so the American troops were divided into three parties. One sought a practicable ascent at the right, one at the left, and the center kept up a brisk fire to attract the attention of the enemy on the heights. Both the right and left parties gained the summit, followed by the center in the face of a galling fire, which they were powerless to return.

On the beach at the place of landing, is now to be seen a large round white rock about ten or fifteen feet high. It is now called "Trask's rock," so named for a fifer-boy who took shelter under its side and did not lose a note in his tune until his company had gained the level above the high bank. It is said at Castine that Captain Hinkley, of Brunswick, stood on this rock and cheered on his men until he was killed by a shot and fell off.

Captain Warren's company of volunteers from Falmouth were the first to form on the heights, when all closed on the enemy, who after a sharp skirmish made their escape leaving thirty men killed and wounded. Of the attacking party of four hundred, one hundred were killed or wounded. Wheeler Riggs, a shipwright, was the only man killed belonging to Falmouth. The engagement was short but great pluck and courage were shown by the Americans. It has been said that no more brilliant exploit than this was accomplished by our forces during the war, but this is the only bright spot in the record of the expedition. After the retreat of the enemy, some slight entrenchments were thrown up by the sadly weakened little detachment, within seven hundred yards of the enemy's main works. These entrenchments were held by our men and thus was made a good beginning.

The same morning a council of war was called of the land and naval officers. The former were for summoning the garrison to surrender, but the commodore and the most of his officers were opposed to the measure. It was next proposed to storm the fort, but the commodore refused to land any more of his marines as those at the first landing suffered severely. The land force alone was deemed insufficient for a successful attack on the works, and a whale boat express was despatched to Boston for a re-enforcement. General Lovell now commenced a regular investment of works by zigzag trenches for Revere's insufficient cannon, and approached to musket shot distance of the fort, so that not one of the garrison dared to show his head above the embankments.

It was afterward ascertained that if a surrender had been demanded, when first proposed, the commanding general was prepared to capitulate, so imperfect were his defences. Commodore Saltonstall was self-willed, and disagreed with Generals Lovell and Wadsworth. During the two weeks delay the British strengthened their defences, and enclosed their works with a cheval-de-frise with an abatis outside of all, which rendered the storming project impracticable, if the expected re-enforcement had arrived. The American commodore kept up a daily cannonade with a show of an attempt to enter the harbor, but it was only a show. A deserter from the Americans informed the British commander of an intended attack the next day, which prevented any success.

On August 13, a lookout vessel brought General Lovell news that a British squadron of seven sail was entering Penobscot bay, in answer to General McLane's application to Halifax on the first discovery of the American fleet. A retreat was immediately ordered by General Lovell, and conducted by General Wadsworth in the night, with so much skill that the whole of the troops were on board the transports undiscovered by the enemy. The British squadron entered the harbor the next morning, consisting of one seventy-four gunship, one frigate, and five smaller vessels all under the command of Sir John Collier, with one thousand five hundred troops on board. Saltonstall kept his position until the transports retreated up the river, when a general broadside from Collier's ship caused a disorderly flight, and a general chase and indiscriminate destruction of the American fleet. Several were blown up by their own crews to prevent their falling into the hands of the enemy.

The troops and crews of the vessels left them for the woods. Most of the officers and men of the fleet and army made their way through the woods guided by the Penobscot Indians, who were friendly to the provinces through the war for independence. These struggling parties suffered every privation before reaching the settlements, subsisting on such game and fish as they were able to obtain. A large number were piloted by the Indians to Fort Halifax, where they were recruited and returned home by the Kennebec.

A court of inquiry as to the cause of the failure of the expedition gave as their opinion, "That the principal reason of the failure of the expedition was the want of the proper spirit on the part of the Commodore. That the destruction of the fleet was occasioned, essentially, because of his not exerting himself at all in the time of the retreat, by opposing the enemy's foremost ships in pursuit." "That General Lovell, throughout the expedition and retreat, acted with proper courage and spirit; and had he been furnished with all the men ordered for the service, or been properly supported by the Commodore, he would probably have reduced the enemy." The court spoke in the highest terms of General Wadsworth. Upon this report the general court adjudged "That Commodore Saltonstall be incompetent ever after to hold a commission in the service of the state, and that Generals Lovell and Wadsworth be honorably acquitted."

In answer to General Lovell's appeal for assistance by the whale boat express to Boston, a regiment under Colonel Henry Jackson proceeded to Falmouth on their way to Penobscot, when they heard of the disaster of the expedition.

When I was a boy, sixty years ago, many of the men of Cumberland County who had been in the Bagaduce expedition were then living; some of them were my own relatives. I have often heard angry discussions between those of the land and those of the naval service. The landsmen always assumed the aggressive, and had the best of the argument. It was the opinion of both, that if General Wadsworth had been in chief command on shore, that the gallant detachments which first gained the heights could not have been restrained until they had crossed bayonets with the garrison of the half built fortress, and that was the time to have carried the works.

After the failure of the Bagaduce expedition the British pursued a system of outrageous plundering on the shores of Penobscot bay and the neighboring coast, in which they were piloted and assisted by the numerous Tories who had gathered at Bagaduce and in the vicinity. To protect the people from this plundering, the continental congress, in 1780, ordered six hundred men to be detached from the three eastern brigades of the state, for eight months service. Every soldier was ordered to march well equipped, within twenty-four hours after he was detached, or pay a fine of sixty pounds currency, which was to be applied to procure a substitute. The command of the whole eastern department, between the Piscataqua and St. Croix, was given to

General Wadsworth, with power to raise more troops if they were needed. He was also empowered to declare and execute martial law over territory ten miles in width, upon the coast eastward of Kennebec, according to the rules of the American army. His headquarters were established at Thomaston. For the purpose of protecting his friends, the General found it necessary to draw a line of demarkation, between them and their foes. He issued a proclamation prohibiting any intercourse with the enemy. This paper, of which I have a copy, is dated at Thomaston, April 18, 1780, and declares the penalty of military execution for any infringement of it. The people of the islands east of Penobscot to Union river, "from their exposed situation," were ordered to hold themselves as neutrals. All persons joining the enemy were to be treated as deserters from the American army.

This proclamation did not have the desired effect. The most bitter of the Tories supposed that they would be protected by General McLane, but he disapproved of their plundering. Captain Mowatt of detestable memory, who was in command of the British squadron, was of a different character, and encouraged the depredations, when they became very aggressive. A staunch friend of the American cause at Broad bay, named Soule, was shot in his bed, and his wife wounded. This drew from General Wadsworth another proclamation denouncing death to any one convicted of secreting or giving aid to the enemy. Soon after a man named Baum was detected in secreting and aiding Tories to reach Castine. He was tried by court-martial, found guilty of treason, and General Wadsworth ordered his execution by hanging the next morning, which was carried into effect. This effectually checked the intercourse with Bagaduce. A daughter of General Wadsworth in writing of the circumstance, to a son-in-law in 1834, said, "My mother has told me that my father was greatly distressed at being obliged to execute the penalty of the law." General Wadsworth's wife was with him at the time.

After the term of service of the six hundred troops had expired, General Wadsworth was left with only six soldiers as a guard at his house, it being his intention also to leave within a week or two. His family consisted of his wife and son of five years, and Miss Fenno of Boston, a particular friend of Mrs. Wadsworth's.

Made acquainted with his defenceless condition by spies, General McLane at Bagaduce, dispatched a party of twenty-five men under Lieutenant Stockton, to take him prisoner. They left their vessel four miles off and marched to his residence, arriving at about midnight February 18, 1781. The General had plenty of firearms in his sleeping-room, and when his house was entered by the enemy he made a determined defence, until he was shot in the arm, when he surrendered and was hurried off to the vessel. When he became weak from the loss of blood, he was set on a horse for the march. He suffered much from cold and pain from his wound. He was taken across the bay to Castine and imprisoned at Fort George. For two weeks he knew nothing of the fate of his family, who had been exposed to the firing. At the request of General Wadsworth, General McLane sent a lieutenant with a boat's crew to Camden across the bay, with letters to his family and to the governor of the state, which were inspected previous to sealing. Finally, a letter was received from Mrs. Wadsworth containing an assurance that they were unharmed. General McLane treated his prisoner very politely, inviting him to eat at his own table, with guard of an orderly sergeant, but refused him a parole or exchange. In the spring, four months after his seizure, Mrs. Wadsworth and Miss Fenno, with a passport from General McLane, arrived at Bagaduce and were politely entertained at the fort for ten days. In the meantime orders had arrived from the commanding general at New York, in answer to a communication from General McLane. Their purport was learned from a hint conveyed to Miss Fenno by an officer, that the General was not to be exchanged, but would be sent to some English prison. When Miss Fenno left she gave the General all the information she dared to; she said, " General Wadsworth, take care of yourself." This the General interpreted to mean that he was to be conveyed to England and he determined to make his escape from the fortress if possible. Soon after a vessel arrived from Boston with a flag of truce from the governor and council, asking for an exchange for the General and bringing a sum of money for his use, but the request was refused.

Major Burton, a resident of St. Georges river, who had served the previous summer under General Wadsworth, was a prisoner in the same room with him. After a long preparation, and by obtaining a gimlet from the fort barber, they made their escape on the night of June 18, by passing through an opening previously and laboriously made in the board ceiling with the gimlet, the marks of which were filled with bread. They adroitly evaded the sentinels, but got separated in the darkness, both, however, getting off safely. They kept much in the shoal waters of the shores, to prevent being tracked by the blood-hounds which were kept at the fort for that purpose. The two friends came accidentally together on the next day. Major Barton dropped a glove in the darkness which pointed out to their pursuers the route they had taken on leaving the fort. They, however, found a canoe, got across the river, and pursued their course through the woods by a pocket compass to the settlements, and were assisted to Thomaston, after much suffering. On arriving at his former residence, General Wadsworth found that his family had left for Boston, whither he followed them after a brief stop at Falmouth, where he finally fixed his residence.

In some of the states, the Loyalists or Tories, as they were called, were numerous, active, and troublesome to the great majority who were fighting for independence. In September, 1778, in Massachusetts, a law was passed, by which the estates of three hundred and ten persons, late inhabitants of the state, who had retired to the protection of the enemy, were confiscated. It was called the "absentee act." In it, the name of each of these persons was given. Of these, only seventeen were from Maine, and all but one belonged to Falmouth. Their names were Francis Waldo, William Tyng, John Wiswell, Arthur Savage, Jeremiah Pote, Thomas Ross, James Wildrage, George Lyde, Robert Pagan, Thomas Wyer, Thomas Coulson, Joshua Eldrige, Thomas Oxnard, Edward Oxnard, John Wright, and Samuel Longfellow.

There was a commissioner appointed in each county to look up absentees' estates and return their lists to the secretary of state. The commissioner for Cumberland County was John Waite. The judges of probate appointed administrators upon the estates, and they were settled the same as if the late owners were in fact dead. Should any absentee return, he was to be arrested and transported to the dominions, or some military post of the enemy, and on the second return, he was to suffer death. There were many others in the town in more humble circumstances, who held to their Tory principles, but did not make themselves obnoxious to the ruling sentiment. The property of Loyalists, sold under the absentee act, did not usually sell for its full value, and in some instances it was recovered by its original owners, after the war, for a small sum.

Several of these Loyalists had sought protection in Boston. Arthur Savage, the collector of customs, was there at the time of the battle of Bunker Hill. In 1789, Savage was in London, and gave to Rev. William Montague, who was then Rector of Christ's church, Boston, a leaden ball with the following account of it:

On the morning of the 17th of June, 1775, [said Mr. Savage], I with a number of other Royalists and British officers among whom was Gen. Bourgoyne, went over to Charlestown to view the battlefield. Among the fallen, we found the body of Dr. Joseph Warren, with whom I had been personally acquainted. When he fell he fell across a rail. This ball I took from his body, and as I shall never visit Boston again, I will give it to you to take to America where it will be valuable as a relic of the Revolution.

The ball is preserved in the library of the New England Historic Genealogical Society. Mr. Savage died in England of apoplexy in 1801, at the age of seventy.

The whole effective force that withdrew with General Howe from Boston was eleven thousand. The Loyalists, classed as follows, were more than one thousand in number. One hundred and thirty-two who held official stations; eighteen clergymen; one hundred and five persons from the country; two hundred and thirteen merchants; three hundred and thirty-two farmers, traders, and mechanics; total nine hundred and twenty-four. These returned their

names on their arrival at Halifax, whither the fleet sailed.
It was a sorrowful flight for most of them; for men of property left all behind, and almost every one relied for daily
food upon rations from the army stores.

One or two extracts from the letters of Benjamin Faneuil
junior, nephew of Peter Faneuil, of Faneuil Hall memory,
will furnish a correct idea of the state of the Loyalists in
their exile, and will show their confidence in the subjugation
of the colonies. London, March 9, 1777, he writes to his
aunt Mary Ann Jones, at Halifax, thus:

I cannot say I am very sorry for your disappointment, in missing
your passage for England, for unless you could bring a barrel of
guineas, you are much better anywhere than here. . . As soon as the
Christmas holidays were over, we presented a petition to the Lords
of the Treasury, setting forth our suffering and praying for a support
till the affairs in America are settled. This method was taken by the
council, and indeed by all the refugees. Within these few days, the
Lords of the Treasury have agreed to allow for the present, Chief
Justice Oliver £400 a year, Lieut. Governor Oliver and Mr. Flucker
£300. The council, (Mr. Botineau among the rest) £200; the refugees in general £100, some only £50. Our affair is not yet absolutely
determined, on account of Lord North's illness; but we are told we
shall be tuckt in between the council and the refugees, and be allowed
£150 a year. This is a very poor affair, and we can by no means live
upon it; but there are such a counfounded lot of us, to be provided
for, that I am told no more will be allowed. . . . When we shall be
able to return to Boston I cannot say; for sooner or later, America
will be conquered, and on that they may depend.

May 14, 1777, he writes from London thus:

We were promised three months ago, that some provision should
be made for us; and about ten days since, we were assured at the
Treasury that in a very few days, something should be done for us.
As soon as there is, we propose to set out for Bristol and fix ourselves
there, or at least, in that part of the country, till the American affairs

are settled, which from the last advice from New York, we flatter ourselves will not be longer than this year; though I am not without my doubts, at least as to the time, but submit they must, sooner or later. . . . All us Yankees are well, but growl at each other most confoundedly, for want of money. We hope to see you in Boston in the course of another year. . . Mrs. Faneuil is sitting by me, trying to transmography an old gown. No money to buy new.

After the construction of the works for defence on the Neck, Falmouth was a quiet town during the war. The enlisting and mustering of soldiers was the principal business carried on. I think all the enlisted men from the eastern towns were mustered in here. After Major Daniel Ilsley, Major Benjamin Waite served as muster-master. About all of the able-bodied men of the town were in the army at some time during the war. The first was a dark year for the provincials. The surrender of General Burgoyne and his army in September, 1777, was the first victory that caused sincere rejoicing throughout the new states. If the home government had discovered that the colonies could raise needed revenue, the Provincials had also discovered that they possessed military power, and at Louisburg and Quebec they had learned something of the art of war. Parson Smith recorded October 26, "Sunday. We had the news by the post, authentic, of the astonishing victory of Gen. Gates in taking Gen. Bourgoyne's army. Our people were hereupon mad in their rejoicing."

Although Parson Smith does not mention it, this rejoicing terminated disastrously. Benjamin Tukey, a young married man of twenty-eight, was killed while firing a cannon near Mrs. Grele's tavern at the head of Hampshire street. A brother of young Tukey who was present, and assisting at the firing, and who lived to be more than ninety years old, related to me the circumstances of the accident and described the "mad rejoicing." The leading Whigs of the town (the leading Tories had left), gathered at Mrs. Grele's long, one story tavern on the east corner of Congress and Hampshire streets, to celebrate the victory by eating and drinking, accompanied with the discharge of a small cannon in front of the house on Congress street. There was a general illumination of what few houses Mowatt's bombs had spared. A party was sent round with strings of candles and when they found a house without extra lights, a pane of glass was broken, and a string of candles thrown in, with orders to "light up." Some families with Tory sympathies did not immediately obey the order, but a second call, with anxiety for the safety of their windows, brought the desired illumination. The cannon had been repeatedly fired; the weather was warm and the windows were open. Those who wore red coats and cocked hats were inside in the midst of jollity; buckets of punch and bottles of wine were freely passed out of the windows to the noisy crowd. The firing was resumed. Young Tukey was ramming down a cartridge when it was prematurely discharged, carrying away his right arm at the shoulder, and causing a mortal wound. He had married Hannah Stanford less than two years before.

There was a similar accident on the first of April, 1783, while the same people were celebrating the success in compelling George III. to acknowledge the independence of the states. This was a similar celebration. The man killed was Samuel Rollins, by the bursting of a gun. He lingered four days; he left a wife and four children; his age was forty years.

There were several attempts at privateering from Falmouth during the Revolution. A sloop named the Retrieve sailed from here 1776. She was poorly equipped, having only one gun and a swivel obtained from the fort at Windham. The same that Major Ilsley recommended in his order-book to have got down to arm some of his batteries. The privateer was soon captured and carried to Halifax. The History of Portland gives a description of the private armed ship Fox and her career. Beside those there named as owners, Brigadier Preble owned a part of her. In his journal while in Boston in attendance at the council board he records, "September 8, 1780, I went to Wheelwright's wharf where the prize ship lay, taken by the Fox, and where her cargo was stored. I found the indigo and some of the deer-skins much damaged." In the last part of Major Ilsley's order-book is the schedule of the materials and the dimensions of a letter of marque to have sixteen ports and a list of the men's names who were at work on her in 1777. This list shows who were the shipwrights of Falmouth in the Revolution. Their names were, Life Morse, John Tukey, Josiah Riggs, Benjamin Moody, Josiah Berry, Benjamin Fickett, Mark Wilson, Jonathan Fickett, David Hall, Isaac Sawyer, Matthew Pennell, Amos Merrill, Mark Knights, Jonathan Lowell, Wheeler Riggs.

CHAPTER XI.

DURING the complications of France and England, in 1793, President Washington issued a proclamation of neutrality, to which the people of Portland heartily responded in a public meeting. For this they were much better prepared than for defence; there was not a gun mounted on the shores of the harbor, nor at its entrance.

In March, 1794, Congress appropriated one hundred and seventy-two thousand dollars for defensive works on the eastern coast. Colonel Rochefontaine, a French officer of engineers in the employ of the United States, in rebuilding the fortifications of West Point, was sent to Portland to lay out and build fortifications. A town meeting was called, at which a committee was chosen "to confer with the engineer and to purchase land for the use of the United States."

After consultation, a square work without bastions was laid out on the highest point of Munjoy's hill, at the southwest of the present North street, and south of its junction with Cumberland street. A deep and wide ditch, or moat, was excavated on the four sides of the enclosure. A leaning wall of boulders, of about fifteen feet high, was built from the bottom of the ditch to the top of the parapet. This was surmounted by a heavy wooden capsill and palisade, with a jointed projecting cheval-de-frise from the outside of the capsill. The entrance gate was at the southwest side, the approach to which was over a draw-bridge. The principal building was a large square block-house, intended both for barracks and defence.

Colonel Jonathan Williams, who was superintendent of West Point military academy, in company with Captain Alexander McComb, inspected the New England forts in 1808. A copy of their report is at West Point. They say of "Fort Sumner, Portland, Maine, a square block-house." In his report to Congress the secretary of war called this fortification a "citadel," and it was so considered by the citizens of the town. In 1801 the selectmen advertised that they had arranged with Captain Henry, the commander, that his sentinels should "watch for fires, and discharge a six-pounder pointed towards the town if fire was discovered between eleven P.M. and four A.M., and also give notice to Mr. Burns of the second parish, and Mr. Fernald of St. Paul's, to ring the bells." Evidently this idea was borrowed from Quebec or Halifax, both having high citadels, which always performed this service.

So enamored were the people with the music at the evening parade of the garrison, the outlook from the fort, and the sunset gun, that crowds gathered on the glacis each fair evening. This interfered with the drill of the soldiers, and became a serious inconvenience to the officers, to such a degree that in the autumn of 1802, the commander, Captain Henry, published in the papers of the town an order forbidding "the citizens from coming within the limits of the fortress."

The plan of Colonel Rochefontaine included a battery on the brow of the hill between the burying-ground and the observatory, facing the harbor, to be connected with the

26

citadel by a covered way. The battery had an earthern breastwork on three sides with ten heavy guns mounted; but the covered way was never completed, owing to the loose kind of earth through which it was to pass. Within the work was a brick furnace for heating shot. The battery overlooking the harbor and within short range, to repel an attack by water, would have been a very effective work.

The report to the President of the secretary of war, in 1796, gives a reliable description of those fortifications. He says:

At Portland is built a fort — a citadel, a battery for ten pieces of cannon, an artillery store, a guard-house, an air furnace for heating shot, and a covered way from the fort to the battery. The works are substantially executed except the covered way. To complete this, (the earth on the spot being of a bad quality,) with the necessary support of stones and sods, is estimated at four hundred dollars. Leveling earth round the works, fencing the land, a pump for the well, painting the woodwork, four hundred and seventy-one dollars.*

These works remained without any name except " citadel, the fort, or the battery," until 1799, when Increase Sumner, governor of Massachusetts, died. His warm partisans conceived the idea of giving the fort on the top of the hill his name, which was carried out in July of that year. The Portland Gazette says, July 1, " Fort Sumner was christened by a salute of fifteen 24 pounders, and a smart peal from two brass six-pounders taken with Burgoyne. An oration was delivered by Capt. Stoddard its commander."†

* In July, 1794, says the Eastern Herald, " While Col. Rochefontaine was proving some pieces of ordnance on Munjoy's hill, an eighteen pound cannon burst and killed Andrea Zeldstedt, captain of a Swedish vessel lying in the harbor and wounded Jeremiah Colby."

† Captain Amos Stoddard was a lawyer from Hallowell. He had served in the army of the Revolution. When war with France was

In December, 1800, Captain John Henry, the commander of Fort Sumner, advertised for proposals for the erection of a house for officers' quarters, which was built outside of the moat.

The Duke de la Rochefoucauld Liancourt, in company with Talleyrand, Bonaparte's future prime minister, made a tour of the United States and Canada, in 1795, 1796, 1797. He published an account of his travels, in London, in 1799. He visited Portland during the time of the building of Fort Sumner. He thus notices it:

They are at present constructing on the site of an old earthern breastwork,* a fortification which they expect to command the town, and to render it at least secure from the invasions of an enemy. This new fortification stands at the extreme point of the peninsula on which Portland is established, and consists of a battery of fifteen or twenty heavy cannon of large calibre, commanding that wide entrance to the bay, which was above mentioned. This battery is to have, by means of a covered way, a communication with a small fort, at a distance of four or five hundred toises, which it has been thought necessary to erect on the highest point of the isthmus. The fort is sufficient to hold two hundred men.

apprehended in 1798, he joined the army as captain. At the battle of Fort Meigs, in 1813, he was wounded by a shell, and died soon after at the age of fifty-four. He was a man of education. He had published in London, a work called "The Political Crisis," and afterward "Sketches of Upper Louisiana." He delivered the oration at the celebration of the fourth of July, in Portland, in 1799. The late Colonel William P. Stoddard was his son.

* After considering Rochefoucauld's assertion, that the lower battery (then intended to be connected with Fort Sumner) was built on "the site of an old earthern breastwork," I am in doubt about whether Fort Allen or this old breastwork was the "great fort on the hill," mentioned by Major Ilsley and by Governor Sullivan as the one whose guns caused the man-of-war "Cerebus" to leave her anchorage and go to sea in 1775.

Fort Sumner and its battery below were the only fortifications in the town or vicinity until the erection of Forts Preble and Scammell in 1808–1809. The height on which Fort Sumner was erected obtained the name of Fort hill and is so called in the notice of fireworks exhibited there on the fourth of July, 1808. That year the fort was offered for sale or for exchange for a site for another fort. It however remained intact until the war of 1812, when the guns were remounted and it was occupied by a garrison.

During the war two deserters were ordered to be shot there on a Sunday morning. They were carried there in a cart with their coffins. Their graves were dug on the spot chosen for the execution, and the coffins placed by their side on which the condemned men were made to kneel. The whole garrison were on duty and the squad to do the execution was drawn up with guns charged, at the proper place, when an officer rode up holding a commutation of the punishment in his hand. None but the officers in command knew of the interruption until the horseman's arrival on the ground. It was previously so arranged to make the scene impressive. One of the condemned men was afterward for many years an industrious mechanic of the town.

My first personal knowledge of Fort Sumner was as it stood sixty years ago. Then all the woodwork, buildings, and guns were gone, but the walls and earthworks were perfect. A description of the fort and battery as they stood at the commencement of the century I received from an aged gentleman who recollected it at that time. In 1827 the late John Neal set up a gymnasium within the old fort, after setting a high paling round the parapet. He had just returned from a long sojourn in England and was the first to set up the parallel bars and leaping poles in New England, and this was the last occupation of the fort.

The battery originally intended to be connected with Fort Sumner was made a very formidable work for defence when there were fears of an attack in 1814. Sixty years ago, on its parade stood two gun houses for the field pieces of the artillery companies of the town, but one company had disbanded. There was also a long range of low buildings filled with the cannon belonging to Massachusetts, and so remained until the erection of the State Arsenal, where the Maine General Hospital now stands, in about 1830, when they were removed with the small buildings to that enclosure. The old battery was finally undermined to obtain earth for filling at the foot of India street.

In about 1830, Fort Sumner was sold to Hon. John Anderson, while he was a representative to Congress, for about fifty dollars. The lot contained about three acres, and is now covered with buildings. The Shailer schoolhouse lot takes in the northern corner of the fort lot. A few rods south of the schoolhouse, in a yard, a part of the original wall of the fort can now be seen in its place.

The British army evacuated New York, November 25, 1783, thereby acknowledging the victory of the infant states over royal power. The commander, Sir Guy Carleton, did not submit this last stronghold with a good grace. When General Knox and George Clinton entered Fort George on that day, they found the British flag flying, the halyards and cleats of the staff gone, the flag nailed, and the staff slushed, showing spite against the victors, and a belief that the absence of British authority in the United States would be only temporary. But their painstaking did not avail. A sailor-boy of sixteen, John Vanarsdale by name, using sand, climbed the slushed flag-staff and pulled down the hated British ensign, which had floated there more than seven years, and in its place unfurled the flag of the new nation.

Although George III. tacitly acknowledged our independence, he also acknowledged to our minister, John Adams, that he was the last to admit it, and that it was the most disagreeable act of his life. Many of the American loyalist refugees continued to fan the British hatred of the people of the new states, and it cropped out in the policy of the regency ministers. They refused to execute a treaty of amity, or even to send a minister to the United States, until France, Holland, and Spain had sent representatives to the seat of our general government, and they were compelled to yield to expediency.

Under the authority given by Congress, in 1797, President Adams ordered the building of four frigates, one of which was the famous "Constitution," which was launched at Boston, October 21, 1797. The President also authorized an increase of the number of national troops, which were denominated a provisional army. General Washington had retired to private life, and was then aged sixty-eight; nevertheless he was induced, from motives of patriotism, to accept the command of it, but on condition that he was not to take the field in person, unless there was imminent danger of an invasion by the French, who had threatened to make war upon the United States. The general officers designated for command in the provisional army from Massachusetts were Henry Knox as major-general, and John Brooks as brigadier-general. Both had been favorite officers in the army of the Revolution, under Washington. A part of the newly raised army was stationed at Oxford, in Worcester County, where they remained about a year, when they were disbanded. The number of officers commissioned in the provisional army was in proportion above that of the privates. Several of these officers were from Portland, and when I was a boy, "Adams' Oxford army" was a by-word with the Democrats.

The French revolution had a disturbing effect on the people of the United States. Many professed to see in it an imitation of our own. France had been our ally in the struggle, which created a strong sympathy with her. A powerful French party sprung up in the United States. Lossing says:

The contagion of that bloody Revolution had so poisoned the circulation of the social and political system of the United States, that, strange as it may appear to us, when the proclamation of the French Republic, with all its attendant horrors of August and September (1792), was made known here, followed speedily by the intelligence of the conquest of Austrian Netherlands by a French army, there was an outburst of popular feeling in favor of the Gallic cause that seemed to be almost universal. They were blind to the difference between their own Revolution and that of France. With a similar spirit, the death of the French king was hailed by leaders of the Republican party in the United States, and the declaration of war against England and Holland, by France, awakened a most remarkable enthusiasm in favor of the old ally of the Americans, aroused old hatreds toward England, and called loudly for compliance with the letter and spirit of the treaty of 1778.*

Dr. Franklin said, "The French having served an apprenticeship in America had set up for themselves."

* A treaty of alliance, friendship, and commerce, was entered into by the United States and France, February 6, 1778, by which the former was bound to guarantee the French possessions in America, and by a treaty of commerce executed at the same time, French privateers were entitled to shelter in the American ports, while those of the enemies should be excluded. See Article XVII. of the Treaty. This provision of the treaty was canceled in 1801 by Buonaparte, in offset for the assumption by the United States of the liability for the "French claims" for spoliations.

The stirring events, following each other in France, were celebrated in the cities of the United States with great enthusiasm. There was a grand fete held in Boston, January 24, 1793. An ox was roasted whole, then decorated with ribbons and placed on a car drawn by sixteen horses; the flags of the United States and France were displayed from its horns. It was paraded through the streets followed by carts bearing sixteen hundred loaves of bread and two hogsheads of punch. These were distributed among the people. At the same time, a party of three hundred, with Samuel Adams, lieutenant-governor of Massachusetts, at their head, assisted by the French consul, sat down to a dinner in Faneuil Hall. Bradford says, that " when the President had occasion to address the servants who attended upon the company, he used the familiar language of citizen Cuff, or citizen Cato, and was addressed with the same familiarity, citizen Adams, what is your desire." To the children of all the schools, who were paraded in the streets, cakes were presented, stamped with the words *Liberty and Equality*. By public subscription, the sums owed by prisoners in jail for debt were paid, and the victims of that barbarous law set free. In Philadelphia, the anniversary of the French Alliance of 1778 was commemorated by a public dinner, at which Governor Mifflin presided. At the head of the table, a pike was fixed, bearing on its point the *bonnet rouge*, with the French and American flags intertwined in festoons, and the whole surmounted by a dove and olive branch.

The French Jacobins, as they were called, affected the simplicity of the republics of Greece and Rome. All titles were abolished, and the term *Citizen* was universally applied to men. When the King was spoken of, his family name of

Capet was used. He was called "Citizen Capet," or "Louis Capet."

The people of Portland did not escape the French mania. French fashions, French phrases, and French manners were adopted as if they represented a principle. In imitation, though faint, of their friends in Boston, the admirers of France here celebrated the twenty-second of February in a similar spirit. The Eastern Argus, February, 1793, says:

On the birthday of our illustrious fellow citizen, George Washington, President of the United States, a number of gentlemen met in this town in the afternoon, at Citizen Motley's, at the sign of the Freemason's arms, where was displayed the flag of the United States. After a Federal salute of fifteen cannon, and the partaking of a bountiful supper, the president of the meeting, Nathaniel F. Fosdick, called to order. Speeches were made by several gentlemen. They were the genuine effusions of hearts warm with the love of their country, and rejoicing in the emancipation of their sister republic, France.

The following toasts were given, at each of which a cannon was discharged, under the direction of Citizen Weeks of the artillery company, followed by three cordial cheers.

There was a list of thirteen regular toasts, from which three are selected.

6th. Our great and glorious allies, the French; may their victorious struggle for liberty be attended with all the success that the stores of heaven can shower down.

9th. The enlightener of the world, Thomas Paine. May the "Rights of Man" be understood and speedily practiced by the benighted corners of the earth.

13th. Brave Irishmen! May the sword of justice, once drawn, never be sheathed till they have obtained equal liberty and laws.

It is with pleasure we mention that there was only one unfortunate

persou confined in the jail in this town, and amidst the conviviality
of the company his distresses were by no means forgotten.*

After the peace of 1783, the United States was considered
by the Barbary powers as a weak nation, without a navy, on
whose commerce they could prey with impunity. Between
1785 and 1793, the Algerine pirates captured and carried
into Algiers, fifteen American vessels, confiscated the property, and made one hundred and eighty officers and seamen
slaves. In 1795, for the lack of a navy, the United States
agreed by treaty to pay eight hundred thousand dollars for
what were left of these captives, and in addition, to make the
Dey a present of a frigate worth one hundred thousand dollars. An annual tribute was also to be paid of twenty-three
thousand dollars.† The frigate was built at Kittery navy-
yard ; she was launched in July, 1797.

It is a humiliating fact that up to 1801 all the Christian
nations as well as the United States paid tribute to, and purchased the forbearance of the Barbary Powers by shipments

---

* The tavern with the "sign of the Freemasons Arms," was the jailer's house or "county-house," which stood where the eastern corner of
the old City Hall now does. It was of two stories and was afterward
removed to Federal street. "Citizen Motley," who kept it, also kept the
jail for a small compensation. He was the grandfather of Motley the
historian. The jail where the "one unfortunate person" was confined
was connected with the house by a yard.

† Colonel Ebenezer Stevens, an active merchant of New York, who had
been a meritorious officer during the Revolution, was employed by the
government as its factor in forwarding the stores to Tunis. In May,
1801, Secretary Madison wrote to Mr. Stevens on the subject, saying, "It
is desirable that the remaining cargo of maritime and military stores
due to the Regency of Tunis should be provided and shipped without
loss of time. The powder will be given to you from the public maga-
zines, and the Navy Department will give orders to its agent at New
York or elsewhere, as may be most convenient, to supply the cannon
and such other articles as you may want and can be spared."

of specie and goods to the Bey of Tripoli, the Dey of Algiers, and the Bey of Tunis. In May, 1800, Commodore Bainbridge, in command of the George Washington of twenty-four guns, went out with the usual tribute to the Dey of Algiers. He arrived at the port of the capital in September, and with courtesy paid over the money. He was about to leave when the Dey commanded him to carry an Algerine embassador to the Sultan, at Constantinople. The Commodore politely refused, when the insolent Dey said, " You pay me tribute by which you become my slaves, and therefore I have a right to order you as I think proper." Bainbridge could not pass the castle for home without a permit from the Dey, so he was compelled to submit, and was obliged to carry the Algerine flag at the main, but after leaving port he placed his own ensign in its usual place. His was the first ship to display that flag at Constantinople, and Bainbridge and the Turkish Admiral became friends, and, when the American ship was about to leave, the Admiral gave Bainbridge a *firman* to protect him from further imposition. On his return to Algiers the Dey was about to send him again to Constantinople, but the Turkish Admiral's firman caused the haughty tyrant to desist.

The Bashaw of Tripoli, not content with the sum that had been paid him by the United States, when he learned that his neighbors had received larger tribute than himself, demanded a further sum, and threatened war if his demand was not complied with. He waited the stipulated time without any return to his demand, when he cut down the flag-staff of the American Consulate and declared war.

General William Eaton, of Brimfield, Massachusetts, then consul at Tunis, led a force of Egyptian troops, furnished by a brother of the reigning Pasha, over the desert in a long and wearisome march, and took the city of Derne, a seaport of Barbary.

In anticipation of war, Commodore Dale had been dispatched with a squadron of three frigates, and the afterward famous Enterprise, then a schooner of twelve guns. After passing Gibralter, the Enterprise captured a Tripolitan corsair, called the Tripoli, after an engagement of three hours, without the loss of a man on board of the Enterprise, while twenty were killed and wounded on board the corsair.

A relief squadron was next sent, in 1802, of five ships, under the command of Commodore Morris. A blockade of the ports of the Barbary powers was kept up until November, 1803, when the fleet returned home.

The conduct of affairs in the Mediterranean, under Commodore Morris, was not satisfactory, and after a court of inquiry, the President dismissed him from the service without further trial.

The government of the United States had determined to act with more vigor against the Barbary powers, and in May, 1803, Commodore Preble was appointed to the command of a squadron consisting of the Constitution of forty-four guns, the Philadelphia of thirty-eight, Argus and Syren of sixteen guns each, and the Nautilus, Vixen, and Enterprise of twelve each. Commodore Preble chose for his flagship the Constitution, then six years old. He had been off duty for a year on furlough on account of ill health. He sailed in August, and was followed by the other vessels of the squadron as fast as they could be made ready.

Preble had an interview with the Emperor of Morocco, who professed to desire peace, and he sailed for Tripoli. In chasing a native ship into Tripoli, the frigate Philadelphia got aground, and was captured by the Tripolitans, and Commodore Bainbridge, her commander, officers and crew were made prisoners. The officers were treated as prisoners of war, but the crew were made slaves. Two days after the accident the frigate was got off by the Tripolitans and taken into the harbor, under the guns of the castle, to be fitted for sea. Commodore Bainbridge found means to inform Commodore Preble, at Malta, of his misfortune, and to suggest the destruction of the Philadelphia where she lay.

The Enterprise, in whose history all Portlanders take an interest, then a schooner, was commanded by Lieutenant Decatur, afterward a commodore, who was killed in a duel by Commodore Barron, in 1820. She sailed in company with the Constitution, and in the Mediterranean she captured a ketch belonging to the Tripolitans, bound to Constantinople with a present of female slaves for the Sultan. The ketch was taken into the service under the name of the "Intrepid," and was the same vessel used by Decatur and his volunteers in the attack on and burning of the Philadelphia, in February, 1804, within half gunshot of the Bashaw's castle. The final destruction of this ketch, Intrepid, was coupled with the death of one of Portland's brave sons.

On the third of September, Commodore Preble's bomb-vessels commenced a heavy bombardment of the city of Tripoli and its defences, while he, in the Constitution, ran in within grape-shot range of the castle and city, and delivered eleven broadsides; the smaller vessels were continuing the bombardment at a greater distance. A rising gale compelled the Commodore to withdraw the squadron.

Lossing gives the following description of the disastrous attempt to destroy the Tripolitan cruisers in the harbor:

The ketch Intrepid used in the destruction of the *Philadelphia* had been converted into a floating mine for the purpose of destroying the enemy's cruisers in the harbor of Tripoli. One hundred barrels of gunpowder had been placed in a room below deck, and immediately above them a large quantity of shot, shell, and irregular pieces of iron were deposited. In other parts of the vessel combustibles were placed, and she was made in every way a most disagreeable neighbor. On the night succeeding the fifth bombardment of Tripoli, she was sent into the harbor on her destructive mission, under the command of Captain Somers, who had behaved gallantly during the recent attacks on the town. He was assisted by Lieutenant Wadsworth, of the Constitution, and Mr. Israel, an ardent young officer, who got on board the ketch by stealth. These, with a few men to work the Intrepid, and the crews of two boats employed in towing her, composed the expedition.

At nine o'clock in the evening the Intrepid entered the harbor on her perilous mission. The night was very dark and she soon disappeared in the gloom. Many eager eyes were turned in the direction where the shadowy form was last seen. All hearts in the squadron beat quickly with anxiety. Suddenly a lurid light streamed up from the dark bosom of the waters like volcanic fires, and illuminated with its lurid gleams the rocks, forts, flotilla, castle, town, and the broad expanse of the harbor, followed instantly by an explosion that made all surrounding objects tremble. Flaming masts and sails, and fiery bombs rained upon the waters for a few moments, when all was again silence and darkness three-fold greater than before. Anxious eyes and ears bent in the direction of the dreadful explosion. The boats were waited for until the dawn with almost unsupportable impatience. They never came, and no man of that perilous expedition was heard of afterward.

Waldo in his life of Decatur, page 146, says that an eye-witness informed him that the evening was unusually calm; that as the Intrepid moved silently into the inner harbor, two of the enemy's heaviest galleys with more than a hundred men in each, captured the "infernal," wholly unconscious of her character. The impression was that Somers, knowing that their fate would be miserable captivity if taken prisoners into the city, where Bainbridge and his men had suffered for eleven months, considered death preferable, and with his own hand fired the magazine of the Intrepid. It is evident that Commodore Preble entertained the same opinion of the cause of the explosion.

On the southeast face of the cenotaph to the memory of Lieutenant Wadsworth, in the Eastern cemetery, in Portland, is this inscription: "Determined at once they prefer death and the destruction of the enemy to captivity and torturing slavery. Com. Preble's letter." The letter of Commodore Preble referred to was probably written to Lieutenant Wadsworth's father, who was the Commodore's friend and neighbor. It might have been his official letter to the secretary of war. The monument referred to was erected in the Eastern cemetery by General Wadsworth, father of the Lieutenant.

Lack of powder, and the approach of the stormy season of the year, induced Commodore Preble to cease operations on the dangerous Barbary coast, other than the maintenance of the blockade of Tripoli. On September 10, 1804, Preble was relieved by the arrival of Commodore Samuel Barron, and he returned home in February, 1805. The reason for his supersedure was because it was thought necessary to increase the force of the squadron, and there were no captains, junior to him, who could be employed on that service, and his retention would necessarily involve his being placed over captains who were his seniors. The news of his five attacks on Tripoli were unknown at home when the change was ordered. He differed from the administration in politics.

The year 1799 was made memorable by the sudden death of General Washington. He died at Mount Vernon on the fourteenth of December, after an illness of only twenty-four hours, in the sixty-eighth year of his age. It was a great shock to the whole country as his illness was not known until the announcement of his death. He died of inflammation of the windpipe caused by exposure to rain.

The following is a copy of the letter of Tobias Lear, the General's private secretary, announcing the sad event:

MOUNT VERNON, Dec. 16, 1779.

Sir: It is with inexpressable grief that I have to inform you of the death of the great and good Gen. Washington. He died last evening, between 11 and 12 o'clock, after a short illness of about twenty-four hours. His disorder was an inflamitory sore throat, which proceeded from a cold of which he made but little complaint on Friday. On Saturday morning about three o'clock he became ill. Dr. Dick attended him in the morning, and Dr. Craik of Alexandria, and Dr. Brown of Port Tobacco were soon after called in. Every medical was offered without the desired effect. His last scene corresponded with the whole tenor of his life. Not a groan nor a complaint escaped him, though in extreme distress. With perfect resignation, and a full possession of his reason he closed his well spent life.

I have the honor to be, &c.,

TOBIAS LEAR.*

To the President of the United States.

*Colonel Lear was a native of Portsmouth, New Hampshire. His widowed mother was called upon by Washington when he visited that town in 1789. On his entrance into the town, General Washington was on horseback, and following him came his carriage, occupied by Colonel Lear, his secretary. As they passed, many supposed the secretary was the President. After the General's death, Colonel Lear was appointed to the diplomatic service. In his last place he spent eight years as consul-general at Tripoli. He had but one child, Benjamin Lincoln Lear, who graduated from Dartmouth College and read law with Prentice Mellen, in Portland, in 1811. Mr. Mellen's law office was on the corner of the entrance to the Preble property, now occupied by the Casco National Bank. Ezekiel Whitman occupied the opposite corner office, with whom John Mussey and Nathaniel Deering were law students at the same time. Young Lear afterward married a daughter of Colonel Bomford, of Washington. He died in the city of Washington in 1831. The elder Lear's second wife was Miss Custis, niece of Martha Washington. In the old Lear house at Portsmouth, hangs a framed piece of black satin on which

A resolution was passed by Congress, " That a marble monument be erected by the United States in the capitol of the City of Washington, and that the family of General Washington be requested to permit his body to be deposited under it, and that the monument be so designed as to commemorate the great events of his life."

In her letter consenting to the removal of her husband's remains, Mrs. Washington closed with these words: " I need not, I cannot say what a sacrifice of individual feeling I make to a sense of public duty." The feeling resolution of Congress was never carried out.*

Congress recommended that the next anniversary of Washington's birth, be set apart for a day of public mourning for his death, which was so done throughout the country. Portland did not wait for the President's proclamation, but observed the event on the eighth of January by a military parade by the Federal Volunteers, the only uniformed company in the town. In his diary, on January 8, 1800, Dr. Deane records: "At 8 o'clock A.M. Military mourning." The eccentric Parson Bradley of Stroudwater, in his journal on the same day says, "Spent the day in Portland. The volunteer company undertook to bury General Washington, and such an irregular, confused, and erratic piece of business, I believe no man ever saw before — harum scarum." The celebration was in accordance with a vote of the town.

When Napoleon Buonaparte, then first consul of France, heard of Washington's death he ordered black crape to be

are wrought four lines of poetry, with General Washington's hair, and four other lines with the hair of Martha Washington, who forwarded for the purpose, both packages of hair to Colonel Lear's niece.

* A lofty and elegant monument was erected at Baltimore, but it was from the proceeds of a lottery.

suspended on the flags of the Republic of France, and Fontaine pronounced an oration in the Temple of Mars, commemorative of the event. Lord Bridport, commander of a British fleet of nearly sixty vessels, lying at Torbay, on the coast of France, when he heard of the death of General Washington, lowered his flag to half-mast and signalled the fleet to do the same.

Mrs. Washington continued to live at Mount Vernon until her death, which occurred in May, 1802. The following is the announcement of her death, in a Washington paper:

Died at *Mount Vernon*, on the 22d May, ult., [1802], Mrs. MARTHA WASHINGTON, widow of the late General George Washington. Composure and resignation were uniformly displayed during seventeen days depredations of a severe fever. From the commencement she declared she was undergoing the last trial, and had long been prepared for her dissolution. She took the sacrament from Mr. Davis, imparted her last advice and benedictions to her weeping relations, and sent for a white gown, which she had previously laid by for her last dress — thus in the closing scene, as in all preceding ones, nothing was omitted. The conjugal, maternal and domestic duties had all been fulfilled in an exemplary manner. She was the worthy partner of the worthiest of men, and those who witnessed their conduct could not determine which excelled in their different characters, both were so well sustained on every occasion. They lived an honor and a pattern to their country, and are taken from us to receive the rewards — promised to the faithful and just.

The setting off of the Neck from the parent town, and its incorporation as a separate municipality, should have been earlier mentioned. A petition, signed by sixty of the principal citizens of the peninsula, for an act of incorporation, was presented to the general court late in the year 1785, and, just ten years to a day from the passage of the act by Congress declaring the independence of the colonies, the general court of Massachusetts declared Falmouth Neck to be an independent town by the name of Portland.

The bounds of the new town were thus defined: "To begin at the middle of the creek that runs into Round marsh, thence north-east to Back Cove creek, thence down the middle of the creek to Back Cove, thence across said Cove to Sandy Point, thence round by Casco Bay and Fore river to the first bounds. Together with all the Islands that now belong to the First Parish in said Falmouth." One hundred and eighty acres of land north of Back Cove creek, belonging to the heirs of Moses Pearson, were, by the act of incorporation, annexed to the town. Hence the crooked boundary line on the western limits. A section of the act obliges Portland to maintain "Stroudwater and Pride's bridges."

Early in 1806, there was a proposition to reorganize the naval service, and Congress sustained the proposition so far as to make provision for the building of a "musquito fleet." An act of Congress for fortifying the ports and harbors of the United States, and for building fifty gun-boats, became a law on April 21, 1806.

A flotilla of them, obtained from Naples, had been used effectively by Commodore Preble in the war with Tripoli, in 1804. They were popular in the service because they afforded commands for ambitious young officers. I have heard it asserted that Commodore Preble brought home one or more gun-boats, which he took from the Tripolitans, but I find no documentary evidence of it. In August, 1806, the Commodore received orders to build eight gun-boats and a bomb-ketch, at Portland, for our navy, to be launched in November following.

Among Commodore Preble's papers, is a book of "Indents" for gun-boats and two bomb-vessels. From these "indents" I learn the size, rig, and armament of all these vessels. The bomb-ketch Etna, built at Portland by Moulton, about where the Galt block now stands, on Commercial street, was eighty-three feet long, twenty-four feet beam, four-teen feet depth of hold, and measured sixty tons. Under her largest guns was solid timber from the keelson to the deck.* She was armed with two brass twenty-four pound-ers and ten nine pounders. She was rigged as a brigantine of the present time, with standing royal.† The bomb-ketch Vesuvius, built at Newburyport, and fitted out here, was rigged and armed like the Etna, with the addition of one thirteen inch mortar. Gun-boat Number Eleven was seven-ty-four feet long, breadth of beam eighteen feet, with a depth of hold of only five feet and three inches. Her meas-urement was sixty-five tons. She was rigged as a fore-and-aft schooner. Her armament was two long eighteen pounders, and two five and one-half inch brass howitzers. All the gun-boats built here were of about the same size and

* A gentleman, now living, who recollects the launching of the bomb-ketch, stated to me that her great weight caused her, when launched, to completely bury, so that waves washed the whole length of her deck.

† This style of rig, with standing royal, for a vessel of sixty tons, seems odd to us. The Columbian Centinel of November 28, 1800, published in Boston, contains an advertisement of a vessel for sale, which is thus described: "The complete schooner Mary of 98 tons; she has two top-sails, and two top-gallant-sails, main-sail, fore-sail, jib and flying jib and sails well." Almost all vessels at that time had standing yards, at least on one mast — sloops had them. These top-sails made a promiscuous fleet, leaving the harbor after a storm, look very picturesque; much more so than the present style of long fore-and-aft schooners. While at anchor their three or four naked masts, all alike, look like a contracted line of telegraph poles.

build, with some variation in their batteries. They were built and launched into Clay cove, then an enclosed basin of water which came up to within one hundred feet of Fore street. From these vessels it obtained the name of "gun-boat dock."

On October 9, the ketch Etna, Lieutenant Jones, the Vesuvius, Lieutenant Leonard, Gun-boat Number Eleven, Lieutenant Bainbridge, and Gun-boat Number Twelve, Lieutenant Dexter, sailed from here for New Orleans. This was the beginning of the famous "gun-boat policy" of the government.

On August 23, 1807, nine gun-boats in one squadron, sailed from Portland for New York, under the command of Lieutenant Lawrence, who was killed while in command of the Chesapeake, on the first of June, 1813, in an action with the frigate Shannon.

The secretary of the navy reported to Congress, in December, 1807, that to protect the coast, it would require two hundred and fifty-seven gun-boats to be stationed from Passamaquoddy to New Orleans, six at Portland and fifty at New York. That of the whole number, sixty-nine were built, and that the one hundred eighty-eight to be built, would cost five thousand dollars each. In May, 1813, there were one hundred and seventy-six gun-boats already built, and the work was going on. These small vessels did not answer the expectations of the government. They were laid up in the harbors along the coast; some of them remained in gun-boat dock and were purchased for coasters.

Commodore Preble's honorable career as a naval officer calls for a notice of his early life. He was born on Falmouth Neck, October 15, 1761. He was the third son of Brigadier-General Jedediah Preble, who was one of the foremost men of the town. The history of his services is interwoven with the history of the French and Indian wars and with that of the Revolution.

After the burning of the Neck, in 1775, General Preble retired to his farm at Capissic, in the cultivation of which his sons assisted. One day, when Edward was about six-teen, he suddenly threw down his hoe and declared that he was done farming. He walked to the Neck and shipped on board a privateer belonging to Newburyport, then in the harbor. The vessel went to Europe and had a hard passage home, but it did not cure the young sailor of his love for the sea.

His father, finding he was resolutely bent on being a sailor, procured him a midshipman's warrant in the Massa-chusetts state marine, and he was appointed to the "Pro-tector." On her second cruise she was captured, and the junior officers were put on board of the prison-ship Jersey, at New York. Here young Preble was taken with a fever, was placed on parole, and finally obtained his release through the kindness of his father's former neighbor, Colonel Tyng.

After the peace of 1783, Massachusetts no longer needed a navy, and the officers were generally discharged. Young Mr. Preble was then twenty-two years old. He at once sought employment in the merchant service, in which he continued fifteen years as supercargo, commander, shipper, and owner.

The troubles in France brought Preble into public life a second time, and he was commissioned a lieutenant in the United States navy, in January, 1799. His first service under his commission was as commander of the brig Pick-ering. In June, of the same year, he was commissioned captain. Soon after he received orders to the frigate Essex, which was built at Salem by subscription of the merchants, who received government stock for the money advanced. Captain Preble took charge of the Essex before her rigging was completed. It was while fitting out the Essex at Salem, and only a month before he sailed, that Commodore Preble wrote the following letter to Madam Deering, who was then the widow of Nathaniel Deering, and was living in her mansion house, which stood on a low hillock where the present post-office is. Her only daughter, Mary, and the servants constituted the household.* Mrs. Deering's only son James, with his family, lived on the opposite side of Middle street. I am permitted to publish the letter by the heirs of the lady to whom it was directed.

SALEM, Dec'r 17th. 1799.

Dear Madam: When I last had the pleasure of seeing Mr. Deering [her son James] here, I gave him a snuff-box for you, of which I beg your acceptance, as a token of my respect. I am ordered to sail the first fair wind for Newport, and from thence to the East Indies, this order grieves me exceedingly, as it separates me for at least one year

---

* Mrs. Deering's house was built and owned by William Owen, until it was purchased by Nathaniel Deering. It was a long two-story wooden house, with a common two-sided roof. The knoll on which it stood, was ten or more feet above the street, with a spacious yard in front. The only ornamental shrubbery in the enclosure, was a snow-ball tree on one side of the front steps and a lilac on the other. Mrs. Deering's only man-servant was William Hanse, who had charge of the garden and the cow. Hanse was a celebrity of the town. He served in one of the Falmouth companies in the war for independence, and had an exalted opinion of General Washington. The boys of the town often raised his ire by calling Washington a coward, but before doing it, they looked out a safe way to escape. His armament of "small stones" was almost as dangerous as that of the shepherd-boy who killed Goliath. Mrs. Deering died in 1835, aged eighty-six years, and her old servant Hanse, went to live with her daughter, Madam Preble. He had a house of his own on Crow Alley, between Green and Oak streets.

from the society of your family; you know not how very dear to my heart your amiable daughter is; but I beg leave to assure you she is infinitely more dear to me than my existence. I love her with the tenderest affection, and would sacrifice my life to promote her happiness — for heavens sake Madam, plead for me, and if she should consent to be mine, on my return, my whole future life shall be devoted to a tender and delicate attention to her happiness and your own. You may rely with confidence on my attention to prudence and economy, and a steady adherence to the interest of your family — for I love you all with an unfeigned affection.

You have long known of my attachment to your lovely daughter, and I feel truly sensible of the delicacy with which you have ever attended to my feelings, when ever I have visited at your house. I beg you to accept my thanks for your friendship, and my fervent prayers for the health, happiness, and prosperity of yourself and family. Could my lovely friend know how much I suffer from the thoughts of so long an absence from her, for whom alone I wish to live, I am sure she would pity me. Give my best love to her, and tell her the future happiness of my life rests with her; and may the God of all goodness restore me to the joys of her loved society, and bless me with her affections.

If I possessed a world I would give it freely to pass one hour with your amiable family before I go, but that alas is impossible. Adieu.

Yours with respect,
EDWARD PREBLE.

MRS. DORCAS DEERING, PORTLAND.

Should Mary Deering bless an other with her affections, and not me, *I am lost forever* — for heavens sake plead for me. Adieu.

Pray pardon this hasty letter.

The Essex and Congress, with a convoy of merchantmen, sailed from Newport, Rhode Island, on January 6, 1800, for the Cape of Good Hope. The Essex, Commodore Preble, arrived there on the eleventh of March, but the Congress was dismasted and put back. The Essex was the first public vessel that carried our flag around the Cape of Good

Hope.   On his return voyage, Commodore Preble sailed from Batavia on the nineteenth of June, with a convoy of thirteen laden India ships bound to the United States.   The Essex was a remarkable fast sailer.   The Commodore remarks in his journal, " Run all night under double reefed top-sails on the cap, to keep company with the merchantmen." He called at St. Helena to wait for the convoy, and arrived in New York harbor on the twenty-ninth of November.

He immediately went to Washington to report to the secretary of the navy, and to obtain a furlough.   The secretary replied, "The leave of absence you solicit is granted for such time as may suit your convenience."   Captain Preble's health would not permit him to return to the Essex, and he remained in Portland during the winter.   The nature of his pastime, while at home, we can conjecture from his ardent letter to Madam Deering a year before.   He was married to Miss Mary Deering in March following.   Ever after his return from the East Indies, Commodore Preble's health was precarious.   From this cause he tendered to the secretary his resignation, which was not accepted.

The Commodore's next service was in the expedition to the Mediterranean, and on his return, in building the gun-boats and bomb-vessels, which were all built from his drafts. Of these services I have already written.*   On his return from Tripoli, a gold medal was voted to him by Congress, which is now in possession of his descendants.

In 1806, while his health was failing, the Commodore

* I should have mentioned in the proper place, that on the return of Commodore Preble, from Tripoli, in 1805, his fellow-townsmen gave him a public dinner at Union Hall, at which Woodbury Storer presided. In response to a complimentary toast, the Commodore gave, " The town of Portland; may its commercial interests ever meet with a ready and effectual protection from our navy."

wrote to the secretary of the navy, this message: "If a service of danger presents, I shall feel mortified at not being employed. I stand ready to proceed at a moment's warning on any service which the government think proper to send me, against any nation or people, and to shed my blood in the execution of such service." He made short trips in the bay in one of the gun-boats, without benefit. He died of consumption, on Tuesday, August 25, 1807, ten days before completing his forty-sixth year.

Commodore Preble had for a year been building an elegant residence, which is now the center compartment of the public house that bears his name, but he had not moved into it. It was afterward occupied by the widow, until her death. At the time of his death, he lived in a large wooden house on Middle street, which also became a public house; first called the "Sun Tavern," and afterward the "Casco House." At the time of his death, this house had an open yard with an unobstructed view of the street. At this house, the funeral services were held, Dr. Deane officiating. The coffin was then brought out, and the Masonic service was held in the front yard. All business of the town was suspended on the twenty-seventh, the day of the burial. Such a funeral pageant had never been seen in Portland.

> "Far down the long line solemn music was streaming,
> Lamenting a chief of the people should fall." *

There was not a hearse in Cumberland County at that time. As was the custom, the coffin was carried on a bier on men's shoulders, covered with a black velvet pall, with

---

* A gentleman writes me from New York, as follows: "I recollect Commodore Preble's funeral; I was then nine years old. The march played principally, was 'Roslyn Castle,' which since that time has been a favorite with me."

cords and tassels at the sides, held by the "pall bearers," hence the name. On top of the pall was laid the Commodore's sword.   There was not a carriage in the procession — all walked; even the bereaved wife was supported by her only brother, James Deering, and, owing to the long route of the procession, her strength failed, and she left her place as chief mourner, and was assisted to a neighboring house. This last fact I obtained from a lady, now dead, who was then seventeen years old, and was present, observing all the proceedings with a girl's curiosity.

Commodore Preble's remains were placed first in the tomb of his father-in-law, Nathaniel Deering.   At the time of the death of the Commodore's only child, Edward Deering Preble, in 1846, he had in process of building, a family tomb, in the same time-honored cemetery to which the remains of the father were removed.

CHAPTER XII.

THE affair of the Chesapeake and Leopard, which occurred in June, 1807, was a prominent cause of the ill-feel-
ing between the United States and Great Britain, which
resulted in a declaration of war by the former nation in 1812.

In June, 1807, a British squadron was lying in Lynhaven
Bay, in Virginia. From one of these ships three seamen
deserted and entered on board the American frigate Chesapeake, at the Washington navy-yard. There had been a
formal demand made for the men by the British minister,
and a refusal by the President to deliver them, as they were
proved to be of American birth. When the Chesapeake,
under Commodore James Barron, sailed from Hampton
Roads for the Mediterranean, the British frigate, Leopard,
preceded her to sea, and, after bearing down to within
hailing distance, desired the Chesapeake to lay to and receive a message from the commander of the Leopard, which
was done, when demand for the delivery of the deserters
was made in the name of Admiral Berkley at Halifax.
Commodore Barron refused to have his crew mustered, and
the boat left. After a hail from the Leopard, she fired
several broadsides into the Chesapeake, which was unpre-
pared for action, killing three men and wounding eighteen

on board the Chesapeake, which did not return the fire (except a single gun), but struck her colors. Several officers boarded the American frigate and took out the deserters. The Chesapeake returned to port, and the publication of the account of the outrage caused great excitement and condemnation from all parties, and a general desire was expressed for a declaration of war against England. The outrage was disowned by the English ministry and provision was made for the families of those slain on board the American vessel. The President ordered all British armed vessels to leave the waters of the United States immediately, but not having sufficient power to enforce his order, they were in no hurry to comply. Commodore Barron was tried by a court-martial for neglect of duty, found guilty, and condemned to five years suspension from duty without pay. It was the affair of the Chesapeake that occasioned the correspondence between him and Commodore Decatur in 1820, which resulted in a duel, and the death of Decatur.

The right to search American vessels for British seamen was still insisted upon. War then existed between France and England, and other nations of Europe, in which the Emperor Napoleon had been very successful. December 17, 1807, Napoleon, then at Milan, issued a decree declaring that every vessel that should submit to be searched, or to pay tribute to England, should be seized, if found in any of the harbors of France.

Previous to this time, a storm had been gathering in Europe, which threatened to involve the United States in a war with England. In May, 1806, Great Britain declared the continent of Europe, from the Elbe to Brest, to be in a state of blockade. November 21, Napoleon, seated in the palace of the vanquished King of Prussia, at Berlin,

issued his famous "Berlin decree," declaring the British
Isles in a state of blockade, by which the vessels of neutral
nations, going to or from England, were liable to be captured. January 7, 1807, the British government, by way of
retaliation, issued an "order in council," which prohibited
neutral powers from trading from one port to another of
France or her allies, or with any country with which England might not trade. November 11, 1807, another order in
council was issued, which prohibited all neutral nations from
trading with France or her allies, unless they would pay
tribute to England. Then came the attack on the Chesapeake, which shook the American states from center to
circumference.

December 21, 1807, Congress laid an embargo prohibiting
any American vessel from sailing to any foreign port. The
British orders in council, the Berlin and Milan decrees, and
the embargo, were death blows to American commerce for
the time being. The exports, which, in 1807, were one
hundred and eight millions, in 1808, fell down to twenty-
two millions, and the imports fell from one hundred and
thirty-eight millions to fifty-seven millions. Political parties
were greatly excited; the Democrats threatening war, and
the Federalists, smarting under the embargo, were bitter
against Jefferson and his policy, and accused him of trying
to cripple mercantile interests. During the war between
France and England, and up to 1806, the merchants of the
United States had been growing rich, having, from our
neutrality, been the principal carriers on the seas.

When the counter edicts of Napoleon Bonaparte and the
British government were issued against neutral ships in
1807, the United States was the only neutral maritime
nation in the civilized world, and, of course, was doing

about all the carrying trade. Commerce and its connecting industries comprised about all the trade pursued by the people of Portland. What shipping the Berlin and Milan "decrees," and the British "orders in council" left, was swept away or made worthless by the embargo act of Congress, passed December 21, 1807. It prohibited all vessels in the ports of the United States from sailing for any foreign port, except foreign ships in ballast, or with cargoes taken on board before notification of the act; and coast-wise vessels were required to give heavy bonds to land their cargoes in the United States. In the Senate the act was passed with closed doors, by a strictly party vote — ayes twenty-two, noes six. In the House the final vote was taken at midnight and passed eighty-two to forty-four. It was a southern and western measure.

A supplementary act applying to the navigation of rivers, lakes, and bays, made the original act more stringent and, of course, more odious to the people of New England.

Petitions were showered upon the government from every seaport, for the repeal of the oppressive act, but Congress was deaf to these appeals. A proposition for repeal, and to allow merchantmen to arm and take care of themselves, was voted down by a large majority.

The enforcement of the Embargo act was so ruinous to Portland interests that in many cases it was violated. Cargoes were prepared, and, when all was ready, organized parties loaded vessels in a night, and before morning they were out of reach of government officers. In several cases vessels were loaded and dispatched by daylight, and the government officers, with gun-boats and forts were powerless to prevent it. A great anti-embargo demonstration was got up by the Federalists and those opposed to the measure. A long-boat of a ship was loaded on to a car prepared for the purpose, stern foremost, and rigged like a ship, but made to represent the state of the shipping. All the running rigging was hanging loose. On the stern and quarters was painted a transposition of the word "Embargo," it being spelled backwards, making "O-g-r-a-b-m-e." Then all the truckmen of the town hitched their horses to the car, in single line, and mounted them, each one holding his whip by the small end, at the side of his horse. Then followed a band, playing doleful music, and the unemployed people followed — masters, mates and men, and all the mechanics connected with commerce. The pro. cession marched to the battery, where Monument street now is, and halted. Captain Edward Kelleran, a large and jolly ship captain, delivered a burlesque address, showing how easy it was to starve old England, by shutting our ports and keeping our ships at home. James D. Hopkins, a noted lawyer and wag, had adapted Watts' psalm, beginning "Teach me the number of my days," to suit the occasion, and it was sung with unction by the assemblage, to a solemn tune. While these ceremonies were in progress, a party of riggers had taken the car bearing the ship, behind the gun-house and turned her bow forward, painted over the hull, put the rigging in the best trim, hoisted the American ensign at each mast-head, and a crew of neatly dressed sailors manned her. In this improved condition the procession marched through the town to Union Wharf, and launched the ship, with the crew on board, amid the cheers of a very large crowd.*

* For a description of this and other similar scenes in Portland during the embargo and the war that followed, I am indebted to Captain Andrew Scott, now living at Flushing, New York, at the age of eighty-eight years. At the time of the passage of the Embargo act he was nine years old. His father was a ship-master of the same name, born in Scotland.

The pressure upon the administration against the Embargo act became too great for resistance and on the first of March, 1809, it was repealed. As a sop to those upholding the Embargo, and a bugbear to European belligerents, a Non-intercourse act was passed, by which the commerce of the United States was opened to all the world except England and France, and British and French ships of war were equally excluded prospectively from American ports.

At a large meeting of the inhabitants of the town of Portland held January 18, 1808, to hear the report of a committee chosen at a former meeting to devise a plan for the relief of the distressed poor in the town, they made a long report from which the following is extracted.

Your Committee, from the result of their enquiries, and the best investigation they have been able to make, are unanimously of opinion that such are the calamities of the times, the house provided by the town will not afford shelter, and that the most prudent expenditure of all monies which can possibly be realized by the Overseers of the Poor from the specific appropriations of the town, will be greatly inadequate to meet the extent of the calamities we now feel and which are increasing upon us to such an alarming degree.

Your Committee could not in the short time allowed them, ascertain the number of our fellow citizens who have heretofore been able by their own industry in their several employments to accumulate more than a sufficiency for the support of themselves and families, and are now by reason of their present public distress not only deprived of business and without the means of subsistence, but your Committee are painfully compelled to say that they are already very numerous and daily increasing.

Your Committee further beg leave to report that from a statement of the finances of the town furnished by the Chairman of the Selectmen, it appears that by reason of the late heavy misfortunes of some among us, who have until now contributed very largely towards the aggregate sum of our taxes, a very considerable deficit will be exhibited at the settlement of the town accounts for the present year.

28

And your Committee would further suggest, that the Market-House standing on the town's lot, near Dr. Coffin's building, being a place which can be occupied without cost to the town, and situated near the center, can be with a very little expence, furnished with a Chimney and Apparatus for cooking, and that therefrom might be distributed daily, at least one meal of wholesome and cheap food for that part of the poor of the town which our Overseers may not be able to relieve.

The committee give information that the *Market-House* is open to carry all the objects of the foregoing Votes into effect, and will be continued open as long as their funds shall enable them. And it is requested that all Donations of Money, Provisions, Wood, &c. may be deposited in the Market-House, where two of the Committee will daily superintend the distribution of provisions, record the names, donors and their donations, and attend to any other business which may come within their commissions. It is further suggested by the Committee that as many individuals are supplied daily from private families with cold provisions, which if sent to the Market-House, would furnish relief for many more than are really benefited by such assistance it is an object of importance that such private relief be withheld and that all cold provision, &c. &c. be sent to the Market-House, where it will be an important object with the Committee that nothing shall be wasted but that all should be used with economy.

The "market-house" here mentioned stood about where the eastern corner of the present "Old City Hall" now does. To clear the lot for the present building in 1825, the market-house (a small one story building), was moved to the west corner of the North School lot and became an engine house for a fire engine. "Dr. Coffin's building," mentioned in the report, was of brick, and is now the south corner of the United States Hotel.

A long cooking-range of large kettles was built in the "market-house," and there hundreds who had formerly lived in affluence obtained a large part of their daily food. This establishment for the feeding of the people who had no employment was kept up until the restrictions were removed from commerce, and its white sails were allowed to come and go with freedom. Like the food of the Israelites "The manna ceased on the morrow, and they did eat of the fruits of the land of Canaan that year."

This was the beginning of the "soup charity" in Portland, and twice at least since, from the building now on this hallowed spot, have the hungry people obtained food for the asking, without money and without price; first during the severe depression in business in the winter of 1837 and 1838, and again after the great fire of 1866.

The following extracts relating to the time of which I have been writing, are from a letter from Captain Andrew Scott, who has been already mentioned. In his prime he was a ship-master, sailing from Portland. His wife was a niece and adopted daughter of Dr. Coffin, the younger.

FLUSHING, N. Y., August 14, 1880.

MR. GOOLD,

Dear Sir: In reply to yours, I have to say, I recollect Commodore Preble's funeral in 1807. I was then nine years old. The march played was "Roslyn Castle," which since that time has been a favorite with me. With other boys I followed the procession. I was intimate with Capt. Enoch Preble, his brother. He was an antiquarian, full of old tales — most interesting in conversation, especially with the young. I was with him and Samuel Freeman in advising about the publication of the first edition of "Smith's Journal." The map of the town in Willis' History is my drawing. I was on board the Enterprise when she came in with her prize, the Boxer, as well as the fitting out of privateers — the alarms and occurrences of the war of 1812. I used to go often to the observatory — saw through the *tele-

---

* The telescope in the observatory was of peculiar interest to young Scott, from the fact that it was made in London, under the direction of his father, who was a ship-master, and formerly a resident of London; and was brought to Portland by him. The captain's family always had a free pass to the tower, which the son writes, "is good yet."

scope the blockading ships, Lahogue, Acasta, Shannon and others; counted their guns, and could almost count their crews.

I send you enclosed a story of "Derring do," from the Massachusetts law reports, in an attempt to recapture the ship Mary Ann from the French. Paper blockaders were actual pirates upon American ships at the time. The ship belonged to Captain Arthur McLellan of Portland. You will notice that the names of the Captain, Eben McIntosh of Portland, and Bacon, mate, of Freeport, are not given in the report. They were suppressed at the time for fear of trouble, but everything about it was known by McIntosh's friends, though he refused to ever speak of it.

In detail it was said that thirteen Frenchmen who refused to leave, were killed, and that two of the American crew left on board, were seen hanging at the yard-arm when the French got re-possession. I think the story will bear repeating in Portland.

The McIntosh family came here from Scotland, in 1774. They lived some years on Bang's Island, — afterward at the head of the Duckpond, in Windham. There were four sons and five daughters. Eben was next to the youngest, born on Bang's Island, made his first voyage with my father, in a ship belonging to the Fox's. Peter and John became sailors, but never rose higher than mate. Both of them were of extraordinary strength, as were all the family, as well as of terrible tempers; both lost their lives by violence. James kept the farm. Eben was married but left no children. He continued in the employ of Arthur McLellan and his son until loss of sight prevented his wonted usefulness. He had never laid up much of his earnings. The lawsuits which he had to encounter every voyage took a great part, and his liberality the rest, so that he died poor. He was a perfect gentleman in soul and conduct—friendly to a fault, but "sudden and quiet in quarrel," of courage that never counted the numbers of his enemies, or his own danger, and of irresistible strength in encountering them. Yet he had a peculiar kind of cowardice as a ship-master; fearful of carrying sail — reefed down every night; jealous of trusting to his officers or men — always severe with his mates. He was so fearful of accidents or short supplies that he overloaded his ship with spare spars, sails, rigging and anchors, which he never found use for.

In his affair with the Frenchmen, it was said that Captain McIntosh commenced the attack alone, and unarmed, killing the prize-master with his own sword. Bacon, whose courage and character were like his, coming in with a handspike. The others of the American crew being confined below, and the prize-crew partly aloft taking in sail, and the time so short, the French shore and the lugger so near, that escape was all but hopeless.

The boat very narrowly escaped the fire and chase of the lugger, and arrived at Dover, England, in the night. The captain and crew were carried in triumph to London — exhibited as lions at the theatres, and provided for in the most liberal manner and claimed by the clan McIntosh as cousins.   Yours,

                                        ANDREW SCOTT.

There is no reason to doubt that the lugger was one of Bonaparte's commissioned cruisers. It was said at the time that Captain McIntosh claimed that if they acted like pirates he was excusable for treating them as such, and it will be seen that the court justified him in his action. It was said that the Captain finished by driving two or three overboard.

It is noticeable that two of the opposing counsel, Whitman and Mellen, became chief justices of the supreme court of Maine.

          12th Mass. Reports, p. 246. May term, 1815.
     Arthur McLellan vs. Maine Fire and Marine Insurance Co.
Policy dated March 29th, 1811. Ten thousand dollars on ship Mary Ann, of Portland. To, at, and from Charleston, S. C. To, at, and from London to a port of discharge in the U. States; with liberty to touch and trade at St. Ubes; Ship valued at 15,000 dollars.
Averment, — Ship taken by the French, — By force of arms, — Lost by perils of the sea; taken and carried to ports unknown, &c., &c.
Case tried Oct. term. — Judge Putnam.
Master testified:—
Proceeding up the English Channel, American colors hoisted, March 8th 1811; descried an armed lugger making for the ship; on

her coming up, she hailed us in French also in English; ordered us to alter our course, threatened to fire &c.; lugger hoisted French colors; witness obliged to comply; lugger accompanied ship towards French coast; when just under the land, ran along side, and put prize-master and two men on board; — soon ran the ship ashore near the harbor of Calais, and then ten or twelve men came on board — the tide rising, the ship beat off. Prize-master told witness that he intended to carry the ship into Dunkirk; threatened him and his crew that they would run them through if they would not assist in working the ship. During this time no inquiry was made from the lugger, " what ship it was ? " " where from, or where bound ? " No reason given why the ship was taken or as a prize; only inquiry " what cargo ? " Lugger had about six guns and sixty men; gave no notice who she was, or what nation, or whether commissioned or not by Belligerent powers. At the time of capture boats might safely have passed between the vessels.

Finding the ship in possession of these people, continually threatening and acting like ruffians, breaking open and robbing stores and cargo, He, with the assistance of part of his crew, rose upon the captors, seized a dirk from one, and in a few minutes killed or disabled all but two of them, and got a complete victory; retook the ship and steered her towards England. Afterwards, becoming calm, the lugger again gave chase with sweeps, and, it being manifest that she would retake her, the witness, with all his crew (except three, who would not assist him for fear of losing their lives if retaken), left the ship and took to the boat. The ship was again taken and carried towards the French coast, but to what place the witness did not know. He, and those in the boat with him, with great peril, arrived at Dover. Nothing has been heard since, either of the ship or of the three American seamen left in her. Witness sent his demand over to France to reclaim the ship; did not know what became of it. Papers and documents all remained on board.

Testimony of the master confirmed by one of the seamen. William Widgery, President of the Company, said that he considered it a loss which the Co. was bound to pay. Several of the Directors were of the same opinion. Three thousand, two hundred and sixty eight 50-100 dollars were paid up to January 1812. The Secretary's account confirmed the payment.

Jury charged by Judge Putnam.

Belligerent ships have a right to search vessels on the high seas; to ascertain whether they belong to an enemy, or if neutral, if they have contraband or enemy's property on board; may send into port for above, or for breach of blockade. Rescue taken for such alleged cause is violation of duty of a neutral, and such a cause of forfeiture of the property would exonerate underwriters. But Belligerents have duties to perform as well as rights to enjoy and enforce. It is their duty to make known their character and the cause of detention. When they omit to do so, masters are not bound to know them as lawfully commissioned Belligerents. Neutrals are not to be attacked at first in a hostile manner, but first examination is to be made. Neutrals have a right to resist assailing thieves. It is their duty, if the laws of nations are disregarded, if they act like pirates, resistance is a right and duty. The jury are to decide whether the capture was by pirates, enemies, rovers or assailing thieves; and if there had been an adjustment as for total loss, with full knowledge of facts; if so, verdict should be for the plaintiff. If total loss, or partial with benefit of salvage? if the captain was for examination and lawful search? Against.

Verdict for the plaintiff, Total loss.

Exceptions for the Def't.

Rescue of ship, especially after arrival in France, was breach of Neutrality and discharged underwriters from liability.

Abandonment not proved.

Part payment no evidence of adjustment.

Mellen and Stover, Defs; Whitman and Potter, Plfs

Judge Jackson.

Law of rescue correctly stated by the Judge to the jury. The principle contended for by the defts would expose every Neutral ship to pirates without right of self defence. If the Captain could not resist untill after capture, resistance would come too late and be ineffectual. The argument supposes that the capturer was a French commissioned cruiser; no evidence to the master. Capturers may have plundered the ship and sunk her with the three men, and neither the owner nor the government could have demanded indemnity from the French government. Defendants were seasonably apprised of the loss and all circumstances. In the course of eight months they made sundry payments without suggestion that they were not bound to pay the whole for want of abandonment. Testimony of the president &c. is that both parties considered the prospect of saving hopeless. Abandonment is usually an idle ceremony. Deft's are bound and cannot object.

Judgment according to verdict.

At the commencement of the war of 1812 there was one vessel belonging to Portland of man-of-war build, and very suitable for a privateer. This was the brig Rapid, of one hundred and ninety tons, and only three years old. Her speed had saved her in more than one instance before the war. She was a full rigged brig with standing royals, and all the flying kites that could be set with a reasonable hope to catch a zephyr. The account of her voyage up the Baltic, and her escape from the harbor of Memel I received from the officer who sailed her.

During the European war the French and English blockades of each other's colonies made it a rich prize to run a cargo out of the West India Islands for a European market. This state of Europe was the means of producing in the Atlantic states a class of clipper built vessels which have never yet been excelled for speed, and which became useful to the United States in the war of 1812.

In 1809 Deacon James Jewett and his nephew, William Jewett of Portland, employed Moulton, who had a shipyard where the Galt block now is, to build them a fast brig to run the English blockade at Guadaloupe, but the island had surrendered before her arrival there. John Curtis was master and William Cammett was first mate. The brig was appropriately named the Rapid. William Jewett, one of the owners, was a passenger in the vessel, and was determined to make a good voyage at all hazards, notwithstanding he had been disappointed in obtaining a cargo of coffee. He decided to purchase a cargo of cotton at Charleston, South Carolina, and to seek a market in Europe. The brig had ninety-six bales of cotton on deck. On the arrival at Falmouth, England, he learned that cotton was wanted at Memel in Prussia, at a dollar per pound. The brig joined a convoy of seven hundred sail of merchantmen at Gottenburg, all bound up the Baltic under a British convoy of several frigates and two line of battle ships, one of which was the Victory, Nelson's flag ship, on whose deck he lost his life at the battle of Trafalgar in 1805.

On the arrival of the Rapid at Memel in November she was seized by Bonapartist officials, as the city had a few days before surrendered to him, and a guard of sixteen French soldiers was put on board. After several days' trial on shore by Mr. Jewett and the captain to have the brig released, Mr. Jewett came on board without the captain, and was much affected at the loss of his vessel and cargo, which were confiscated, as the vessel was from a British port and under a British convoy. Mr. Jewett's state of mind excited Mr. Cammett's sympathy, and he proposed to him that with his permission he would retake the brig and run her out by the forts, to which Jewett gladly assented, and the crew as gladly promised their assistance, as they would lose their wages if the vessel remained a prize to the French. That day a crew of pilots came on board to take the brig up to town, to avoid the ice. The cook could speak French, and was of great service in the project. The pilots attempted to weigh anchor, but found it foul of some obstruction, when Mr. Cammett proposed through the cook, to set some of the lower sails, which would assist them in clearing the anchor, to which they agreed. The time to act had now arrived.

The wind was favorable and the sails were set except the jib. When the vessel headed right, Mr. Cammett told the men to hoist the jib, which the Frenchman tried to prevent, suspecting the intention, and ordered the soldiers to fire on the crew, but their guns would not go off, as the faithful cook, by Mr. Cammett's order, had removed the flints. Mr. Cammett seized an axe from its hiding-place, and at one blow cut the hemp cable on the windlass and held the axe for future use if necessary. The soldiers and pilots went over the side into their boat, and with a swift breeze the Rapid ran by the forts, under fire, but without receiving a shot.

The Rapid arrived and wintered at Riga, in Russia, where her cargo was sold for a large price, and she sailed for Boston by the way of London, making the passage from London to Boston in the unprecedented time of fifteen days.

Early in the summer of 1812, the owners of the Rapid put a heavy battery of fifteen guns, with one hundred men on board of her, and dispatched her as a privateer, under the command of Captain William Crabtree. She had very little success, and returned to port. She was again sent out under the same captain, with Joseph Weeks, a spirited young sailor of the town, as first lieutenant, but the favorite Rapid returned from her cruise with no better success. Prizes were arriving every week, sent in by the Baltimore, New York, and Salem privateers, which led the owners of the Rapid to the conclusion that there was some fault in the commander, who had a good reputation as a merchant captain. The lieutenant, Weeks, had shown some impatience at the management of the captain, and the owners put Weeks in command for the next cruise.

But after making one prize, the Rapid was caught at a disadvantage by a fast-sailing frigate, and was captured. Like many other privateers the Rapid was overloaded by her battery. The particulars of her capture are given in the captain's letter to his owners, which I am pleased to be able to give :

Extract of a letter from Captain Joseph Weeks, dated Halifax, Nov. 5, 1812.

I am sorry to give you the disagreeable news of the capture of the Rapid, on the 18th ult. by the Maidstone frigate, (the Spartan in co.) after a chase of 10 hours; — 17th, thick foggy weather — at 8 a.m. the fog scaled off — we discovered two sail in the N. E., the wind then at W. N. W. and light — we immediately held our wind to the northward — at half past 8 discovered them to be men-of-war. tacked ship and made all sail to the westward, the wind hauling in to N. N. W. The frigates not more than 4 miles distant, also tacked and made sail after us. At 12, finding that one of the frigates was gaining on us — cut away our stern boat and one anchor — at 8 p.m. 18th Oct. threw eight guns over — at 3 a.m. the frigate hoisted American colors, and fired a volley of musketry at us — At 6 p.m. being under the cover of her musketry, and continued showers pouring in upon us, we finding further attempts to escape vain, struck to the Maidstone, Capt. Burdett. During the chase, we gained 6 miles of the Spartan. The wind was light, with a very heavy sea; had not this been the case they never could have caught us — We have received the best of treatment from the commanders and officers of both ships.

Extract of a letter from one of the Lieutenants of the Rapid, dated Halifax, Nov. 15, 1812.

Great credit is due Capt. Weeks for his calm and deliberate conduct during the whole chase. I was told by one of the officers of the Maidstone that the captain of her while in chase said if he came up with the privateer, he would give the captain of her his sword again after receiving it, for the skill he displayed during the chase, which he actually did when we arrived at the mouth of Halifax harbor.

A sea-captain of eighty-six years, now living on Long Island, New York, who during the war of 1812 was a boy living neighbor to Captain Weeks, in King street, writes me these words about the officers of the Rapid:

Captain Crabtree made several cruises in the Rapid with little success. It was said by the boys that every sail he met he ran away from, fearing it was a British 74. But when Jo Weeks took command it was "Hurrah for the Rapid! Success to Jo Weeks!" But Capt. Jo had hardly made a cruise when he was taken, with the pick of Portland for a crew, who were in Dartmoor Prison until the end of the war.

The officers of the "Maidstone" and "Spartan" frigates had seen what the Rapid was capable of under favorable circumstances, and reported her sailing qualities to the admiral at Halifax. He ordered her to be fitted as a brig of war, and she was entered on the list of the English navy.

The Halifax papers of December 30 (less than two months after her capture), report her as sailing with a convoy up the Bay of Fundy as "H. B. M., gun brig Nova Scotia, formerly the privateer Rapid, of Portland." Her final fate might be traced by the English navy lists.

Notwithstanding Captain Weeks' sword was returned to him for his skill in the chase he was sent prisoner to England with his crew, where he remained until the end of the war. He witnessed the cruel shooting of prisoners in the yard of Dartmoor, by order of Captain Shortland. After his discharge Captain Weeks returned to Portland, and was in command of merchantmen for many years, and died a bachelor at an advanced age. He found a pleasant home in his last days, in the family of his brother, Joshua F., who occupied the old homestead on India street.

During President Jefferson's administration the army and navy had been allowed to run down, for the sake of saving money, but in 1807 it was apparent that the national safety required the strengthening of both these arms of the public service. One million dollars was placed at the disposal of the President for coast and harbor defences. There were no military engineers in the government service, and civil agents were appointed by the war department, for the construction of fortifications.

The secretary of war at that time was General Henry Dearborn of Maine, who had been appointed by Jefferson at the beginning of his administration. His chief clerk in the department was General Joshua Wingate junior, who married the daughter of the secretary, and who afterward made Portland his home until his death in 1843. As agent for the war department for Maine, General Dearborn appointed his son, H. A. S. Dearborn, the elegant and eloquent gentleman so well known in Portland in after life. Mr. Dearborn immediately entered upon the duties of his office. In May, 1808, he advertised in the Portland papers as follows: "To be exchanged for a site for a fort between Jordan's Point [now occupied by the Portland Company] and the extreme north-east point of the town, the land, building, and battery of Fort Sumner, in this town." This shore of the harbor was abandoned as a proposed site, and Spring Point was fixed upon for the site of the principal fort.

"Spring Point" was so named for a spring of water just above high-water mark; it is now enclosed by the outworks of Fort Preble. The point formerly belonged to the ancient White family. A daughter married a Thrasher, a tanner, who occupied the property. The Thrashers sold the site for the fort to the government in 1808, and afterward sold another piece of land to enlarge the fort lot. It was on this lot that the ancient log meeting-house stood, and the burying-ground, connected with it, adjoins on the shore.

Mr. Dearborn also purchased of John Green Walden,

father of the late Captain Green Walden of the revenue service, "For twelve hundred dollars to me paid by Henry
Alexander Scammel Dearborn agent for the U. S. all the
south west part of *Howe's*, alias *House Island*, containing
twelve acres more or less."

On the highest point of this purchase, Dearborn erected
an octagonal block-house of timber, with a pointed roof of
eight sides. On the low upright center timber of the roof
was placed a carved wooden eagle with extended wings. On
each of the eight sides of the block-house was an embrasure
or port-hole, and a gun. The upper story contained the battery, and projected over the lower story two or three feet.
All the buildings, including the block-house and barracks
were clapboarded and painted white. The works were
enclosed in an earthen rampart and presented a picturesque
appearance. When the modern extensive earthwork was
begun in 1860, the block-house was taken down, to the regret
of all the lovers of the beautiful in the landscape. Fort
Scammel is now built to mount seventy guns.

Fort Preble was a more extensive fortress. As originally
built the ramparts facing the ship channel were faced with
brick and whitewashed. It originally contained but twelve
mounted guns. There were several one story cottages with
verandas, used as officers' quarters. All the original buildings and the brick walls have disappeared; the enclosure has
been very much enlarged and contains a large number of
casemates. Its armament when completed will number
seventy-two guns. In an attempt to improve the ancient
boiling-spring, the blasting opened seams in the ledge, which
admitted the sea water, by which the spring was greatly
damaged.

One of Dearborn's several newspaper advertisements for material for the forts was this :

Wanted for the war-department, ten or fifteen pieces of best sound white oak timber of the following dimentions, viz.

28 feet long,	32	inches wide, and	36	inches thick.	
24 " "	26 "	"	30	"	"
20 " "	20 "	"	24	"	"
16 " "	14 "	"	14	"	"

Dearborn probably knew that this large timber could be obtained then, but the largest sticks could not be procured now in Maine.

It will be recollected that in 1746 " Captain Pearson's two great guns " were mounted at Spring Point to drive back D'Anville's fleet.

By reference to the extracts from the regimental order-book of Major Ilsley, ante, page 364, it will be seen that in January, 1776, Captain Bryant Morton had forty-eight men and one commissioned officer beside himself engaged " every day on the fort at Spring Point," and that a guard of eight men were stationed at " Portland Point," to watch for armed vessels and fire alarm-guns if necessary. This was the point where the Portland light-house now stands. The government have within a few years built a battery at this point.

The late venerable General J. G. Swift wrote in 1860, " It is worthy of remembrance that the sites upon which these small works were built, were those selected in the Revolutionary struggle, and they remain to this day the best for their purpose." He referred to the coast forts in general.

In 1813 there was a battery at Jordan's Point, with mounted guns, belonging to the United States. Its " pent-houses " and " old gun-house " are mentioned in the newspapers of that time. I find no mention of the time of its construction.

A communication from Captain Atherton to the officer of
the regular army then in command of Forts Preble and
Scammel, shows that the town was considered safe from
bombardment as long as the enemies' ships could be prevented from passing those forts. He said, "Should the
enemy make an attack and succeed in passing the forts, with
wind and tide favoring him, this post (Jordan's Point),
would be the last stronghold for the defence and protection
of the town." Improved ordnance has changed the military
ideas. The last defensive work built (a few years ago),
was a battery near the light-house, which was considered
necessary to prevent an enemy's ships from taking shelter
behind Bang's Island and shelling the town from that point.

In 1813 a draft of militia was called out to build an earthwork fort a short distance westerly from Jordan's Point.
This was a state fort. The citizens of the town subscribed
nearly five hundred dollars to build a range of barracks for
the quartering of the garrison. The building was one hundred and thirty-six feet long, with small gables on the roof
facing the parade. This fort was built under the superintendence of Captain Abel W. Atherton, who commanded the
detachment of militia who built it. He was also the commanding officer of the Portland Rifle Company, who afterward volunteered to garrison the fort. On November 14,
1813, the fort was with some ceremony, named "Fort Burrows," in honor of the slain captain of the brig Enterprise.
This fort and barracks were perfect within my recollection,
and I think they stood about where the brewery building
now does, opposite the machine shop of the Portland Company. The fort was sold by the state, and the barracks were
occupied several years as tenements for families.

While the British squadron was blocking the harbor in

August, 1814, it was decided by the "committee of public safety," to throw up a battery for heavy guns at Fish Point, the most easterly point of the neck, "for the use of the Sea fencibles." This was a company of ship-masters and mates, whose commander was Captain John L. Lewis.

These water batteries were alluded to by Longfellow in these lines:

> "I remember the bulwarks by the shore
> And the fort upon the hill."

Captain Daniel Tucker, chairman of the committee, published a notice to all patriotic citizens to assemble at Fish Point on August 23. Every citizen was desired to bring with him "a pick-axe, crow-bar, spade, shovel, or hoe." A week later the citizens of Stevens' Plains and Back Cove to the number of one hundred and twenty, marched into town and gave a day's work on the battery, many of them bringing their teams.

I have heard the excitement of that time described. The rich men and ministers took their entrenching tools on their shoulders in the morning and marched through the town gathering recruits for the work as they passed along. While the people were throwing up ramparts, the carpenters of the town were building the platforms for the cannon. When completed, the battery consisted of five or six long forty-two-pounders. These guns remained there many years, and were occasionally fired on Independence Day. When the Atlantic and St. Lawrence Railroad was begun in 1845, the first ground broken was on the fourth of July, on the parade of Fish Point battery.

All the defensive works of Portland except the light-house battery were built before the great improvements were made in heavy ordnance, consequently their sites were chosen with

29

a view of arming them with short-range guns. As late as 1858, the formidable looking castle on Hog Island ledge was begun, to complete this system of defences, by a strong work that would command all the entrances to the upper harbor as well as the principal ship channel. Fort Gorges was begun that year, under the direction of Captain Casey, of the United States Engineer Corps. In bombproofs and in barbette it was intended to receive one hundred and ninety-five guns. A modern ironclad ship would soon batter down those frowning granite walls, and make the tiers of casemates untenable. If it is of little value for defence, it is an ornament to the harbor. The future harbor defences will probably be built on the highlands of Bang's Island and the Cape shore. The forts and water-batteries at the entrance are good of their kind and situation.

The act of Congress declaring war against Great Britain was signed by President Madison, and a formal proclamation announcing the fact was issued on June 19, 1812. Then the United States, as a nation, was at peace with all the world, yet there was much feeling remaining against France. When the war act was considered in the House of Representatives, a proposed amendment to the bill, to include France also, received ten votes.

At this time the navy of the United States consisted of three small frigates, and nine smaller men-of-war, and one hundred and sixty-five gun-boats. The British navy at that time consisted of one hundred and fifty-four ships-of-the-line, thirty-five fifties and forty-fours, two hundred and forty-seven frigates, and five hundred and six smaller vessels of war, making a total of one thousand and thirty-six. Of these, eighty-one vessels of all sizes were on the "American station," whose home port was Halifax.

At the time of the declaration of war, we had very little commerce exposed at sea, owing to restrictions and dangers which had prevailed. Seventy-eight days before the declaration of war, Congress passed an act prohibiting the sailing of any American vessel for any foreign port within ninety days. This was preparatory to the passage of the war act. On the passage of this embargo act, the merchants of New York, Philadelphia, and Baltimore despatched a fast pilot-boat to Hamburg with orders to their ships to remain in the ports where the orders found them. This saved many from being captured unawares. On the twenty-sixth of June, Congress passed an act authorizing the issue of letters of marque and reprisal, and a few days later the collector of the port of Portland, Isaac Ilsley, was prepared to issue them here.

At the commencement of the war Portland harbor contained numerous dismantled ships and other vessels; some hauled up in the secure coves, some swinging at anchor in the stream, while the wharves were lined with others in the same state of inactivity. This state of the town's principal industry was caused by the restrictions upon her commerce by our own government, and by the belligerent nations of Europe. The officers and men who had sailed these vessels were idle and ready for any adventure which would afford them remunerative employment.

When the war was declared Portland had but few vessels which were built for speed. She had no first-class pilot boats, and the fishing vessels were very much inferior to those of the present day. With one-half the present New England fishing fleet, each vessel with a long pivot gun amidship, the Americans would have cleared the Atlantic waters of all British merchantmen and of all their cruisers, except the largest ones, in six weeks. Portland had two or three clip_ per brigs and schooners which were previously built to run the English blockade of the French West India Islands, but they were not in port, as their owners thought them able to take care of themselves among the belligerent cruisers of contending Europe; and they were pursuing their precarious business in any sea, where a venture promised success.

For want of a suitable navy we were compelled to suffer from the insolent attacks on our shipping by France and England. The government was compelled to depend chiefly on private armed vessels to protect in a measure the coasting trade and the fisheries.

Encouraged by the government, the owners of any small, fast vessel, in any port from Maine to Georgia, began to think of making her a private cruiser, and at the start men were not wanting to enter on wages, or to take a share in the profits the same as on a fishing trip. They were not all seamen, but many idle landsmen with a taste for adventure, able to handle a musket, and to pull and haul, shipped as marines.

Where facilities were at hand green timber was taken from the woods and keels laid down for cheap vessels, for which the only object or quality sought seemed to be speed, to enable them to overhaul or escape from an enemy, as the circumstances might require.

One of these vessels hurriedly built was the three-masted schooner "Dart." This vessel was built, armed and fitted for a cruise, in five weeks from the declaration of war. She was built on the Cape Elizabeth side of the harbor, and was owned by Joseph Cross and others of Portland. Of course she was not built of the best materials, and was only of forty tons burthen. Contrary to the fashion for vessels of the time, she was built low and long, and with a pink stern; and for the facility of hiding from an enemy in a cove or at sea, her three masts were jointed above the deck, allowing them to be dropped like those of a canal boat. She carried four guns. This description I obtained years ago, from an old privateersman, but the log book does not mention the lowering of the masts — perhaps they had no necessity for it. I find by the log that she carried flying topsails on yards that were sent down or up at pleasure. The commander of the "Dart" during her career was Captain John Curtis. I have the journal of her first cruise with this caption:

"LOG BOOK FOR THE PRIVATE ARMED THREE-MASTED SCHOONER DART OF PORTLAND, JOHN CURTIS, COMMANDER."

The "Dart" does not appear to have been a desirable vessel to serve on board of, in the estimation of the sailors, although men were plenty. Perhaps from the joined masts, low gunwale, and long sweeps, they discovered that she was intended to depend much on "white ash breezes," as they called rowing, from the species of wood of which the sweeps were made. The first entry in the log is:

Monday, July 27, 1812. — This day begins with a calm. At 12 meridian, got underway and beat out of the harbor — the wind at SW. The crew amounting to 27 in all, bound to Townsend (Boothbay) to recruit men. At one p.m. passed Fort Preble. Latter part calm — took to our sweeps. At 11 at night, came to anchor 2 miles below the harbor.

July 28. — At sunrise, got under way and came up to town. The captain went on shore, but could not get a man. Got under way bound to Thomaston, to recruit men.

The Dart arrived at Thomaston on the thirtieth.

On Saturday, Aug. 1, got all hands on board, amounting to 46 in all.

The next day the schooner went to sea, and on the twenty-

third of August took two English brigs from Ireland. Put
prize crews on board, and ordered them to Portland. On
the twenty-seventh captured the brig Eliza of Lancaster,
bound to Mirimichi; manned her and ordered her to Portland.

The next capture made the Dart famous, and *raised the
spirits* of all Portland. It is thus recorded:

Aug. 31, 1812. — At 5 a.m., Cape Ray bearing NNE, distant four
leagues; at 8 saw a sail; at 9 she proved to be a brig, standing to the
Northward. We hauled our wind, but could not fetch her. At 10
tacked ship and at 11 came up with her; gave her two shot and
brought her to. She proved to be the brig Dianna, Capt. Alexander
Thom, from London bound to Quebec, with 212 puncheons of rum on
board. Put Mr. Thomas (Wm. first officer) on board as prize master,
with pilot and nine men, and ordered her for Portland.

The captain of the Dianna, with his crew, wished to be
landed, which was done the next day at Cape La Have.
From the constant drain on his crew to man prizes, Captain
Curtis judged it prudent to run in. The Dart arrived in
Portland on the eleventh of September, after a cruise of
forty-one days. Whether the prizes had arrived before him
or not, the journal does not say, but from undoubted tradition I know that the Dianna did finally arrive, and her cargo
proved famous as the " Old Dart Rum," which became more
celebrated for the peculiar flavor than any cargo of spirits
ever landed in the country. It had probably lain for years
improving, in the vaults of the London docks, until some
Canadian merchant had discovered its quality and purchased it.

Sixty years ago Old Dart rum was retailed in Portland
from " the original casks " at fancy prices, but some of them
had undoubtedly been refilled several times. I have in mind
a worthy old gentleman who kept a house of entertainment,

who would show his appreciation of a few special friends occasionally by setting before them a bottle labeled "Old Dart," and if there were any youngsters present who did not know its history, he would dilate on and magnify its peculiar oily character, not forgetting to caution them against its deceptive strength, and while doing it one eye would close, and his lips would moisten, showing that he appreciated its flavor himself.

Soon after the discovery of the desirable properties of the "Dart" rum, a rival appeared in a waif puncheon of rum picked up at sea by Captain Lemuel Weeks. It was called the "Admiral Rum," from what circumstances I know not. While on a homeward passage Captain Weeks, or some of the ship's company, discovered an uncommon object floating near the ship. The top sails were laid to the masts and a boat lowered, and on his return the officer reported it to be a puncheon full of some liquid, seemingly tight, but with every appearance of having been long in the water, covered with barnacles, and the hoops badly damaged. The officer doubted the strength of the chimbs to admit of hoisting it in the usual way with can-hooks. The captain's curiosity became excited and he ordered it to be enclosed in a sling, and hoisted carefully with a tackle from the yard arm, which was done and it was safely swung inboard and broached with the above result. The captain distributed much of it to his friends and it became a doubtful matter which had the most admirers, the Admiral rum, or the Dart brand.

All the spirits used by our forefathers were undoubtedly of a different manufacture and quality from those sold at the present day. If they had produced the same effects as modern spirits, the race must have degenerated to people of no more intelligence than the ape, from whom Darwin argues we descended; for all classes drank habitually, and on all occasions. What would Portland now do with five times the population with two hundred and twelve puncheons of rum?

How many cruises were afterward made by the Dart, I have no means of knowing, but it is well known that she finally sailed from Portland under the command of Captain Curtis, and the fate of vessel and crew was never known. She probably foundered in a gale, from her faulty construction.

Another of the early and hastily built privateers of the war was the sloop "Yankee." She was built by a boat builder by the name of John H. Hall, who had a shop near Richardson's wharf, and lived at the corner of Fore and Cotton streets. He was best known as the inventor of "Hall's breech loading rifle," the first, I think, of the breech loaders. He sold his patent to the United States government and went to Harper's Ferry to superintend its manufacture.

The model of the Yankee was as long a step from the beaten track as was the cutting off of the rifle barrel and making it spring up to be loaded. The sloop was about one hundred tons, flat bottomed, and having a keel nearly six feet deep, bolted through and through to the keelson, intended to have the same effect in sailing as the modern center-board, and might have been the first suggestion of it; but unfortunately it could not, like the center-board, be drawn up in a heavy sea.

The Yankee was owned in shares by a company as were most of the privateers. She sailed in command of Captain James Brooks, an Englishman by birth, who had sailed from Portland several years in the merchant service. He was the father of James Brooks, who was once the editor of the Portland Advertiser and afterward established the New

York Express. He was subsequently a representative to Congress. His brother, Erastus, was associated with him in the management of the Express. He was a printer, and served his time with Day and Frasier, of Portland.

A mate of a merchantman, named Veazie, was an officer in the Yankee. He was a brother of General Samuel Veazie, who died in Bangor, a few years ago, very wealthy; the General then was a baker's apprentice and drove a bread cart in Portland.

Captain Crabtree in the privateer "Rapid," in coming in, passed the "Yankee" off Portland light, going out, and cheered her. This was the last ever heard of her or her company, who repeatedly cheered the "Rapid" in passing, seeming in high spirits. Her deep keel probably caused her to founder in a gale, as it gave the seas a great purchase on the fastenings and started a plank.

> "It was not in the battle,
> A tempest gave the shock."

The brig Dash was the most efficient and successful of the private armed fleet owned in Portland during the war of 1812, until her final catastrophe in the last few months of hostilities.

The Dash was built at Porter's Landing, Freeport, by Brewer. This was the native place of her principal owners, Seward and Samuel Porter, merchants of Portland, on Union wharf, both of whom had been ship-masters, and well knew the proper model for a vessel of her class, and for the business for which she was intended, namely, to carry a fair cargo, sail well, and fight her way to her intended port, without a heavy and cumbersome battery. She was of two hundred and twenty-two tons burthen, pierced for sixteen guns, and was launched early in 1813. She was first rigged

as a topsail schooner with a top gallant sail and all the light
sails possible to set. Her armament was originally a long
thirty-two pound pivot gun, and six broad-side guns. The
other ports had wooden guns to make a good show to an
enemy when her ports were opened. Her crew numbered
forty.*

The first commander of the Dash was Captain Edward
Kelleran, who came from Thompson, and was long an active
shipmaster after the war, in the employ of Captain Asa
Clapp and Matthew Cobb, and died in Portland in about
1850. He made the voyage in the Dash to St. Domingo and
returned safely laden with coffee and logwood — enough of
the latter for "dunnage" to stow the coffee. The journal of
the first voyage of the Dash is not to be found in the Custom House, but I learned some particulars of it from one of
the owners, Captain Seward Porter, in whose family I passed
the first year of my married life. He never tired in describ-

---

* There was an amusing story in circulation about the pivot-gun of the
Dash. Some years before the war which produced the Dash, William
McLellan kept a variety store on Temple street, and also kept piano-
fortes to let, which were obtained second-hand from Boston. Needing
an additional one, he gave an order to Captain John L. Lewis, who sailed
a packet sloop between the two towns, to purchase for him a second-hand
"forte-piano," in Boston, which was then a common way of writing the
name of the instrument. On his return from the trip, and making the
sloop fast at Long wharf, Captain Lewis went immediately to McLellan's
store, and said to him: "I could n't find a forty-pounder, but I got you
a long thirty-two, which was the biggest I could find; and I want it
taken away, as it lays right across my hatch."

The captain supposed that McLellan had an interest in some vessel
for which he wanted a gun, as all were then armed. The gun lay on the
wharf several years, and was referred to as " Billy Mac's piano," until
guns came to be more salable than pianos, and the "long thirty-two,"
from an object of ridicule, became a terror to John Bull, as the pivot-
gun of Portland's crack privateer.

ing the sailing qualities and career of his favorite clipper. Captain Kelleran evaded or ran away from the British cruisers that infested our coast, before our own armed vessels became numerous, and was on his passage home with a cargo of coffee. When near his home port he was chased by an enemy's vessel, and escaped by carrying sail until he sprung his foremast, but being a good pilot he ran into shoal water, where the enemy dared not follow. He delivered the cargo safely to her owners, and it was sold at war prices.

The Dash had now been tested in all weather, and under all circumstances, and it was found that she would bear more head sail, and it was decided to replace the broken mast with one suitable for an hermaphrodite brig, and the whole rig was changed to that of a long-legged brig. Captain Cammett, who commanded the Dash after Captain Kelleran, has often described to me the rig of the vessel, which he considered perfect for speed when in the proper trim. To balance the increased spread of canvas on the foremast a long sliding spar was fitted to the mainboom, to which a "ring tail" was attached to be hoisted to the gaff when needed, which increased the size of the mainsail one-third. A longer main topmast with a gaff topsail to correspond, replaced the old ones. With these improvements, and a wholesale breeze, the Dash could overtake or run away from anything of her class. There was one advantage the English cruisers had over ours — we had no sheathing copper, and all kinds of compositions were prepared to lay over vessel bottoms, to increase their speed, and prevent their getting foul.

I have the journal of the second voyage of the Dash under the command of Captain Kelleran. It commences at Castine, from whence she sailed August 31, 1813. She called at Deer Island and Owlshead to ship men, and sailed for Port-au-Prince on the sixth of September, arrived at Jacquemel September 22 and at Port-au-Prince October 1. Sold and discharged cargo (probably lumber). Payed over the bottom of the vessel with soap and tallow, to do which the vessel was careened. Took on board coffee and logwood on the vessel's account, and five hundred and fifty bags of coffee on freight. Sailed for Portland on the seventeenth of October. October 31 was chased by an English brig and was compelled to throw overboard four hundred bags of coffee, the spare spars, and the two bow guns. November 3 the chase continued and the Dash threw one hundred and twenty-two more bags of coffee, two more iron guns, and all the wooden ones, ten in number, which brought the brig into proper sailing trim, and she escaped after a two days' chase, saving all the cargo belonging to the brig. The next day the Dash was chased by a seventy-four gun ship and a brig, from which she escaped by her superior sailing, and arrived in Portland, November 5, 1813.

At the time of the arrival of the Dash, the townspeople were fearful of an attack from a British squadron which was hovering on the coast, and the owners of the cargo of the Dash had it carted to Gorham village for safety. The coffee was divided into three lots and was left in charge of Nahum Chadbourne, Nathaniel Gould, and Captain Harding. This cargo of coffee was returned to Portland and stored in the Porters' warehouse on Union wharf, and on January 22, 1814, the block of four wooden stores was burned. In this fire the Porters lost beside the cargo of coffee, which was worth one dollar per pound, two gangs of rigging for new vessels, all uninsured.

On December 13, 1813, Captain Kelleran again sailed from Portland in command of the Dash for Port-au-Prince. To

evade the enemy's cruisers was not the only care and anxiety
of the navigators in a winter passage on our coast. There
were then no chronometers, and the vessel must be navigated
by "dead reckoning." Beside they were frequently caught
in storms on a lee coast — no "indications" being then
published a day in advance. This was the case with the
Dash on the next day after sailing. The day she sailed
ended with a thick snowstorm and there were no fog horns.
I give the vessel's log for the next day after sailing:

Tuesday, 14th Dec., 1813. Commences with stiff breezes accompanied with squalls of snow and hail. At 3 p.m. in foretop gallant sail
and jib, and reefed the mainsail. At 5 in main topmast staysail and
close reefed the foretop sail. At 10 in mainsail, and scudded under
the foretop sail and fore sail. Wind hauled to the north. Middle
part a hard gale with snow and sleet — a very bad sea; latter part a
very heavy gale. At 6 a.m. reefed the fore sail, and at 10 sent down
the topgallant yard, ends with thick squally weather.

The wind being off shore gave him sea room to scud.

The Dash arrived at Port-au-Prince December 31. Sold
and delivered cargo and gave the vessel the usual soap and
tallow bottom. Took on board thirty thousand pounds of
coffee, and sailed for home in company with privateer
schooner Flash of New York, on January 16, 1814; same
day saw an English frigate, and both vessels returned to port
for protection from the frigate, which proved to be the
Leonidas, which anchored in the outer roads. The two privateers hauled alongside of each other and kept all hands at
quarters all night to repel any attack from the frigate's boats,
although it was a neutral port.

To show the lack of respect for the laws of nations by
British naval commanders, it is only necessary to mention
the case of the privateer brig General Armstrong of New
York. She was a very powerful vessel, with a daring cap-

tain (Reid). He had boldly attacked and beat off in the night, an English frigate, supposing that she was a letter of marque, and captured the ship Queen of sixteen guns, with a cargo invoiced at one hundred thousand pounds sterling. These daring acts had excited the hatred of the whole British navy. On September 26, 1814, the General Armstrong anchored in the Portuguese port of Fayal. At sunset the same day the British naval ships Plantagenet, Rota, and Carnation anchored in the roadstead. Fearing an attack the Armstrong warped up under the guns of the Castle; yet she was twice attacked by boats from these vessels — the last time by twelve boats. In both attacks the boats lost sixty-three killed and one hundred and ten wounded, with the loss of several boats. On the twenty-seventh one of the ships hauled in and commenced a cannonade on the privateer. Finding that the Armstrong would be taken, Captain Reid abandoned his vessel, after firing a six-pound shot down the hatchway and through her bottom. This sinking gun was fired by Captain Thomas B. Parsons, who was sailing master on board. He afterward taught navigation for years in Portland, and died here in 1870, aged eighty-three.

But to return to the Dash. During the next day the officers of the frigate made some threats to cut out the American vessels. The armed schooner Chancey of New York was also in port and hauled alongside of the other two vessels, and all three were moored and lashed together in the form of a cross, so that they could fire in all directions in case of an attack from the frigate's boats. In this state, with shotted guns, and every man at his station, they waited in vain for the threatened attack. The frigate saw the preparation and made no demonstration, but sailed the next day. The Dash sailed for Portland on the twenty-second, in company with the two schooners, and arrived home in safety on the fifteenth of February, except the cargo was shifted in a gale, but was replaced the next day.

We must now take leave of Captain Kelleran as commander of the Dash. He came here from Georges river. The paternal mansion was to be seen high up on the bank of that stream two years ago. He came to Portland early in the century. I have before me a newspaper of December, 1810, containing his arrival at Portland, as master of the ship North America from Cronstadt, Russia, "with iron and sail duck to Asa Clapp." This was a twin ship to the South America; they, with several others in the Russian trade, were owned by Asa Clapp and Matthew Cobb. Within eighteen months after Captain Kelleran left the Dash, the war was ended, and he went back to the Russian trade. Those who recollect the presidential campaign of 1840, will recall Captain Kelleran's jolly face and figure, which would rival Hackett's personification of Jack Falstaff. Singing was relied upon as a means of conversion in that contest, as much as it ever was at a camp-meeting. Captain Kelleran was then well along in years, and an enthusiastic Harrison man, with a powerful voice. Those who took a part in that campaign will recollect his voice and appearance at the Whig meetings, when, with his arm aloft, he led the chorus in these closing lines :

> "We 'll sing the Harrison songs by night,
> And beat his foes by day."

And then his ringing shout of "hip-hip-hurrah!" after the English fashion. He was then probably seventy years old, six feet and more in height, and weighed two hundred and fifty pounds. On the fly leaf of the journal of his last voyage in the Dash is a stirring, patriotic song in his own handwriting.

Hitherto the Dash had not been aggressive, but had been sailed in the regular St. Domingo trade, and wasted no ammunition except in self defence. Her next two cruises were made under the command of Captain William Cam. mett, then twenty-eight years old, and like his predecessor, almost a giant in stature. He had seen some war service. He was first lieutenant of the brig Rapid when she went to sea in company with the Teazer " to try her sailing." This was in August, 1812, as mentioned in the log of the Teazer. At the time William Crabtree was captain. Lieutenant Cammett well knew the speed of the Rapid, as he sailed as mate on her first voyage, in 1809, and while the captain was on shore he ran her out of the harbor of Memel, Prussia, after having been seized by Napoleon's officers, whom he drove into their boat, and saved the brig and cargo. He made the passage home from London to Boston in sixteen days, and yet the captain of the Teazer claimed to have beat her in a two hours' trial.

The log book of Captain Cammett's first cruise in the Dash is not among those discovered in the Custom House. The brig arrived from her previous voyage on February 15, 1814, and Captain Cammett's arrival in Portland is reported in the " Gazette," as occurring on Tuesday, July 11, so the cruise must have been made during the intervening time. In later years Captain Cammett was a daily and welcome caller at my place of business, and was always ready to relate his experience as a privateersman in the Dash, and being a little " web-footed " myself, I made brief notes to refresh my memory if I should ever need them. I only noted the years, not the months, and these log books fix all dates.

The four small iron guns thrown overboard by Captain Kelleran in October, to escape from the English gun-brig, were not replaced, but Captain Cammett, the new commander, wanted a heavier battery, and the remaining small guns were taken out and two eighteen pounders substituted, retaining the pivot-gun. The number of men was increased to sixty. George Bacon of Freeport was first lieutenant. He was mate with Captain McIntosh, and so ably seconded his gallantry in the recapture of the ship Mary Ann.

Captain James Slater, of Portland, was a prizemaster. The Dash sailed to the south of Bermuda, where she fell in with a British man-of-war which gave chase. The Dash steered for North Carolina, outsailed the Briton, and arrived in safety at Wilmington. The brig's bottom had become foul, and she was careened and cleaned. While looking for the ingredients to pay over the bottom, a merchant called the captain's attention to a lot of crude plumbago in his store which was purchased and mixed with the usual soap and tallow, and put on. This proved to be a good compound and gave the brig more speed than ever.

Captain Cammett found that the store houses of Wilmington were full of flour which was offered very low, as there was great risk in its transportation, while it was high at home, and he concluded to purchase a small cargo on the vessel's account. He took fifteen hundred barrels at four dollars per barrel, and twenty-four hogsheads of tobacco at three cents per pound. I find by the advertisement of the cargo for sale at auction, that the vessel also had "140 barrels of tar, fifty tierces of rice, and 4000 Carolina reeds." With this lading the Dash sailed for Portland, and after beating off one vessel with her guns, and running away from another with the aid of the plumbago bottom, she arrived at

30

her home port as before mentioned, on the eleventh of July.
The newspaper report of her arrival says "she was repeatedly chased by British cruisers and escaped only by superior
sailing, after throwing overboard a part of her cargo."

The owners of the Dash, S. and S. Porter, had by the depre-
ciation of the value of shipping and by the burning of their
storehouses on Union wharf in the previous January, become
crippled in their business. It will be remembered that they
lost in that fire a cargo of coffee, and the rigging for two
new vessels, without insurance. To satisfy their creditors
it was decided to sell the Dash and her cargo at auction.
Brig and cargo were advertised to be sold one week after her
arrival by "Eleazer Greely, auctioneer." From my notes of
conversation with Captain Cammett I find that flour which
cost at Wilmington four dollars, sold for fifteen dollars per
barrel, and tobacco which cost three cents, sold for fifteen
cents per pound, and other goods at similar war prices, net-
ting a large sum. So well satisfied were the creditors with
the sum realized from the sale of the cargo, that the vessel
was withdrawn from the advertised sale, and the owners were
allowed to retain her. Captain Seward Porter summed it
up in this concise sentence: "One Dash at John Bull saved
our bacon."

I find in the Custom House the journal of Captain Cammett's second cruise in the Dash. It is evident from this
document that the owners were so well pleased with the
Wilmington voyage that they sought to repeat it. The journal is headed "Letter of Marque brig Dash from Portland
towards Wilmington, North Carolina," but she did not reach
there. The captain hit upon a more profitable venture than
the last, and one which also crippled the enemy, and which
would tend to make the war unpopular with the British
merchants.

August 7, 1814. Got underway in Portland harbor with brig Grand Turk (of Salem, privateer.) Nothing remarkable occurred until the 21st when the brig was in sight of the island of Bermuda, bearing north. Saw two sail bearing N. W. distant 6 leagues, bore down for, and discovered them to be a sloop and a ship. At 7 p.m. brought to the sloop and boarded her. She proved to be the sloop Emily of Charleston, prize to H. M. Ship Lacedemonian; took all hands from on board and manned her; gave chase to the ship, and came up with her; gave her a shot which she returned and hauled down her colors.

Aug. 22. The ship proved to be the " Five Sisters " from Jamaica, for Bermuda with a cargo of rum. At 1 p.m. commenced taking the cargo of the ship on board the Dash. Got out 32 puncheons of rum, the sloop remaining in company.

Aug. 23. All hands employed in taking rum from the prize. Found one barrel of dry goods. Threw overboard from the Dash all the cargo, consisting of 200 barrels of beef, and took on board this day 100 puncheons of rum.

24th. At 2 o'clock p.m. got all the cargo of the ship on board the brig, and gave up the ship to the captain and passengers. Put on board the ship the former British prize crew of the sloop and ordered her for Bermuda. Put the American captain of the sloop in prize master of his own vessel with four men from the Dash, and ordered her for the island of Nantucket.

Captain Cammett's ludicrous description of the scene on board the ship, years after, is fresh in my memory. The weather being hazy, the near appearance of the Dash and her gun was a surprise to the passengers of the ship, about thirty in number, male and female. They were about to sit down to dinner, which Captain Cammett described as very bountiful and well cooked, but the captain was drunk, and it was considered dangerous to leave so large a number of unknown persons on board their own vessel, and they were immediately transferred to the Dash without their dinner, where they were provided for.

When Captain Cammett told them that he should return

to them their ship, the ladies cried out, " *Oh, don't!* " and begged to be protected from their own drunken captain. To compromise the case their captain was made a prisoner in his own vessel, and the English prize master of the recaptured sloop was put in master over him. The passengers returned to the ship with thanks to the officers of the Dash. The Five Sisters went on her way for Bermuda, and the Dash sailed for Portland. I find by my memorandum of Captain Cammett's narrative, as related to me, that the Five Sisters had on board six thousand dollars in specie, but the log book does not mention it. It was probably got on board the Dash as secretly as possible. In all the journals of the privateers which I have examined, I find only one mention of specie among the proceeds of a prize.

I find by Marshal Thornton's notice for a hearing on the libel of the cargo of the Five Sisters that there were " 170 puncheons of rum, 20 bags of cocoa, and one barrel of merchandize." All this could not be stowed under deck and leave room for the swinging of sixty hammocks, so a part of the casks of rum were secured on deck. All went well until the first of September, when the Dash was chased by a frigate and a schooner in company. With all her lading the Dash out-sailed the frigate, but the schooner gained on the privateer. The log book does not mention the ruse practiced to escape, but Captain Cammett related it to me in his old age with many embellishments in his entertaining manner. When he saw the schooner was gaining on the Dash and began to fire, he found he must surrender or fight. In her usual sailing trim the Dash would be a match for the schooner, but deep laden as she was, she would probably be crippled. She could use her two eighteen pounders, but the pivot-gun was encumbered by the puncheons of rum, which he could not afford to throw overboard at the then high price. Captain Cammett had in his ship's company some of the most spirited young men of the town. In the emergency they were consulted, and it was decided to show fight, and if the schooner persisted, to bring her to close quarters and board her. Every man was ordered to arm himself accordingly. They were then within sight of the headlands of the coast, and did not like the idea of occupying a Halifax or Dartmoor prison. The two broadside guns were cleared away and loaded, one with a double charge of grape and canister, and when all was ready, the brig was luffed up to bring a gun to bear, and a round shot was fired, which went uncomfortably near the chaser. The captain of the schooner evidently concluded that the Dash meant to fight, and had led him into a trap. Much to the surprise and gratification of Captain Cammett the schooner tacked ship, got out her sweeps and made every effort to get away from the Dash, whose sweeps were also got out, but were pulled in the opposite direction, which the enemy in his fright did not discover, but kept his course in his flight. "The wicked flee when no man pursueth." The Dash was the same day on "Cashes Bank," where a fisherman was spoken, who informed the captain "that the British had taken the city of Washington."

The next day, September 3, the Dash arrived in Portland harbor, and found the town alarmed, fearing a visit from a British squadron. To save the cargo it was carted out to Saccarappa, and sold there at auction, the rum at two dollars and fifty cents per gallon. This was probably the largest "single sale" of rum ever made in that village. On the arrival of the Dash Cammett found that her owners had completed at Freeport the hull of a much larger brig, which they named the "Tippoo Saib," for that noted son of the Maharajah of Mysore, who was slain at the battle of Serringapatam in 1799. She was intended by her owners for a heavily armed privateer, to be rigged the same as the Dash and to be commanded by Captain Cammett, who left that vessel to superintend the rigging, arming, and fitting out the new one. After the Tippoo Saib was ready for sea and was hauled into the stream the long hoped for news of peace arrived.

The advent of peace released the dismantled merchant ships, and Captain Cammett returned to that trade in which he became one of the most successful and skilled shipmasters of the port. For fifty years he had sailed the ocean, in every station, when he was appointed inspector of customs under President Lincoln, which was his last active business. The captain had a happy faculty of describing scenes and transactions in his eventful life, and always had an amusing anecdote to relate in the proper place. Age did not have its usual effect on his sturdy frame and active mind. He was my friend when I was but a boy, and so continued until his death. He died in April, 1880, at the great age of ninety-seven years.

> " And the stately ships go on
> To their haven under the hill;
> But oh, for the touch of a vanished hand,
> And the sound of a voice that is still."

The Dash remained in port two weeks, and sailed on another cruise September 13, while the town was full of troops for its defence. The first lieutenant of the brig, George Bacon, was promoted to be captain. His journal of the cruise is among those in the Custom House. It purports to be the journal of a voyage "towards Wilmington, N. C.," but like the previous cruise, the vessel did not get there.

On the 29th of Sept. the Dash captured a schooner from Yarmouth, N. S., took out the crew and sent her in. On the 3d of October took an English ship from Tobago laden with rum. Took the rum, all but two puncheons, which belonged to the Captain, on board the Dash, replacing it with ballast, and gave up the brig with her officers and crew.

Oct. 20 ran into Wiscasset.

26, Got under way and swept down the river; spoke a sloop which had been captured by the tender of the British ship of war " Feureuse." Saw a sail which we supposed to be a privateer; made all sail in chase; gave her a gun, when she hove to — found her to be the Thinks-I-to-myself, tender to the Feureuse. Put a prize master and crew on board and ordered her to keep company.

Both vessels arrived in Portland.

There is in the Custom House a log book of the man-of-war ship Feureuse, which was probably found on board of the captured tender.

The Dash remained in port a few days only, during which she was again fitted for a cruise under the command of John Porter, a younger brother of the owners, who had just arrived from Europe in one of their ships. His log is in the Custom House.

The Dash sailed from Portland Nov. 9th on a cruise to the coast of Nova Scotia, and was off Cape Sable on the 12th. On the 16th captured the schooner Polly from Halifax, bound to Martinique, laden with fish and lumber. A prize crew was put on board and ordered for the United States. The next day took another schooner of the same class and ordered her for Portland. On the 7th of Dec., a sea carried away the jibboom and flying jibboom, but saved the sails. The next day the lost spars were replaced by new ones. On the 12th of Dec., re-captured the letter of marque schooner Armistice of New York, captured by the English frigate Pactolus. 19th captured a sloop bound to Bermuda. 20th, took an English brig from the West Indies, laden with rum and sugar, put a prize crew on board and ordered her to keep company with the Dash. 31st of Dec., took possession of brig Mary Ann of St. John, bound home. Took out of her one cask of shrub and one cask of lime juice and let her proceed

Arrived in Portland January 4, 1815, having taken six prizes from the enemy.

We have followed the fortunes of the Dash through seven successful cruises, made under four commanders, during which she made some fifteen captures and there is no record of the loss of one of them. She lost some spars, but not a man; no shot ever struck her in all her trials of speed with men-of-war in chase. We now come to the final cruise of which there is no journal, no record of her fate, no survivor to tell the sad story. Alas! she sailed to destruction with all her laurels thick upon her. Soon after her arrival on the fourth of January, it was known that the Dash was being put in order for another cruise, under the command of John Porter. He had won a good name although he was but twenty-four years old. He was one of a family of eleven brothers, all sailors at some time of their lives. Two of them, younger than himself, were to be his first and second lieutenants in the vessel. The Dash had become a favorite privateer, and all the young men of spirit were anxious for a position on board of her, even some who had once sailed in command. The Porter Brothers chose their own ship's company, most of whom were from the best families of Portland and the sea-board towns. No vessel had ever sailed from the port, which had the prayers of such a multitude for her safety. Everything being ready, the Dash with a cloud of canvas and bunting, got up her anchor, fired a gun for the captain, and stood up and down the harbor like a race-horse in check. The while the captain was with his young wife to whom he had been married only a few months. She had not left her father's, who lived in what is now the Federal street side of the Park. After the lady had arrived at the age of more than eighty years, she described to the writer, with much feeling, the leave taking. The captain seemed depressed, as if he had some sad foreboding. He left his wife on the steps, and hearing the gun he hurried away, and was about to turn the corner of Essex (now Franklin) street, when he hesitated and turned round, but hearing a second gun, he waved a final adieu and disappeared.

> "The ship was cheered; the harbor cleared,
>   Merrily did she drop
> Below the church, below the hill,
> Below the light-house top."

The privateer schooner Champlain had been built and fitted out here by Portsmouth parties, and by arrangement was ready to sail with the Dash, to test her speed. Each with a press of sail passed the light-house in company, and not till then did the crowd leave the hill. For what more is known of the Dash we are indebted to the officers of the Champlain. For more than twenty-four hours the Dash led the way, and at dark the second day she was a long distance ahead, steering nearly south, but the Champlain kept her light in sight. Soon a gale sprung up and the captain sounded and found the water shoaling, and fearing Georges Bank he changed his course. When last seen the light of the Dash bore the same by the compass. It was the opinion of nautical men that after the gale sprang up, Captain Porter underrated his speed and went on to Georges Bank. What that shoal is in a January gale, we learn from a newspaper announcement, that two weeks ago, a fleet of Gloucester fishing vessels were, by the sudden rising of the wind, compelled to slip their cables and make sail, losing all their anchors.

The loss of his three brothers and so many other valuable lives in the Dash was a continual trouble to Captain Seward

Porter in after life. He insisted that he should live to see a light-house on the bank, and represented its feasibility to a congressional committee. His theory was to sink a large number of stone-laden hulks at one time, in a circle on the shoalest part of the bank, which he thought would form a sufficient breakwater to admit the driving of long piles, perhaps some of iron, within the enclosure, and still continue to add to the number of old ships with stone, and whole trees with limbs. These he thought would form a nucleus for an Island of sand, which would finally rise out of the water, and on which a light-house of iron might be erected.

The Dash was not given up for lost for many months after the usual time had expired for her return. Those having friends on board scanned every signal which was hoisted on the observatory, hoping that it was the private signal of the Dash, indicating her coming. At last the fears of her loss came to be accepted as a certainty. Then came cruel and groundless rumors that some of her company had been heard of on desolate islands. The knowledge that vessels had been captured by the Algerines a few years previous, and their crews enslaved, kept a hope alive in some cases, that this might have been the fate of the Dash and her company, and that they would yet be found alive in some of the Barbary States. This theory was revived several years after her disappearance, showing what high hopes went down with the missing vessel. At last all hope died out. Many wives were compelled to feel that they were indeed widows. The wife of the captain was one of these. She had a son born after the loss of her husband, whom she named John Porter, for his father, and he lived to be a source of happiness to her. Years after Mrs. Porter married Captain John Dunlap of Brunswick, afterward of Portland, a shipmaster and owner.

A daughter of the second marriage was the wife of James Russell Lowell, the poet. Mrs. Dunlap died in October, 1882, at the age of ninety-one years.

The ship Hyder Ally was of the most force of any of the privateers fitted out in Portland. She was built here by Samuel Fickett, a noted shipwright who had a yard and dock near the foot of Park street. She was not especially built for a privateer but was constructed to carry a battery, as no vessel was then safe on the high seas without one. Her register at the Custom House says she was of three hundred and sixty-seven tons. She was built for speed as most vessels of her time were; drogers were sure to be picked up by the armed vessels of some nation, and during Napoleon Bonaparte's time, it was hard to comply with the restrictions of all the belligerents.

The Hyder Ally's keel was laid before war was declared. Although there was no sale for ships in the ordinary trade, Fickett concluded to finish her and trust to luck for a purchaser. When she was completed and ready to launch, Sturgis, of the firm of Bryant and Sturgis, merchants of Boston, being in Portland on other business, was invited to look at the new ship and to make an offer for the hull. After an examination and learning that the asking price was forty dollars per ton, he told Fickett that if he would rig her into a ship he would take her at that price. The rigging at that time would cost as much as the hull, yet Fickett accepted the offer as it was the only one he would probably get. The ship was immediately launched and rigged.

The purchasers now looked about for guns for an armament, and found that the guns and all the armament of the prize brig Boxer had been sold at auction by the government, and could then be purchased at private sale. A bargain was closed for them. With these and some new guns from Boston the ship was fitted out with twelve eighteen pound carronades, two long eighteen-pounders, and two long nines. She is registered at the Custom House as carrying only ten guns, but I received the history of this ship twenty years ago from a reliable man, who sailed in her during her whole career as a privateer. This was Mr. Isaac Fickett, of Portland, who died in 1877 at the age of eighty-three. Mr. Fickett was a relative of the builder of the ship, and had just completed an apprenticeship as a caulker, and shipped on board of the Hyder Ally in that capacity with some other duty specified.

The captain of the ship was Israel Thorndike of Beverly; first lieutenant, Henry Oxnard of Portland; second and third officers, Perry of Salem, and Noah Edgecomb, a rigger, of Portland. The ship carried a crew of fifty men, among them Alexander Paine, Aaron Jordan, John Raynor, and others of Portland. She sailed from here for the Indian Ocean in January, 1814. When near the Cape of Good Hope, she was chased all day by a sloop-of-war belonging to the British East India Company, but got clear of her in the night. Soon after getting round the cape in the latitude of the Isle of France she captured a British East Indiaman with a very valuable cargo. She was manned with a prizemaster and crew and ordered to Portland, but was recaptured by the privateer "Tom" off Cape Elizabeth.

The Hyder Ally steered for the coast of Sumatra, and fell in with and captured two English ships with cargoes of pepper in bulk. Lieutenant Oxnard was put in charge of one ship, and Lieutenant Perry of the other. Oxnard made the coast off Penobscot bay, and passing the enemy's cruisers, ran into Castine, which proved to be a trap, as that port had been taken possession of by the enemy after the Hyder Ally sailed. As soon as the ship had dropped her anchor several armed boats came off to take possession of her, when Oxnard began to look about and saw that every vessel in the harbor bore the British flags, but it was too late to save the ship. The ships' boats were lowered and into one Oxnard jumped on a mattress, into which he had put all his valuables, including a rich India shawl for his sister. All hands gained the shore. The enemy's boats fired on the retreating boat and wounded Lieutenant Oxnard in the leg, but he managed to get into the woods with his crew, who helped him to save the articles taken from the ship. The shawl was in the possession of his family a few years ago. Of course Oxnard was vexed at the loss of the ship and valuable cargo, when so near home.

After the two lieutenants had sailed in the prizes, and the ship being short of men, the captain adopted the practice of several other private armed vessels in those waters, which gave privateers a bad name. He used a flag to suit all occasions. The discipline of the ship from the start had been very severe.

In the Indian Ocean the privateer overhauled two Chinese junks loaded with betel-nuts, silks, and other China goods of immense value, bound to Penang. The captain condemned these goods as British property, and confiscated the whole, and took them on board of the privateer, giving the junks his ballast in return.

The Hyder Ally next fell in with the British frigate Salsetta. Both ships lay nearly becalmed twelve hours. In the long chase which followed, the frigate continued to fire her bow guns without effect. By knocking away some of the wood-work of the stern of the Hyder Ally, Captain Thorn-

dike managed to work two guns as stern chasers, not much
expecting to damage the frigate, but to propel his own ship.
This was done by rigging long breechings with which he
held the recoil of the guns, and increased the headway of
the ship. I have never heard another instance where gunpowder was pressed into service to propel a ship. Finally a
squall gave the Hyder Ally the advantage and she escaped ;
but soon after the privateer was becalmed within dangerous
distance of another frigate. Both ships lay becalmed several
hours looking at each other, but powerless to move. The
frigate caught a breeze first, which brought her down within
gunshot of the Hyder Ally, who was compelled to surrender
with all her ill-gotten cargo. The frigate proved to be the
"Owen Glendower," and no doubt Captain Thorndike
wished her where Prince John of Lancaster wished her
Shakesperian namesake. On making sail in company Captain Thorndike found that the privateer could sail round the
frigate with the same breeze, which was not a pleasant discovery after being captured by her.

Both ships sailed for Penang, where the privateer's crew
were imprisoned four months. When the East India fleet
came in, having lost a large number of men by sickness, they
offered the crew of the Hyder Ally wages if they would do
seamen's duty until they arrived at Whompoa, and from
there to London, which was accepted. At Whompoa Fickett's ship was discharged, when he learned that three of the
crew of the Hyder Ally were to be exchanged for the same
number of English prisoners. Lots were drawn, when Fickett drew a prize, and was liberated with two others, but
those remaining prisoners went on with the fleet to London
under wages, and yet on their arrival they were imprisoned.
After he was exchanged Fickett found that the merchant ship

America, of New York, was in port, dismantled and housed over to protect her from the sun, with her crew on board, waiting for the end of the war. He went on board of the America and remained a month, when he obtained a passage to Canton, where the American Consul supplied his wants. There were three Boston ships at Canton, letters of marque, all bound home. Fickett shipped on board the Bramble and arrived safe at Boston. I think every one of the rich prizes captured by the Hyder Ally were recaptured by English vessels before they could be got into an American port.

Lieutenant Henry Oxnard of Portland, the first officer of the ship, remained in the employ of Bryant E. Sturgis of Boston, and was put in command of a good ship after the war, in which he made one voyage to Batavia. He finally went into mercantile business in Boston. His first venture was the importation of a cargo of tea in company with William Appleton, which paid a large profit, materially increasing his capital. He next built two ships at Medford, of the same size and model. He became wealthy, and died in Boston in 1844, aged fifty-four.

Early in the war a most daring act was performed off Cape Elizabeth by privateersmen. Somewhere at the south, the British ship Rolla captured a Philadelphia ship, put a prize crew on board and ordered her to Halifax. Five days after capture, the prize ship stood in near Cape Elizabeth and sent in the prisoners. She was all day becalmed in sight from the Cape. A few daring men from that side of the harbor planned to retake the ship after getting particulars from the released crew. A whale-boat was procured and a crew of eight men under Captain John Chity rowed off near the ship, which was becalmed, and pretended to be fishing, until night came. When it was dark enough for their purpose, they rowed stealthily alongside of the ship and climbed on board ; some at the bow and some at the companion ladder and suddenly appeared on deck and demanded the surrender of the ship to the boats of a well-known privateer, with threats of what they would do in case of refusal. The astonished prize master surrendered at discretion.

After securing the arms of the ship, the captors threw off their disguise as belonging to an armed vessel, and ordered the prisoners to help them hoist their whale-boat privateer on board, which was done. A breeze sprang up in the night and the captors worked the ship into Portland harbor, with the whale-boat on deck, and cast anchor.

Of this whale-boat crew Captain Chity was afterward in command of the privateer sloop Lilly of Portland. "Jot" Sawyer of Cape Elizabeth was afterward boatswain of the Teazer of New York. Ezekiel Jordan and Wormal were Cape men.

Beside the private armed vessels owned in Portland, cruising sometime during the war, of which I have given an extended notice, there are thirty-four others registered at the Custom House belonging here. Their rig, tonnage, number of guns, names of owners and officers are recorded.

Aside from the privateers owned here, there were several very successful ones whose owners made Portland their home port, and kept agents here to look after their prizes as they were sent in.

One of the most successful of these vessels was the schooner Teazer of New York. The "Teazer" was originally a New York pilot boat with the regular rig of such vessels. When war was declared she was armed with a long gun amidships and one short gun. She was licensed in New York, and sailed from that port very soon after the commencement of the war. Although she belonged there she had an agent in Portland. In the journal of her second cruise is the closing loose leaf of her log-book for the first cruise, which shows that her crew entered on shares, and that from some cause three left the vessel at Portland at its close, thereby forfeiting their shares, although they had taken the brig " Hero " as a prize. The leaf from the first journal shows that the " Teazer " arrived in Portland harbor on the twenty-fifth of July from her first cruise, only thirty-seven days from the declaration of war. Her commander was C. W. Wooster. The first cruise was probably considered unsuccessful, which was the reason why the men threw up their shares.

I have the full journal of her second and very successful cruise. She sailed from Portland August 3, 1812. Nothing remarkable occurred after sailing until the ninth, when the schooner came up with a brig, which surrendered without firing a gun. She proved to be the " Peter Waldo, Capt. Ralph Wilkes Herbert, from New Castle, England, bound to Halifax, with a cargo of sundry articles." " Mr. Charles Warren was put on board as prize master with six men, and ordered to Portland. Brig first discovered by Francis Gifford." The " Peter Waldo " arrived safe, and proved to be a very valuable prize. Cogshall says she netted the captors more than one hundred thousand dollars. A part of her cargo was clothing and blankets for the British troops in Canada. She also had crates of crockery ware, which was sold at auction to retailers, and pieces of it are still remaining among the descendants of old families, and are still known as " Peter Waldo ware."

Prominent as a part of the cargo of the brig, were several very large cattle, purchased in England for a Canada farm;

they were purchased here by John Gordon of Stroudwater. By whatever name the breed was known in England it was not perpetuated here, but they bore the name of the vessel that brought them, and they became so famous for their size that during the visit of President Monroe to Portland in 1817, he made a special visit to Gordon's farm to see the herd of " Peter Waldo cattle." They were driven to Winthrop to a cattle show, and also to Brighton, Massachusetts. There have been crosses of the blood in the State within a few years, still bearing the vessel's name, but their reputation was never high.

There were two passengers on board the Peter Waldo, a Mr. Wilson and his wife, English Quakers, who for several years after kept a confectionery store on the south side of Exchange, opposite Milk street.

On the eighteenth of August, after exchanging several shots from the long gun, and receiving several broadsides, the " Teazer " captured the British ship Osborne of Hull, from Gibraltar bound to St. John ; armed with ten eighteen pound carronades and having a crew of twenty-five men. The log book thus describes the close of the fight :

At 7 ship ceased firing — came within a quarter of a mile, found her topgallant sheets flying and topsail yards on the cap. Fired a shot over her which she returned. Continued firing from the Teazer until 10. Ceased and sent a boat and asked them if they had struck. They would give no other answer than that we should not board them until morning. Continued firing for half an hour — then sent a boat well armed, with the following orders, that if they did not permit the boat to board her, that the privateer would haul alongside of them and put every man to the sword; upon which message they permitted the boat to board and take possession.

On the twenty-fourth the Teazer arrived in Portland harbor and was saluted by the prizes which had already arrived.

On the next cruise of the Teazer she was captured by Admiral Warren's fleet, and one of the officers, at least, broke his parole by entering on board another privateer at New York, called the "Young Teazer."

In the spring of 1813, the first lieutenant of the Teazer, which had been captured by Admiral Warren's fleet late in 1812, whose name was W. B. Dobson, sailed from New York in command of another private armed schooner called the Young Teazer. The number of her guns or the number of her crew are not mentioned in her log book, which is in the Portland Custom House. By law all private armed vessels were obliged to make oath to the truth of the journal of each cruise, and to deposit it in the Custom House where the cruise ended. The rig of the schooner is not easily made out from the journal, yet of course she carried a standing topsail, as there is mention of "taking in the lower studding sail." Neither is her tonnage mentioned; but the want of these facts is not important. It is her capture of the enemy's vessels, and her final fate that is now interesting.

The Young Teazer left New York for a cruise to the eastward on May 10, 1813. May 13, after a chase of five hours, "came up with a large black schooner with two topsails, and a sloop in company, apparently an American; commenced action with the schooner, and expended twenty-one twelve pound, and fifteen nine pound shot; found she was a man-of-war, and knowing that the government would not pay us for our capture, would not try to board her. The schooner kept her course; we supposed her damaged as we saw several shot strike her.

"Same day. Saw a sail from the mast-head, made all sail for her; came up with her, she laying to for us. After exchanging two broadsides she struck. The prize proved to be the ship Invincible Napoleon, mounting sixteen guns, with a crew of one hundred men ; formerly a French privateer, cap-tured by H. B. M. brig-of-war Native ; recaptured by the American privateer Alice, and again captured by H. B. M. frigate Tenedos. Manned the prize and ordered her to Port-land." Captain Cogshall calls this ship a " Corvette." From a Portland paper I find that all three of these vessels arrived here safe, and were sold for the benefit of the owners, offi-cers, and crew of the privateer. Two of them were valuable prizes, being large vessels and coppered.

The following is an extract from the Portland Gazette of May 31, 1813.

Arrived the French privateer ship Invincible Napoleon, prize to the Young Teazer. The Invincible Napoleon mounts sixteen guns, and is the same ship which on the 3d of April last captured the American brig Two Brothers, of New York, and ransomed her for $5,000. On the 9th of April she also captured the American ship Mount Hope, Capt. McCobb of Georgetown, Me., from Charleston, for Cadiz, with a cargo of rice, and ordered her to France. Shortly after the Invincible Napoleon captured the above named American vessels, she was herself captured by the English and ordered to an English port. On her passage thither she was fallen in with and re-captured by the privateer ship Alexander, Capt. Crowninshield of Salem, who ordered her to an American port. She was chased into Cape Ann by the Shannon and Tenedos, English frigates, who went in with their launches and cut her out, and again ordered her for an English port. She was shortly after fallen in with and captured by the Young Teazer.

On the twenty-sixth of June Marshal Thornton advertised for sale at auction at Long wharf, Portland, as prizes to the Young Teazer, " the ship Invincible Napoleon, burthen about 310 tons, coppered to light water mark, with her arma-ment consisting of twelve 18 pound carronades, two long 9 pounders and two long 6 pounders." Also at the same time the brig Ann, of two hundred tons, coppered to the bends — one pair of nine pounders and one pair of six pounders. Also the schooner Greyhound, with cargo of dry fish and lumber.

May 24 the Young Teazer engaged and captured, after a short action, H. B. M. brig Ann, packet of Falmouth, having been captured by the privateer Yorktown, and re-captured by the British ship of the line Lahogue.

May 26 the Young Teazer was chased by a frigate off the Seal Islands, and escaped by her superior sailing, and arrived in Portland harbor on the first of June.

After a short time spent in port in refitting, the Young Teazer again sailed from Portland under the command of Captain Dobson, on a second cruise, and the first report of her where-abouts after sailing was a report of her destruction by the explosion of her magazine. I have gathered the following particulars of that catastrophe. It is mentioned in Halibur-ton's history of Nova Scotia but no particulars are given.

It subsequently transpired that Johnson, who fired the mag-azine, was a lieutenant on board the old Teazer when she was captured by Admiral Warren's fleet, and was released on his parole. Without waiting to be regularly exchanged he entered as first lieutenant on board the Young Teazer.

Captain Cogshall gives this reason of the blowing up of the privateer :

By letters from several of the crew [prisoners in Halifax] to the agents of the privateer, we learn the following particulars of the sad catastrophe: While the Young Teazer was closely pursued by an English man-of-war and in great danger of being taken, Capt. Dawson [should be Dobson], who commanded the privateer, called his officers aft to consult on what was best to be done. While they were delib-erating on the subject, one of the sailors called aloud to the captain that Lieut. Johnson had just gone into the cabin with a live brand of fire in his hand. In another instant the Young Teazer was blown up.

Johnson knew that if he was taken in arms, under the circumstances, his fate would be death, and he did not think of his shipmates — only his own sure fate.

Of the twenty-nine persons who lost their lives by the explosion, the carpenter Mr. Gunnison and Mr. Carlow, prize-master, were both of Portland.

That the Young Teazer had been an active and trouble-some cruiser is shown by the following, copied from a Boston paper of the time. A fishing boat was boarded off Cape Ann by a boat from the line-of-battle ship Lahogue and her register taken on board the ship on which the following was indorsed and returned :

His Majesty's Ship Lahogue — At sea, 8th of July, 1813. I have warned the fishing boat Sally of Barnstable to return immediately to her own coast, and in consequence of the depredations committed by the Young Teazer and other American privateers upon the British fishing and coasting vessels belonging to Nova Scotia — but more particularly from the inhuman and savage proceeding of causing the American schooner Eagle to be blown up after having been taking possession of by H. B. M. ship Ramalies, an act not to be justified on the most barbarous principles of warfare — I have directed H. B. M. cruisers on this coast to destroy every description of American vessels they may fall in with, flags-of-truce only excepted.

Given under my hand, etc.,

THOMAS B. CAPEL, Captain.

The brig Grand Turk, of Salem, was one of the fighting privateers, and made her home in Portland. She was one of the larger class which were fitted out to replace the small ones hastily sent to sea at the beginning of the war, many of which were captured by the enemy. She came into Portland in May, 1813, from an early cruise, perhaps her first one, having an agent here to look after her prizes. She was fitted out from here for another cruise. The Custom House books give her tonnage as three hundred and ten, with fifteen guns and one hundred men. Joseph Endicott, Joseph I. Knapp, Samuel Cook, Samuel B. Graves, and twenty-five others, owners; Nathan Green, commander; Ebenezer Meacom, lieutenant. Captain Holben J. Breed, of Salem, commanded her on one cruise. Her agent here was Joseph I. Knapp, one of the owners.

The journal of one cruise is in the Custom House. From the record of making and shortening sail, I learn that she was a full-rigged brig with royals and sky-sails. She left Salem and " took her departure " from Thatcher's Island, bearing northeast by north, six miles distant, on Tuesday, February 9, 1813. Two days after, in the night, John Mason fell from under the maintop, went overboard and was lost; as it was blowing a gale they could not save him. The Grand Turk was a good sailer. I noticed that she logged for five successive days, severally in miles, two hundred and three, two hundred and nine, two hundred and nineteen, two hundred and thirteen, two hundred and sixteen, and this without the stimulus of a chase.

She was off the coast of Brazil in March and April, in the track of Portuguese merchantmen, many of whom were chased and brought to, but, as they were neutrals, the time was lost. On the third of April, the Turk had a streak of good luck, which is thus described in the log book :

At 5 a.m., saw a sail on our weather bow; tacked ship to the eastward. At 6, tacked ship to the southwest. At 8, saw another sail. Made all sail in chase. April 4, at 5 p.m., came up with the two vessels and commenced a smart cannonading with both. After an action of ten or fifteen minutes, both ships struck to us. At 6 the two ships were manned out, and the prisoners were on board of our brig. During the action we had two men killed and four wounded. The enemy had two killed and a number wounded. The ships proved to be from Liverpool, bound to Buenos Ayres, with assorted cargoes. Wm. Malloy was put on board the ship Paragon, as prizemaster, with eleven men, and Wm. Vickery was put in charge of the ship Williams, with eleven men. I ordered them to some port in the United States, giving Salem the preference.

April 5 commences with pleasant breeze and clear weather. The two prizes still in sight. At 8 a.m. saw a sail bearing north, steering southwest. At 11 a.m., discovered her to be an English ship from London, bound to Buenos Ayres. She proved to be the ship Apollo, from London, out 60 days. Put John Gage on board as prizemaster, and twelve of our people, and ordered her for America, giving Salem the preference of any port.

April 14. At 3 p.m. came up with the chase, which proved to be a Spanish schooner from Montevideo, bound to Paraguay. After our prisoners had signed a parole we put 30 of them on board the said schooner, and supplied them with all necessary provisions to last them to the port.

April 23. At half-past 5 p.m. departed this life Mr. Jacob Abrahams, sailing master of the brig, who was wounded in the action of April 4th, aged 28 years.

I have a list of thirty-nine prizes which were taken and sent into Portland, by privateers belonging to different ports from Baltimore to Portland, with the names of the capturing vessels.

During the war there were two hundred and fifty licensed privateers. These private armed vessels were a great scourge to British commerce. Meetings of merchants were held in several of the ports of Great Britain, to petition their government to devise some means of protection from American privateers. These meetings had great influence in bringing about the peace measures. The system of letters of marque and reprisal is liable to great abuses in the hands of unscrupulous officers, whose acts are frequently little better than piracy.

No battle during the war, on land or sea, so excited the

people of Portland as did that between the Enterprise and Boxer, which was fought on the fifth of September, 1813.

The Secretary of the Navy wrote to the Portland committee of safety, that the Enterprise with the brig Syren had been ordered here in May, "for the protection of the coast in the neighborhood," but she did not arrive here until the thirtieth of June, and the Syren did not come at all. The Enterprise was again ordered to Portsmouth and Captain Blakeley, her commander, was sent to the lakes. He afterward was in command of the sloop-of-war Wasp, and captured the English sloop-of-war Reindeer. Lieutenant Burrows succeeded Blakeley in command of the Enterprise, and arrived in Portland harbor on the thirty-first of August, in chase of a suspected British privateer. The brig Boxer had been a troublesome cruiser on our coast and had captured on the fourth of August, at the mouth of the Sheepscot, the schooner Industry, Captain Redden, of Marblehead. With her prize and some others, she sailed for St. John, New Brunswick. The following letter from a well-known merchant formerly of Portland, but then doing business in Portsmouth, New Hampshire, explains what brought the Boxer to the mouth of the Kennebec:

CAMBRIDGE, MASS., Sept. 9, 1873.

At the commencement of our war with Great Britain in 1813, the United States had but few if any factories for the manufacture of woolen cloths and blankets, and the soldiers were clad in British cloths and slept under British blankets. It was understood no captures would be made of British goods owned by citizens of the United States, and many American merchants imported, via Halifax and St. John, N. B., their usual stock of goods. In 1813 I went with others in the "Swedish" brig Margaretta to St. John, N. B., and filled her with British goods, intending to take them to Bath, Maine, and enter them regularly and pay the lawful duties thereon. All we had to fear was American privateers; and we hired Capt. Blyth, of H. B. M. Brig Boxer, to convoy us to the mouth of the Kennebec river, for which service we gave him a bill of exchange on London for £100. We sailed in company, and in a thick fog, off Quoddy Head, the Boxer took us in tow. It was agreed that when we were about to enter the the mouth of the river two or three guns should be fired over us, to have the appearance of trying to stop us, should any idle folks be looking on. Capt. Burrows, in the U. S. Brig Enterprise, lay in Portland harbor, and hearing the guns got underway, and as is well known captured the Boxer, after a severe engagement, in which both captains were killed. Our bill of exchange we thought might in some way cause us trouble, and we employed Esquire K. to take 500 specie dollars on board the captured ship and exchange them for the paper, which was found in Capt. Blyth's breeches pocket.

Yours respectfully,

CHAS. TAPPAN.

Capt. Preble.

The statement of Mr. Tappan that Captain Burrows, in the Enterprise in Portland harbor, heard the sham cannonading of the Margaretta, as she entered the Kennebec, is not in accordance with the facts. I have heard the circumstances which led to the sailing of the Enterprise in pursuit of the Boxer, related by different persons of the town who all agreed that a fisherman saw the Boxer fire at the Margaretta, and arrived in Portland Saturday morning, and immediately reported the fact to Captain Burrows, who was expecting to hear of the Boxer on the coast. There were several young men of the town in the crew of the brig, and, as this was her home station, much interest was expressed in the expected contest. Another cause for the excitement which prevailed, was the means resorted to by the enemy to draw out the Chesapeake for a fight before she was prepared. Captain Broke, of the Shannon, had obtained a draft of men from his consorts to strengthen his ship's crew for the fight, and had sailed daily up to Boston light to menace Captain Lawrence, who had an untrained crew, but he accepted the challenge and lost his life and his ship. The loss of the Chesapeake occurred but a few weeks before the news of the presence of the Boxer in our waters was known here, by the arrival of a fisherman. At the time the wind was light and southerly and it was flood-tide, so that the brig could not sail out between the forts. She was immediately got underway and ran down to Spring Point, but when she came to change her course she could not stem the tide. As if by magic every boat dropped into the water, full of men, and they were ranged in a line ahead of the brig, and, with exciting songs, towed her out clear of the land, and she bore away for Seguin.

Of what occurred on that memorable Sunday morning I give the official account. Of the arrival of the vessels after the battle and the funeral of the slain captains, I give the account published in the Portland Gazette of September 13th. The Captain Hull, who followed next to the coffin of Captain Burrows as one of the "chief mourners," was the famous commodore who was in command of the frigate Constitution when she captured the Gueriere. He was naval commander at this station at the time of the capture of the Boxer.

PORTLAND: Monday, September 13, 1813.
GALLANT NAVAL ACTION & VICTORY.

On Monday last, 6th inst. anchored in this harbour, the U. brig *Enterprize*, (late WILLIAM BURROWS, commander) accompanied by H. B. M. brig *Boxer*, (late Capt. SAMUEL BLYTH, commander,) her prize, captured on the 5th inst. after a well fought action of 45 minutes. The following particulars of the engagement are given by the Officers of the Enterprize.

" Sept. 5th, at 5 A.M. light winds from N. N. W. Penmaquid bearing North, 8 miles distant, saw a brig at anchor in shore, and made sail on a wind, with the larboard tacks on board. At half past 7, the brig weighed and fired 3 shot at a fishing boat, for the purpose of ascertaining what we were, (as we have since learnt.) At half past 8, the brig fired a shot as a challenge, and hoisted three English Ensigns, and immediately bore up for us. At 9 we tacked, kept away South and prepared for action. At half past 9, it fell calm, the enemy bearing N. N. W. distant four miles.—At half past 11, a breeze sprung up from the S. W. which gave us the weather gage, we manœuvered to the windward, until 2 P. M. to try our sailing with the enemy, and ascertain his force. At a quarter past 2 P. M. we shortened sail, hoisted 3 ensigns, and fired a shot at the enemy. At 3 P. M. tacked and bore up for the enemy, taking him to be one of H. M's. brigs of the largest size. At a quarter past 3, the enemy being within half pistol shot, gave three cheers and commenced the action, by firing her starboard broadside. We then returned them 3 cheers, with our larboard broadside, when the action became general. At 20 minutes past 3 P. M. our brave commander fell, and while lying on deck, refusing to be carried below, raised his head and requested, *that the flag might never be struck.* At half past 3, we ranged ahead of the enemy, fired our stern chaser, rounded too on the starboard tack, and raked him with our starboard broadside. At 35 minutes past 3, the enemy's main topmast and topsail yard came down. We then set the foresail, and took a position on his starboard bow, and continued to rake him, until 45 minutes past 3, when he ceased firing and cried for quarters; saying, that as their colors were nailed, they could not haul them down.

We then took possession of the prize which proved to be H. B. M's. brig Boxer.

64 prisoners were taken including 17 wounded. The number of the enemy killed cannot be exactly ascertained as many were hove overboard before we took possession, Capt Blyth being one of the slain who fell in the early part of the action.

When the sword of the vanquished enemy was presented to the dying conqueror he clasped his hands and said, " *I am satisfied, I die contented.*" And then consented, nor till then, would he consent to be carried below.

The Enterprize had two men killed and 12 wounded in the action, among the latter, were her Commander, who expired on the night following, and midshipman Waters, supposed mortally.

The number killed on board the Boxer, is unknown; the number wounded was 17.

The brave BURROWS was wounded in the early part of the engagement, and the command devolved on Lt. M'CALL; the result of the action furnishes an eulogium upon the skill and bravery of the officers and crew of the Enterprize, highly honorable to themselves and country.

The two vessels suffered much in the action, but the injury done to the Boxer was incomparably the greatest, & shows that the fire of the Americans was much superior to that of the English. The Boxer had her main and fore-top mast shot away; her rigging and sails cut to pieces, and received a great deal of damage in her hull.

FUNERAL HONORS.

The remains of the intrepid and gallant WILLIAM BURROWS, late commander of the U. S. brig Enterprize, and his brave competitor, SAMUEL BLYTH, late commander of His B. M. brig Boxer, were buried in this town on Wednesday last, with military and civic honors. The procession was formed in front of the Court-House, at 9 o'clock A. M. under the direction of Robert Ilsley, and Levi Cutter, Esq's, assisted by twelve Marshals, and proceeded under escort of the Portland Rifle Company, Capt. Shaw's Infantry, & Capt. Smith's Mechanic Blues — the whole commanded by Captain Abel W. Atherton — to the lower end of Union Wharf, where the corpses were landed from each vessel, from barges, rowed at minute strokes, by ship masters & mates, accompanied by many other barges and boats. During the approach of the barges from the vessels to the shore, solemn music was performed by a full band, and minute guns were fired alternately from each vessel.

From Union Wharf the procession proceeded in the following Order:—

Military Escort.
Selectmen of Portland.
Town Treasurer and Sheriff of the County.
Town Clerk and other Municipal officers.
The Rev. Clergy.

Remains of Capt. Burrows.

Mr. Le Saffier, Mr. Shields, Mr. O'Neal, Mr. Turner, Mr. Tilling-hast, Mr. M'Call, Pall-bearers.

Chief Mourners.

Dr. Washington — Captain Hull.

Officers of the Brig Enterprize.

The Crew of the U. S. Brig Enterprize.

Remains of Capt. Blyth.

Lem. Weeks, jr., Wm. Merrill, Seth Barnes, James Coombs, Joshua Knight, John Alden, Pall-bearers.

Officers of the Brig Boxer, as mourners, and officers on parole.

Crew of the brig Boxer.

Officers of the United States Navy.

Ship Master and Mates.

Marshal of Maine.

Navy Agent— and The late Consul General to the Barbary Powers.

Collector of the Port and Surveyor.

Superintendent General of Military Supplies.

Officers of the Army of the United States.

Military Officers of the State in Uniform.

Judges & other Civil Officers of the U. States.

Members of Congress.

Judiciary of the Commonwealth.

Members of the State Legislature.

Civil Officers of the State.

Portland Marine Society.

President, Directors, and Officers of the Banks, and Insurance Officers.

Citizens in General.

Through Fore and Pleasant Streets to High-street, thence through Maine and Middle streets, to the Meeting-house of the Second Parish. The corpses being placed in the broad aisle, the solemnities of the sanctuary commenced by singing an appropriate Hymn — the Throne of Grace was then addressed by the Rev. Mr. Payson, in a Prayer adapted to the melancholly occasion — couched in language to command the attention and affect the feelings of his numerous auditory, and expressive of the feelings and sentiments of a Christian and

Minister of Peace. An Anthem was sung by a full choir, and this part of the solemnities was closed with a Benediction. The procession was again formed and moved through Middle & King-streets to the burying ground. Two Artillery Companies commanded by Lt. Barnes, fired minute guns, which were repeated at Forts Preble and Scammel, by direction of Col. Learned.

As the funeral escort arrived at the graves, the ranks were opened to the right and left, halted, and faced to the centre, & rested on arms reversed, during the placing of the bodies in the graves, which were deposited side by side. The escort then discharged six vollies by battalion over the graves, with a pause after the three first designating the fires for each corpse.

The colors were then unfurled — the music struck up quick time, and the procession returned to the Court House, when it dissolved.— Business was suspended, and the doors of the Ware-houses and shops were closed. The shipping at the wharves and in the harbour wore their colours at half mast.—And the Bells were tolled at proper intervals. A great concourse of people assembled from town and country; the wharf and streets were lined with people on both sides; tops of houses and windows were filled with men, women and children, anxious to gaze on this new and interesting spectacle.—The highest degree of order prevailed and solemn silence was kept. The command of Escort was ably conducted by Capt. Atherton, and orders were promptly and strictly executed by all officers and soldiers. It would be invidious were it just to make up any distinction between the companies composing this escort — suffice it to say that all the officers and soldiers discharged their duty in a style which would honor veterans.

The thanks of Commodore HULL were tendered to the Escort of the day, in the most polite and satisfactory manner.

On the next day, after the sailing of the Enterprise, there was great excitement manifested in town to learn the result of the expected battle. Captain Eben M. Corry, in after life, gave me the most minute account of the sailing of the Enterprise, the excitement on Sunday, and her return on Monday with her prize; also a description of the funeral exercises and burial. He was then twenty years old.

Early on Sunday people began to gather at the Observatory. Its keeper, Captain Moody, was as anxious to make discoveries as any one. He admitted a few friends and the proprietors of the tower, but excluded all others. Seguin light-house is plainly seen with the telescope in a clear atmosphere, which was the case at that time. Captain Moody kept his practiced eye to the glass, and that directed to Seguin and the open water beyond. In the forenoon he saw the smoke of the Boxer's challenge-gun and that of the Enterprise accepting it. This discovery he communicated to the anxious crowd below, when a cheer went forth notwithstanding it was Sunday. It was several hours before the vessel obtained sea-room and ceased maneuvering for the advantage of position. The crowd on the hill began to leave, thinking the battle was over. Soon Captain Moody announced that he saw smoke of guns; the fight had begun, but no vessels could be seen.

The battle was fought on the open water inside of Monhegan, forty miles in a direct line from Portland, which accounts for the failure to hear the guns at the Observatory. The excitement culminated on Monday when the Enterprise was signaled, leading her prize under the same flag. The vessels came up to Union wharf where all who wished went on board. The Boxer was very much cut up in hull and rigging. Years ago a ship master said to me that "there was no place on one side of the Boxer where he could not reach two shot holes at the same time by extending his arms."

The dead commanders were each wrapped in his own flag. The flag of the Boxer, which was defiantly nailed to the mast, is now one of the trophy-flags at the Annapolis Naval

School. Captain Blyth was instantly killed by an eighteen
pound shot. Captain Burrows lived eight hours after receiving the wound.

The surviving officers and crew of the Boxer immediately
placed a monument over the remains of their dead commander, by permission of the town authorities. His age was
twenty-nine. The grave of Captain Burrows remained
unmarked until "a passing stranger" (Silas M. Burrows, of
New York), erected a substantial monument to his memory.
His age was twenty-eight.

These monuments were erected by permission of the
authorities of the town. Who has the right to remove
them, as has been proposed?

By the side of his gallant commander rests the body of Lieutenant
Kervin Waters, a native of Georgetown, District of Columbia, who
received a mortal wound September 5th, 1813, while a midshipman on
board the U. S. brig Enterprise, in an action with His B. M. brig
Boxer, which terminated in the capture of the latter.

This is an extract from the inscription on a table monument standing beside that of Captain Burrows. It was
written by the Rev. Dr. Ichabod Nichols. Young Waters
lived until September 25, 1815, cared for by the young men of
the town, who erected the monument over his grave. Mrs.
Catherine Shanks, a surviving sister of Lieutenant Waters,
after the fire of July, 1866, sent three hundred dollars to the
mayor for the relief of the sufferers, and expressed "great
interest in the city, and sympathy with its suffering people."

A week after the capture of the Boxer, the British sloop-
of-war Rattler, Captain Gordon, and two smaller vessels, stood
in to the mouth of the harbor under flags-of-truce, and sent
a boat in charge of a lieutenant with a letter from Captain
Gordon to the commander of Fort Preble, asking for the

32

exchange of the officers and crew of the Boxer. There was no officer there to give the proper answer, but finally one was returned by Colonel Learned and United States Marshal Thornton that they were unauthorized to comply with the request, and the vessels stood off again. If Captain Gordon had known of the absence of the garrison of the fort he could have taken quiet possession. There was only a sergeant's guard in charge; the troops of the garrison having been sent to the Lakes.

On the fifteenth of September a public dinner was given by the citizens to Lieutenant McCall and the surviving officers of the Enterprise at Union Hall. Captain Robert Ilsley presided and "John Mussey, Jr., Esq.," acted as toast-master. He is now probably the only survivor of that dinner party. His age is ninety-five years. An original ode, "a fine specimen of splendid thought and tasteful fancy," was sung at the table by Mr. Nathaniel Deering. The crew of the Enterprise went in procession to receive a public dinner at Mechanics' Hall, corner of Fore street and Burnham's wharf.

From the papers of United States Marshal Thornton, I learn the following facts: The Boxer was sold at auction to Thomas Merrill, Junior, for five thousand, six hundred dollars. Ten eighteen pound, and two six pound cannon were sold at the same time. Also thirty-six tons of "kentlege"—iron ballast. The whole amount of sales was nine thousand, seven hundred and fifty-five dollars. The heirs of Captain Burrows received eleven hundred and fifteen dollars prize money. The seamen's shares were fifty-five dollars.

The Boxer went into the merchant service in command of Captain William McLellan. The accompanying cut of her is from a painting done at Marseilles and now in possession of Captain Jacob McLellan. The removal of her hammock-

BRIG BOXER, AFTER SHE WAS MADE A MERCHANTMAN.

nettings made her appear much lower than she did when she was captured. Her final end is uncertain. The Enterprise made only one more cruise during the war, under the command of Lieutenant Renshaw. On the coast of Florida, she was chased by an English seventy-four, and her commander was obliged to throw all his guns overboard during the chase of seventy hours. A fortunate change in the wind saved her. She finished her career as a guard ship at Charleston, South Carolina.

During the first week of September, 1814, an express was sent here by General King, who was in command of the eastern coast, with a message to the committee of public safety and defence, saying that " a large fleet with troops " had left Castine, steering westward, and apprehended that their destination was Portland. The blockading squadron with the Bulwark, seventy-four, as flag-ship, had become more bold than formerly, sailing up daily to the light-house.

All this caused alarm in the town. The specie in the banks, and valuable stocks of goods were removed to places of safety in the country. A large number of families left the town with their household goods. On the sixth, Governor Strong ordered " the whole of the militia to hold themselves in readiness at a moment's warning," for the defence of the state. He also called a special session of the general court for the fifth of October. The militia of the counties of Cumberland and Oxford were ordered to repair to Portland for the defence of the town. The infantry and artillery numbered between six and seven thousand, and were placed under the command of Major-General Alford Richardson, of North Yarmouth. He was in after-life cashier of the Bank of Portland.

I was then old enough to now recollect the excitement in

the country while the troops were mustering and to assist my
mother all night in making bullets for my father's company,
which had orders to appear the next morning at nine o'clock,
at the gun house on Munjoy's hill; and they were there
promptly, with their own arms and ammunition, as the laws
then directed.

The troops were about all in camp on the seventeenth, and
Colonel Sumner, aid to Governor Strong, arrived from Boston
to assist in the arrangements for the defence of the town. A
company of "exempts," numbering sixty, was organized in
the town under Brigadier-General John K. Smith, who was
a captain in the Revolution. A man from Halifax reported
that an expedition was fitting out there, supposed to be
destined for Portland or Boston. This served to increase
the alarm. The town appropriated ten thousand dollars for
the public defence.

The Portland Rifle Company was ordered by General
Richardson to take the battery of the prize ship San Jose
Indiano, and put it on board the captured brig Boxer, whose
guns had been removed, and haul her into position and moor
her so as to command the roadway of Vaughan's bridge;
and, in case of the appearance of an enemy, to defend the
bridge. For days the company amused themselves with the
practice of gunnery. The steep declivity of Bramhall's hill
stopped their balls.

Redoubts were thrown up and guns mounted at all the
entrances to the town, and a picket line of sentinels established on the whole shore of the peninsula. The troops were
kept in camp about two weeks; as no enemy appeared, they
were dismissed and the town assumed its usual quietness. It
was only a few months after this that the war closed. In
the treaty which followed, not a word was said about the

British right to search our vessels, which was the ostensible cause of the war. Both nations were glad to make peace.

New England experienced very little of actual war on its soil, yet it felt its pressure heavily in the annihilation of its peculiar industries, and the continual drain upon its wealth of men and money.

CHAPTER XIII.

EARLY COUNTY BUILDINGS. CEMETERIES. LIGHT-HOUSES. WRECKS. ISLANDS. SIMONTON'S COVE. CUSHING'S POINT. MARKETS.

IN 1735, an annual session of each, the "Inferior Court" and "The Court of General Sessions of the Peace," was established in Falmouth. The first session was held June 9, 1735. At that date Parson Smith records, "I prayed with the court."

The town, in its associate capacity, erected the meeting-house on King street. Willis' History of Portland says, "There was no court-house, nor regular place for holding the court before the Revolution." This is a mistake. After the abandonment of the old house as a place of worship in 1740, the second story was fitted up at the expense of the town for a "court-house" — so named in the vote. The consideration was that the town might use it when the court was not in session.

In the history of early county buildings, occupied under the old county of York, before the separation in 1760, when the whole state comprised but one county, as at the building of every court-house and jail the committee, having charge, had been directed to use the materials of the old in the construction of the new, it is very probable that in the basement of the county wing of the city building is some of the iron work, or doors of the jail, erected at the junction of Middle and India streets in 1752, so we will begin there.

A court held at York, in 1752, ordered a jail to be built at

Falmouth, on the north side of the "court-house." The next year after the fitting up of this court-house in 1747, Parson Smith records, "I prayed with the Court in the afternoon. Justice came drunk."

In 1753, in answer to a petition of the selectmen of Falmouth, the court of quarter sessions of the county of York appointed a committee of five, all of Falmouth, to let out the building of a new jail in Falmouth, and directed them "that if they can purchase the block house and the land thereunto belonging, near Benjamin Larrabee's, for a sum not exceeding £45. 6 shillings, and 8d lawful money, at the county charge for a prison house, a deed for the same is to be transmitted to the county treasurer." In case this block-house was purchased, the committee was desired to remove the jail already begun and join the same to said block-house, and finish the same according to a former order. This order is as follows: To be joined to the court-house on King street, "linter fashion." That is a corruption of the phrase "lean to," or with the court-house for one side wall, with a one-sided roof. The same kind of an addition to a barn at the present time is called a "linter" from the two words "lean to." The order says it is to be thirty-five feet long, fifteen wide and seven stud, with one stack of chimneys of four smokers. The building is to be of good, square, sound, hewed or sawed timber, well boarded, clapboarded and shingled outside, with a lining inside of good, sound oak plank, spiked on, and eighty pounds was allowed for building it.

There was something here that bore the name of the prison at Falmouth as early as 1661. At the commissioners court held at York that year, the record says, John Phillips, of Falmouth, "accused for the suspicion of felony, by the unfitness of the prison to receive him, is confined to his own house as a prisoner and engageth to appear at the next court." The county records mention the building of a jail at York, in 1651, and one at Wells, in 1654. In the record of a court of the commissioners which was held at Falmouth, in 1669, a jail is mentioned as having been built at that place, and delinquent towns were ordered to pay their share of the expenses. The location of the jail is now unknown. It must have disappeared prior to 1685, as in that year the general assembly ordered that Fort Loyal shall be appointed as a prison or jail for the four associated towns. These were Saco, Scarborough, Falmouth, and North Yarmouth.

The block-house was purchased and the "lean to" was removed and joined to it. The Larrabee house stood where the portico of the old city hall now does, and the block-house, which was built for defence against the Indians, stood about where the north corner of that building does. Parson Smith records, June 13, 1746, "This neighborhood are building a block-house near Mr. Larrabee's for the common defence." The treaty of Aix-la-Chapelle, concluded in 1747, put an end to the war of 1774, with the French and Indians. This block-house had been garrisoned with provincial troops, who were now discharged, and it was of no further use, hence it was sold to the county. There was a jail-keeper's house built on Middle street, in front of the jail, at the expense of the county, in which the jailer kept a public house, as the county paid him only fifteen pounds as jailer. Thomas Motley, the grandfather of Motley the historian, kept this block-house jail from 1781 to 1793. His tavern was called the "Freemason's Arms" and had a swinging sign in front, inscribed with a representation of the square and compasses. Mr. Motley's sons, for many years the distinguished Boston merchants, were born in the old jail tavern, and also the youngest son Charles, who was a sailor, was born there in 1785, and was twelve years old when the block-house jail was removed. When he was ninety-five years old, he described to me the old timber-jail and the jail-house in which he was born and lived until he was eight year old. The jail is also described by a letter from Nathaniel Gardiner, a sea-captain and a loyalist of Pownalborough. He was taken prisoner in 1780, while loading his vessel (the armed schooner Golden Pippin) with iron from the wreck of Commodore Saltonstall's fleet at Penobscot. He writes, "I was thrust into Falmouth jail, where I had neither bed, blanket, or anything to lay on but the oak plank floor, with the heads of spikes an inch high and so thick together that I could not lay down clear of them." After remaining a prisoner four months he broke jail and escaped.

The old meeting-house on King street served for a court-house from 1746 to 1774, when the town presented the lot to the county of Cumberland, which had been established in 1760, on which to erect a new court-house. This new court-house was a handsome building, not quite finished when the town was bombarded by Mowatt in 1775, when both the old and new court-houses were burned. The old one had been removed to Hampshire street for a town house. During the Revolution the courts were held at Mrs. Grele's tavern on Congress street. In 1777, she was paid two pounds, eight shillings "for a room for the use of the court." In 1787, Samuel Freeman was paid nine pounds "for his great chamber for the use of the courts." After the happy termination of the Revolutionary struggle, the county officers looked forward to better accommodations. The block-house jail had escaped the burning and a lot was sought for a court-house in that vicinity. A committee of the Court of General Sessions reported in 1785, " that the land between the jail and the hay market appears to belong to the county; that the land on the north side of the street, opposite the hay market, is not to be procured. Mr. Larrabee's land near the jail is not to be purchased. Voted to take Mr. Plummer's lot on Back street, four and one-quarter rods in front and four and one-half rods back." On July 18, 1785, Moses Plummer, of Falmouth, cordwainer, executed a deed to the county of this lot of four and one-quarter rods on Back street, for eighteen pounds lawful moneys, paid by Joseph McLellan, Treasurer of Cumberland county. It is described as the " south corner of the three acre lot, I lately bought of Rev. Thomas Smith." The lot was granted in 1720 to the first settled minister, and extended to Back Cove. The lot then conveyed to the county is the central part of the site of the present city building.

Moses Plummer, who sold this land, kept a store and obtained the nickname of " Old Way," from his rigid adherence to the barter system of dealing, when all others were abandoning it. On this small lot of about four rods square, a wooden court-house of forty-eight by thirty-four feet in size, with twenty-four feet posts, was commenced. Parson Smith records the raising, October 3, 1785. The Court of General Sessions of the Peace, composed of all the justices of the peace in the county, then exercised the same functions as our present board of county commissioners. They ordered "the roof to be so framed that a belfry may be built upon it at some future time." The second story, containing the court room and offices, was finished in 1788. The belfry or cupola was soon added. It was surmounted by a carved weathercock. St. Peter's testimony in denying his Master may have suggested to the county fathers the propriety of

CUMBERLAND COUNTY COURT HOUSE. — 1785-1816.

surmounting the new temple of justice with a representative of the historic bird, as a caution to the witness, when he entered the portal, not to deny the truth, whatever might be the provocation from contending counsel.

This weathercock was carved in Portland. Mr. Benjamin Radford, after he became aged, described the carver's process to liven up the living bird which served for a model. He had him confined to the end of a treadle, and when he wanted to make a line he put his foot on the near end, which lifted the living model. This historic cockerel, after several removes, now surmounts the clock-tower of the First National Bank.

The picture of this court-house was taken before it was taken down and is correct. The first floor was an open hall, in which were kept in sight the gallows and the stocks, ready to be erected for use. Near the front of the house stood the whipping-post, with cross bars for securing the arms of the culprit. The whipping-post was removed to the parade ground, now covered by the north part of the Eastern Cemetery in about 1800.

The Eastern Argus of October 6, 1803, contains the following: "George Peters, a black fellow, who broke open the shop of Abner Rogers, watchmaker, will receive his punishment on the training field between twelve and one o'clock to-day." On this training field were grouped the town pound, the whipping-post, and the pillory. The latter was a tall post about twenty-five feet high. About half way up from the ground was a square platform, and two planks crosswise of the post, with an opening for the neck, and two below for the wrists. Two culprits could be pilloried at once. Boys were allowed to pelt them with eggs.

Another mode of punishment was to set the criminal on

the gallows with a rope around his neck. When this was done the gallows was taken from the court-house and set up near the pillory. It had one upright post and a projecting arm on each side.

Corporal punishment was abolished in Massachusetts by the recommendation of Governor Gore, in 1809.

In this court-house of 1785, in 1790, Thomas Bird, a foreigner, was sentenced to be hung for piracy and murder, although his trial had been in the meeting-house near by. He had been confined in the old block-house jail more than a year, waiting for the organization of the District Court of the United States and for a session to be held here. The aged Mr. Motley, before mentioned, described to me Bird's demeanor and habits while in prison. He (Motley) was five years old at the time, and, with his older brother Edward, at the request of Bird, was often admitted by his father to the cell and spent much time there. The prisoner made them toy ships and boats. The execution took place at the junction of Congress and Grove streets (Haggett's Hill,) June 25, 1790.* At the time of the execution, Mrs. Motley, the mother of the boys, took them over back of the Neck to be out of sight of the gallows, as the whole family had become interested in the fate of Bird. The captain of the vessel, whom he killed, was noted for cruelty to his men. Bird admitted that he fired the gun which killed the captain, and justified himself on the ground of his cruelty.

* This gallows had stood in this very public place since Goodwin's execution on it, in 1772, for murder in throwing a man overboard from a boat. He had been three times reprieved. This was the first execution in town. Nathaniel Gardiner, of Pownalborough, previously mentioned, says, on his way to Falmouth jail in 1781, he was carried past the gallows and was told that was his place. In lowering the grade of the street in 1819, the crossed bed-sills of this gallows of 1772, after being buried forty-seven years, were dug up in a sound state, by a man now living.

Bird's council, Syms and Frothingham, made application for a pardon on the ground of its being the first capital conviction in the United States Courts, after the adoption of the Federal constitution. The petition was immediately forwarded to President Washington, who then resided in New York, but he declined pardoning or suspending the time of execution. The jailer Motley and his family thought the prisoner should be pardoned, and it was with sadness that he was surrendered to Marshal Dearborn to be executed. General Henry Dearborn, of revolutionary memory, was the marshal and superintended the execution.

It is a rare circumstance in historical investigation to find a man with clear intellect and memory, who is able to describe a prison and the life led by a prisoner, ninety-one years after his execution. It is the minute description which I obtained from the very aged Mr. Motley,—the last of a distinguished family,—which leads me to dwell so long on the old block-house jail. Although it was used as the county jail twelve years after the court-house was erected, the History of Portland makes it a one story building, and does not mention the purchasing of the block-house by the county for a prison, although the one story part was joined to it.

This was the first capital trial in a United States Court. Prisoners frequently escaped from the wooden jail and it needed frequent repairs. In 1792, a committee of the court reported that it would be more expensive to repair the old jail than it would be to erect a new one, and, thereupon, it was decided to build a stone jail for the use of the county.

A committee reported that the town wanted the land on which the old jail stood for a "market place," and would purchase a piece of land adjoining the court-house lot for the jail in exchange. In 1795, the county treasurer took a deed of another piece of the Plummer lot in the rear of the court-house, five rods wide and ten rods deep. The consideration was twenty pounds, which was paid by the town, which received a deed of the old jail lot, restricting its use for "market purposes."

The county treasurer reserved the buildings and the right to occupy until the new prison was completed. The building committee were directed to use the iron work and other material in the old jail in the construction of the new one.

On the new lot in the rear of the court-house, after several postponements for the lack of money, was built in 1797 a cut stone jail. The building was fifty by thirty-four feet in size and two stories high, with a gambrel roof and rooms in the attic. Granite was not then the manageable material that it now is, which made the erection of such a building then a formidable job. This was the first dressed stone building erected in the county and, I think, in the state. The building committee were Samuel Freeman and William Gorham, both members of the court of sessions. The superintendent of the building was John Park, of Groton, Mass., who had recently erected a similar prison at Concord in that state. The jail had dormer windows on the front roof. A gentleman, now dead, who built those windows, related to me the talk which he had with the building committee. He inquired if he should finish the back roof in the same style, when they replied, "No, make it entirely plain; there never will be any settlement on that side." The cost of the building was about eight thousand dollars. From this prison, in 1808, Joseph Drew, of Saccarappa, walked to the gallows, near the observatory, a full half mile, with the sheriff on one side and Parson Bradley, of Stroudwater, on the other. He was executed for the murder of Ebenezer Parker, a deputy sheriff of Westbrook. This was the last execution in Portland. This jail of 1797 was taken down in 1859, after the erection of the present county jail. Over the principal door was an inscription, cut in the lintel, giving the date of its erection. At the conclusion is an odd character of which the meaning in late years has not been known. That it is a part of the inscription is shown by its being separated from the date by a semicolon only, and is followed by a period.

FAC-SIMILE OF THE INSCRIPTION.

This lintel is built into the partition wall of the basement of the county wing of this building, and has the original iron door yet swinging beneath it.

The next building erected on this lot was a jail keeper's house. It was called the "county house," and was built in 1799. It was of brick and two stories in height. It stood between the court-house and the jail. With my grandfather I dined in it at the invitation of Mr. Gerrish, the jailer, when I was about nine years of age. After dinner we were shown through the jail. The old-fashioned "dungeon," with its chains, shackles, and ringbolts, impressed me deeply. The debtors' rooms in the attic were not so repulsive, yet those who were then confined in them, for no crime but poverty, did not appear as if they were happy. Imprisonment for debt was then common. A Portland paper of January 10,

1806, says, "Andrew Hanson has been in jail for debt nine months. He has only one shirt and no shoes."

In 1816, for two hundred dollars, the county purchased the right to lay a drain from the jail through the Plummer lot to Back Cove. Seven years later I recollect that there was the same complaint of this single sewer, which had its outlet on the flats, as there has been of late years of the "Back Bay nuisance." During the embargo and the endless lawsuits which were its results, the old wooden court-house proved too small for the county business. After the peace of 1815, commercial business wore a brighter aspect, and the county ventured to erect a more spacious and elegant court-house.

The old one was sold to the Free Will Baptist Society for a house of worship, and, in 1816, it was hauled with oxen to the south side of "Court," now Exchange, street, between Congress and Federal streets. The center of the second story floor was removed and railed around, leaving a gallery on each of the four sides. In 1827, the society vacated it for the then new Casco street church, and the next year it was sold for a soap factory and was moved to Green street, where it was taken down in about 1875.

In 1815, an additional piece of land on the northeast side and adjoining the court-house lot, twenty feet in width and one hundred and fifty-five in length, was purchased of Henry Titcomb for four hundred dollars.

In 1846, under the direction of the committee, consisting of Sheriff Hunnewell, Barrett Potter, and Albert Newhall, was erected, on the county lot, a brick court-house, sixty by fifty feet, of pleasing architecture, and with a cupola, which was surmounted by the scales of justice.* It was directly at

* These scales are now in the Cabinet of the Natural History Society.

CUMBERLAND COUNTY COURT-HOUSE.—1816-1858.

the head of Exchange, then called Court street, making a
fine appearance from all parts of that street. In 1831, two
projecting wings were added at the ends, of about twenty
feet each, and containing fire-proof rooms for the county
offices. The additions gave it an improved appearance.

When the vote of 1819 was found to favor the separation
of the District of Maine from Massachusetts, there was a
warm feeling in nearly the whole state to make Portland the
capital. To do this, the county of Cumberland tendered to
the new state the free use of the court-house, whereupon a
company of the leading citizens of Portland proposed to
erect on the county's lot, adjoining the court-house, a separate building, to be gratuitously occupied by the state government, with apartments for the state officers. This land
was purchased by the county at a "vendue" sale, in 1817, it
being the remaining part of the front of the Plummer lot,
fifty-seven feet on Back street to Myrtle street, and being
one hundred and fifty feet on Myrtle street. On this lot was
a stable, which was occupied by the owner, John Plummer.
On this part of the county lot, in the spring of 1820, was
erected, by those gentlemen, a two story wooden building
with a hipped roof and high stories. The front was finished
with a pediment supported by pilasters, sheathed and painted
white, and, at the time, it was considered an elegant building. The state officers had their apartments in the lower
story, and the upper story was occupied by the senate
chamber and the rooms for the governor and council. This
building was dignified by the name of the "state house,"
which it bore while it was occupied as such. The court room
of the court-house was occupied as the representatives' hall.
Thus equipped the legislature held its sessions here until
1831. It seems odd to us, but it is true, that as late as 1822

33

spirituous liquors were sold in the court-house.   In that year
the court of sessions ordered the sheriff to forbid it "during
the sitting of the court or the legislature."

At the time of the visit to Maine of General Lafayette,
in June, 1825, an awning was spread from the front coving
of the state house to the elm trees in front, and a platform at
the entrance was built of two steps in height, and on this,
after a brief rest inside, the General held his reception.   After
the removal of the seat of the state government to Augusta,
the city became the owner of the state house and leased it to
several tenants until it was wanted for municipal purposes,
when it was used for the offices of the city government.   To
make way for the erection of the new city building, it was
moved to the east corner of Congress and Market streets,
and was occupied for city purposes.   The lower story was
the police office.   It went down in the great fire of 1866.

After the chaste old brick court-house had served the
county forty-two year, the courts and county officers began
to feel straitened for room, and to think of increased
accommodations.   At the same time the city government
was in a like condition, the city officers having their rooms
in detached buildings.   In 1858, the city government concluded an arrangement with the county, which owned this
lot, to take a long lease of it and to erect a building which
would furnish all needed accommodations for the public
offices for the city, ample room for the courts and county
offices, and, at the same time, sufficient apartments to receive
the state legislature and executive government, on the same
spot where they first organized in 1820, if at any time they
should please to return to Portland.

The county lot was at that time occupied by the brick
court-house of 1816, the old state house of 1820, the stone

jail of 1797, and the jail-keeper's house of 1799. In March, 1858, the county authorities leased to the city this lot at a nominal rent, for a term of nine hundred and ninety-nine years, with all the buildings thereon. As a consideration, the city was to provide suitable accommodations for the county courts and officers during the construction of the building and during the terms of the lease, free of charge. This lease was executed and a plan was drawn of a building of brick, to cost about eighty thousand dollars, during the mayoralty of William Willis. The next city council altered the design, enlarged the plan, provided for a dome, and changed the material for the principal front, from brick to Albert sandstone from Nova Scotia. As a part of the arrangement for the enlarged structure, the county purchased an additional piece of land on the southwest side, from the heirs of Judge Emery, on which, for many years, he had a one-story law office. For the Emery lot the county paid seven thousand dollars. The new and enlarged plan was perfected under the mayoralty of Jedediah Jewett, and the building was completed under his administration. The architect was James H. Rand, of Boston. The building was completed in 1862, at a cost to the city of about two hundred and sixty-five thousand dollars.

I now come to the sad story of the destruction of the spacious and beautiful city building, only four years after its completion. It is an unpleasant theme to dwell upon. During that dreadful night of the fourth and fifth of July, 1866, the ruin was accomplished. It was hoped that the force of the fire had passed by, and that the structure was safe. It was this hope and belief that was its destruction. There was a misunderstanding between those who desired to guard and protect it. There was no one on the roof to report the

danger — if any one had been there they had left too soon.
The burning cinders from the Natural History building
above, and on the opposite side of the street, were blown by
the strong wind against the dome, and slid down on the
copper sheathing, until a sufficient mass had collected at the
base to melt the copper and fire the woodwork beneath. The
devouring element had sought a vulnerable spot and found
it here. The dome was first destroyed and then the roof,
and finally the whole interior. The only public records
destroyed were those of the Probate office, which was a great
misfortune of itself. The re-erection or restoration of the
building is so recent that it has not ripened into history.
It is, perhaps, sufficient to say that the restoration was completed in 1869, at a cost of three hundred and fifty-seven
thousand dollars, and, in the words of the prophet, " the
glory of this latter house shall be greater than of the former."

THE EASTERN CEMETERY.

For two centuries from the first settlement of the Neck,
this now " Field of Ancient Graves " was the only common
burial place. Probably some families buried their dead in
their own enclosures. The last Anthony Brackett, who
owned the land where Brackett street now is, died in 1785,
aged seventy-eight. He was buried in his own field, on the
slope of the hill, above Brackett street. Within my remembrance, his grave was found and his bones removed, by his
descendants, to Peaks Island. This was, probably, the burial
place of that ancient family. George Cleeves, the first settler
on the Neck, who died about 1670, was probably one of the
first who was buried in the old burial-ground on the hill.
His grave and that of his wife may have been the nucleus
around which those for the fathers of the hamlet were made.

They may have been buried in the ancient burial-ground on his own Hog Island. In the many years that fishing ships summered in our harbor, before Cleeves came, or during the stay of Levett's men, some, in the natural course of life, must have died here. Prudent men would bury their friends near their huts or tents on shore, to be safe from Indian desecration. I am convinced that the old farm on the south shore of Hog Island was the common landing-place of the fishing ships, and was the place chosen by Christopher Levett, in 1623, for his home farm. The little burial place, with its mossy stone-wall, probably encloses the graves of the first persons who died within the bounds of old Falmouth.

The central point near which all the ancient settlers seem to have sought to bury their friends, in the oldest part of the eastern cemetery, was a very large pine tree of the Norway species, which stood about six feet south from the grave of the Rev. Thomas Smith. This lone tree is represented on all the early plans of the locality. From its situation and great height, it was a landmark on entering the harbor by the main channel, which was brought in range with other prominent objects further inland, by all vessels on rounding Spring Point and Stanford's Ledges, before these were marked with buoys. This tree was blown down in about 1815. In later years its site was marked by planting another tree, which flourished until the fire of July, 1866, when the great heat killed it. Within my own knowledge, some of the pitchy roots of the original tree were dug up in making a grave.

Near this spot, undoubtedly, were buried the twelve men who were killed in the battle with the Indians, near the Deering mansion, beyond the oaks, on September 21, 1689. The famous Colonel Benjamin Church, of Plymouth, was in command. In his account of the battle he says, " By this time the day was far spent, and marching into town about sunset, *carrying in all their wounded and dead men;* being all sensible of God's goodness to them in giving them the victory, and causing the enemy to fly with shame, who never gave one shout at drawing off." From a deposition on record* we know that the wounded were carried to Captain Tyng's house near Fort Loyal, the site of which is now occupied by the passenger station of the Grand Trunk railroad. At and near the fort all the people of the little settlement were gathered for safety, as here were the three or four companies of Colonel Church's soldiers, who had helped to put the Indians to flight " with shame," the day before.

Let us contemplate, in imagination, the sad funeral — the first with martial escort to this now crowded enclosure. George Burroughs, the martyr, was then minister of the town,— he who, three years later, suffered on the gallows at Salem for witchcraft; on which occasion one of his judges, Sewall, of Boston, in his diary, says, " Mr. Burroughs by his speech, prayer, and protestation of innocence, did much move unthinking persons, which occasions their speaking hardly concerning his being executed." We can picture to ourselves the scene: this godly man's earnestness in prayer at the burial for the families of the slain, and for further protection from the savages ; the British flag at half staff within the stockade, floating over the solemn assembly. After the military escort followed the hastily constructed biers, supporting the rough coffins of the dead, borne by their comrades, and then at the head of the long line of relatives, some of them wounded in the fight, came the athletic form of the minister. When all were ready, the martial figure of Colonel Church,

* See ante, page 143.

who, two years before, had hunted the noted King Philip to his death, passes up the line and gives the word " Forward ! " his men take up the time from the muffled drums, and the first military funeral procession takes its way up the foot-path to the tall pine on the hill.   Here, under its shadow, were a few unmarked graves, whose number was doubled that day.   Probably there were no volleys fired over the dead, as every charge of powder was found to be needed for the defence of the living.

In May of the next year, after a siege of five days and a brave defence, Fort Loyal, under the command of Captain Sylvanus Davis, surrendered to a force of between four and five hundred French and Indians, and every building on the Neck was destroyed.   In his report to the governor, after his return from captivity, Captain Davis says, " They killed and wounded a great part of our men."   These bodies, with Lieutenant Thaddeus Clark and his thirteen men, who were killed in a lane near the burying-ground, by a party of Indians in ambush, a few days before, lay exposed to wild beasts and the bleaching storms, until Sir William Phips and Colonel Church, on an expedition to Pemaquid, came into the harbor in August, 1692, and buried the bones of the slain.   Lieutenant Clark and his men were probably buried by the side of those who fell in the battle of 1689, as they were killed near the burying-ground.   But those who were killed at the fort would be more likely to be buried nearer where they were found.   It would be a satisfaction to know that the dust of Thaddeus Clark was really enclosed in the ancient burial place.

I think the oldest inscription on any stone in the burial-ground is that to the memory of Stephen Larrabee, who died in 1718, aged sixty-six.   There are many other

slate stones marking the graves of those who died early
in the century. A more expensive stone is one of slate
with an elaborate inscription, at the head of the grave
of Major Samuel Moody, who came here from Portsmouth,
in about 1716. He graduated at Harvard College in 1699,
and from his education and force of character, he was
employed in the military service of the province, and had
command of the fort at New Casco, which was dismantled in
1716, after which he lived between India and Hancock streets
on the north side of Fore street, and was the leader of the little
settlement. He died in 1729, in the fifty-second year of his
age. His grave is a few feet west of the site of the ancient
pine.

There is a very wide and heavy slab of blue slate near that
to Major Moody, which is the headstone to the grave of
Joseph Stockbridge, " of Hanover." He was a graduate of
Harvard (1755), and was the first Register of the Court of
Probate for Cumberland County. He died in 1761. At the
top of this stone is cut the figure of a man in a bag-wig, to
indicate his judicial office.

A noticeable and ancient monument is that erected to the
memory of Allon McLean and John Fleet, two Scotchmen,
each twenty-six years old. They were killed by the over-
loading with corn of an attic floor, which fell and carried
down the floor below it, in the house of Captain Ross, in
1760. Fleet was killed in the kitchen, and McLean in the
room over it. This is a table monument, of Welsh slate, with
armorial bearings and long inscriptions, artistically cut, in
Scotland, and, although it has stood there more than a century
and a quarter, it shows no mark of age; every line is as perfect as when it was cut. Captain Alexander Ross, in whose
house these young men were killed, has a marble monument

near theirs. He was also from Scotland and was a merchant in extensive business. He died of a cancer in 1768, aged fifty-nine. At the foot of the graves of Captain Ross and those of Fleet and McLean, is the grave of Thomas Cumming, another Scotchman, who was a merchant having a store on the north corner of King and Middle streets. He died in 1798, aged sixty-nine.

Here also was buried, in 1784, Brigadier Preble, a foremost man of the province, who was, in 1775, chosen by the provincial congress major-general and commander-in-chief of the Massachusetts forces, which honor he declined on account of the infirmities of age. His monument has been removed to Evergreen by his grandson.

At the north, and near the pine tree as was possible to dig, was the burial lot of the truly venerable Parson Smith. He died May 25, 1795, aged ninety-three years, and in the sixty-seventh year of his ministry. A monument of brick, supporting a horizontal slab of slate, was erected over his grave. On this slab were the inscriptions to all his family who died before him. The slate became broken into three pieces and the whole monument was renewed in the same style by his heirs in about 1860.

A similar monument to that of Captain Ross, and near it, is that over the grave of John Chipman, a lawyer of Marblehead. He was seized with apoplexy while pleading in the court-house here, and died in two hours, July, 1768.

The stateliest monument that stood under the shadow of the old pine tree was that erected to the memory of Colonel William Tyng. He received his commission as colonel from the British General Gage, at Boston, in 1774. He was the second sheriff of Cumberland County, having been appointed in 1768. He was a loyalist and fled to New York and from

there to Nova Scotia.   He returned in 1793, and settled in
Gorham, where he died much respected, in 1807.   The monument was erected by his widow, who was the only child of
Captain Alexander Ross.   It is an imposing one for that
time, of red freestone with marble panels, and is nearly ten
feet high.

Within the circle formerly marked by the shadow of the
ancient pine, are many unpretending slate headstones with
inscriptions, showing that they mark the resting places of the
prominent men and women of the town, who died during the
first half of the last century, and after that, graves began to
be made outside of this charmed circle.

There are probably more graves of early settlers, like that
of George Cleeves, unmarked, than there are with inscribed
headstones.   In those days, the larger number of families
were poor, and even stones of slate (which is really the most
lasting material,) were expensive; they must be procured in
" the Bay."   I think Bartlett Adams was the first that did
monumental work here.   He came early in this century and
advertised as " stone cutter and sculptor."

The first tomb built in the old burying-ground was that of
Joseph H. Ingraham.   The monument is oblong, built of
granite blocks and surmounted by a horizontal slab of white
marble.   This tomb probably contains more bodies than any
other in the enclosure.   It was built in about 1795.   Sixty
years ago, it was said that the site was chosen to prevent the
laying out of a street direct from the then new Tukey's
bridge to the lower wharves, which it was proposed to cut
through the burying-ground.   The bridge was finished in
1796.   Then the enclosure had not more than one-quarter of
the width at this point that it now has.

The next tomb built here was that of Nathaniel Deering,

which is a few rods west of the Ingraham tomb. It has no monument, but a small upright stone at the entrance with the owner's name only. He died in 1795. In this tomb were deposited the remains of Commodore Edward Preble, whose wife was the only daughter of Nathaniel Deering. Commodore Preble died 1807. After the death of their only child, Edward Deering Preble, in 1846, the widowed mother caused a new vault to be built near the northeast boundary of the enclosure, and a massive monument of white marble to be placed over it, and the remains of the Commodore and his son were removed to this new tomb.

Deacon James Milk, the father of the wife of Nathaniel Deering, senior, has a monument, rich for that time, near the Deering tomb; he died in 1772, aged sixty-one.

I have named only the monuments that first strike the eye in looking over the oldest part of the cemetery, but these are a small part of the number of the graves of the fathers of the town. There are resting here, in graves less expensively marked, many others just as worthy, who, in their time, ruled the destinies of the little town and served the state in the councils, in the field, and on the ocean.

The ancient burial-ground was very small for many years after its commencement, and has been several times enlarged on the northwest side. In 1789, a vote was passed by the town to "fence the burying-ground." In 1795, the committee on enlarging the burying-ground reported that they had purchased of Rev. Mr. Smith land on the southeast side of Smith street (now a part of Congress street), for seventy-one pounds, five shillings. The same year the burying-ground was enlarged on the northwest side "to a line from the easterly line of the school lot parallel with Smith street." Previous to this enlargement, a lane had been laid out from the present Congress street gate to the old burying-ground, called "Funeral Lane." At the time of the first enlargement of the ground, a lane one and a half rods wide was laid out from the eastern end of Funeral lane, northeast "to stone wall," where Adams street now is. This with Funeral lane now forms the open passage from the gate on Congress street to that on Adams street. From the new lane six others, "each half a rod wide, to run on a course south 16 degrees east," were laid out, "within which no grave shall be dug." There seems never to have been any attention paid to the vote establishing these six narrow passages.

At a town meeting held in 1795, a vote was "that the selectmen be directed to set off to the Friends or Quakers, twenty-five square rods in the northerly corner of the bury-ing ground, and at the southward of the new street, and to give them a quit claim deed." This spot is on the Adams street front, and next east of the gate. At the time of the purchase from Parson Smith, only a few weeks before his death, of the land between the old burial-ground and Congress street, it was an open training-field with the town pound at the eastern end, and the pillory and whipping-post in about the middle. At the time of my first knowledge of this spot, sixty-five years ago, the pound and the machinery for punishment had disappeared, but it was still an open smooth field, common for military exercises, ball playing, and a grazing place for cows. The burying-ground fence inclosed one row of tombs northwest of the Adams street lane and gate, and ran parallel with Congress street to the school lot, where there was a small tool-house, one end of which was filled with the openwork wooden gates, on which were the owners' names; these were set up at the entrance to the vaults when they were opened. These two or three acres, now covered thickly with graves, remained an unclosed common until about 1825, when the fence between it and the burying-ground was removed to the Congress street line, and the living gave up their play-ground to the dead. The eastern section of the new ground, has, by common consent, been devoted to tombs, many of which are surmounted by elegant monuments. In the enclosure there are seventy-five tombs. There is not, in the old or the new ground, a tomb with the entrance above the surface of the ground. There are in the cemetery now about seven acres completely covered with the mansions of the dead. There are streets on three of the four sides, and that looking seaward is some fifteen feet above the street, and is protected by a very permanent wall of stone from the street to the surface. From all parts of the enclosure, there is an unobstructed view of the islands, forts, and light-houses, and the open sea beyond. This was well chosen for a place of burial, whoever did it.

One of the principal ornaments of this time-honored burial place is the monument to Admiral Alden, placed there by his direction to his executor. It is of polished red granite, with bronze panels on each of the four faces with inscriptions and the proper emblems. The front bears a bronze medallion likeness of the Admiral, with this inscription:

REAR ADMIRAL
JAMES ALDEN,
Born in Portland, March 31, 1810.
Died in San Francisco,
Feb. 6, 1877.

The monument is about twenty feet high.

Admiral Alden was not only one of the bravest in action, but one of the most courtly and accomplished men in the navy. In his last sickness he expressed a wish that his body should be brought home to Portland and buried beside those of his parents, and his wish was complied with. Edward Motley, another Portland boy, who achieved a fortune as a merchant in Boston, came home to die. On the last day of his life, he sent for his old acquaintance, James R. Mitchell, then superintendent of burials, and said to him, "Do you know where the Motleys are buried?" After being answered in the affirmative, he added, "I want to be buried by the side of my mother." It was done, and, at his request, a plain slate head-stone like hers was set up in the old cemetery at the side of that of his mother, to mark his own grave.

Dickens said of an old woman, whom he met on the dock in New York, whose two sons were sending her to Ireland to end her days, and to have her bones laid among her people in the old grave-yard at home, " God help her and them, and every simple heart, and all who turn to the Jerusalem of their younger days, and have an altar-fire upon the cold hearth of their fathers."

A similar sentiment was expressed by Jacob, the patriarch of old, when he found his end was approaching. He said to his son Joseph, " Bury me not, I pray thee, in Egypt; bury me with my fathers," and he required of him an oath. Joseph, under similar circumstances, required an oath of his children, and said, " Ye shall carry up my bones from hence." And from that time to the present, human nature has been the same. When we come to contemplate our end of earth we wish, if possible, to be buried with our own people, amid the scenes of our earliest recollections. I appreciate the sentiment of the brave Admiral in his dying request. When sickness had come upon him, although surrounded by affluence in a distant state, he thought of the quiet and secluded resting place of his good mother and father, overlooking the broad ocean on which he had obtained fame and fortune, and there he wished to be laid. The writer of this has often, in boyhood, played ball with James Alden on the spot where now is his grave. This part of the ancient enclosure was then a play-ground.

I never enter that hallowed enclosure but I feel an impulse to remove my hat, recollecting the declaration of the voice from the burning bush to Moses, " The place on which thou standest is holy ground." Here not only repose the rude fathers of the hamlet but also the eminent men, who for two centuries have adorned the town, and those who have built ships and sailed them, seeking fortune in every clime,— the honored dead of seven generations. It was a small enclosure at its commencement, with a tall pine in the center, a relic of the "forest primeval." All will acknowledge the fitness of the place chosen. It was the principal place of burial belonging to the town until 1829, when it was estimated that the dead here interred outnumbered the living within the corporate limits.

And here I want to say a word against the removal of the dust of its tenants. This was the chosen spot for their burial. Its beauty is marred in some places by partially filled graves, where relatives have sought (often in vain) for the bones of ancestors, and were compelled to be content with the removal of the head-stones set up by their immediate families. And these stones are not permitted in most cases to be set over the scanty dust in its new place of burial, but they are left in stone cutters' yards, monuments of a lack of veneration and good taste, and, perhaps, to be used as flag stones, making false the first line of the inscription,

"Sacred to the memory of." If any remains are found, their consequent exposure is to be deprecated.

Milton's grave in the chancel of St. Giles, Cripplegate, was opened, in making repairs on the church in 1790. The lead coffin was not immediately covered up. In the night, the coffin was cut open and teeth were knocked out of Milton's jaw, with a paving-stone, to be shown as relics.

A frequent excuse given for the removal of remains from the Eastern cemetery is, "It is liable to have a street cut through it at any time," but it should be recollected that this is the very way to hasten such a desecration; but the ground is not needed for that purpose. If the dust of ancestors is removed to another cemetery, perhaps in a few years another generation may think that this dust is not yet in its proper place, and then there will be another removal, without the respect shown by Edward I. to his beloved queen. On the several spots where her body rested on its way to Westminster Abbey, he erected a stately cross — hence "Charing Cross." Under ordinary circumstances I think no one has any better right to remove the remains of a relative from their chosen place of burial, and change the monument, than they have to disobey his attested will and change the disposition of his other former property.

The dust of Columbus has been removed from city to city, until, I think, it is not quite certain where it now rests. It was Shakespeare's malediction, said to have been written by himself, and which is inscribed over his grave, which has prevented the removal of his dust from the bosom of his native valley of the Avon, to enrich Westminster Abbey.

"Good friends for Jesus sake forbeare
To dig the dust enclosed here.
Blessed be he who spares these stones,
And curst be he that moves my bones."

I think it not unreasonable to suppose that the disembodied spirit, for a time at least, retains a knowledge of its former mortal tenement. This probability should be an incentive to us to surround our places of burial with all pleasant associations, and that they should be well cared for as a duty to the dead, and as attractions to the living.

To inspire his squares of infantry, when about to be charged by the Mamelukes on the banks of the Nile, Napoleon cried out, "From yonder pyramids twenty centuries observe your actions." So, from this cemetery two centuries look down upon the people of the city and plead for its preservation and care.

As early as 1811, it was thought advisable to secure a lot of land at the west end for a burial-ground. In accordance with this sentiment a large lot, west of the present Vaughan street, was purchased of David Ross for the purpose. The war came on and people lost their interest in the proposed burial ground, and the town voted to place the land under the care of the overseers of the work-house. In about 1824, a part of the lot was sold to the state, and on it a large brick arsenal was erected. In 1868, the movement was originated to build the Maine General Hospital. The old building had ceased to be occupied as an arsenal by the state, and the buildings and lot were donated by the state to the trustees of the hospital corporation, on which was erected the splendid and sightly buildings of that institution, which is a monument to the foresight and kind heart of the late Dr. John T. Gilman, its originator. No part of the original large lot was ever used for burial purposes, for which it was purchased.

There is a public burial place near the alms-house in which many worthy but unfortunate people have found a resting-place since that public charity was opened in 1804.

34

WESTERN CEMETERY.

For several years, as the town increased westward, there had been a growing desire by the people of that part of the town, many of whom were new-comers, to have a place of burial at the west end and to abandon the ancient burial ground which was fast filling up. In 1829, about fifteen acres of land on the southern slope of Bramhall's hill were purchased for a burial place, which was then called the Western burying-ground, which, within a few years later, came to be called the Western cemetery.

There was then manifested by discontented people, the same eagerness to have the remains of their relatives removed from the old to the new burial place, that has since been shown to remove from the old enclosure to the out-of-town cemeteries; in fact, some have been a second time removed.

The land enclosed in the Western cemetery was a part of the farm of George Bramhall, who had a tanyard by the road leading to Vaughan's bridge. He was mortally wounded in the battle with the Indians near the Deering Oaks, in 1789. From him the hill took its name. During the first years of the present century, all the land on this hill down nearly to State street, about four hundred acres, was owned by William Vaughan. Included in the cemetery on the southern side, is the small private burial ground of the Vaughan family, containing a clump of pitch pines and enclosed by posts and chains. Here is buried William Vaughan, who was seated on the hill above in landed dignity, and died in 1826, aged eighty-one; and also the most of his family. In this private ground is buried "Rev. Ichabod Nichols, for forty years minister of the first church in Portland." He died in 1859, aged seventy-five. Also Judge Nicholas Emery, who became the owner of a part of the

Vaughan land.   Here, also, is the grave of Isaac Riley, who owned and lived in the house on the north corner of Danforth and Brackett streets.   He was proprietor of the unincorporated township of "Riley," in Oxford County.   He died in 1824, aged fifty-five.   Sixty years ago, this private burial place, with its tall pines, which seem no taller now, was a conspicuous object in the center of a cow-pasture.

The Western cemetery is finely situated on the southerly slope of the hill, which rises abruptly at the north to the highest point in the city.   This bank makes a convenient situation for a range of tombs, with the entrance door entirely above the surface of the path.   Of these there are about twelve, — all there are in the cemetery.

The most conspicuous monument in the enclosure is one of granite, about twenty feet high, erected to the memory of Henry Jackson, long a teacher of the High school for boys, by those who had been at different times under his instruction.   He died in 1850, aged sixty-seven.

There is an expensive and massive monument of marble in the south part of the cemetery, " erected by the Bar of Maine to the memory of Prentiss Mellen, first Chief Justice of the Supreme Court of the state."   This was erected in 1850.

William Willis, Charles Stuart Daveis, and many others, whose graves and monuments would add honor and interest to any cemetery, are buried here.   Here, also, are the burial places of many of the industrial classes — the sailors, soldiers, mechanics, builders, both of ships and buildings, not to be overlooked for lack of sculptured marble.   Especially worthy of veneration and kind recollection are the graves of the working men and working women, who, with faith and good will, assisted with their small savings to build the railroad to

Canada; and it is a matter of congratulation that their faith and their savings were not misplaced.

Notwithstanding the beauty of its situation, the cemetery is marred by numerous small enclosures of wood, stone, and iron around single family lots. Removals from this to more modern cemeteries in the neighboring towns are now very rare.

Of the two more modern cemeteries, owned by the city, in adjoining towns, I have not space to write in this connection, but hope to at another time.

MARKETS.

Hawthorne, in his "English Notes," says, "The English people really like to think and talk of butcher's meat, and gaze at it with delight; and they crowd through avenues of the market houses, and stand enraptured round a dead ox." The remaining English blood must have caused the people of the town to establish a market, and to pass the following vote in 1768, when there were only one hundred and thirty-six dwelling-houses on the whole Neck: "Voted that no person shall purchase any flesh meat for food, saving such as shall be exposed in the lower part of the town house on the Neck, which is hereby appropriated for that use, under a penalty of six shillings." Before that the market people, like the mourners, "went about the streets." Until about 1815, there were no horse-wagons. The common way of carrying meats, butter, and eggs to market, was in large leather "saddlebags," or paniers, on the back of a horse. It was considered the best time to go to market in "court week," as it now is in the new counties.

The next market house was the one previously mentioned as standing where the east end of the old city hall now is.

A vote passed in town meeting, in 1805, throws some light on the origin of this market-house. It is as follows: "Voted that it is best that the old market-house remain on the land given for that purpose." Soon after this vote, Joseph H. Ingraham presented to the town for market purposes, the lot on the west corner of Milk and Market streets. In town meeting it was voted to accept the land, and to erect suitable stalls to accommodate the butchers, to extend the length of the lot, and that they be rented. From this market the street took its name. Afterward, a two story building of brick was erected on this lot for a watch-house, and two fire engine houses with a firemen's hall in the second story.

In 1825, the "market-house" in Market square, now old city hall, was built. The town owned the old jail lot, but the narrow "heater lot," reaching to the junction of the two streets, was owned by two separate proprietors. The extreme point at the junction was owned by Woodbury Storer, who had rented it to the town to accommodate the high framed hay scales, and the surrounding streets were occupied for the hay market. Arthur Savage contracted to erect the "hay-machine," to weigh three tons, in 1769, "for 27 pounds lawful money." The load of hay was raised from overhead by a lever purchase, connected by chains to the hubs of the wheels. The small lot between the hay scales and the jail lot was owned by Jonas Mills, who demanded an exorbitant price. He was brought to reasonable terms by a proposition to lay out a street over it.

The building committee chosen by the town were Albert Newhall, Joshua Richardson, and John Mussey.

The same men were the parish committee in charge of the building of the present stone church of the first parish, the same year. Joshua Richardson had the principal direction

of the building of the market-house, and John Kimball, a
joiner of the town, was the principal architect and overseer
of the carpenter work. The truss roof was planned by Mr.
Mussey, to leave the upper story unobstructed for a drill hall
for the military. This was the first truss roof built in the
town. Except two rooms, at the sides of the stairway, the
whole second story was a town hall. The entrance door
was in the lower story where the present portico stands,
from which an inside stairway led to the hall. The stairs
were a mass of solid timber, each stair a separate square
piece. The exterior walls were very plain, with no attempt
at ornament. The projection at the eaves was very narrow
with copper gutters. The lower story was finished into
market stalls, which were readily rented.

On the western gable was a large open cupola or belfry,
surmounted by a weather vane. The cupola was that now
on the front of the Westbrook Seminary in Deering. This
was the only ornament on the building, and was not in keeping with the other parts of the exterior. Owing to the
economical ideas of the committee, and the small appropriation, the general appearance was unsatisfactory as the principal public building of the town, and, in about 1832, after
the : doption of the city charter, it was decided to remodel
the front. Charles Q. Clapp was appointed to draw a plan
and superintend the improvements. The projecting piers,
or pilasters, were built at the corners and the handsome
portico added as it now stands. The capitals of the columns were carved by Nathan Chapman. The expense was
a large outlay for the city at that time, and the government
was slow in appropriating the funds to pay the balance.

For a long time this was the only large public hall of the
city. Here the first city government in Maine was organ-

Wm Goold

At the Age of 76 years.

ized.   Here, in 1844, was considered in a series of public meetings, the project of building a railroad to Canada.   In 1850, was held here the most noted assemblage of public and business men ever gathered in Maine, to consider the plan for a railroad to St. John, New Brunswick.   Most of the leading men of the lower provinces were in attendance.   No one who was present will forget the speech of General Dearborn, of Roxbury.   When he alluded to the truly venerable Admiral Owen, of Campobello — his rising with the assistance of his staff, and his graceful acknowledgement of the recognition.

It is true that all the gatherings at this building have not been peaceful.   The early antislavery advocates were mobbed here.   In 1850, a furious mob, urged on by designing men, assailed the building, to get possession of liquors stored in the cellar.   By the pluck and energy of the mayor the mob was dispersed and the building saved.   This was the only serious mob in the town which was dispersed by the authorities before it had accomplished its purpose.

One of the committee of the town, who, sixty years ago erected this building, is yet in good health — pray save him the pang of witnessing its proposed destruction.

The lack of time and space will not admit of the finishing of this chapter according to the headlines.   The deferred matter will subsequently appear in another connection.

> Many a vanished day and year,
> Of cruel sack and scourge severe,
> Have swept o'er Portland, yet she stands,
> A city formed to Freedom's hands.

INDEX.

35

SUBSCRIBERS.

Where more than one copy was ordered the figures at the end of
the name represent the number wanted.

PORTLAND, MAINE.

City of Portland, by vote of the city government, 100.
Charles Burleigh.
Charles B. Rogers, 3.
Wm. Senter.
Henry F. McAllister.
Wm. Senter jr.
Maine Historical Society, 2.
Hubbard W. Bryant, 5.
R. O. Conant.
Franklin J. Rollins.
W. W. Thomas, 5.
B. F. Chadbourne.
John E. Dow.
Thos. L. Merrill.
Charles Morrill.
M. G. Palmer.
Philip H. Brown.
John C. Proctor.
E. Corey.
M. F. Hammond.
E. M. Thompson.
Sidney Thaxter.
Henry Deering, 3.
Jas. R. Lunt.
H. E. Bacon.
Neal Dow, 2.
J. S. White.
C. Way.
Geo. F. Morse.
T. C. Hersey.
Chas. M. Gore.
Thomas Shaw, 2.
Geo. A. Thomas.
Edward H. Thomas.
Mrs. G. F. Hitchings.
L. Clifford Wade.
Frederic H. Gerrish, 2.
George C. Peters, 2.
B. C. Somerby.
Arthur B. Morrill.
John M. Adams.
W. W. Thomas jr.
George Trefethen.
N. O. Cram.
Charles D. Brown.
Nathan Webb, 2.
R. T. McLellan, 3.
Z. K. Harmon.
C. M. Rice.
J. A. Merrill.
Moses Gould.
Sidney B. Stewart.
George H. Moore.
P. B. Burnham.
Stephen Berry.
H. H. Hay.
M. N. Rich.
Brown Thurston, 2.
Rt. Rev. Bishop J. A. Healey.
Rev. E. H. Doherty.
C. E. Somerby.
Walter Corey.
H. W. Hale.
Henry Fox.
P. W. Neal.
George F. Lewis.
J. B. Fickett.
Jeremiah Dow.
A. Cummings.
George A. Wright.
W. S. Dana.
W. Y. Pomeroy.
J. Hall Boyd.
Edward H. Daveis.
George S. Hunt.
Granville M. Stevens.
Ambrose Giddings.

James Noyes.
E. A. Noyes, 3.
H. T. Blackstone.
Edward Gould, 4.
Wm. P. Preble, 2.
Henry Littlefield.
Miss Ellen M. Baker.
George H. Holden, 2.
Wm. Edward Gould, 3.
James S. Marrett.
Fred N. Dow.
F. W. Libby.
H. N. Jose, 2.
Charles Cook.
Arthur S. Gilson.
Eliza A. Jones.
Fred J. Ilsley.
W. H. Milliken jr.
Charles W. Ford.
C. T. Libbey.
W. D. Little.
William G. Hart.
J. E. Gilman, 2.
Mark P. Emery.
D. W. Clark, 3.
Andrew Hawes.
Lendell Osgood.
John H. Russell.
Daniel Goodhue.
William H. Clifford, 2.
Aretas Shurtleff.
Charles Edwards.
Hall L. Davis.
William S. Edwards.
John Cammett.
Theodore C. Woodbury.
L. C. Gilson.
H. K. Hinkley.
Geo. W. Beale, 2.
Isaac F. Sturdivant, 2.
F. A. Boothby.
Sylvan Shurtleff.
James H. Baker.
Samuel Waterhouse.
John C. Soule.
Nathan Cleaves, 2.
H. A. Thompson.
Mrs. Joel Whitney.
S. H. Colesworthy.
A. S. Fernald.
George H. Cook.

William Wood.
J. P. Baxter, 4.
J. B. Thorndike.
W. Roberts, 3.
Miss Greely.
George C. Burgess.
J. J. Gerrish.
P. C. Manning.
Oren Ring.
John Marshall Brown, 5.
Stephen Scamman.
Charles Fobes.
J. B. McDonald.
Albert A. Waite.
Rufus Cushman.
Charles C. P. Paine.
H. M. Maling.
E. A. Norton.
Philip Henry Brown, 5.
Charles Davis jr.
Dr. Warren.
Geo. S. Hay.
A. L. Gilkey.
W. E. Russell.
Lewis Pierce, 2.
Albert C. Dam.
A. A. Kendall.
G. F. Sparrow.
S. B. McLellan.
Dr. J. T. Gilman.
Lewis A. Goudy.
William H. Wood.
Daniel Evans.
Miss Con. S. Blake.
George Hall.
Edward R. Colcord.
James A. Day.
C. H. Burr.
Will E. Carter.
William L. Billings.
T. B. Reed.
John Russell.
Irving Blake.
Alex. T. Laughlin.
Mrs. F. C. White.
Edward P. Oxnard.
Asa Dalton.
John Pike.
Chas. B. Varney.
James E. Carter.
C. O. Leach.

Samuel Hanson.
C. H. Boyd.
Henry S. Burrage.
Frank A. Elwell.
George E. B. Jackson, 2.
Edward A. Marwick.
M. C. M. Library Association.
Francis Cushing, 2.
Isaac Cobb.
Harry Brown.
Mrs. Charles C. Hall.
I. P. Farrington.
John Sparrow.
D. W. True.
Edward A. Jordan.
Lewis Bunce.
Joseph Webster.
George C. Codman.
J. G. Whittier.
Rev. Robert Kyle.
W. M. Sargent.
W. M. Rose.
Mrs. H. N. Wetherbee.
George S. Hay, 4.
Albert Brackett.
W. H. Smith.
Frederick Odell Conant.
Frank S. Morton.
J. W. Deering.
George H. Libby.
H. W. Hersey.
Nahum Libby.
Herbert G. Briggs.
L. A. Gray.
Henry Nutter.
David W. Snow.
Seth L. Larrabee.
Henry C. Peabody.
Andrew J. Rich.
J. E. Blabon.
W. H. Milliken.
George W. Woodman.
Seth B. Hersey.
Alfred Woodman.
J. B. Coyle.
Stephen Johnson.
C. F. Williams.
Charles B. Merrill.
William H. Moulton.
C. J. Farrington.
F. R. Farrington.

W. Chenery.
R. C. Robinson.
F. E. Woodford.
Dorville Libby.
Andrew J. Chase.
Isaac W. Dyer.
J. Withanger.
George S. Goodwin.
Charles H. Ford.
Alpheus Griffin.
H. B. Wilson.
J. L. Farmer.
William Allen jr.
Augustus Champlin.
Augustus H. Ford.
Jotham F. Clark.
H. M. Payson.
J. W. Waterhouse.
Charles Payson.
W. S. Jordan.
F. G. Messer.
S. T. Pickard.
E. H. Elwell.
W. R. Anthoine.
Hugh J. Chisholm.
Joseph A. Locke.
George P. Westcott, 2.
John J. Perry.
Benjamin Kingsbury.
Samuel Rolfe.
George F. Gould.
Public Library.
C. S. Walker.
A. H. Berry.
J. T. Leroy.
D. F. Emery jr.
B. B. Farnsworth, 2.
N. J. Sanborn.
George W. Perry.
A. E. Lucette.
Charles A. Staples.
S. C. Strout.
George E. Bird.
Edward M. Rand.
Thomas Tash.
C. H. Baker.
L. W. Cleveland.
William D. Jones.
A. A. Strout.
Edward P. Payson.
W. D. Hatch.

George Brock.
Albro E. Chase.
Annie McKenzie.
George M. Goold.
Henry C. Lovell.
David Moulton.
Lewis B. Smith.
N. W. Allen.
B. F. Hinds.
Henry S. Trickey.
Charles W. Roberts.
William C. Howe.
James Crie.
Isaiah Daniels.
John Welch.
James Quinn.
Edward Moore.
J. B. Donnell.
Charles J. Chapman.
A. H. Files.
William A. Winship.
William F. Small.
Rufus Stanley.
George L. Kimball.
Charles Walker.
Benjamin Thompson.
T. A. Foster.
Josiah H. Drummond.
S. E. Spring.
William H. Looney.
W. B. Irish.
William F. Todd.
John Morgan.
Alfred L. Kyser.
S. H. McAlpine.
Portland Gas Light Company.

Charles McCarthy jr.
N. E. Redlon.
J. H. Hamlin.
Charles L. Jack.
Edward R. Lincoln.
L. W. Fobes.
H. N. Burgess.
Charles F. Guptill.
S. R. Lyman.
Charles E. Jose.
F. A. Smith.
A. M. Smith.
W. G. Soule.
H. B. Hill.
H. S. Melcher.
George H. Buxton.
James F. Hawkes.
E. A. Sawyer.
Clarence Hale.
H. M. Sylvester.
George Milliken.
William H. Smith.
Albert Brackett.
William Deering.
David F. Corser.
Emery C. Chase.
C. T. Varney.
J. S. Ricker.
E. G. P. Smith.
George McAllister.
M. A. Blanchard.
J. S. York.
F. C. Emery.
F. Nash.
R. H. Boynton.
John Higgins.

SUBSCRIBERS IN OTHER PLACES.

Samuel L. Boardman,	Augusta.
J. A. L. Whittier,	Boston, Mass.
Henry J. Edwards,	Chicago, Ill.
Lewis McLellan,	Gorham, 2.
Elijah Kellogg,	Boston, Mass.
Manasseh Smith,	Woodfords.
Geo. H. Preble,	Brookline, Mass.
Edward Johnson,	Belfast.
Mrs. C. C. Stevens,	Framingham, Mass.
Rev. A. S. Packard,	Brunswick.
Hiram P. Hunt,	Gray.
Granville Loud,	Baltimore, Md.
James W. Harmon,	Cape Elizabeth.
James Appleton,	Manlius, N. Y.
Thomas B. Haskell,	Cape Elizabeth.
Dr. Charles E. Banks,	Portland, Oregon.
Charles Anderson,	Windham.
Edward Clark,	N. Y. Tribune.
Otis Sawyer,	Shakers.
J. S. Soule,	Freeport.
C. H. Cram,	Gorham.
Clinton M. Hamilton,	Chebeague Island.
Frank C. Goold,	Boston, Mass., 2.
John G. Whittier,	Amesbury, Mass.
Frank Hanson,	Lynn, Mass.
Thomas P. Foster,	Saccarappa.
Greely Cutter,	New Gloucester.
Mr. Elder,	Lewiston.
Prof. Chapman,	Brunswick.
Judge Williamson,	Belfast.
R. C. Pennell,	Lewiston.
Mrs. C. A. Clark,	New York.
A. D. Warren,	Worcester, Mass.
S. A. Holbrook,	Freeport.
Josiah Pierce,	London, Eng.
W. N. Richards,	Yarmouth.
John Bailey,	Washington, D. C.
Mrs. James Greenleaf,	Cambridge, Mass., 5.
John Frank Pratt,	Chelsea, Mass.
Caleb H. Libby,	Brooklyn, Iowa.
Alvin Woodbury,	Duck Pond.
Henry T. Clark,	Cumberland Mills.
Robert S. Boyd,	Cambridge, Mass.
Abba Goold Woolson,	Concord, Mass., 2.
George E. Ross,	San Francisco, Cal.
Cyrus T. Parker,	Windham.
Robert M. Weeks,	Riverside, N. J.
Lois W. Emery,	Limerick.
Rev. R. J. Kyle,	Windham.